CIVIL WAR ARKANSAS, 1863

CAMPAIGNS & COMMANDERS

GREGORY J. W. URWIN, SERIES EDITOR

CIVIL WAR ARKANSAS, 1863

THE BATTLE FOR A STATE

Mark K. Christ

University of Oklahoma Press : Norman

Also by Mark K. Christ

(ed.) *Rugged and Sublime: The Civil War in Arkansas* (Fayetteville, 1994)
(ed.) *Getting Used to Being Shot At: The Spence Family Civil War Letters* (Fayetteville, 2002)
(ed.) *All Cut to Pieces and Gone to Hell: The Civil War, Race Relations, and the Battle of Poison Spring* (Little Rock, 2003)
(ed.) *The Earth Reeled and Trees Trembled: Civil War Arkansas, 1863–1864* (Little Rock, 2007)
(ed.) *The Die Is Cast: Arkansas Goes to War, 1861* (Little Rock, 2010)

Publication of this book is made possible through
the generosity of Edith Kinney Gaylord.

Library of Congress Cataloging-in-Publication Data

Christ, Mark K.
    Civil War Arkansas, 1863 : the battle for a state / Mark K. Christ.
        p. cm. — (Campaigns & commanders ; 23)
    Includes bibliographical references and index.
    ISBN 978-0-8061-4087-2 (hardcover : alk. paper) 1. Arkansas—History—Civil War, 1861–1865—Campaigns. 2. United States—History—Civil War, 1861–1865—Campaigns. I. Title.
    E470.4.C47 2010
    973.7'34—dc22

                                                                2009017622

Civil War Arkansas, 1863: The Battle for a State is Volume 23 in the Campaigns & Commanders series.

The paper in this book meets the guidelines for permanence and durability of the Committee on Production Guidelines for Book Longevity of the Council on Library Resources, Inc. ∞

1 2 3 4 5 6 7 8 9 10

Contents

Illustrations

Maps

Preface and
Acknowledgments

This book examines the struggle for the Arkansas River Valley in Arkansas in 1863, a conflict that cost Confederate forces in Arkansas and the Indian Territory thousands of men and the capital of a rebellious state, resulting in the return of Unionist state government and nominal Federal control of everything north of the river. Scattered articles have been written about the battles and campaigns of 1863, but never a book-length treatment. The intent of this volume is to provide both an accurate account of the events of 1863 in Arkansas and the immediacy of the eyewitness reports of the men and women who were there.

In quoting from the many letters and diaries of the men who campaigned in Arkansas and the civilians and politicians who were affected, I have left their often creative spelling and punctuation—or lack thereof—intact unless I judged it too confusing for twenty-first-century readers. Their accounts of what they felt and observed provide a depth and insight that I could not hope to improve upon.

In gathering the materials cited in this book, I received the assistance of many archivists from repositories across the country, and I give them my profound thanks for their help. In particular I want to thank Brian Robertson of the Butler Center for Arkansas Studies, Central Arkansas Library System, Little Rock, who kept me abreast of new additions to the Butler Center's holdings and encouraged me to press on with the book, and Judi King at the Arkansas

State Library for her prompt attention to my numerous interlibrary-loan requests.

Others assisted in various ways. Kirk Montgomery created the maps that appear here, and I cannot adequately express my thanks for his generosity. My niece Beth Wimer Macias took time from her studies at the University of Illinois to travel to Springfield and research the manuscript collections of what was then the Illinois State Historical Library. My friend Jack Baxter read an early draft, and his critique strengthened the content of this book considerably. Doyle Taylor of Pine Bluff provided insights into the propaganda value of the CSS *Pontchartrain* and the possible fate of the steamer *Blue Wing*. Connie Langum of Wilson's Creek National Battlefield, another old friend, scoured the battlefield's collections for photographs. Anthony Rushing and Don Hamilton provided photographs of key players in the events of 1863. Others helped in many ways, and if they are not named here specifically, it in no way indicates that I am any less grateful for their assistance.

Special thanks are due to series editor Greg Urwin, and Chuck Rankin at the University of Oklahoma Press, for their patience and guidance during what turned out to be a much longer project than expected. Alice Stanton, Bobbie Drake, and Emmy Ezzell of the University of Oklahoma Press also provided invaluable advice and assistance. Kevin Brock's insightful editing improved this manuscript considerably, for which I am grateful.

Above all I want to thank my wife, Kim, for her steadfast support during the course of this project and for her incisive suggestions for improving the manuscript. I would never have finished it without her.

CIVIL WAR ARKANSAS, 1863

Prologue

"A Muddy, Red, and Brackish Stream"

The Arkansas River Line, January 1863

The first day of January 1863 dawned clear and warm in the western theaters of the American Civil War. The sun rose on thousands of men in blue and gray scattered along the Mississippi and Arkansas river valleys, some facing each other on the bluffs of Chickasaw Bayou, others manning the works at Arkansas Post or the riverport at Helena, still others scattered in miserable camps as they retreated from their defeat at Prairie Grove in northwest Arkansas. Illinoisan William Kennedy recorded it as "a fine day, so warm that the men went without coats and were a little warm at that." Samuel Gordon of the 118th Illinois Infantry Regiment hailed: "Welcome New Year, thrice welcome. Our prayer to God is that long before thy close that peace may reign upon our beloved *country*." W. W. Heartsill, a soldier with the W. P. Lane Rangers from Texas, found January 1 "a pleasant day to begin a new year with, and we can only hope that our journey through the coming year may be so bright and lovely as this its first day." Aaron Estes of the Tenth Texas, snug in his cabin at Arkansas Post, wrote that "this is Newe Years morning and a butiful morning and wee are all well and doing very well. Wee are in ower house and got plenty bread and meete."[1]

But this new year changed the nature of the war, as Texan Flavius Perry lightly observed, writing, "It is eighteen hundred and sixty three that Lincoln proclaims the negroes free." The U.S. president had announced his Emancipation Proclamation following the bloody

3

nightmare of Antietam the previous fall, and as of January 1 all slaves within the Confederate States of America were declared "then, thenceforward, and forever free." The proclamation was for some Unionists a bright spot amid reports of a disastrous Federal defeat at Fredericksburg, Virginia, and the failure of Maj. Gen. William Tecumseh Sherman's attempt to flank Vicksburg via Chickasaw Bayou. A historian of the Forty-second Ohio Infantry recorded that "there was nothing encouraging, anywhere on the long line of the army of the union on that New Year's night unless it might be the fact that on that day President Lincoln had issued the Proclamation of Emancipation; and the hopefulness springing from this was of a moral rather than of a military nature."[2]

Many of the primarily western and midwestern men who fought for the Union in the Trans-Mississippi were not enthusiastic about Lincoln's proclamation. Indianan John Cumer wrote: "[T]here is a great dissatisfaction here about the order of old Abe. I could endure the hardships of a soldier pretty well before the first day of Jan. 1863 but there is such A dissatisfaction that soldiering is a drag to me. I don't know what our country is comeing to." John Harrington of Kentucky declared angrily to his sister, "I enlisted to fight for the Union and the Constitution, but Lincoln puts a different construction on things and now has us Union Men fight for his Abolition Platform and thus making us a hord of Subjugators, house burners, Negro thieves, and devastators of private property." David Massey of the Thirty-third Missouri Infantry wrote to his father, "[t]his has got to be a terrible thing freeing the negro is not what I set out to do and I don't expect to fight very hard for them." A soldier in the 118th Illinois Infantry stated, "that [emancipation] is all we are fiting for now and as soon as I can get Out I will and let them fite . . . for me," while another Illinoisan sputtered, "as for the Negroes they are not worth the powder to blow them up with."[3]

Not all of the Yankee soldiers shared those sentiments, seeing instead the military potential of the newly freed bondsmen. Pvt. Minos Miller of the Thirty-sixth Iowa Infantry wrote to his mother: "[W]e got the news last night at 8 oclock that all the negros was free and them that was able for servis was to be armed and set to guarding foarts. I think now the union is safe and all will be over by the forth of July. I feel like fighting now for we have something to fight for." Prentice Barrows of the Twenty-ninth Iowa reasoned: "I don't see we could carry out Lincoln's emancipation proclamation without some plan being adopted to find employment for the slaves when they are liberated and I know of no better plan or one that would suit me better than to have them help do the fighting."[4]

Confederate leaders in Richmond expressed outrage at the Emancipation Proclamation. Jefferson Davis called it "the most execrable measure in the history of guilty man." A Texas Rebel shared this sentiment: "I have red old Abes messidge and it is all humbugry. He has not got one principle thats fore the truth." Other Rebel troops in Arkansas saw a bright side to it. One soldier from the Twelfth Texas noted "flying reports in camp that the western men are all deserting [Lincoln's] standard. We all hope that it may have the effect to produce an explosion in his own magazine." Yet another Texan declared: "The Feds is deserting the Northern Army and coming over to be payrolled. . . . They said they sat out to fight for the Union but it has run into the *negro question* and they ain't going to have anything to do with it. . . . They wont going to fight to free the negros."[5]

Eighteen sixty three also would witness a change in Union strategy in the central Trans-Mississippi. Following the signal Confederate defeats at Pea Ridge and Prairie Grove in northwest Arkansas and Union occupation of Helena on the Mississippi River in 1862, and amid the ongoing siege of Vicksburg, Mississippi, Federal strategy turned toward control of the verdant Arkansas River Valley. The region was the key to control of Arkansas and Indian Territory, splitting both down the middle, and provided not only an opportunity to bisect the Trans-Mississippi Confederacy but also to close Arkansas as an avenue for Confederate invasion of Missouri. The capture of Little Rock, the state capital, would also further President Lincoln's political goal of reestablishing loyal state governments throughout the South.[6]

For the Federals, the Arkansas River presented its own set of strategic and tactical difficulties, caused in part by its unique hydrology. The river begins its long journey to the Mississippi at ten thousand feet above sea level in the mountains of Colorado, thundering from mountain streams into a series of rapids and waterfalls in a five-thousand-foot elevation drop over its first 150 miles. Entering the flatlands of Kansas, a Federal engineer noted, "the water becomes brackish, and below the mouth of the Cimarron assumes a blood-red color." Continuing into Indian Territory, the Arkansas is joined first by the clear waters of the Grand River, a junction overlooked by the Federal post at Fort Gibson, and then by the brown-tinted flow of the Verdigris. "These streams float together for more than twenty-five miles, the Verdigris and Grand Rivers keeping the left bank, and the Arkansas the right, without losing their distinctive colors," the engineer observed.[7]

Nearly three decades earlier, Albert Pike—poet, teacher, Mason, and sometimes soldier—wrote of the river as it entered Arkansas Territory:

> Above Fort Smith, the river is generally about a quarter of a mile wide; and, in fact, its width is much increased from that point to its mouth. Above that place the river is shallow and not navigable by steamboats. Below Fort Smith the river continues of about the same size and depth—passing, in succession, through the counties of Crawford, Johnson and Pope to Pulaski. . . . Below Fort Smith the Arkansas is a muddy, red and brackish stream—though much more so at one time then another, according to the stages of water, or the places where the rises come from. At low water it is the worst river of the West, except Red River, for snags and difficult navigation.[8]

As it runs through the area, the Arkansas is fed by three navigable streams—the Big Piney, Petit Jean, and Fourche LaFave—and innumerable smaller creeks. It passes the towering eminence of Petit Jean Mountain through bottoms three to four miles wide, then flows by Pinnacle Mountain and on to Little Rock, named for a stone ledge that protrudes into the river. From the state's capital—a prosperous city of 3,127 souls in 1860—the Arkansas leaves the mountainous areas behind and becomes a far more sinuous stream. A Federal engineer noted that "bends of a loop-like form are very common below Little Rock . . . [T]hey are so exceptional that their occurrence attracts attention."[9]

Meandering into the vast, flat Arkansas delta, the river passes Pine Bluff, a flourishing village near some of the rare high ground in the eastern part of the watershed. "In this part of its course the river is very tortuous, bending back upon itself in a repetition of loop-like forms, which are constantly cutting through at the narrowest part of the neck, or otherwise changing the course of the channel," a surveyor observed. It soon passes Arkansas Post, the state's territorial capital.[10]

About 8 miles before ending its 1,500-mile journey to the Mississippi, the Arkansas encounters the state's other major navigable river.

The White River originates some 720 miles from its junction with the Arkansas, flowing from the Boston Mountains into southern Missouri and then southeast through Arkansas. Unlike the Arkansas, the fast-moving White River scours a generally clear channel along its course. But as it nears its exit into the Mississippi, the White "is little more than a narrow, crooked ditch, which seems designed only for draining an immense swamp." The two rivers linked via a cutoff, which Albert Pike thought "a most singular sight. Here is a mass of red or chalky water, there a mass of water that appears to be black—boiling and whirling around, and seeming as distinct as though the latter was not water but oil. A little further on, and the waters mingle and discharge themselves into the great Mississippi." Below the cutoff, the Arkansas finally finishes its long journey from the Colorado mountains.[11]

A Texas soldier observed in late 1862 that "the [Arkansas] river chanel is broad and shallow crooked and full of snags and very poor for navigation." Indeed, travel on the Arkansas was often problematic, with the river frequently blocked by sandbars formed by the tons of silt picked up during the journey through the flatlands of Kansas and Indian Territory—one Confederate soldier remarked that "in the fall of each year it is reported that 'the cat fish have to employ the turtles to tow them over sandbars.'" The river's propensity to change course caused it to rip into its banks, dropping trees that created snags in the channel that could puncture the fragile hulls of unwary steamboats. High water during the winter and in late spring allowed vessels carrying up to seven hundred tons of cargo to ascend as far as Fort Smith, but low water could easily trap boats between sandbars, forcing them to wait until a new freshet allowed passage. A Union engineer summarized river traffic on the Arkansas: "Boats drawing from five to six feet of water are generally employed between Memphis and Little Rock. Between Little Rock and Fort Smith three and a half feet draught is more suitable, and between Fort Smith and Fort Gibson small steamers drawing, when not loaded, one foot are usually employed."[12]

Despite the unreliability of boat travel, the river was a strategic route for military operations in the Trans-Mississippi region. The U.S. government had recognized this as early as 1832, when it added the Arkansas to the national strategic system, joining the Mississippi, Ohio, and Missouri rivers as part of the country's infrastructure for providing national defense. This move led to the initial clearing of snags from the channel, which in the waters below Little Rock averaged around two hundred per mile. During the war the river provided an avenue for moving troops and supplies and for communications between the Mississippi River and Indian Territory. Union leaders realized that by bisecting Arkansas and the territory, the river created a natural boundary to split those areas and their resources from the rest of the Trans-Mississippi Confederacy, a possibility that became increasingly realistic after the 1862 victories at Island No. 10 and Memphis won the Union control of the upper Mississippi and easy access to Arkansas's waterways. The almost complete lack of railroads in the state and the execrable condition of most of its roads increased the river's strategic significance.[13]

But the chief importance of the Arkansas River was not its navigability, nor necessarily its strategic value. The rich soil of its forty-mile-wide valley produced a high proportion of the state's food crops, a particularly important fact as 1863 followed the drought year of 1862 and a devastating hog-cholera epidemic that decimated the state's swine population. In 1860 the twelve counties that bordered the Arkansas River were home to 20 percent of the state's farmland, both improved and unimproved. That year's production included 28 percent of the Irish potatoes, 18 percent of the sweet potatoes, 17 percent of the wheat, 21 percent of the Indian corn, 16 percent of the peas and beans, 24 percent of the butter, 27 percent of the cheese, 26 percent of the honey, a whopping 38 percent of the hay, and 24 percent of the cotton grown in Arkansas. As one Texas soldier observed: "[T]he valleys of the Arkansas and White rivers are the great granaries of the state and the seat of its greater wealth. . . . There are few if any extremely poor people in the valley of the Ark."[14]

The prize, then, in 1863 was control of the strategic, political, and agricultural wealth of the Arkansas River Valley. The New Year found Union troops controlling the Mississippi River at Helena and cordoning the Trans-Mississippi Confederacy south of Missouri and Kansas, while Confederate troops of varying quality held most of Arkansas and Indian Territory. Just how this strategic situation came to be, though, is important to understanding the 1863 campaigns in Arkansas.

1

"THE DIE IS CAST"

Arkansas Goes to War

Arkansas had been reluctant to join the Confederacy. In the tense months following Abraham Lincoln's election as U.S. president, opinions on the state's course of action polarized, with the slave-holding delta and lowland counties favoring secession and the mountainous regions supporting the Union. Henry Rector, Arkansas's newly elected governor, voiced the tension facing his state and the nation in his inaugural address: "the states stand tremblingly upon the verge of dissolution." That tension increased on December 20, 1860, as South Carolina pushed the issue by withdrawing from the Union. The next day Rector asked the Arkansas legislature to follow suit; the house of representatives on December 22 voted to hold a convention to chart the state's course, and the state senate followed suit on January 15, 1861. A public election on calling a secession convention was set for February 18.[1]

The regional divide between the yeomanry of the northwest and slaveowning planters of the east and south became even more apparent as public rhetoric heated up in the weeks preceding the election. As upland Unionists struggled to get word of the election to likeminded people in the remote hills and hollows of the Ozark and Boston Mountains, a resolution from Van Buren County stated what many across the region felt: "We follow no secessionist . . . nor any set of disunionists who have nothing in view but their own selfish and hellish designs." Robert W. Johnson, one of Arkansas's U.S.

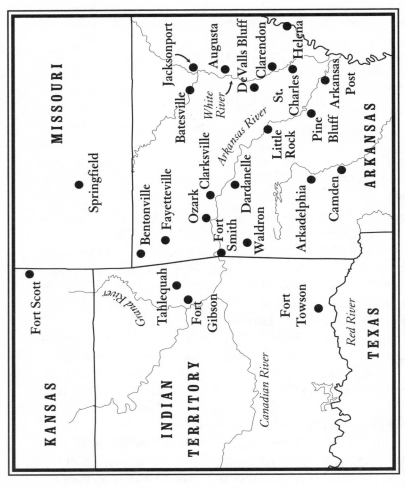

Arkansas River Valley. While elements of the Union and Confederate armies were active throughout the state, the major focus of operations in 1863 was control of the valley. *Map by Kirk Montgomery.*

senators and a leading proponent of secession, summarized the fears of the planter class, saying that Lincoln's election meant "the extinction of four thousand million dollars of southern property and the *freedom, and the equality with us* of the four million negroes now in the South." Even as this debate raged in Arkansas, six more states—Alabama, Georgia, Texas, Mississippi, Louisiana, and Florida— followed South Carolina out of the Union between January 9 and February 1. An independent Confederate States of America was declared on February 4.[2]

As the situation became ever more volatile, a new crisis erupted in Little Rock. Capt. James Totten and sixty-five soldiers of the Second U.S. Artillery had quietly manned the old U.S. arsenal complex on the edge of town since the previous November. On January 28 Governor Rector notified Totten that the small garrison should not attempt to remove or destroy supplies at the arsenal and that reinforcements would not be permitted. The captain stiffly replied that he took his orders from the U.S. government, not the state of Arkansas, but that no reinforcements were anticipated. Despite his assertion, a rumor in early February electrified Arkansas secessionists, who flocked to Little Rock on a report that Federal troops were approaching the capital aboard the steamer *S. H. Tucker.* Rector sent Little Rock volunteers armed with cannon to the banks of the Arkansas to repel any attempts to reinforce the arsenal, though they were disbanded once the rumors proved false.[3]

On February 5, amid secessionist demands that the governor seize the arsenal, nearly one thousand volunteers from Phillips, Prairie, White, Saline, Montgomery, Hot Spring, Monroe, and St. Francis counties poured into Little Rock, itching for action. A shaken Rector disavowed having called for the militiamen, but on February 6 he again contacted Totten, this time asking him to surrender the arsenal. Later events in the war would show Totten to be a somewhat flaky individual, but his judgment now was sound as he considered the odds of his tiny force withstanding an assault by hundreds of armed men. He would agree if Rector would hold the arsenal and its equipage in trust for the U.S. government and allow the garrison to evacuate, bringing with them their ordnance and equipment. The governor accepted these terms, and the Federal garrison marched from the arsenal on February 8, camped for a few days at Fletcher's

Landing, then steamed to St. Louis on the twelfth. A shooting war in Arkansas was averted, at least temporarily.[4]

The elections held on February 18 reflected the continued uneasiness of Arkansans on secession: voters elected to hold a convention but overwhelmingly rejected withdrawal from the Union by sending a clear majority of Unionist candidates to the meeting. Delegates gathered at the state capitol on March 4, the day Abraham Lincoln took office as president of the United States. Pro-Union members won the office of chairman of the convention and headed all of the major committees. For some two weeks, as secessionists railed and such luminaries as Governor Rector and Senator Johnson pleaded the case for disunion, the majority remained united. Finally, amid concerns that the planter counties of the delta would secede from the state, the convention determined to hold a referendum on secession on the first Monday in August. Delegates thus offered a reprieve from disunion, but the core divisions in the state remained. In Van Buren in western Arkansas, thirty-nine guns were fired in honor of Crawford County's thirty-nine pro-Union votes; at Pine Bluff and Napoleon in the delta, cannon were fired on steamboats believed to be carrying supplies for Federal forces.[5]

Ultimately, the results of the convention were moot. Early on the morning of April 12, 1861, Confederate artillery at Charleston, South Carolina, opened fire on Fort Sumter after the garrison's commander refused to surrender the U.S. post. After two days of bombardment, the stronghold fell. On April 15 President Lincoln issued a call to the states for 75,000 men to crush the rebellion. Rector refused the request for 780 troops from Arkansas, telling Lincoln that "the people of this state are freemen, not slaves, and will defend to the last extremity, their honor, lives and property against Northern mendacity and usurpation." Instead the governor ordered Mexican War veteran Solon Borland to take a thousand militiamen and steam upriver to seize the Federal post at Fort Smith. They arrived to find that the small garrison there had already quietly withdrawn into Indian Territory with all of its equipment. Borland's expeditionary force was cheered from the banks of the Arkansas River as it returned downstream. David Walker, the secession convention chairman, gloomily called for the delegates to reassemble at Little Rock on May 6.[6]

Unlike the earlier convention, the gathering in the house of representatives chamber was marked by no heated debate or lengthy discussion; one chronicler noted that the "intensely excited throng could not brook the ordeal of discussion." Walker began the roll-call vote, and only five of delegates, mostly from mountain counties, voted against secession. The chairman addressed the dissenters: "Now, since we must go, let us all go together; let the wires carry the news to all the world that Arkansas stands as a unit against coercion." Four of the pro-Union delegates changed their vote, then Isaac Murphy of Madison County rose to his feet: "I have cast my vote after mature reflection, and have duly considered the consequences, and I cannot conscientiously change it. I therefore vote 'no.'" The chamber erupted with howls of rage against Murphy, but a Little Rock widow seated in the balcony threw the Unionist a bouquet of flowers in recognition of his principled stand. It was a gesture of civility that would soon be alien in the divided state.[7]

In the days following the vote, thousands of men flocked to join local companies, leaving their homes amid cheers and with flags hand sewn by local women. One young recruit from southwest Arkansas spoke of the men's mood in a letter to his sister: "The Northern States are every where preparing for battle. Lincoln says the United States Flag shall *float* over every seceding state, a *glorious* time he will have in placing it over them." Mustered in to state or Confederate service, many were sent to training camps in northwest or north-central Arkansas while others were immediately sent east of the Mississippi. The new troops learned the rudiments of drill, the boredom of camp life, and the horrors of disease as childhood illnesses swept through the close-packed camps and killed hundreds of men never before exposed to them. One regimental surgeon recorded: "[M]easles are making sad havoc with all the troops, and some of our Arkansas regiments have lost several men with them. . . . [T]he mumps came in by way of variety I suppose, just to keep the measles company." Nonetheless, the Arkansas regiments began to take on the appearance of viable military units.[8]

Not everyone in the state rushed to the Confederate cause, however. In the mountains of north-central Arkansas, Unionists formed an underground movement called the Arkansas Peace Society. This group, which may have numbered as many as 1,700 members who may have been motivated mainly by a desire to protect their homes, drew immediate and draconian reactions from pro-Southern authorities. Militiamen in Searcy County arrested seventy-eight Peace Society members, who "were chained together two and two, with an ordinary log chain fastened around the neck of each, and for twenty-four hours prior to their departure . . . were thus guarded, in two ranks, as it were, with a long chain running down the centre of the column." The prisoners were marched to Little Rock and, along with thirty-nine other Ozark Unionists, forced to choose between standing trial or service in the Confederate army. One hundred two were formed into two companies and shipped east of the Mississippi; the other fifteen were never tried. The majority of these galvanized Rebels eventually deserted, and many ultimately joined Missouri Federal units. Arkansas's traditional Unionist strongholds would remain loyal to the United States throughout the war, and, historian Thomas A. DeBlack notes, "despite having the third-smallest white population, Arkansas would provide more troops for the Federal army than any other Confederate State except Tennessee."[9]

While many of the new Arkansas regiments were sent east of the Mississippi, those that remained behind would see action first. Rebel troops had been concentrating in northwestern Arkansas since June, when Brig. Gen. Ben McCulloch had joined his Texas and Louisiana regiments with about two thousand Arkansians in state service under N. Bart Pearce. On August 4 the combined force entered Missouri, where a mixed bag of state troops under Sterling Price was being hounded into the state's southwestern corner by a tough army of 5,600 Yankees under Brig. Gen. Nathaniel Lyon. Price and McCulloch linked up at Carthage, then bivouacked their combined army of some 15,000 troops at Wilson's Creek southwest of Springfield. While numerically superior to Lyon, many of the Arkansas troops were indifferently armed with old muskets and shotguns; a large number of Price's men had no weapons at all. McCulloch planned to move on the Federals in Springfield on the night of August 9 but cancelled the advance because of heavy rain, withdrawing the pickets from around the Rebel camps in anticipation of a morning march. Lyon took advantage of this on the morning of the tenth, splitting his small force to hit the Rebels from front and rear. The attack caused pandemonium initially, but then Union troops under Brig. Gen. Franz Sigel fled after mistaking gray-clad Rebel soldiers for an Iowa unit wearing similar uniforms, allowing them to fire on the Yankees at point-blank range. The combined Rebel force then converged on Oak Hill, where Lyon was killed leading a counterattack. The exhausted Federals broke off the battle and returned to Springfield as the Rebels "watched the retreating enemy through our field glasses, *and we were glad to see him go.*" The fields around Wilson's Creek were littered with 279 dead and 951 wounded Rebels; Lyon's force suffered 258 dead, 873 wounded, and 186 missing or captured. "I don't see how any of us escaped being killed that was in the Battle," a green Arkansas sergeant wrote to his parents in Clark County, "We have drilled but very little."[10]

Following the victory at Wilson's Creek, McCulloch, who had never been comfortable about entering a state that had not formally seceded, withdrew to northwest Arkansas. The general left his troops there and hurried to Richmond to defend this decision. Price took his Missourians to Springfield, then headed toward the Missouri River, envisioning a popular uprising that would bring the state into the Confederacy. After defeating the Federal garrison at Lexington, however, many of his troops left his army, some returning home while others joined guerrilla bands. Price and the remnants of his force soon fell back to southwest Missouri. The Arkansas State Troops, meanwhile, were met on their return to Arkansas by Thomas C. Hindman, a fire-eating secessionist who had entered Confederate service as a colonel and would rise to the rank of major general. Hindman urged the soldiers to move to Pitman's Ferry in northeast Arkansas and there enroll in Confederate service under Brig. Gen. William J. Hardee. The prospect of leaving Arkansas and fighting east of the Mississippi was not attractive to these veterans, and whole companies disbanded, leaving the service and heading for home.[11]

The fate of the Arkansas River Valley was not wholly dependent on activities within its namesake state, however. Moving upriver from Fort Smith, the Arkansas flows through Indian Territory, an area that had seen as much division over whether to ally with the Confederacy as had its eastern neighbors. It also was a strategically important area, with the lands occupied by the Cherokees, Creeks, Choctaws, and Chickasaws providing a buffer between Confederate Texas and pro-Union Kansas. Confederate officials moved quickly in 1861 to woo the Indian nations to the Southern banner.

The tribes themselves were ambivalent. Having been forced to leave their homelands in the southeastern United States and move to Indian Territory in the 1830s, many of the members of the so-called Five Civilized Tribes identified with Southern values, with many owning slaves. Economically the tribes had strong trade and banking ties with the South. At the same time, their active treaties with the United States provided them with annuities and U.S. Army protection. As Texans armed for war under the Confederate banner, however, the army abandoned its posts at Forts Washita, Cobb, and Arbuckle, violating treaties and leaving Indian Territory without an organized Federal presence. Into this void came Albert Pike, an adventurer and poet who at age fifty-two was already well known in the territory, having represented Creek and Choctaw clients as a frontier lawyer before the war. Pike's mandate from the Confederate government was to negotiate new treaties binding the Indian nations to the Rebel cause.[12]

Pike entered negotiations aggressively, reminding the Indians that it had been the U.S. government that had forcibly removed them from their homelands. Targeting the slaveowning minority, he slammed the activities of abolitionist missionaries in the territory. Promising that the Confederate government would take up the annuities lately offered by the United States, that the tribes would retain their status as sovereign nations, and that any troops raised would not be asked to serve beyond the borders of the nations, Pike cemented treaties with the Chickasaws, Creeks, Choctaws, and Seminoles by August 1, 1861. Within the Cherokee tribe, however, long-fermenting tensions again rose to the surface. Principal Chief John Ross sought to maintain neutrality even as Stand Watie raised a regiment to serve the Southern cause. Facing the reality of being surrounded by pro-Confederate forces, Ross too signed a treaty with the South on October 7. Pike also won agreements with the Osage, Quapaw, Seneca, and Shawnee tribes, which lived in the northeast corner of Indian Territory. Appointed a brigadier general in the Confederate army in recognition of his efforts, Pike became commander of the Department of Indian Territory.[13]

Despite the treaties, many tribal members did not embrace the new relationship with the Confederacy. The debate had not centered solely on whether to remain loyal to the Union, but had also revived bad feelings that dated as far back as removal. Some simply wanted nothing to do with the new war in the East. In mid-November Opotholeyahola, an aged Creek chief, led some five thousand men, women, and children toward Kansas. His band consisted mainly of Creeks and Cherokees but also included Seminoles and blacks, both slave and free. Col. Douglas Cooper led a force of Creeks, Choctaws, Chickasaws, and Texans in pursuit of the refugees, catching up with them near Round Mountain north of Red Fork. Setting fire to the horseshoe-shaped prairie, Opotholeyahola's warriors ambushed the Confederates and set them to flight. The refugees continued moving northeast, camping near Tulsey Town, while Cooper retreated to the east to lick his wounds. By November 30 the Rebels were again in pursuit, closing in on Opotholeyahola's camp on December 7. Cooper sent Cherokees from Col. John Drew's regiment to negotiate, but the old chief's arguments were apparently more persuasive: 400 of Drew's 480 men deserted that night, most to the enemy camp. Although Cooper again retreated, Opotholeyahola attacked his rear guard, goading the Rebel force into pursuit. The refugee force again selected the battlefield, this time at a bend of Bird Creek. After four hours of fighting, the battle ended in a draw, with Cooper falling back to Fort Gibson to resupply and Opotholeyahola, also running low on food and ammunition, continuing northwest and digging in on a ridge at a place called Chustenahlah.[14]

Having suffered two reversals at their hands, Cooper determined to destroy Opotholeyahola's column lest it give heart to others in Indian Territory who opposed an alliance with the Confederacy. From northwest Arkansas Col. James McQueen McIntosh answered his call for help, bringing with him some 1,600 mounted Arkansans and Texans, many of them veterans of Wilson's Creek. Cooper and McIntosh intended to coordinate, with Cooper hitting Opotholeyahola from behind as McIntosh struck their front. At noon on December 26, with Cooper nowhere in sight, McIntosh and his men splashed across Shoal Creek as the defenders voiced their defiance by "barking like a dog howling like a wolf & yelling and gobbling like a turkey." The attacking Confederates swept through the Seminole skirmishers and closed with the refugees' main line. The old chief's Unionists broke and scattered across the prairie. Col. Stand Watie, at the head of his Confederate Cherokee cavalry, arrived as the battle ended and began pursuit. Desperate rear-guard stands were swept aside as Opotholeyahola's column, now hopelessly destitute of supplies, fled through the bitter cold and sleet to Kansas, finally finding sanctuary at Fort Scott. In the fighting at Chustenahlah and the flight to Kansas, the refugees lost more than 260 men killed and 380 women and children and twenty slaves or freedmen captured, while also losing dozens of wagons, seventy yokes of oxen, and hundreds of horses, cattle, sheep, and dogs. Southern losses were a mere eight killed and thirty-two wounded. The Indian Territory was now firmly in Confederate control.[15]

The beginning of 1862 found Ben McCulloch's Confederate infantry resting in winter quarters in northwest Arkansas while his cavalry and artillery enjoyed comfortable berths south of the Boston Mountains in the Arkansas River Valley; Sterling Price's Missourians remained in their home state, wintering at Springfield around a hundred miles to the north. The former Texas Ranger took advantage of this lull to travel to Richmond to complain to Confederate president Jefferson Davis about Price. The Texan and the Missourian who had fought well together at Wilson's Creek were now feuding furiously, and their quarrel had spread to partisan newspapers. Davis, in a move that would become depressingly familiar over the next few years to Trans-Mississippi Confederates, responded by appointing an incompetent friend to make things right. On January 10 he created the Military District of the Trans-Mississippi and appointed fellow Mississippian Earl Van Dorn to head it. Van Dorn had graduated fifty-second of fifty-six in the West Point class of 1842, served with distinction in the Mexican War, and risen to the rank of major in the prewar regular army. By the beginning of 1862, he was a Confederate major general. Despite this record, as historian William L. Shea has noted, "Van Dorn was a poor choice. . . . He was impulsive, reckless, and lacked administrative skills." The new Trans-Mississippi commander set up shop in Pocahontas in northeast Arkansas, intent on invading Missouri, his strategy summarized by the declaration, "I must have St. Louis—then Huzza!"[16]

Union forces in Missouri were not going to wait complacently for Van Dorn's invasion. Maj. Gen. Henry W. Halleck, commander of the Federal Department of the Missouri, gave Brig. Gen. Samuel Ryan Curtis command of the District of Southwest Missouri and ordered him and the 12,000 men and fifty cannon of his Army of the Southwest to clear Price's forces out of the state. Curtis, like Van Dorn, was a West Point graduate and Mexican War veteran; he also was a founder of the Republican Party and had resigned a seat in Congress to take the field against the rebellion. Unlike Van Dorn, he would show a strategic and tactical virtuosity that would doom Confederate efforts to bring Missouri out of the Union.[17]

Curtis pushed southwest, and a surprised and shaken Price, his pleas for support unanswered by the absent McCulloch, abandoned Springfield on February 12. The Federal army followed closely, gobbling up stragglers and passing through the nightmare landscape of the Wilson's Creek battlefield, where rain and animals had exposed the skeletons of casualties who had been buried in shallow graves. On February 16 Curtis's advance encountered Price's rear guard, and the first fighting seen in the state of Arkansas occurred as men of the First Missouri Cavalry regiments, Union and Confederate, skirmished across Big Sugar Creek. The Army of the Southwest marched into Arkansas the next morning, following the Wire Road past Elkhorn Tavern to Dunagin's Farm, where it encountered a strong defensive line. After a tough action that left as many as thirty-nine soldiers dead on the field, Curtis withdrew to Little Sugar Creek and set up camp. Price's bedraggled Missourians continued south to McCulloch's winter quarters at Cross Hollows. The Texan, newly returned from Richmond, saw that the winter encampment was not defensible and ordered it burned on the nineteenth. The next day he began distributing supplies from the vast Confederate depot at Fayetteville, unable to move them for lack of transport. Rebel soldiers got into the spirit of the event a bit too much, many of them moving beyond the supply depot to loot homes and businesses in the Ozark village. When McCulloch ordered the remaining supplies burned on February 21, the fire got out of hand, consuming several city blocks. The combined Confederate army continued through the freezing weather to establish camp in the Boston Mountains.[18]

On hearing of Curtis's offensive, Van Dorn had immediately left Pocahontas with a small party and started the two-hundred-mile journey to the Boston Mountains. Despite being dunked in the Little Red River and developing a fever that would plague him during the subsequent campaign, Van Dorn joined the force he now dubbed the Army of the West on March 2. The Federal army was now divided, with one division camped in western Benton County on McKissick Creek and another occupying the old Rebel camp at Cross Hollows. Van Dorn determined to head north, crush the Federals in detail, and then invade Missouri. As for supplies, each Southern soldier would carry his rifle, forty rounds of ammunition, and three days' rations;

after defeating Curtis he expected his army would live off of captured Union provender. Van Dorn also ordered Albert Pike to bring his Indian troops into Arkansas, despite treaties specifying that they would not serve outside Indian Territory. After due consideration, many of the Cherokees agreed to move east as long as they were paid in advance. Van Dorn began his offensive on March 4, leading more than 16,000 men and sixty-five guns—a force that outnumbered Curtis's Federals by three to two.[19]

The advance was a disaster. Troops who had grown soft in winter quarters dropped in droves by the roadside as the Army of the West struggled northward. Curtis, meanwhile, had been warned by a Fayetteville Unionist of the Rebel march and ordered his divided command to consolidate at an unassailable position on the high ground above Little Sugar Creek. A small force under Franz Sigel was almost cut off as the German general tarried over breakfast in Bentonville, but Curtis successfully gathered in his men. Van Dorn, ignoring the miserable condition of his exhausted, hungry soldiers, changed plans and ordered his army to take a road called the Bentonville Detour that would lead them north around Curtis's position to the Wire Road, from which they could attack the Federals from behind. Marching on the night of March 6–7, the Confederates inched along the Bentonville Detour with still more men dropping from exhaustion. By the morning of the seventh, Price's vanguard was just reaching the Wire Road while rear elements had not left Little Sugar Creek. Van Dorn then made a fatal decision to divide his command, ordering Price to head south on the Wire Road while McCulloch's men would go cross-country on Ford Road to Elkhorn Tavern. From there, he imagined, his reunited Army of the West would drive into the Federal position from behind, destroying Curtis's army and opening the door to an invasion of Missouri.[20]

One cannot fault Van Dorn for being unenthusiastic, but his optimistic plans soon turned to disaster. Union patrols already had discovered the Rebels on the Bentonville Detour, and Curtis acted decisively. He sent a division under Col. Peter J. Osterhaus to the west and another under Col. Eugene A. Carr northeast to block the Wire Road at Elkhorn Tavern. Meanwhile Curtis began turning the rest of his command around, abandoning his strong works on Little Sugar Creek to face the impending danger to his rear. Near the few scattered buildings of Leetown (named after a first cousin of Robert E. Lee),

Osterhaus's advance collided with McCulloch's division. Despite being outnumbered, the former Prussian soldier set an artillery battery to work against the Rebels, who charged and captured the cannon. As this attack took place, Pike led his thousand-man Cherokee regiment and two hundred or so Texans against two companies of Iowa cavalrymen to the west of the Union artillery. The Yankee horsemen were easily brushed aside, but several of their wounded and captured were killed and scalped. Osterhaus, meanwhile, deployed the rest of his division facing north and ordered his artillery to send harassing fire beyond the intervening treeline, a strategy that worked as shells landing among the Cherokee broke them up and, despite Pike's pleading, ended their use as a coherent force for the rest of the fight. McCulloch deployed his men for battle, then rode forward to reconnoiter the Federal position. This return to his Texas Ranger roots had fatal results as a company of Illinois skirmishers let lose a volley, one bullet of which pierced McCulloch's heart and dropped him from his horse. On being informed of the Texan's death, General McIntosh assumed command and ordered an advance against the Union lines. Rushing ahead with his troops, McIntosh in turn was greeted with a volley that left him dead on the field. Leadership of the Confederate division now fell to Col. Louis Hébert, who was leading an advance through thick woods on the Rebel left. Becoming confused in the smoke-filled woods, the Louisianan blundered into the Union lines and was captured, the third commander of the division to be lost that day. Pike attempted to take command, a rather ludicrous endeavor that ended with him wandering east on the Bentonville Detour with about two thousand men as the rest of the division either marched in the other direction or lingered on Ford Road. Half of Van Dorn's army was effectively out of the battle, bested by Osterhaus's spoiling attack.[21]

Price's division, meanwhile, was heavily engaged east of Leetown, where Carr had established a position across the Wire Road near Elkhorn Tavern. The Missourians, under Van Dorn's personal command, had marched up from a valley called Cross Timber Hollow to be met by a storm of Federal fire. It was nearly nightfall before Van Dorn, finally realizing that his forces vastly outnumbered Carr's defenders, extended his lines and attacked, driving the Federals back a half mile until massed artillery firing a blistering hail of canister blunted the assault. The spoiling attacks of Carr and Osterhaus had achieved their objectives, stopping the Confederate advance and buying Curtis the time needed to turn his army 180 degrees to face the threat from the north. As the fighting of March 7 died down, the Union commander brought together the troops from Leetown and Little Sugar Creek to join Carr's line. While the Yankees resupplied and filled their cartridge pouches with fresh ammunition, Van Dorn's Rebels lay on their arms with empty bellies and dwindling cartridges, their supply wagons sitting where they had been left that morning along Little Sugar Creek. A confident Curtis told an aide, "In the morning I will attack at Elk Horn Tavern and will whip the rebels there, and when I whip them there, I whip them everywhere."[22]

He was as good as his word. Opening March 8 with a two-hour bombardment by twenty-seven cannon, Curtis placed the 10,000 men of the Army of the Southwest in line of battle and advanced shouting toward Van Dorn's haggard Southerners. The Mississippian ordered a withdrawal, blithely riding away to the east and leaving behind most of his wounded on the field and part of his command actively engaged with the Federal advance. The Army of the West crumbled, fleeing east of the White River to Van Winkle's Mill, where the famished Rebels foraged as best they could from the stark Ozark countryside. "Every living biped and quadruped was immediately killed and eaten," a Louisiana soldier observed. Van Dorn's rapid advance to Little Sugar Creek and up the Bentonville Detour had cost him some 3,500 of his 16,500 men; of those who made it into battle at Pea Ridge, at least 2,000 lay dead, wounded, or missing on the bloody fields and woodlots at Leetown and Elkhorn Tavern. Curtis's losses were also severe, with 1,384 casualties from his army of 10,250 Federals, but he had won a victory that effectively sealed Missouri for the Union.[23]

Van Dorn decided to move the Army of the West south to the Arkansas River Valley, ordering it to Van Buren in an admission of the failure of his grandiose quest for "Saint Louis—then Huzza!" As the wretched Southerners struggled through the forbidding Boston Mountains, many disillusioned men drifted away, never to return to arms. One of the Cherokee regiments, comprised of followers of Chief John Ross, defected in its entirety to the Union, motivated in part after Van Dorn's troops seized supplies in Fort Smith earmarked for Pike's Indians. These men would later fight their erstwhile comrades under Stand Watie in a further schism of the Cherokee Nation. As the desultory Confederates recovered in their camps around Frog Bayou, from which one Arkansas cavalryman wrote to his parents,

"It is almost disheartening to think that our forces are whipped on every occasion hear of late," Van Dorn received a telegram from Gen. P. G. T. Beauregard asking him to transfer the Army of the West east of the Mississippi in a consolidation of Rebel troops against Maj. Gen. U. S. Grant's Union forces in western Tennessee. With typical enthusiasm, the Mississippian ordered his exhausted soldiers to hurry east. Rain and muddy roads slowed their columns so that they were just trickling into Des Arc on the White River by April 6, far too late to join their comrades meeting defeat that day at the Battle of Shiloh. It would be the end of the month before the Army of the West was consolidated with Beauregard's troops. Most of the men would fight the rest of the war with the Army of Tennessee; Van Dorn would enjoy a mixed record before his date with a jealous husband's bullet a few months later.[24]

When Van Dorn abandoned Arkansas, he brought with him not only most of the fighting men in the state but also stripped it of weapons, animals, supplies, equipment, and machinery—whatever his flaws, one cannot fault the Mississippian for not being thorough. These actions also left Arkansas open to Curtis's Army of the Southwest, which marched across southern Missouri until the Union high command was positive that Van Dorn was across the Mississippi and again ordered him to invade Arkansas. The Yankees crossed the border near Salem on April 29 and headed south, occupying Batesville on May 2 after the Iowa Republican personally led a charge against the town's ragged band of defenders. Another Federal column under Frederick Steele, who would make his own mark on Arkansas's Civil War history, entered the state from southeast Missouri and occupied Jacksonport. Absorbing Steele's troops into his own command, Curtis now had an army of more than 20,000 men; Brig. Gen. John Seldon Roane, who Van Dorn had left in hapless command of Confederate Arkansas, led perhaps 1,200 soldiers, many of them unarmed. As Union troops crossed the Little Red River near Searcy, threatening the capital at Little Rock, Governor Rector abandoned the city and fled to Hot Springs, where he sent President Davis an indignant letter threatening to again secede, this time from the Confederacy. Rector's panicky flight would seal his doom as a political force in Confederate Arkansas.[25]

Curtis, however, had gone as far as he could. With their supply line to Missouri hopelessly stretched, the Yankees foraged heavily for supplies, increasing local rancor toward the invaders. This enmity reached a peak on May 19, when a troop of Texas cavalry supported by homegrown irregulars attacked a foraging party composed primarily of Missouri Germans east of Searcy. After a short, vicious fight, the Southerners brutally killed several wounded and surrendered Federals. Curtis angrily issued a terse order to his commanders: "Instruct your scouting parties to take no more prisoners of armed bandits." As Arkansas teetered on the edge of anarchy and collapse, Roane declared martial law on May 17. Nine days later, in a move that would change the nature of the war in Arkansas, Beauregard ordered Maj. Gen. Thomas Carmichael Hindman to take command of all Confederate forces in the state and Indian Territory.[26]

Hindman was committed to secession body and soul, had risen from colonel to major general in less than a year, and was deadly serious about his new assignment. Before crossing the Mississippi he paused at Memphis, where he seized a handful of weapons along with blankets, boots, shoes, percussion caps, and medicine while impressing one million dollars (Confederate) from city banks. Once in his home state, Hindman confiscated more shoes, blankets, ammunition, and medicine from stockpiles at Helena and Napoleon. Despite his shock at the scarcity of nearly everything of military worth in Arkansas, the former Helena lawyer boldly proclaimed, "I have come to drive out the invaders or perish in the attempt." Historian William Shea has observed that "during his brief period of command in Arkansas, Hindman demonstrated what fanaticism and a complete disregard for constitutional rights could accomplish." The general molded an army, nabbing Texas troops in transit through the state, ordering all non-Indian troops in Indian Territory to report for duty in Arkansas, finagling the return of one of Price's Missouri divisions from Mississippi, and conscripting Arkansians into the army. He ordered cotton worth millions of dollars burned to keep it from Federal seizure, declared martial law, and established price controls. To supply his nascent force, Hindman instituted manufacturing facilities that began producing guns, ammunition, and other materiel. A legitimate army began to take form.[27]

Despite Hindman's efforts, Curtis's Federals still loomed as a threat to the state capital. To harass the Yankees and buy time, Hindman issued General Orders No. 17, in which he wrote: "For the more effectual annoyance of the enemy upon our rivers and in our mountains and woods all citizens of this district who are not subject

to conscription are called upon to organize themselves into independent companies. . . . When as many as 10 men come together for
this purpose . . . [they] will at once commence operations against the
enemy without waiting for special instructions." These "Bands of
Ten" were ordered to attack isolated Federal pickets and scouting
parties, to kill pilots on riverboats, and to otherwise cause mayhem
behind enemy lines, "using the greatest vigor in their movements."
Hindman's orders succeeded in raising upward of 5,000 irregular soldiers between its issuance on June 17, 1862, and that August. Many
of these bands were genuine guerrilla fighters who disrupted Union
operations for the rest of the war. Thousands, however, formed gangs
of armed thugs that by the end of the war were opportunistically
attacking Union, Confederate, and civilian targets with equal sav-
agery. The true legacy of General Orders No. 17 is a record of horror
that rivals that of the more publicized—and romanticized—guerrilla
war in Missouri.[28]

Hindman also recognized the impending threat to the state's
waterways after the destruction of the Rebel fleet defending Memphis
on June 6. The Arkansas River was too low for navigation, but the
lower White was easily traveled and was the obvious route for a supply
line to Curtis's increasingly hungry Yankees at Batesville. Hindman
ordered that works be erected on the high ground at St. Charles, the
first defensible ground above the union of the White and Arkansas
rivers. Capt. Joseph Fry brought the gunboat *Maurepas* to St. Charles
and, after removing her cannon, had it and the steamers *Eliza G.* and
Mary Thompson scuttled to block the river. On the evening of June
16, Lt. John W. Dunnington brought his gunboat, the *Pontchartrain*,
to St. Charles, bringing two 32-pounder rifled guns to the earthworks,
before sending his vessel upriver to Little Rock for repairs. With a line
of skirmishers and a second battery below the high ground, a small
contingent of Confederate sailors, bolstered by a handful of soldiers,
settled in to await the inevitable Federal flotilla.[29]

They did not have to wait long. On June 10 and 11, a fleet of four
Union gunboats, two transports, and a pair of tugs towing coal barges
had left Memphis to head up the White River. One transport carried
the men of the Forty-sixth Indiana Infantry, the other was laden with
supplies for Curtis and his men. Capturing a Rebel steamer and easily
removing timbers that had been sunk to block the White's channel,
the little fleet made steady progress upriver. On the morning of June

17, the flotilla, with the ironclad gunboat *Mound City* in the lead, approached the Confederate works at St. Charles. After the *Mound City* encountered Rebel skirmishers, the Forty-sixth Indiana Infantry was set ashore some two and one-half miles below the Southerners to advance overland. But Federal commanders decided to silence the Confederate cannon with their gunboats instead of risking the Hoosier infantry. As the ironclad *St. Louis* pounded the lower battery, the *Mound City* moved upstream to seek the guns on the high ground. One shot from the masked 32-pounder was devastatingly accurate, piercing the *Mound City*'s casemate and bursting her boiler and steam chest. A nightmare of scalding steam burst loose, and the sailors who survived the initial explosion scrambled overboard as the gunboat helplessly drifted downstream. Rebel sharpshooters began picking off the struggling sailors in the water. As the warships dropped back to avoid the *Mound City*'s fate, the Forty-sixth Indiana charged and easily overwhelmed the Confederate positions, killing eight and wounding and capturing twenty-four while suffering no casualties. The carnage the *Mound City*'s 175-man crew suffered was incredible. Eighty-two men were killed by the initial shot through the casemate and the cloud of scalding steam it released. Forty-three others were shot or drowned in the river, while another twenty-five were seriously injured in the hard-earned victory at St. Charles.[30]

The Federal fleet continued upriver another sixty-three miles until falling water levels forced them to turn around. Curtis, in a little-noticed but radical departure from military convention, elected to completely sever his tenuous supply line with Missouri and march cross-country to meet the supply flotilla at Clarendon—an action U. S. Grant would emulate the next year in his operations against Vicksburg. The Army of the Southwest lived off the land with a vengeance. The troops ate everything that could be eaten by them and their animals and destroyed what was left, plundered private property, burned public buildings and private homes, and freed thousands of slaves with eman-cipation papers printed on commandeered presses, despite the fact that the Emancipation Proclamation was still six months in the future. One Yankee wrote, "desolation, horrid to contemplate, marks every section of the country through which the army has passed and an air of sickening desolation is everywhere visible." Historian William Shea declares that "economic devastation, social upheaval, and the collapse of local institutions were the legacy of Curtis's march across eastern

Arkansas. The state felt the impact of 'total war' long before it was visited upon Georgia or other parts of the Confederacy."[31]

Hindman, interpreting Curtis's movements as a retreat, called on the people of eastern Arkansas to rise against the invader, to shoot Federal soldiers whenever possible, and to "destroy every pound of meat and flour, every ear of corn and stack of fodder, oats and wheat that can fall into his hands; fell trees as thickly as rafts, in all roads before him, burn every bridge and block up the fords." Most of the Arkansians of the region, already suffering such treatment at the hands of the Army of the Southwest, declined to comply with the general's zealous entreaties. Hindman, seeking to block the Federals from crossing the Cache River, also pulled together a force of some 5,000 Texas cavalry and Arkansas infantry and sent them against Curtis's army. The Yankees began crossing the Cache near Cotton Plant on July 7, but the Texans caught up with them at Parley Hill's plantation about four miles south of the crossing point and attacked. Curtis's men initially fell back, then reformed along a fencerow on the edge of Hill's cornfield. As the Rebel cavalry charged, Union troops unleashed a withering volley, stopping them dead. Union reinforcements (including two rifled cannon) arrived, and the Texans fled, leaving as many as 136 dead on the field and about the same number wounded; Curtis suffered only six killed and fifty-seven wounded. It was the final organized Confederate attack on the Army of the Southwest.[32]

Having wiped out organized Confederate resistance with this lopsided victory, the hungry Federals continued down the White River to Clarendon. There, to their dismay, they found that the supply flotilla had already left. Curtis fired blasts from his artillery and rushed cavalrymen downriver to catch the vessels, but his efforts were futile. The Army of the Southwest was deep in enemy territory with no hope of receiving Federal supplies. Curtis decided to abandon any hopes of capturing Little Rock and elected to head to Helena, a bustling port on the Mississippi River some forty-five miles to the east. The march of the woolen-clad soldiers across the pestilential delta through the heat of an Arkansas July matched in misery the army's earlier tramp across the prairies as ticks, chiggers, and snakes vied to make the Yankees miserable; one Illinois horseman told his wife that the journey gave him "an idea of how it is in haydes." On July 12 the Army of the Southwest finished the five-hundred-mile march that had started at Pea Ridge just over three months earlier, occupying Helena without opposition and accompanied by thousands of freed slaves. Curtis assuaged his disappointment at not capturing Little Rock by establishing his headquarters in Hindman's stately mansion and freeing the Confederate general's slaves. Food, clothing, and other supplies began pouring in to the riverport, and Helena became the Union's main Arkansas base on the Mississippi. An Iowa infantryman summed up the army's relief at ending the grueling campaign, writing, "we have more fun here [in Helena] that we can stand too[.] we come 65 miles in too days on fore crackers."[33]

While Confederate Arkansas may have drawn its collective breath with the threat to Little Rock averted, major changes in its political and military leadership were looming. Governor Rector, still smarting from widespread criticism of his flight to Hot Springs and failing to halt new provisions that reduced gubernatorial terms from four years to two, announced his bid for reelection. His political foes nominated Harris Flanagin of Arkadelphia. Flanagin, a New Jersey native, was serving east of the Mississippi as the respected colonel of the Second Arkansas Mounted Rifles and had fought at Wilson's Creek and Pea Ridge before leading his men into action in Mississippi, Kentucky, and Tennessee. Rector went on the offensive, claiming that his abandonment of the capital had saved Little Rock from Union capture because "there was nothing to come for" and charging that Flanagin was actually an Irish Yankee, "his descent directly from the original Patrick O'Flanagin of Derry, county Connaught, Ould Ireland." Although Flanagin was on active duty in Tennessee and thus unable to campaign, he easily defeated Rector in the October 6 election, which saw a surprisingly large number of votes cast: 18,187 for Flanagin and 7,419 for Rector; a third candidate trailed distantly with 708 votes. Flanagin's resignation from the Army of Tennessee was accepted on October 25, and he headed west for his new civil duties in Arkansas. Rector resigned his office after addressing the state legislature on November 4, leaving the president of the senate to serve as chief executive until the former colonel took office.[34]

The people of Arkansas also were tired of Hindman's iron-fisted reign, with many of his prewar political foes leading the clamor against his policies. In early July President Davis answered their cries by sending yet another old friend west of the Mississippi River. His choice was, if possible, even worse than Van Dorn. Theophilus Hunter Holmes had failed as a planter in North Carolina before his father arranged his appointment to the U.S. Military Academy. He graduated in 1829—a year behind Davis—and served in the Seminole War and at various posts in Indian Territory. Holmes served with distinction in the Mexican War, earning the rank of brevet major for his actions in the fighting at Monterey; fought Indians in the West; and led recruiting efforts for the army in the years before secession. Resigning from the U.S. Army in the spring of 1861, he returned to North Carolina and helped organize troops. The president appointed him a brigadier general in the Confederate army in June. Holmes led two regiments at the First Battle of Bull Run, though arriving too late to take part in the action, and fought ineffectively at Malvern Hill a year later. As historian Albert Castel observes, "After a year of war all that could be said about Holmes was that he had done nothing either outstandingly good or bad." As he arrived to take command of the Department of the Trans-Mississippi, Holmes was nearly fifty-eight years old, going deaf, a bully to his subordinates, and lacked self-confidence—a poor combination for head of a sprawling command covering Arkansas, Missouri, Louisiana, Texas, and Indian Territory. To his credit the elderly general realized his limitations and would repeatedly ask to be replaced in the months ahead.[35]

Holmes arrived at Little Rock on August 12, 1862. While Holmes the dithering worrier and Hindman the forceful fire-eater could not have been more different in personality, the new department commander admired the results of his subordinate's extralegal activities, which had resulted in an army of some 30,000 troops when he arrived (though at least 5,000 of those had no weapons). Holmes defended Hindman's actions to Richmond, arguing that his policies had been essential to wrest order from the chaos Van Dorn had left behind and to bring reluctant recruits under the Southern standard "as the conscripts have to be hunted down, and in some instances have armed themselves and banded together to resist enrollment." Accordingly, despite their unpopularity, he retained martial law as well as extended price controls. Holmes quickly subdivided his department into three sections. The District of Texas contained Texas and Arizona, while the District of Louisiana consisted of those parts of Louisiana west of the Mississippi. Holmes basically left both of these to their own devices, concentrating his energies on the District of Arkansas, which contained Arkansas, Missouri, and Indian Territory and remained under Hindman's command. Holmes took about half of the troops present in

A personal friend of Confederate president Jefferson Davis, Lt. Gen. Theophilus Holmes was sent to command the Trans-Mississippi after a poor showing in the East. His record did not improve west of the Mississippi River. *Courtesy Library of Congress.*

Arkansas—many of them in new units arriving from Texas—and set them to fortifying positions along the White and Arkansas rivers, including an impressive earthwork at Arkansas Post. This, he hoped, would contain Federal forces at Helena and protect Little Rock from attacks from the east. The rest of his men, under Hindman's direct command, were stationed at Fort Smith and Fayetteville in northwest Arkansas. The ever-aggressive Hindman suggested a drive into Missouri to keep the Yankees off balance. But Holmes counseled him to focus on drill and discipline for the raw recruits and conscripts who made up Hindman's First Corps of the Army of the Trans-Mississippi.[36]

Hindman arrived in Fort Smith on August 24 and took command of the First Corps, numbering roughly 9,100 men and fourteen pieces of artillery. While indeed consisting of mostly untrained and reluctant conscripts, his force also included a brigade of Missouri horsemen under Col. Joseph O. Shelby that would become one of the most storied and effective units in the entire Trans-Mississippi. Regardless of the overall quality of his troops, the general deployed the bulk of his army along Arkansas's northwest border. Establishing his headquarters at Pineville, Missouri, Hindman set plans to clear Federal troops out of Indian Territory and to move on Springfield, once again using southwestern Missouri as an avenue of invasion that could once and for all bring the state into the Confederacy. These bold plans, however, would face a new foe who was an experienced campaigner in the region. Samuel Curtis, newly promoted to major general, left Helena and assumed command of the Department of the Missouri on September 19. Curtis quickly ordered troops under Brig. Gen. John M. Schofield back to the ground through which he himself had campaigned back in the spring. Cobbling together a force he styled the Army of the Frontier, Schofield headed toward the state's southwest corner to drive Hindman out of Missouri.[37]

At this critical juncture, Holmes ordered Hindman to return to Little Rock. Brig. Gen. James S. Rains, an affable Missouri State Guard officer who "was profoundly ignorant of everything pertaining to military affairs," took command during Hindman's absence with orders to avoid combat. Schofield, however, had no such restrictions, and his advance attacked Rebel troops at Newtonia, Missouri, on September 30, driving them back after a day of hard fighting. Some of these men, under Col. Douglas Cooper, fell back to Maysville while the rest, under Shelby, retreated to Cross Hollows in Arkansas.

Schofield sent a division under pugnacious Kansan James G. Blunt to attack Cooper. On October 22 at Fort Wayne in Indian Territory Blunt did just that, smashing the Rebels in a half hour and capturing all of their artillery. Other Federal troops had reentered Arkansas four days earlier and occupied Cross Hollows, Fayetteville, and Bentonville. Schofield withdrew all of the Army of the Frontier except Blunt's division back to Springfield in early November and, feeling ill but satisfied with his accomplishments, returned to St. Louis on November 20, leaving Blunt in charge.[38]

Even as Rains and Cooper bungled the situation in northwest Arkansas—Hindman would remove Rains from command for drunkenness—Holmes was dealing with pressure to again move troops east of the Mississippi. Following Gen. Braxton Bragg's failed invasion of Kentucky and Van Dorn's defeat at Corinth in early October, Richmond authorities were concerned that Union forces would begin a serious offensive to seize control of the Mississippi River and ordered Holmes to send 10,000 men to bolster the defenders of Vicksburg, Mississippi. His initial letter from Secretary of War George Wythe Randolph, which included notification of his promotion to lieutenant general, actually authorized Holmes to "direct operations on the eastern bank," which must have sent the old general into a quivering funk. On learning of these orders, which were issued without his knowledge, President Davis promptly chastised Randolph, who resigned in protest. Holmes, mindful of the disastrous results attending Van Dorn's abandonment of Arkansas, declined the levy of troops for Vicksburg. Fearful of a potential Federal invasion from Missouri and of the powerful gunboats on the Mississippi, Holmes declared that to send men east of the river could result in the loss of the Arkansas River Valley, if not the entire Trans-Mississippi. He also noted that instead of the 50,000 men Richmond thought he commanded in Arkansas, he only had some 22,000 effective troops. He also sent a letter attempting to refuse his promotion, which Davis tore up, though Richmond noted, "it is quite refreshing, amongst the legions of applications rec'd here from officers for this promotion, to find one officer whose modest appreciation of his own merits has induced him to decline a promotion."[39]

While Schofield may have believed the year's campaigning was over, Hindman saw in the divided Federal army a grand opportunity to strike a smashing blow. He decided to send his cavalry, now commanded by Brig. Gen. John Sappington Marmaduke of Missouri, to gather supplies from the fertile area around Cane Hill, southwest of Fayetteville. This activity, he hoped, would draw Blunt's troops deeper into Arkansas, after which he would hit the Kansan from the rear with the bulk of his army. After crushing Blunt, Hindman then intended to turn to Missouri to smash Brig. Gen. Francis J. Herron's Yankee troops as they rushed to Blunt's aid, leaving southwest Missouri open to invasion. Hindman's plans depended heavily on the Union commanders doing exactly as he anticipated and did not adequately anticipate Blunt's belligerent nature. An amateur soldier, Blunt had been a fervent abolitionist before the war, and what he may have lacked in military experience he more than made up for with aggressiveness. Learning that some 2,500 Rebel cavalrymen had arrived at Cane Hill on November 25, Blunt went on the offensive with about 5,000 men and thirty cannon, "determined to strike Marmaduke and destroy him before re-enforcements arrived." By forced marches his force of Kansas, Indiana, and Indian troops camped within ten miles of Cane Hill on the evening of November 27. Early the next morning the Federals attacked the surprised horsemen. Initially checking Blunt's advance, the Confederates were slowly forced back over the rough terrain. Shelby's men covered the rear, placing a company on each side of the road, unleashing a volley, and then dropping behind the next two companies, which would do the same. This gradual withdrawal allowed Marmaduke time to set up a series of defensive positions, which would be abandoned once Blunt deployed his troops for assault. This running battle continued for nine hours, stretching over twelve miles of rugged, tree-covered mountains, and ended with a desperate twilight rear-guard action by Arkansians and Missourians under Col. Charles Carroll. While casualties were light—Blunt lost eight dead and thirty-six wounded, Marmaduke about the same—the Rebels withdrew to Dripping Springs south of the Boston Mountains. Blunt made camp at Cane Hill, now even deeper in Arkansas and farther from reinforcements. Like Schofield, Blunt foresaw an end to campaigning in Arkansas: "the enemy are badly whipped, and will probably not venture north of the Boston Mountains again this winter." But Hindman saw opportunity beckoning.[40]

Blunt was now more than three times closer to the Rebel army than to his nearest reinforcements at Springfield. Although his troops were mostly indifferently armed recruits and conscripts, his artillery pitiful, his draft animals substandard, and his transport decrepit, Hindman decided to attack and headed into the Boston Mountains on December 3 with 11,000 men and twenty-two cannon. To inspire his men, the former politician distributed a printed exhortation warning that the Federal army they were attacking was "made up of Pin Indians, free negroes, Southern tories, Kansas jayhawkers, and hired Dutch cut-throats. . . . We can do this; we must do this; our country will be ruined if we fail." Blunt, aware that the First Corps was on the move, grimly dug in around Cane Hill and sent word to Herron in Springfield that he needed reinforcements. Herron, a veteran fighter who had earned a Medal of Honor during the carnage at Pea Ridge, gamely set out on the morning of December 4 with 7,000 men and twenty-two pieces of artillery on the 110-mile trek to Arkansas.[41]

Hindman's cavalry was the first part of his army to materialize from the Boston Mountains, staging a raucous demonstration at Reed's Mountain on December 6 as the bulk of the infantry struggled north well east of Cane Hill. The Rebel learned that Federal reinforcements were moving fast from Missouri and hurriedly revised his own plans, deciding to hit Herron's two divisions near Fayetteville, destroy them, then wheel and crush Blunt's troops at Cane Hill. He sent Marmaduke's cavalry toward Fayetteville on the morning of December 7; the Rebel advance under Shelby quickly encountered Herron's forward elements—the Seventh Missouri and First Arkansas Cavalry (U.S.)—and hurled them back toward town. Herron halted the rout, reportedly shooting one panicked trooper off his horse, and moved forward, unlimbering the First Missouri Light Artillery and shelling the enemy horsemen. Marmaduke fell back to where he found Brig. Gen. Francis A. Shoup's Missouri division deployed on a tree-covered hill behind the Illinois River near a pleasant little building called the Prairie Grove Presbyterian Church. Hindman, worried by reports that Blunt's troops were beginning to move at Cane Hill, looked over the position and decided that this was the place where the First Corps of the Army of the Trans-Mississippi would make its stand against Herron's foot-sore Yankees. As the Battle of Prairie Grove commenced, both armies were exhausted by the grueling marches they had just completed.[42]

Hindman's army formed in a roughly horseshoe-shaped line atop the high ground overlooking Crawford's Prairie. Herron's attenuated divisions, numbering less than half that of the Confederates, crossed the Illinois opposite the Rebel right and began hammering their foes with rifled artillery fire. He then ordered a charge up the hill toward the wood-frame home of Anthony Borden. When his strike force entered an apple orchard behind the house, however, it was mauled by concentrated musketry from troops under Marmaduke and Shoup. As the survivors—about half of those making the attack—fled down the slope, a mob of Confederates pursued. Now it was their time to die, massacred by the superior Federal artillery. Herron again ordered a charge up the hill, which was again blunted around the Borden House. The combatants afterward maintained their respective initial positions until midafternoon, when Hindman finally decided to swing his left, which had been largely unengaged, across the prairie and crush Herron's exhausted Yankees once and for all. As this maneuver began, Blunt arrived on the field, and the entire situation changed.[43]

The Kansas general had heard the artillery fire to his northeast that morning and immediately set out with his division. A wrong turn brought the Federals in from the northwest instead of from the southwest and into the Confederate rear, but he characteristically flung his 4,500 men straight into action, hitting the Confederates just beginning to move downhill against Herron. Rebel and Yankee fought fiercely around the home of William Morton at the base of the slope until a determined counterattack finally drove the Federals back onto the prairie. In a bloody mirror image of that morning's fighting, Southern troops streamed after Blunt's retreating soldiers and were mauled by canister from the Federal artillery. Blunt and Herron finally linked up and formed a solid line as darkness fell across the battlefield. During the night Blunt brought up 3,000 cavalrymen who had been guarding his supply train at Rhea's Mill, while hundreds of Herron's stragglers rejoined their units. Hindman had no hope of such reinforcements.[44]

The Southern general established a cease-fire with Blunt in order to treat the dead and wounded on the gory battlefield. It was a nightmare scene. Many of the wounded had crawled into haystacks for warmth, then were too weak to escape when artillery fire ignited the hay. "A large drove of hogs, attracted doubtless by the scent of roasting flesh, came greedily from the apple trees and gorged themselves upon the unholy banquet," a Rebel soldier recalled later. A Missouri Yankee remembered the emaciated physiques of the Confederate dead, noting the "sallow cadiverous look" of the "thin and yellow" corpses. Hindman, his men desperately low on ammunition and totally without food, realized that to continue the battle in the morning would be disastrous. Wrapping the wheels of his artillery and wagons in blankets to mask their sound, he quietly withdrew the First Corps back into the Boston Mountains and eventually to Van Buren. The human cost of the fighting at Prairie Grove was high. Herron and Blunt, with less than 8,000 men between them, lost 175 killed, 813 wounded, and 263 missing. Hindman suffered 164 killed, 817 wounded, and 336 missing of his approximately 9,000 Rebels.[45]

The battered First Corps was in sad shape as it limped into Van Buren. Its battle losses were high, and several of its conscript soldiers had deserted; many would later enlist in Federal units. In addition, hundreds of soldiers were sick, which Hindman attributed to the "unprecedented hardships to which the men have been exposed." Marmaduke and Shelby headed east down the Arkansas River to take up winter quarters at Lewisburg while Hindman withdrew the bulk of his infantry across the river to camps near Fort Smith. But Blunt and Herron were not yet done with the First Corps. On learning that Schofield was returning to retake command of the Army of the Frontier, the two generals decided to make one last attack. On December 27 they moved a shock force of 8,000 men and thirty pieces of artillery into the Boston Mountain, moving quickly down the primitive roads. One Union cavalryman reported crossing Cove Creek thirty-three times within a ten-mile stretch, noting, "I felt glad about those times that I was not an infantry man when I saw them splashing through the cold water." The quick-moving Federals burst into the camp of R. P. Crump's Texas cavalrymen at Dripping Springs, driving them in disorder to Van Buren. The Yankees were right behind them and quickly seized control. Hindman ordered his artillery to shell the town—an order that was met with dismay by its secessionist population—and Blunt's cannons returned fire, beginning a duel that lasted until sunset. But Hindman had had enough. He ordered Fort Smith abandoned, along with hundreds of his sick and wounded, and burned two steamboats on his way out of town for a long, bitterly cold march toward Little Rock. The Federals loaded all of the captured supplies they could into wagons, then burned the rest along with three steamers and the ferry. The Army of the Frontier left Van Buren on December 29–30, "quite well satisfied with our Holidays visit to our *friends* in secessia," and returned to Rhea's Mills in time for a New Year's Day party, one soldier writing, "you can believe we made some noise but it was all got over without any trouble."[46]

Hindman's offensive into northwest Arkansas was the final gasp of a year-long attempt by Confederate armies to take the war to the North. In the east Gen. Robert E. Lee's Army of Northern Virginia had invaded Maryland in September, enjoying initial success before locking with Maj. Gen. George B. McClellan's Army of the Potomac at Sharpsburg, Maryland. The carnage there cost the combined armies more than 26,000 casualties, including more than 4,700 dead, and forced Lee to return to Virginia. In the heartland Braxton Bragg and Maj. Gen. Edmund Kirby Smith led Confederate armies from Tennessee into Kentucky, nearly reaching the Ohio River before themselves retreating after the confusing and costly Battle of Perryville in October. Price and Van Dorn, who had failed so miserably at Pea Ridge, attempted a northward thrust in Mississippi that was blunted at Corinth, returning the offensive momentum to Grant, who would bullishly maintain it toward Vicksburg. As the year ended east of the Mississippi, Lee held firm after mauling the Army of the Potomac in the meat grinder that was the Battle of Fredericksburg; Bragg's Confederates and Maj. Gen. William S. Rosecrans were locked in bloody fighting along Stones River at Murfreesboro, Tennessee; and Grant was maneuvering south. The failures of these wide-ranging Rebel offensives gave Lincoln what was perhaps the greatest political opening of the war. On January 1, 1863, he issued a proclamation stating: "I do order and declare that all persons held as slaves within said designated states, and parts of states [in rebellion], are, and henceforward shall be free." With the stroke of a pen, the president changed the nature of the war politically, deprived the South of most of its diplomatic initiative, and opened a vast potential source of labor and soldiers for the North.

As the Federals in the Trans-Mississippi, with Schofield now again in command, withdrew into Missouri and Kansas at the end of the year, northern Arkansas was largely devoid of organized Confederate troops and civilian government. Hindman's "partisan rangers" took advantage of the situation and began victimizing the Unionists of the region. Indeed, as historian Robert R. Mackey has observed, "Rebel authorities discovered that they had lost control of their guerrillas by the winter of 1862–63, and they would never regain it." Morale was low among Confederate troops and desertion rampant. Both soldiers and civilians suffered from food shortages caused by poor harvests in 1861 and 1862 that were augmented by the insistence of Arkansas farmers to grow more-profitable cotton rather than desperately needed staples. A cholera epidemic dramatically thinned the state's hog population, and a critical shortage of salt made it difficult to preserve what pork was available. These miserable conditions continued west into Indian Territory, where many Cherokee and Creek soldiers were leaving Confederate service and joining Union forces. Comanche raids led Rebel commander William Steele to move most of the effective troops in Indian Territory to the Texas border to protect settlements there. A weak line of forts along the Arkansas River provided the main evidence of an organized Confederate presence in the Creek and Cherokee nations. It was within this gloomy scenario that the struggle for control of the rich valley of the Arkansas River would begin in earnest in 1863.[47]

2

"WHILE IT LASTED SHILOH WAS NOWHERE"

The Battle of Arkansas Post

Theophilus Holmes may have had his shortcomings, but he did realize the vital importance of protecting the Arkansas River Valley, which was not only the state's breadbasket but also the road to the capital. On September 28, 1862, he ordered Col. John W. Dunnington, who had helped cause the Union navy so much grief at St. Charles a few months earlier, to develop fortifications along the Arkansas and White rivers to protect them from assault. As the first line of defense on the Arkansas, Dunnington and his team chose to build a fort on the high ground at Arkansas Post, about twenty-five miles from where the river fed into the Mississippi. Slaves from throughout the region were impressed to begin the task of constructing this barrier.[1]

Dunnington was not the first military man to realize the value of the Arkansas Post area. Frenchman Henri de Tonti had left a six-man contingent on the north bank of the river "half a musket shot" from the Quapaw village of Assotoue in 1686 to initiate trade with the Indians, establishing a settlement that would linger for thirty years until the king of France banned fur trapping south of Canada. A French garrison was reestablished in 1721, withdrawn in 1726, and returned in 1732. By 1751 the small garrison realized the need for a stouter fortification so one was built, only to be abandoned in 1756 because it was too inaccessible to boat traffic on the Mississippi. In 1763 Spain gained control of all French interests west of the Mississippi, and in 1781 yet another fort was built. This post was the scene of what was probably the last skirmish of the American Revolution when an English malcontent named James Colbert led about one hundred partisans and a large contingent of Chickasaw Indians against the small Spanish garrison on April 16, 1783. After firing some three hundred cannon rounds at the attackers, Spanish commander Capt. Jacobo Du Breuil counterattacked with ten soldiers and four Quapaws, routing Colbert's motley force. The United States acquired Arkansas Post in 1804 as part of the Louisiana Purchase and placed a sixteen-man garrison there until 1812. Between 1819 and 1820, Arkansas's territorial legislature met there—government functions moved to Little Rock in 1820—and the first newspaper established west of the Mississippi, the *Arkansas Gazette*, began publishing there in 1819. Dunnington and his engineers prepared Arkansas Post for a new chapter in its rich history.[2]

The centerpiece of the Confederate defenses was Fort Hindman, a large, square fort built just below a bend in the Arkansas River. The fort's outer parapets were one hundred yards long, and its walls stood eighteen feet high, protected by a ditch that was twenty feet wide and eight feet deep. On the river side two casemates, braced by three layers of stout oaken timbers covered with sheets of railroad iron, held two Dahlgren cannon, one mounting an eight-inch gun and the other a nine-inch piece. A second nine-inch Dahlgren was placed *en barbette* beside the southeast bastion. The CSS *Pontchartrain* continued her contributions to the Confederate cause by supplying the heavy guns for the post as well as thirty-five tars to man them. Ten-pounder Parrott rifles and 6-pounder smoothbores mounted on the bastions' artillery platforms and firing steps for infantrymen inside the parapet completed the fort's formidable defenses. West of Fort Hindman, a line of trenches ran for some 720 yards, ending near the natural barrier of Post Bayou. To augment the fortifications, pilings held in place with log chains were placed in the river to hinder the passage of any gunboats that ventured upstream. In addition, a line of rifle pits with field works for ten artillery pieces was started two miles below Arkansas Post to menace the river road, while a second line was established above the lower works. To all appearances, Fort Hindman could withstand all but the most determined assaults.[3]

The troops who manned the post, however, had serious misgivings about the location. Col. Roger Q. Mills confided to his wife: "[T]he chiefs here think this is a very strong position but I do not. . . . [I]f they attack us here in high water it will be an accident if we are not all made prisoners. . . . If they attack us in small force, we will certainly defeat them, but they have overwhelming armies and will use them." Another Texan maintained that "had the fort been built anywhere else, it could doubtless have been held successfully against a large force, but . . . there was not a place on the Arkansas River less capable of successful defense against a large force than Arkansas Post, but we were stationed there with orders to hold the place against all hazzards." Capt. Gil McKay of the W. P. Lane Rangers simply dubbed it "Ft. Donaldson No. 2," referring to the Tennessee bastion that had been captured in the spring of 1862. Indeed, one armchair general noted years later, "there is probably no place on the Arkansas River below Pine Bluff with fewer advantages against an invading army, or better adapted for the capture of the troops attempting to hold it, than Arkansas Post."[4]

In Helena the bustle at Arkansas Post did not go unnoticed, and Brig. Gen. Alvin Hovey decided to do something about it. He enlisted the aid of Capt. Henry Walke to supply a gunboat, then set forth on November 16 to "make a dash upon the Post of Arkansas." Walke was concerned that the White River would be too shallow for his heavy ironclad gunboat, the *Carondolet*, to navigate, but Hovey queried "scouts, pilots, deserters, and citizens" who all assured him that the White should have "6 or 7 feet of water in the shoalest parts of the channel." With 6,000 infantry and 2,000 cavalry on steamers, the expedition picked its way down the shallow Mississippi, finally arriving off the mouth of the White River on November 19. Hovey disembarked the cavalry under the command of Col. Cyrus Bussey of the Third Iowa and continued up the White. Bussey and his troopers had orders to seize a ferry at Prairie Landing, but their mission quickly became a nightmare. The area through which they traveled was flooded by recent torrential rains, and the men could not see their horses' heads as they rode in pitch darkness through a thick forest. They rode "single file, floundering through swamps, many of the horses miring down until 8 oclock PM [when they] lost the road and got fast in grape vines. . . . The men dismounted in water ankle deep tied their horses to trees and prepared to pass the night. Before nine oclock a heavy rain came on and continued without intermission during the entire night." Hovey's luck was no better. He reported that "after passing all obstructions known to the oldest pilots we encountered a new bar with only 30 inches in the channel, the river within the last two days having fallen at least 5 feet." The general was gamely preparing to march overland to attack Arkansas Post when he received orders calling off the raid. Hovey then recalled Bussey's soggy horsemen and returned to Helena, arriving on the twenty-first. "I deeply regret that we could not have been permitted to consummate our plans, as I feel confident that we should have captured the Post, with a large number of prisoners and stores," he reported.[5]

Even as the levied slaves and Confederate laborers continued their efforts to fortify Arkansas Post, more Texas troops arrived to man the works. Dunnington initially had direct support from the Nineteenth Arkansas Infantry Regiment under Col. Charles L. Dawson and a battalion of Arkansas infantry under Lt. Col. William A. Crawford. In addition, a brigade consisting of the Sixth Texas Infantry, the Twenty-fourth and Twenty-fifth Texas Cavalry (Dismounted), Lt. William B. Denson's Louisiana cavalry company, and Capt. William Hart's Arkansas Battery was assigned to the area during construction. Col. Robert R. Garland, a U.S. Army officer who resigned his commission in 1861 to raise and train the Sixth Texas, commanded the brigade. During November and December, Col. James Deshler's brigade was transferred to Arkansas Post from Camp White Sulphur Springs near Pine Bluff. One of his men described the West Point graduate and former U.S. Army officer as "a thorough gentleman and every inch the soldier. We all fell right in with him, and the longer we were with him and under his command the more we liked him." Deshler's brigade comprised the Tenth Texas Infantry and the Fifteenth, Seventeenth, and Eighteenth Texas Cavalry (Dismounted). A soldier of the Seventeenth Texas was unimpressed with the garrison: "we have but 2 Briggades at this place, only Garlands and Deshlers, with one or two companeys of Ark Conscripts but they are not worth a curs." The newcomers were poorly supplied as well, Colonel Mills lamenting: "[M]y poor men, many of whom have not a single blanket and it is now winter. Many of them are barefooted. Many with but a single shirt, many with no coats, many on the very verge of nakedness."[6]

The Rebel troops commenced making themselves at home, building winter quarters on some of the high ground north of Fort Hindman. A soldier in the Twenty-fourth Texas noted, "we put up comfortable log houses—make wood chimneys, board roofs—daub the cracks with mud,—make door shutters out of boards &c&c and fix to live comfortable all winter." By the time Deshler's brigade arrived, Lt. Flavius Perry of the Seventeenth Texas reported: "[T]he troops that have been here fore we came had all got their houses finished and have moved in them. They look just like Negro quarters, log houses 16 feet square and the cracks dobed." The newcomers began "making huts of poles fourteen by sixteen, very rough, but they will keep the rain off of us and that is all we want." With the approach of the new year, the Rebels found themselves "eating poor pumpkins, mean sorghum, and coarse corn bread very well contented, as the winter was unusually mild. . . . [W]e felt quite secure from all danger." As the Texans settled into winter quarters, John Arrington of the Fifteenth Texas voiced the frustration that many of the soldiers on both sides felt with their leaders, writing, "I wish that they would stop their fuss so we can all come home and let each other live in peace with all mankind."[7]

The Texas troops had left a trail of graves behind them after entering Arkansas, and diseases continued taking their toll on the men. Isaiah Harlan wrote to his brother, "this place is not as healthy as Camp Nelson," an Arkansas camp where hundreds of Texans had died in an epidemic earlier in 1862. "The atmosphere is close and damp and the water is bad." Their snug quarters did not help any, he noted, writing, "I don think that close cabins are whole some when we are under the necesity of undergoing guard duty and the hardships connected with a soldier's life." The hospital buildings south of Fort Hindman stayed full of sick soldiers, and the continuing stream of disease casualties depressed Robert Hodges, who observed: "[W]e are loseing men every day. It looks as though we are all doomed to die in this detestable country." The mortality rate was so high, "we can hear the dead march nearly all the time of the day and sometimes the night." Another Rebel wryly observed that "the salutes they would fire over the graves of soldiers as they buried them each day was not calculated to brace one up much." Many of the men were looking forward to meeting an enemy they could actually fight as they braced themselves for what they felt was an inevitable attack. A soldier in the Tenth Texas wrote home: "[W]ee are looking for the gun boats up here every day. The river has risen twelve to fifteen feet. Wee are redy for them, let them come."[8]

Theophilus Holmes, meanwhile, was concerned with command issues at Arkansas Post. Dunnington, a captain in the Confederate navy who Hindman had appointed a colonel in his provisional army, was formally given command of the works at Fort Hindman on November 25. In asking that Dunnington's rank be confirmed, Holmes noted that the big guns at the fort came from Dunnington's *Pontchartrain*, and "he is the only officer I have fit to command them. In order that he may exercise command over the very igno- rant colonels who command the two regiments designated to defend the forts I earnestly request that his appointment be confirmed, if only by temporary rank." Holmes may have felt more comfortable when Brig. Gen. Thomas James Churchill assumed command of the defenses at Arkansas Post on December 10. A Kentucky native and Mexican War veteran, Churchill had made Arkansas his home and was the postmaster at Little Rock when hostilities broke out. He raised the First Arkansas Mounted Rifles and fought at Wilson's Creek, after which he received his brigadier's star. Transferring east of the Mississippi and serving in the Kentucky campaign, Churchill led troops in the fighting at Richmond before returning to the Trans-Mississippi. Despite his impressive military credentials, not all of the Texans were excited about serving under an Arkansian, one of them referring to him as "a little bit of a spike-tail, snaffle-bit dude of an Arkansaw Brigadier-General."[9]

Churchill was aware of the heavy Union activity on the Missis- sippi River and ordered his cavalry to harass Federal shipping. These operations disrupted Union supply lines, leading E. Paul Reichhelm of the Third Missouri Infantry (U.S.) to note that "great and constant damage was inflicted upon our transport fleet, and many a day of 'half' or no 'rations' we had to endure . . . may be put to account of the rascally pirates that lurked for spoils behind the walls and cannon of Arkansas Post." Lt. Leroy M. Nutt's Louisiana cavalry company caught a particularly fat prize at Cypress Bend on the Mississippi on December 28, when they fired on the unarmed steamer *Blue Wing.* The captain of the heavily laden vessel cut loose a coal barge and hove to, surren- dering his boat and crew. William W. Heartsill of the W. P. Lane Rangers reported: "[A]t 2 O'clck the captured Boat comes in sight with the Confederate Flag at her mast and lands at the Fort. . . . Captain Nutt's men deserve great credit for their excellent maneuvering which succeeded in capturing the boat." The *Blue Wing*'s cargo was a boon to the hungry, poorly armed Confederates. Lieutenant Perry happily told his wife that the vessel was "loaded with Flour and Coffee, Whisky,

Brig. Gen. Thomas Churchill, though vastly outnumbered at Arkansas Post, tried to fulfill Holmes's futile order "to hold out until help arrived or until all dead." *Courtesy Old State House Museum, Little Rock.*

Salt, Apples and . . . some few Pr [*sic*] cotton cards and Ammunition, Guns and Pistols and several other tricks too numerous to mention." The boat also carried a large quantity of mail, "so we have plenty of Northern papers of the latest dates to read and some of the most interesting letters that I ever saw," boasted a soldier of the Twelfth Texas. "They was written by the young ladies to their sweet hearts in the army. From what I can learn from these papers I think they are as tired of the war as we are." The hapless crew of the *Blue Wing* was "placed in the guard house of our regiment where they were held for a few days and then they were taken to Helena, Arkansas and released on parole." The garrison feasted on the cargo, unaware of events in Mississippi that would decide the eventual fate of Fort Hindman.[10]

General Grant had intended to reduce the Rebel bastion at Vicksburg with a two-pronged offensive, personally leading two army corps in an overland assault while two other corps under Maj. Gen. William Tecumseh Sherman steamed down the Mississippi to attack the Confederates via the Yazoo River. Figuring that one of the assaults would succeed, the Union commander planned to exploit whichever resulted in victory as a basis to take Vicksburg. Confederate initiative, however, doomed both operations. In early December a Texas cavalryman had suggested a raid behind Union lines in Mississippi to plunder the rich stores at Holly Springs and tie up Federal troops that otherwise would be campaigning against Vicksburg. Lt. Gen. John C. Pemberton, the Confederate commander, agreed and placed Earl Van Dorn in charge of the operation. Recent historians of the campaign note that "for the only time during the war, Van Dorn was properly matched to an assignment." The Mississippian's 3,500 cavalrymen raced into Holly Springs on the morning of December 20 and swiftly subdued Union resistance. The town was filled to bursting with supplies, and the raiders equipped themselves in style at Uncle Sam's expense before putting the rest to the torch. The destruction of Grant's forward supply base, coupled with a two-week raid by Maj. Gen. Nathan Bedford Forrest behind Union lines in Tennessee, ended Union plans for an overland assault against Vicksburg. These successes also allowed Pemberton to concentrate on stopping Sherman's drive up the Yazoo.[11]

As Van Dorn's troopers set out on their spoiling raid, Sherman headed south from Memphis with a vast armada of steamers and transports. Additional vessels carrying the bulk of Hovey's garrison joined him at Helena, as did Adm. David Dixon Porter's formidable Mississippi Squadron, which added waterborne firepower for the approximately 32,000 soldiers in the expedition. Despite knowing that Grant's overland drive had been thwarted, Sherman headed up the Yazoo on December 26. His original plan was to strike at Haynes' Bluff, but mines in the Yazoo that previously had sunk the powerful gunboat *Cairo* prevented this. The general instead decided to try to take the high ground on the Walnut Hills near Chickasaw Bayou. Unfortunately for the Union attackers, they had to drag themselves through lowland swamps before reaching the hills, an escarpment that was easily fortifiable and protected by Chickasaw Bayou, which snaked along its base. Rebel troops freed from the defense of Grenada, Mississippi, by Grant's withdrawal were rushed to the Walnut Hills, where Brig. Gen. Stephen D. Lee was in charge. As Sherman's troops steadily forced back Rebel skirmishers between December 26 and 28, Lee continued to fortify the high ground and assemble a force of some 6,000 defenders.[12]

Sherman's men steeled themselves for the assault on the formidable Rebel defenses—on receiving the order to attack, one Union commander murmured, "My poor brigade"—while an ineffectual artillery barrage commenced on December 29. Around noon the Federals advanced. One regiment on the Union left, the Fourth Iowa, managed to capture a section of Confederate earthworks, but the Iowans were soon forced out for lack of support. Near the Union center, the Sixth Missouri managed to cross the bayou only to crouch beneath the escarpment unsupported until nightfall allowed them to slink back to their original lines. The attacking division on the Union right failed to make it past a barricade of fallen trees. This repulse was worsened by freezing temperatures and a driving rain that chilled the demoralized Yankees, many of whom had abandoned overcoats in the warm weather of the preceding days. On December 30 the antagonists warily watched each other, but Sherman declined to launch a second attack, choosing instead to seek a temporary truce to bring in his wounded and bury his dead. Sherman's forces lingered for a few days as the general considered a move up the Yazoo after the navy improvised a minesweeper that could open the way to Haynes' Bluff, but the Union troops ultimately withdrew to the Mississippi. The dismal assault against the Walnut Hills cost the Federals 208 dead, 1,005 wounded, and 563 missing, while the victorious Rebels lost only 187 killed, wounded, and missing. A few years after the war, Sherman wrote to a friend, "the whole position from Vicksburg to Haine's Bluff is as strong as nature ever made anything, and could not have carried as I attempted it, but the troops were raw, and [George W.] Morgan had not the nerve to go in with his whole command, but left it to two brigades." A more honest assessment came in a letter to his wife shortly after the battle, in which the

Ohioan confided, "we have been to Vicksburg, and it was too much for us, and we have backed out."[13]

With the failure of Grant's strategy east of the Mississippi, Union attention turned toward the troublesome little garrison at Arkansas Post. The battered survivors of the futile attack at Chickasaw Bayou would not, however, be under Sherman's command in the move against Fort Hindman. Instead a wily Illinois politician who President Lincoln valued as much for his political skills as for his military abilities would command the attacking forces. John A. McClernand had helped maintain pro-Union attitudes in southern Illinois during the secession crisis and was rewarded with a brigadier's star in 1861 and a major general's rank in 1862. The amateur soldier had fought well at Belmont, Missouri, and in the campaign to take Forts Henry and Donelson in Tennessee, and he had served creditably alongside Sherman in the bitter fighting at Shiloh. But he had earned the enmity of Grant and other Union commanders for his popularity with the press and his tendency toward self-promotion. Sherman was one of his harshest critics, referring to McClernand as "the meanest man we ever had in the west—with a mean, gnawing ambition ready to destroy everyone who could cross his path."[14]

Since late August 1862 McClernand had been stationed in Illinois, where he was sent to oversee the formation and training of troops raised by Lincoln's August 4 call for 26,148 additional Illinois volunteers. The politician-general also took time to lobby the president, both by letter and during a lengthy visit to Washington, for a campaign against Vicksburg under his own command. In October Lincoln directed that "an expedition may be organized under General McClernand's command against Vicksburg" utilizing the new regiments then mustering in Iowa, Indiana, and Illinois. But through the machinations of Grant and General in Chief Henry W. Halleck, McClernand's role was changed in mid-December to that of a corps commander under Grant. As the thwarted general hurried toward Memphis to assume his new command, eight of his regiments were placed under Sherman and engaged in the doomed assault at Chickasaw Bayou. The troops McClernand would command on the lower Arkansas were exhausted and dispirited by the fighting. "It was a thoroughly discouraged army; had [spent] one week in the Chickasaw and Yazoo bottoms fighting, wading in the mud, cold, wet, and defeated, with great loss and nothing gained," the historian

Maj. Gen. John McClernand led the Union force that crushed the Confederate bastion at Arkansas Post in what was perhaps the high point of the Illinois politician's military career. *Courtesy Library of Congress.*

of the First Wisconsin Light Artillery remembered. Col. Marcus Spiegel of the 120th Ohio Infantry despaired, "Men, Officers, who 60 days ago were in favor of fighting till the last man and last Dollar is gone, are now in favor of Compromise strongly on most any terms; I never in my life saw such a change in an Army in two weeks." Another Buckeye was glad to hear of the change in command, noting, "the report [rumor] is currently circulated that our own withdrawal from the Chickasaw Bayou and return down the Yazoo and up the Mississippi was on account of the arrival of General McClernand and there being no chance for Sherman to distinguish himself at the expense of other men's lives much better than his own." "We must have hope in [McClernand]," an Iowa soldier concluded fatalistically, "for it is all we can do."[15]

McClernand left Memphis on December 30, stopping at Helena to meet with Brig. Gen. Willis A. Gorman, commander of the Eastern District of Arkansas. Gorman now led a much-reduced garrison, the majority of his troops and gunboats having joined the excursion against Chickasaw Bayou. At this meeting, McClernand reported, he suggested "the reduction of Fort Hindman, which had been laboriously and skillfully enlarged and strengthened . . . , which formed the key to Little Rock, the capital of the State of Arkansas, and the extensive and valuable country drained by the Arkansas River, and from which hostile detachments were sent forth to obstruct the navigation of the Mississippi River and thereby our communications." Sherman and Admiral Porter met aboard the *Black Hawk* on January 2, 1863, and discussed a similar plan as well as a report that McClernand waited at the mouth of the Yazoo to relieve Sherman of command of the Federal force. The temperamental Sherman was not pleased with this news, confiding to his senator brother, "I never dreamed so severe a test of my patriotism as being superseded by McClernand, and if I can keep down my tamed spirit and I live I will claim a virtue higher than Brutus." Porter did not care for the politician-general any more than did Sherman, complaining that "any admiral, Grant, Sherman, or all the generals in the army, were nobody in [McClernand's] estimation."[16]

It was thus a tense group that met aboard Porter's flagship on January 4 to discuss upcoming operations. McClernand proposed that the army attack Arkansas Post, irritating Sherman and Porter, who also had previously discussed such a maneuver. The admiral, who a

Harper's Weekly reporter described as "a man of wiry, muscular frame, handsome features, of medium height, and, a few years ago, universally admitted to be the strongest man in the navy," bridled at what he saw as McClernand's condescending attitude toward Sherman as the discussion began. "Porter's manner to McClernand was so curt that I invited him out into a forward cabin . . . and asked him what he meant by it," Sherman recalled in his memoirs. "He said that 'he did not like him,' that in Washington before coming West, he had been introduced to him by President Lincoln, and he had taken a strong prejudice against him. I begged him for the sake of harmony to waive that, which he promised to do." Returning to the cabin, the three men got down to business. McClernand would command what he now called the Army of the Mississippi, with Brig. Gen. George W. Morgan in charge of the XIII Corps (which must have rankled Sherman, who blamed Morgan for the failure of the Chickasaw Bayou attack) and Sherman leading the XV Corps. Each corps consisted of two divisions, with Brig. Gen. Peter J. Osterhaus and Brig. Gen. Andrew J. Smith leading those under Morgan and Brig. Gen. Frederick Steele and Brig. Gen. David Stuart commanding Sherman's troops. McClernand's steamers would tow Porter's ironclads, which were low on coal, and the admiral would direct the naval operations against Fort Hindman, wielding the frightful firepower of the ironclad gunboats *Louisville, Cincinnati,* and *Baron DeKalb.*[17]

The fleet left Milliken's Bend and started up the Mississippi on January 4, with many of the blueclad troops' spirits buoyed by the arrival of a boat carrying mail from home. Union commanders planned to deceive Rebel scouts by passing the mouth of the Arkansas and entering the White River, suggesting that they were targeting St. Charles. They would travel about twenty miles upriver before sidling through the White River cutoff to enter the Arkansas and invest Fort Hindman. The vessels stopped often to disembark work crews to gather wood and, as soldiers will, to forage. Thomas Marshall of the Eighty-third Ohio Infantry ran into slaves from a local plantation "who were so delighted they could not contain themselves. They chuckled all the time, showed us where the overseer's chicken coop was, where we *gobbled up every feathered biped. . . .* They wanted us to set fire to the owner's house, but we would not." The fleet traveled by day—one Hoosier soldier citing it as "one of the most interesting sights that a man can behold, the river perfectly crowded with boats in the misty twilight, all apparently approaching some dreaded spot"—and tied up to the shore at night. By the eighth the Federals had reached the mouth of the White River, where one Yankee reported that "*hundreds* of rumors [were] afloat [that] we were going into *white river* on a regular old . . . *Indian bush-whacking expedition.*" John Roberts of the Eighty-third Indiana Infantry recorded in his diary another grim duty the flotilla performed almost nightly: "Still laing at the mouth of white river[.] wet day [.] Ulis sus Johnson died and bered there[.]" Confederate cavalry reported to General Churchill on January 8 that a Union gunboat was taking depth soundings at the White River cutoff, the first alert that an attack was imminent. As the news spread among the Arkansas Post garrison, one Texan summed up the mood: "The atmosphere begins to smell a little gunpowderish around here."[18]

As the Federal fleet tied up for the night on January 8, McClernand contacted Porter with orders to cast off at 8:00 A.M., noting that a staff officer from Col. Giles A. Smith's First Brigade reported that the "gunboats might find a favorable landing for the protection of the disembarkation of the land forces, at Nortribs farm, three miles below the fort." It was an impressive force that prepared to enter the cutoff. Porter's fleet included the *Baron De Kalb, Cincinnati, and Louisville*—all city-class Eads ironclads—and the timberclad *Lexington*, which collectively carried forty-four cannon, including fourteen that were 8-inch guns or larger. The *Black Hawk*, a heavily armed converted side-wheel steamer, and four tinclad vessels—*Rattler, Forest Rose, New Era,* and *Glide*—were armed with thirty pieces of artillery, including six smoothbore 32-pounders, six rifled 30-pounder Parrott rifles, and a number of 24-pounder howitzers. The stout Ellet ram *Monarch* stood ready to blunt any Confederate naval sorties against the fleet. McClernand commanded some 30,000 infantrymen and around 1,000 cavalrymen in addition to artillery batteries armed with forty cannon, all transported aboard sixty steamers. As the fleet steamed through the area around the lower White and Arkansas rivers, Asa E. Sample of the Fifty-fourth Indiana noted in his diary that the country was "the wildest that I ever saw, being low-land covered with heavy forests of timber with cotton wood and cane underbrush. I know not how circumscribed the limits of civilization in our enlightened land are, but I am inclined to believe from all manifestations that *this part of Ark.* is not found within her borders."

On January 9 the Union vessels entered the cutoff, which they soon found was "not so crooked and winding but very full of snags, making the navigation difficult and dangerous." A Missourian on one of the ships observed that "the passage of the 'cut off' was not without its little misfortunes such as getting fast on snags, or large steamers getting stuck in the abrupt and sudden bends in this narrow canal." Despite the obstructions the Federals made their way into the main channel of the Arkansas, "the navigation [of which was] quite difficult on account of snags and sand banks." The sheer size of some of the vessels hindered them, one soldier contended, writing, "our progress is very Slow as the Gun Boats leading the advance draw almost all the water in the River." Still, the massive armada lumbered toward Arkansas Post.[19]

Soon Confederate scouts raced to Fort Hindman and reported to General Churchill that "the enemy, with his gunboats, followed by his fleet of seventy or eighty transports, were passing into the Arkansas River. It now became evident that their object was to attack the Arkansas Post." As the news circulated among the Rebel troops, "the whole camp went into an uproar all at once." A Texas sergeant lamented that "ammunition was given out, and we had to leave our steaming kettles who were filled with back bones, Hogs heads, feet, ears and hog meat in general." Churchill ordered his Louisiana and Texas horsemen forward to observe the Federal horde, then sent Deshler and Dunnington to occupy the lower line of rifle pits, with Garland's Texans held in reserve. But before reaching their destination, this order was countermanded and the troops were directed to the middle line, "as the enemy were supposed to be already landing in large force in the immediate vicinity of the lower pits."[20]

The upper line of rifle pits extended from the Arkansas River to a large pond. Deshler placed his command on the right and Dunnington on the left while Capt. William Hart's six-gun Arkansas battery was positioned near the river; other cannon were sited at intervals between Deshler's companies. Five companies of Garland's brigade accompanied the troops and were advanced as skirmishers. Deshler immediately ordered his men to improve their fortifications, which were "far from being completed." He extended the works toward Dunnington's position and ordered the trees in front felled to form an abatis, noting that "the want of tools, axes, spades, &c., was a very serious drawback to this work." As the Rebels settled down for the night, they paid for their haste as "nearly all of the soldiers left their heavy clothing in their cabins and fell into ranks but thinly clad. . . . [B]ut few marched away from camp prepared for cold weather or exposure of any kind." Nor had they thought of food, as one Texan remembered: "As we have had nothing to eat since morning but . . . three 'flint' crackers, we are becoming quite ravenous, and with three of the greatest causes in the world; hunger, rain and excitement, we do not sleep one wink during the night." About 9:00 A.M. on January 10, the fog lifted on the Arkansas River, revealing the Union gunboats. Many of the Rebels slipped into the woods for a "quick, hawk-eyed glimpse" of the Federal fleet, finding that "one could hardly see anything in the background but smokestacks." They rushed back to the cover of their works as the warships began randomly hurling shells in their direction. Pvt. Franz Coller of the Sixth Texas recalled, "every five minutes we could hear the report of the firing which indicated to us that another bombshell was coming. We lay flat on the ground until the bombshell had flown away over us."[21]

While Deshler and Dunnington hurried to their rifle pits on January 9, McClernand's host began to disembark from their transports. He ordered Sherman's XV Corps to advance and form the right wing of the attacking force, followed by Morgan's XIII Corps, which would compose the Union left. As the historian of the Fifty-fifth Illinois Infantry recorded, "the plan of attack was to stretch a cordon of troops from the river below entirely around the rebels to the river above, and in conjunction with the gunboat fleet, belabor them into surrender." McClernand also ordered Morgan to "debark two regiments of infantry, one company of cavalry, and three pieces of artillery at a suitable point on the right bank of the river and near and below the Post, . . . to ascend the right bank . . . to a point on the river above the Post giving control of the river," an order that would both prevent Rebel reinforcements from arriving via the Arkansas and block any retreat from Arkansas Post. Sherman's troops began leaving their transports at 5:00 P.M. on the ninth at Col. Frederick Nortrebe's plantation, about three miles below Arkansas Post. "A general labyrinth of troops, wagon parts, horses, donkeys and everything possible began to form, until each regiment was provided with 4 wagons and 5 days of rations," a Federal Missourian noted. Morgan's transports tied up on the opposite bank of the Arkansas about nine miles below Nortrebe's to await their turn at the landing. Col. Daniel Lindsey's brigade, made up of the Third Kentucky Infantry, the Forty-ninth Indiana Infantry, and the 114th Ohio Infantry, as well as a section of 10-pounder Parrott rifles of the Chicago Mercantile Battery and a company of the Third Illinois Cavalry, were set ashore at Fletcher's Landing early on January 10 to march cross-country to Col. James Smith's plantation and guard the Arkansas. Setting out with the cavalry as skirmishers, flanked on both sides by a company of infantry, Lindsey drove through the woods to Smith's, scattering Rebel pickets and capturing two men, a six-mule team loaded with supplies, and some freshly killed cattle that were then issued as rations to the men. Lindsey dug some light earthworks to protect his troops from sharpshooters and scattered cannon fire from the opposite shore and then settled in for the night, his men sleeping on their weapons.[22]

Sherman's troops remained aboard their transports at Nortrebe's on the night of the ninth, hunkered down against a driving rain that cleared up at about 4:00 A.M. They began disembarking, completing the task seven hours later. Even as the men were emerging from their transports, McClernand and a staff officer rode up the river road and observed the Rebels preparing to abandon their works under fire from the *Rattler* and *Black Hawk:* "The gunboats slip[p]ed up gave them a few rounds which put them in the double quick," a soldier in the Fifty-fifth Illinois reported. The general sent Col. Warren Stewart and forty men of the Third Illinois Cavalry forward to do a more detailed reconnaissance at 9:00 A.M. Passing the Rebels' forward line of works, Stewart approached the second line and found it abandoned except for some dismounted cavalrymen who surrendered. McClernand determined to send Sherman's First Division on a flanking maneuver from Nortrebe's while his Second Division advanced up the river road.[23]

Accordingly, Sherman ordered Steele's First Division to cut to the right in order to hit Arkansas Post from the north and west. With Hovey's Second Brigade in the lead, guided by runaway slaves, the Yankees entered the woods behind Nortrebe's around 11:00 A.M. and advanced into what "soon became a deep, ugly swamp," plowing forward "through the mud, very near knee deep." Confederate pickets lurked about a half mile into the woods and soon, Texan W. W. Heartsill reported, "here come the Yankees dashing and splashing straight through it, and so perfectly at home as an alligator in the Red River." Hovey ordered his artillery forward and scattered the Rebels, though "small squads of the enemy's artillery hovered in

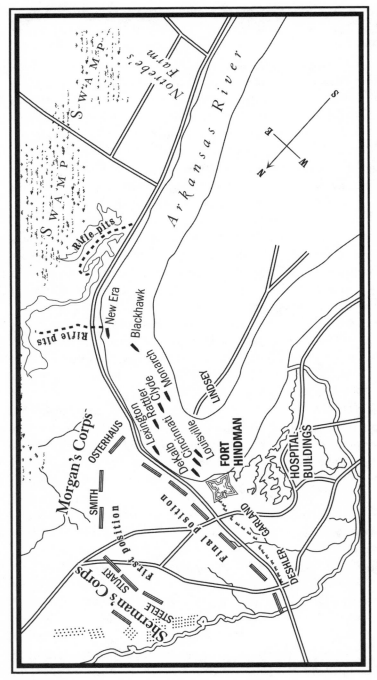

Battle of Arkansas Post, January 11, 1863. A massive Union army and navy assault overwhelmed the Confederate defenders of Arkansas Post in January 1863. *Map by Kirk Montgomery.*

our advance, and several were captured." Following an old road to the right, the Yankees slogged forward until they "reached an apparently impassable bayou, but a crossing was at last effected and the route pursued for several miles." The Federals finally reached high ground and, on questioning the occupants of a cabin there, realized that to reach the Confederate camps they would have to "march a circuit of 7 miles, although in an air-line the distance did not exceed 2." Sherman sent a staff officer back to report the futility of advancing by that route, and McClernand hurried forward to see for himself. Deciding that "for General Steele's division to go forward on a line so extended and remote from the enemy's works would be virtually to retire it from the pending fight, . . . I instantly decided that the division ought to return, and so ordered." An Iowa soldier recalled: "Our Division marched all day through brush and swam where mud and water was shoe mouth deep all over the ground and sometimes knee deep, to get in position in rear of the enemy. We finally came to a swamp that was perfectly impassable, and had to go back to the river, which we reached about dark."[24]

As Steele's men floundered in the swamp, Sherman's Second Division under Stuart, a former congressman and lawyer who had been wounded at Shiloh, moved forward, with Giles Smith's First Brigade at its head. The Eighth Missouri Infantry led the way as skirmishers and soon ran into a Confederate rear guard, five companies of the Tenth Texas. The Missourians scampered forward from tree to tree, driving the Texans back to the works at Fort Hindman "under a heavy skirmishing fire"; the Eighth, joined by the Sixth Missouri, halted within sight of the fort to await reinforcements. Following a reconnaissance by an engineer, McClernand ordered Sherman to shift Stuart's division to the right and Steele's hapless troops even farther right—again through a bayou—so they would end up on the extreme left of the Confederate works. Stuart's artillery, several batteries of the First Illinois Light Artillery, rushed forward with the First Brigade, "under quite a heavy fire from the fort," as the division began cutting a road through the woods. Col. Thomas Kilby Smith ordered the Fifty-seventh Ohio, Fifty-fifth Illinois, and Eighty-third Indiana forward to support the Missouri skirmishers, who still huddled before the guns of Fort Hindman. "The contest opened in the usual desultory way," an officer of the Fifty-fifth Illinois recorded. "Occasionally an enormous shell whipped through the timber, seeking out the blue line. The enemy was pressed back toward their works . . . and occasionally a squalid, dead Confederate was passed who had met a swift messenger of reconstruction." The midwesterners moved into position, then the Fifty-fifth Illinois and Eighty-third Indiana were ordered "to show ourselves in the front, advancing our lines as far as possible to draw their fire." The Rebels in Fort Hindman complied, firing a shell from its pivot gun that "passed not over six feet high and exploded with a terrific splitting sound to the rear of the regiment and among the troops massed behind," Lucien Crooker of the Fifty-fifth Illinois remembered. One Illinoisan was mortally wounded, another's leg was broken, and "among the other regiments several were hit, the loss from the single explosion being stated at the time as three killed and fourteen wounded." As darkness fell, Giles Smith sent the Fifty-seventh Ohio to the far right, where they advanced "unobserved by the enemy almost up to their very works," completing the Federal deployment along this section of the line.[25]

Morgan's XIII Corps began filling in the line to the left of Stuart's men. Having left Colonel Lindsey's troops at Fletcher's Landing on the evening of the ninth, the XIII Corps had arrived too late to disembark that night, then waited on the tenth until Sherman's corps unloaded and began moving forward. Leaving their transports by about 1:00 P.M. on the tenth, Morgan's troops advanced toward Nortrebe's, arriving there just as Steele's men slogged their way back from their unsuccessful swamp march. Amid some confusion caused by congestion on the primitive roads, A. J. Smith's First Division caught up with Stuart's command. Smith, whose tough division historian Shelby Foote would characterize as "gorilla-guerrillas," ordered the Sixtieth Indiana "to the right of the line to be established, and the remaining divisions coming up were ordered into line of battle to the left and front, to relieve those of General Stuart's division that were to move farther to the right." His men continued to deploy before Fort Hindman throughout the night of January 10. The Second Division, under Pea Ridge veteran Peter Osterhaus, advanced and "found all the roads crowded with parts of different commands; and [with] orders . . . to keep in rear of everybody," bivouacked in an open field "whence the river and all the roads in front and on our right could be completely commanded." After sending two 24-pounder Parrott rifles of the

First Wisconsin Battery to reinforce Lindsey's little force at Smith's plantation, Osterhaus settled in for the night.[26]

In midafternoon on the tenth, McClernand "hastened back and requested Rear-Admiral Porter . . . to advance the gunboats and open fire on the enemy's works for the purpose of diverting his attention while the land forces should gain the positions assigned them." So, as one Union tar remembered, "at about 3:30 word was passed to clear the deck for action, and quicker than I can write it, the crew became active, gun tackles were cast loose and each gun's crew was in place." At 5:30 P.M. the *Baron de Kalb, Louisville,* and *Cincinnati* steamed toward Fort Hindman. As the ships rounded the bend, Dunnington's gunners opened fire, having "put their range marks at 500, 700, and 1,100 yards." Justin Meacham, a sailor on the *Cincinnati,* reported that the first shots "went wild," and the vessels continued forward under increasingly heavy fire. Porter, though, had ordered the gunboats to get close to fort before responding. "We had excellent range, and I shall never forget how impatient all were in not being allowed to return their fire," Meacham remembered. "We informed the captain several times that we had good range and asked permission to open fire, but each time his answer was, 'Keep cool, I will tell you when to fire.'" Finally, at about four hundred yards from the fort, "orders came to 'Let go,' and every gun that had range belched forth." Another sailor on the *Cincinnati* wrote that "bullets as well as shells fell about us like hail" as the warships closed to within seventy yards to trade fire with the Rebels. Porter ordered the *Black Hawk* and the *Lexington* forward to fire shrapnel and light rifled shells at Fort Hindman in support of the ironclads, which they did "with great effect."[27]

"We fought them two hours in the dark," seaman Frederick E. Davis of the *Baron de Kalb* reported, treating the Yankee soldiers on the shore to a magnificent fireworks display. "The sight was beautiful," John Harper of the 113th Illinois told the folks at home. "When they would fire the boats would look like they were on fire we could see the shell as they would make a curve through the air and then burst in or over the fort." Another Illinoisan noted the havoc the naval fire caused on the Confederate works, writing, "our cannon balls knocked it in every direction and the rebels had to scamper from under it to keep from being buried alive." One Hoosier cavalryman, "a close spectator to the whole affair," wrote that "the sight after Dark was grand, terrific, and sublime," while Illinoisan William Kennedy stated simply that it "was the most interesting sight I *ever* see[n]." For the Confederate troops, though, the experience was different. "How the roar of the shot jarred a fellow!" Capt. Samuel Foster of the Twenty-fourth Texas wrote. "Swisher—swisher—swisher—swisher, and the shell passed over our heads. . . . Their first shell passed just over the top of the fort. It struck the ground about forty feet behind us and kept rolling along, breaking bushes. It scared us all near to death. . . . The roar and the noise of the cannonade became awfully terrible. We had never heard anything like it." A soldier in the Fifteenth Texas reported that the "gunboats threw shells as big as wash-pots with tails of fire as long as a clothes line." Jim Turner of the Sixth Texas remembered that "the bombardment continued until about nine o'clock and was of terrific grandeur. The large shells, some of them twelve inches in diameter, came thick and fast, and burst around us with a noise equal to the loudest thunder." The Rebel command in the trenches, "although unprotected, maintained its position during this trying ordeal with firmness," Colonel Garland reported.[28]

Fort Hindman took a terrific hammering. Meacham on the *Cincinnati* reported that "in one instance, we saw the inside of one of the casement[s] of the Fort lit up, and felt sure that one of our 10-inch shells had entered the port hole and disabled a gun, which we afterwards learned was true." A later writer stated that, "owing to the terrific fire and superior guns of the enemy, in a short time the fort ceased firing, nearly all the guns being disabled." While casualties among the men were light, the artillery horses in and near the fort were slaughtered by the naval fire. "It was hardly dark when the Yankees began to shoot again with their gunboats," Franz Coller of the Sixth Texas wrote. "They shot various horses down in the vicinity of the batteries. Some lost only a leg and were thus abandoned to their fate." The warships also had suffered, though Porter reported that "the vessels were not virtually damaged, the iron casemates of the gunboats, being covered with a thick coating of tallow, turned many of the enemy's shot and shell." Seaman Daniel Kemp noted that while the *Cincinnati* suffered no casualties, "our boat was struck several times once on the forecastle tearing up a portion of the timbers and bursting in the port. Another struck the hammock netting going thro' a ventilator then on thro' our smoke stack and down thro' the Cook's galley knocking down a slush barrel and spilling grease over the deck then down thro' the hawser box and across to the other hammock netting and out to the bank." Two other vessels were not so lucky, with the *Louisville* suffering eleven killed and wounded and the *Baron de Kalb* losing seventeen men. Around 7:30 P.M. the attacking vessels broke off the engagement, but Porter decided to take advantage of the darkness and battered condition of the fort to slide the tinclad *Rattler* past Fort Hindman to hit the defenders with an enfilading fire. There was still fight in the Rebels, however, and the *Rattler* took a pounding as it got "jammed among the logs" of the pilings the Confederate engineers had placed in the river. "She was only 50 yards from the fort, and at one time there was every prospect of her being destroyed, the enemy's shot hitting her every time and going completely through her," Porter reported. The battered tinclad fell back and rejoined the fleet. With the failure of the *Rattler*'s sortie, "the firing ceased as suddenly as it began and during the remainder of the night everything was still."[29]

Steele's division, meanwhile, was on the move to complete the right of the Federal line. Having fallen back from their earlier attempt to traverse the swamp northwest of Nortrebe's, one Iowan recalled, "we prepared supper and dispatched it with unusual celerity and good will. Coffee and hard tack never tasted so good." E. Paul Reichelm of the Third Missouri Infantry wrote that his regiment had just settled down to cook dinner when "the infernal drums must beat 'fall in'!—peevish fortune—aching stomachs—so horribly fooled, O cherished hopes now balked." Once again the First Division set forth, "moving along the river bank for about one mile, which was illuminated by the flash of guns from the Iron Clads and bursting shell," until they reached the first line of rifle pits. They then turned into the woods, soon encountering "mud and water and underbrush, which we concluded was universal in Arkansas." It was another brutal march for Steele's midwesterners. "In order not to mire down in the swamp, it was necessary to cut down trees and so make a road," John T. Buegel of Missouri wrote. "Our field pieces had to be carried through on the shoulders of men." An Ohio soldier remembered that "the road through the woods was narrow and the late rains had left great pools of water. The heavy artillery and transportation wagons made a perfect mortar bed of it and the column moved slowly through the darkness. A night march over an almost impassable road with artillery and heavy trains stuck in the mud will ever be remembered by the supperless oldier." "This whole country consists of marshes, water, and low-land," Calvin Ainsworth of the Twenty-fifth Iowa sourly concluded. While taking a break during the march, one Missourian recorded, "some of the men and one or two of the Officers amuse themselves by endeavoring to capture a lot of small Porkers that are scampering through the woods, but in this laudable undertaking they are not successful." Paul Reichelm advanced with General Hovey and his staff toward an opening in the woods, where they "beheld to our infinite astonishment the rebel camp. It presented the usual appearance of a camp at this time of night. Fires were burning at the foot of Company streets, here and there a light would show through tent canvas . . . [but] we could infer that the rebels had got wind of our approach and had evacuated this camp in the evening to reinforce the defenders of Ark. Post. A few sick and wounded [and] also a dozen half dead 'Sambos' were all the rebels we could find." As the exhausted troops filed into the abandoned camp, they found "a large amount of clothing, arms, cooking utensils, cornmeal and beef and bacon, &c." Indeed, David James Palmer of the Twenty-fifth Iowa noted in his diary, the Yankees "fared well on [the Confederates'] provisions. they seem to be well supplied with provisions beyond our expectations."[30]

The majority of the Confederates occupied a 720-yard line west of Fort Hindman toward Post Bayou, and they spent the night strengthening their unfinished defenses. "We were as busy as busy could be in throwing up earthworks, each man working fully impressed with the opinion that every shovel of dirt he piled in his front might save his hide from being perforated by a bullet in the morrow," a soldier in the Fifteenth Texas remembered. Deshler's Texans, occupying the extreme left of the Confederate lines, faced the log huts of the Nineteenth Arkansas, which "I had . . . torn down in order to destroy the cover that they would otherwise afford the enemy; the logs were used in making breastworks." As had happened earlier, Deshler reported, "we were very much delayed by the scarcity of intrenching tools; we were compelled to use pieces of board for shovels, &c." Nevertheless, a soldier in the Tenth Texas recorded, "we built a brestwork all knight." The Yankees lying in front of this position "could hear formidable preparations going on within the enemy's lines," a historian of the Forty-second Ohio Infantry remembered. "Wagons and artillery were moving, and the whole garrison was at work tearing down houses, building rifle trenches, extending the outer parapet and making ready for the morrow." General Sherman "crept up to a stump so close that I could hear the enemy hard at work. . . . I could almost hear their words, and was thus listening when, about 4 A.M. the bugler in the rebel camp sounded as pretty a reveille as I ever listened to." Hart's Arkansas cannoneers periodically shelled the Federal lines. J. C. Grecian of the Eighty-third Indiana Regiment remembered, "we lay all night under the mouths of their guns, and they continued for several hours to throw shells into our ranks, killing some in ours, and other regiments." Another Hoosier recalled, "when one of the shot or shell from one of them came toward us, the cry would be 'look out here comes a camp kettle.'"[31]

As the Rebels desperately strengthened their lines, Churchill received a telegram from General Holmes ordering the Arkansas Post garrison "'to hold out until help arrived or until all dead,' which order was communicated to brigade commanders, with instructions to see it carried out in spirit and letter." The command was heartened, perhaps, by the arrival of Capt. Alf Johnson and his redoubtable Texas Spy Company. The Texans slipped past the Union pickets and into the Confederate works at about 10:00 P.M., though the fewer than fifty men provided scant reinforcement against McClernand's host. As the Rebels prepared for the expected Union onslaught on the morning of January 11, they were organized as follows: Dunnington commanded Fort Hindman and its garrison of the Marine Battalion (the sailors from the *Pontchartrain*) and four companies of the Nineteenth Arkansas Infantry. Moving from right to left outside the fort were the other companies of the Nineteenth Arkansas under Col. A. S. Hutchinson, Hart's Arkansas Battery, Garland's Brigade (Sixth Texas Infantry, Twenty-fourth Texas Cavalry [Dismounted], and Twenty-fifth Texas Cavalry [Dismounted]), and Deshler's Brigade (Tenth Texas Infantry, Fifteenth Texas Cavalry [Dismounted], Seventeenth Texas Cavalry [Dismounted], and Eighteenth Texas Cavalry [Dismounted]). "This new position was entirely exposed, not being protected by an intrenchments whatever," Deshler reported, and the thin gray line left "a space of about 200 yards from my left to the bayou, thus leaving that flank completely open." In addition, he noted, Post Bayou "was fordable along almost its entire length, thus leaving my rear also exposed." Marshall Pierson of the Seventeenth Texas was also concerned about the Rebel deployment, writing in his diary that their position left "but one way by which we might escape, and that a bad one, being a narrow space to our left up the river across a boggy bayou into an almost impenetrable swamp."[32]

Captain Foster of the Twenty-fourth Texas was concerned with the quality of the Confederates' weapons: "Garland's Regiment was armed with Enfield rifles. Our own regiment having Mississippi rifles. The Twenty-fifth Regiment was using the old United States muskets with percussion caps for the flintlocks. The rest of the troops were armed with double-barrel shotguns. The muskets and the shotguns were loaded with cartridges made up of three buckshots packed behind an ounce musket ball." Despite the Rebels' concern for their firearms, their works posed worries for the Federals. General Sherman wrote, "when daylight broke it revealed to us a new line of parapets straight across the peninsula, connecting Fort Hindman, on the Arkansas River bank, with the impassable swamp about a mile to its left or rear." John E. Wilkins of the Sixteenth Indiana Infantry, gazing at the Rebel fortifications, grimly predicted, "it is likely we will have a hard and bloody fight before we take it."[33]

The men of the two armies—or at least those of them who had slept during the night—awoke to a beautiful morning on Sunday, January 11. An Ohio soldier remembered "the sun shining like a spring day. The birds were singing as they would in the north in the month of May. All was peaceful and quiet." Another Buckeye wrote: "The Confederate reveille was blown, clear and shrill, at dawn. The Federal bugles took up the strain, and the eventful day was opened with as tuneful a morning call as ever woke an army to battle." On a more practical level, the Ohioan noticed that "an amazing amount of fresh dirt had been thrown up, and from behind the new parapet the guns of two field batteries popped out." William Bentley of the Seventy-seventh Illinois Infantry noted more sourly that "the day . . . was the Sabbath—clear calm and beautiful. It was a day made for rest and the worship of God, and not for human slaughter." A Southern soldier concurred, writing, "Sunday, the 11th, dawned bright, beautiful, and clear, and it seemed a sacrilege that such a day should be devoted to the bloody drama that was there to be enacted." As the two armies faced each other, the numerical superiority was clearly in McClernand's favor. Churchill's command totaled some 4,500 men, though only 3,000 were effective, the remainder being on the sick list or on detached duty. They were backed by the six artillery pieces in Hart's Battery as well as the surviving guns of Fort Hindman. McClernand's army boasted 33,000 men and forty cannon.[34]

At daybreak General Steele ordered Hovey's tired Second Brigade to leave the Rebel huts (which they had reached at 2:00 A.M.) and complete the investment of the Confederate left. The Yankees would not leave, however, before enjoying the spoils of war. "We found fat pigs, chickens and corn meal in their well-constructed log huts for our morning's breakfast," Charles Miller of the Seventy-sixth Ohio remembered contentedly. Calvin Ainsworth of the Twenty-fifth Iowa wrote in his diary: "We got a good sleep and we got up in the morning refreshed and ate a hearty breakfast out of the stores the rebels left in their hurry to get away from our advanced guard. Laurenburg and I cook[ed] a chicken and while doing so a cannon ball knocked a section off the roof but it was just as safe in the shanty as outside, so what's the use of losing our dinner. We cooked the chicken and ate it and never did chicken taste so good." After their repasts, Hovey sent his men ahead, where soon, he reported, "we met the enemy in force his works being in full view." Deshler immediately observed the advance and detached two companies from each of his regiments to form a skirmish line from his left to the bayou. Churchill also placed all of his available cavalry under Alf Johnson and sent them to Deshler, who posted the roughly 120 horsemen along the bayou, finally relieved that he could keep "the enemy from coming in the rear of my left without my knowledge." Six companies of the Nineteenth Arkansas also moved to support the colonel, who placed them behind the men of the Fifteenth Texas, and two sections of Hart's Arkansas artillery were moved to his left-center. The Federals advanced to Deshler's left around 8:30 A.M. and "almost instantly recognized the traitor flag saucily floating in our front," E. Paul Reichelm of the Third Missouri Infantry remembered. "The Regiment was now deployed into line of battle, but scarcely was the movement completed when we were roughly greeted by a hail of shot and shell from a rebel redoubt not 300 yards from us." John Buegel watched as "the first shot passed high over us. The second shell, however, passed two and half feet over the ground so that both legs of Captain Green of Company K were cut off, and our ensign as well as a corporal of the color guard were killed on the spot." Buegel picked up the fallen colors as the regiment "lay down flat on the ground. . . . The third shell came so low, however, and tore my hat off my head so that it flew back." Hovey's men grimly found what cover they could, hunkered down, and waited.[35]

The rest of the Army of the Mississippi spent the morning massing for the assault on Arkansas Post. On the right, Brig. Gen. John M. Thayer's Third Brigade of Steele's division moved into position beside Hovey's men, with four guns of the Fourth Iowa Artillery deploying between the two brigades. Frank Blair's brigade, which had been chewed up in the assault on Chickasaw Bayou, was held in reserve, a duty the men "performed with cheerfulness and alacrity." Stuart's division was next in line, with G. A. Smith's First Brigade forming to the left of Thayer. T. K. Smith's brigade moved into position to the left and rear of the First Brigade. George Morgan's XIII Corps held the next positions in the Union line. Brig. Gen. Stephen G. Burbridge's men massed in front of T. K. Smith's brigade. This double line of battle would attempt to bludgeon its way into the Confederate works, which a soldier of the Sixty-seventh Indiana described: "We could see in our front that all the trees had been felled with the tops pointing toward us and having their limbs sharpened outward, forming a thick abattis, while just beyond was a cleared space terminating at the deep ditch in front of their works." Col. William J. Landram's Second Brigade moved into position to T. K. Smith's left. Col. Lionel A. Sheldon's First Brigade of Osterhaus's division completed the Federal line, forming at the extreme left across the river road. Osterhaus detached John DeCourcy's brigade to guard the Union transports, and Col. Daniel Lindsey's brigade remained in position across the Arkansas River, where they had deployed on the evening of January 9. McClernand ordered two 20-pounder Parrott rifles of the First Wisconsin Battery to the extreme left of the Union line to take on the Rebel's 9-inch Dahlgren in the lower casemate of Fort Hindman, "which had seriously annoyed the gunboats on the previous evening." The Wisconsin gunners masked their cannon behind fallen trees as they awaited the order to fire.[36]

The Confederates watched as the Yankees took their positions, the morning quiet except for the occasional crack of a sharpshooter's rifle or the boom of a cannon when Hart's artillerists spotted a target through the woods. "While all was calm Gen. Churchill on his charger rode up our line in full Confederate uniform and said: 'Boys, we will hold the fort or all will be shot down in these ditches,'" Texan L. V. Caraway remembered. The area in front of the Rebel lines "was covered as thick with blue coats as ever you saw blackbirds on an oat stack in mid-winter," another Texan wrote, adding, "we found what we had been looking for—an opportunity to whip ten to one." S. W. Bishop remembered Churchill's orders: "You will instruct you men having short-range guns to hold their fire until the Yankees come in thirty or forty yards. The buck and ball guns will commence firing at seventy-five to one hundred yards. Minie rifles will fire on them from the time they come in sight." Finally, at about 1:00 P.M., the Union gunboats again advanced up the Arkansas against Fort Hindman.[37]

David Porter, directing the attack from the tugboat *Ivy,* had learned to respect the firepower of Dunnington's big guns and decided to try something new to protect his fleet. In his general order of battle, he instructed that "the front casemates and forward part of the pilot houses of the ironclads must be covered with tallow or slush; it will make the shot glance."[38] Justin Meacham of the *Baron de Kalb* remembered: "At one o'clock, Admiral Porter, smoking a meerschaum pipe, came along side in a tug and sung out, 'Capt. Walker, slush your boat and attack the batteries at once.'" The *Baron de Kalb* led the way, followed by the *Louisville, Cincinnati, Lexington, Rattler,* and *Black Hawk.* The gunboats closed up to within sixty yards of Fort Hindman and commenced to rain hell on Dunnington's gunners. "Their first shots knocked the iron off the fort," Texan Samuel Foster recounted. "It scattered in every direction. The big square logs flew as if they were fence rails." Robert Chalk of the Sixth Texas wrote: "[O]ne shell from the gunboats fell in our lines, just under my feet. It killed and wounded 7 of our company. Little Frank McLaughlin was laying just in front of me, he had a big leather belt on. The shell cut him in two and his belt was left laying in the ditch. It also cut Andy Sutton's legs off about half way between knees and hips. . . . It was awful to see the great streams of blood gushing from his wounds." The Confederate tars from the *Pontchartrain* fought hard. Sailor Frederick Davis recounted to his parents: "[I]t has been a most desperate fight. A harder fought battle than Fort Donaldson. . . . Our 11 inch port bow gun was struck on the muzzle, and a peice [sic] a foot long knocked out. The shell came in the port, and after striking the gun, bursted, killing two and wounding 13 men. . . . Another shell, entered another port, dismounting the 3" gun off its carraige, passed aft, struck a stanchion, which glanced it, and it passed aft, struck on our 'cylinder timber,' and bounded through an aperture on to the . . . deck, passing through the privy, and went over board." On the *Cincinnati* Daniel Kemp observed: "Two shots struck our bow casemate making a couple of dents in the iron plating. Another struck the Pilot House making a dent and splintering the roof a little. Another struck one of the stanchions going thro' the Wheel House, thro' the Ward Room into the Captain's cabin and lodged in the casemate." "Such a terific scene I have never witnessed," Sam Bartlett of the ram *Monarch* declared. "The fort was riddled and torn to pieces with the shells. The iron clads, which could venture up closer shot into their portholes and into the mouths of their cannon, bursting their cannon and dismounting them." Admiral Porter noted with the eye of a professional that "the new-fashioned casemates" at Fort Hindman, "and they were the strongest I had ever seen," were "no better than the guns *barbette*. They were perfect slaughterhouses and were piled up with dead and wounded" under the concentrated fire of the Yankee fleet.[39]

Meanwhile, Col. Daniel Lindsey's regiment, bolstered by Capt. Jacob Foster's two 24-pounder Parrott rifles from the First Wisconsin Battery, had spent a quiet night on the riverbank opposite Fort Hindman, capturing loose horses and guarding against Rebel reinforcement. At about 2:00 P.M., Foster reported, "to our surprise and great joy, we saw one of the gunboats passing the fort." Lindsey ordered Foster and Capt. Charles Cooley's pair of 3-inch wrought-iron rifled cannon to move into position opposite the Confederate lines to fire on them from behind. The historian of the Forty-second Ohio Infantry recorded what happened next: "[A] fierce artillery fire opened from the point of land across the river. . . . [T]he guns beyond the river were firing into the fort and along its West front, enfilading the rear of the Rebel outworks with terrible effect. It was FOSTER. . . . His fire reached the vitals of the Confederate position, set fire to the buildings hitherto sheltered by the Fort, swept the plain in its rear." Trooper Heartsill of the W. P. Lane Rangers observed the destruction caused by the Federal cannoneers: "At half past three o'clock a new Battery opens on us, it is situated over the river near our old camp; this Battery enfilades our breastworks and is doing us more injury than all the day's conflict." Lieutenant Caraway sadly reported, "They disabled all the cannon of our battery and killed all our artillery horses, as their cannon were directed by a man with much skill." Jacob Foster was indeed a man with much skill, fussing about fuse lengths and wreaking maximum havoc on the Confederate positions. And he was effective, Samuel Foster attested, writing that the battery's "first shot passed directly over the flag of our regiment. The second shot cut the flag's staff in two. Their third one came still lower. It bounced into a ditch. Two men were killed. One of them was knocked outside, clear over the breastwork."[40]

As the guns of Fort Hindman fell silent, smashed by the combined Federal cannon fire, Porter ordered the light-draft gunboats *Rattler* and *Glide* and the ram *Monarch* to steam past the fort and cut off the garrison's only line of retreat. As the vessels steamed past the fort, "nothing but musket balls hit our boat which could do no harm," Sam Bartlett of the *Monarch* smugly reported. Steaming downriver, they paused to pick up the men of the Third Kentucky Regiment on the opposite side of the Arkansas. The heavy *Monarch* had to pull up after running aground four times in the increasingly shallow water, but the *Rattler* and *Glide* pressed on and destroyed a ferry after a handful of Rebels had used it to escape the Union trap. The back door was now closed to the Confederates at Arkansas Post.[41]

The Union army had not been idle while the gunboats battered the Rebel lines. McClernand had ordered all of the field artillery to open fire on the Confederates as soon as Porter's fleet commenced its attack, with the infantry moving forward after the bombardment had softened the Rebel defenses. Marshall Pierson of the Seventeenth Texas Cavalry (Dismounted) described the effect of the combined assault as how one "might easily imagine an earthquake, though showering something more substantial than molten lava." Sherman's artillery opened up first, at about 1:00 P.M., throwing shells into Deshler's position. "The 'ball opened' along the whole line and from the gunboats and the roar of the cannon for half an hour was awful; it shook the ground for miles," an officer of the Twenty-fifth Iowa Infantry reported. A Missouri Federal agreed, writing that "the gunboats hurled their fiery shots into the fort and from the land side fifty cannons fired. It seemed as if the elements were in rebellion and made the earth tremble." The two sections of Hart's Arkansas Battery positioned with Deshler returned counterbattery fire. "One of their guns seemed to have my gun for a special mark," remembered Samuel Black of the First Iowa Battery. "The moment it fired we could see the smoke from it and would drop flat upon the ground;

then 'up and at em,' giving them a shot before they could reload."
The Union fire "was kept up quite rapidly and continuously, but
with scarcely any effect excepting the killing and wounding of some
of our artillery horses," Deshler reported. Sherman observed the
ground in front of his corps, finding one hundred yards of clear space
immediately before his troops followed by a three-hundred-yard-
wide belt of gullies and timber, both standing and felled, in front
of the Rebel earthworks. He ordered his artillery to cease fire after
fifteen minutes, and his ground assault to begin; "the infantry sprang
forward with a cheer," he reported.[42]

Hovey's brigade, on the extreme right of Sherman's corps, led
the assault, fronted by the Third Missouri and Seventy-sixth Ohio
Infantry, which were followed by the Thirty-first and Twenty-fifth
Iowa. "The men were ordered to fix bayonets and make the charge
without firing a shot," Ohioan Charles Miller remembered. "The
prospect looked anything but inspiring and all felt that of necessity
there must be fearful slaughter." As the midwestern troops advanced
toward the broken ground in front of Deshler's position, it was the
Rebels' turn to strike. A Texan reported, "We did not open fire on
this column with small arms until its head was within 80 to 100
yards from our line; then we gave them a very deadly fire, firing by
file and with marked effect." Lt. Robert M. Collins of the Fifteenth
Texas remembered that "our boys raised up and gave what was called
a rebel yell, but it did not sound anything like such as we gave when
we were on the march and some pretty Southern woman would
shake a white rag at us, but sounded weak and had a hollow, graveyard twang to it"; nonetheless, "our shot-guns and buck got in their
work and the enemy went down like grain before the mower." "The
enemy allowed us to approach to one hundred paces," John Buegel
wrote in his diary. "But then the blue beans flew into our ranks,
bringing death and destruction. Since it was impossible to get over
the barricade, we were all crowded into the trap, and our boys fell
like flies." A captain of the Twenty-fifth Iowa wrote that "the bullets
came like hail, mixed with grape canister and shells. It actually
seemed that there was not one foot of ground that was not struck by
a bullet." A German soldier in the Thirty-first Missouri breathlessly
reported to his spouse that "they had heavy guns that greeted us
with cannon-balls the size of a man's head (110 lbs.)." The heavy
fire stopped Hovey's assault. Iowan Calvin Ainsworth wrote that

"there were a few scattering trees, logs, brush heaps and stumps. Every man made for some tree or other object immediately." His comrade Adoniram J. Withrow noted: "Some got where they could See Something to Shoot at and kept popping away. . . . Some did not fire a gun, others fired forty or fifty shots." Ainsworth, who personally loosed thirty-nine shots during the battle, noted smugly: "[T]he Rebs are not having it all their own way now. We have them surrounded, the gunboats are demolishing their Fort in their rear and dropping grape and canister among their ranks."[43]

Thayer's brigade of Iowa troops advanced as Hovey's men went to ground, plowing through the thick underbrush in column of regiments until reaching space clear enough to deploy into line of battle. Again Deshler let them come to within eighty to one hundred yards before ordering the Fifteenth Texas to unload a barrage of buck and ball. The Twenty-sixth Iowa, a green regiment in its first battle, occupied an advanced position on Thayer's left and took a terrific beating. H. L. Walker of Company C wrote to his brother that "the Iowa 26th suffered severely. We lost in killed on the field 22 men, some four or five more mortally wounded, and some disabled for life. . . . We were in a very exposed position and I think for a new regiment behaved very well indeed." A soldier in the Thirty-fourth Iowa recalled that "our line of infantry was thrown forward in the face of a tempest of shot and shell and musketry from the enemy. We advanced over stumps, brush, and abatis, until within one hundred and fifty yards of their works." The Iowans, as had Hovey's troops, now "found shelter from the enemy's missiles in some ravines lined by underbrush and fallen timber" and commenced sniping at the Texans' earthworks. Deshler, observing that the Yankees "were continually pressing toward my left flank, evidently with the intention of passing around it through the interval between it and the bayou," moved his reserve, six companies of the Nineteenth Arkansas, to cover the gap. The Arkansians took position in a belt of woods adjacent to Post Bayou, but Deshler nervously noted that "there was still an unoccupied and comparatively open space of about 100 to 125 yards between the left of my trench and the right of the Arkansas battalion."[44]

To Steele's left, David Stuart's division charged forward soon after Thayer's brigade advanced. With G. A. Smith on the right and T. K. Smith on the left, the brigades formed "under a perfect hurricane of shot and shell." G. A. Smith's men immediately ran into trouble, hammered by the muskets of the Seventeenth and Eighteenth Texas Cavalry (Dismounted) and the 6-pounder guns of Hart's Arkansas Battery. "When we had marched a little way towards them we got orders to fall down and protect ourselves the best we could . . . behind stumps, rocks and little knolls," Solomon Woolworth of the 113th Illinois remembered. The Yankees began firing individually, and one of Woolworth's comrades stated that a fellow soldier was wounded "in the back part of his head. It was done by a ball from one of our own guns. Some of the men that did not come up as fast as the rest would lay down behind and fire over us." The colonel's troops hugged the ground as he ordered sharpshooters of the Sixth and Eighth Missouri and Fifty-seventh Ohio to creep forward and take out the offending artillery. "They advanced to within 100 yards of the guns, which they effectively silenced, not only picking off every gunner who showed himself above the works, but killing every horse belonging to the battery," G. A. Smith reported. The Union infantry was supported by Batteries A and B, First Illinois Light Artillery, and the Fourth Ohio Artillery Battery. Battery A's captain reported that they deployed about five hundred yards from the Rebel works, "where we remained keeping up a steady but not rapid fire."[45]

Deshler, meanwhile, continuing to fear a thrust around his left flank, requested reinforcements from Garland's brigade. Garland sent twelve companies of the Twenty-fourth and Twenty-fifth Texas Cavalry (Dismounted) and the Sixth Texas Infantry to fill the gap between the Nineteenth Arkansas and the rest of Deshler's command. "These companies had to pass through a very galling fire almost the entire length of the line . . . and it was necessary to crawl on all fours in our shallow trench the whole distance," the general reported. Robert Chalk of the Sixth Texas remembered that he "ran the full length of our line, exposed to the enemy's fire all the way. The balls whistled very close to me. I now hardly see how one could live and pass under such a fire from a quarter of a mile to half a mile—perhaps Divine Providence was with me."[46]

As G. A. Smith's brigade began its advance, the first elements of Morgan's XIII Corps entered the battle. Brig. Gen. A. J. Smith ordered Burbridge to move his regiments forward. Accordingly, the Eighty-third Ohio and Sixteenth and Sixtieth Indiana Infantry (from left to right) moved forward, and they were hit hard by the Confederates. Ohioan Frank McGregor later described the charge: "[W]e formed our line in the woods and maneuvered a little first to get our men calm and cool and then advanced to the open field in front of the fort. With a shout, the enemy immediately poured in their deadly fire. We all fell flat on our faces near a fence." John Wilkins of the Sixteenth Indiana recorded: "[W]e rushed forward to the charge with shouts and fierce discharges of muskets and we were [met] with a storm of shell, canister grape and musket balls from the enemies works, which sent many a brave fellow to his long account." A soldier in the Sixtieth Indiana noted that the regiment, "being last on the field at V'ksbrg was placed in front and . . . was the first to charge, when they lost in a very few minutes, in killed and wounded, 60 men." As the troops clustered under the cover of the fence, "the line could not be kept, and when we all got over the fence the regiment looked like a mob, no order, no discipline," Thomas Marshall of the Eighty-third Ohio wrote. His comrade Frank McGregor reported, "We were ordered to *retreat*, and back we rushed pell mell for the woods, all in confusion." There, Marshall noted, "we were rallied and cursed by Genl. Smith, and again started forward."[47]

Much of the fire that had stunned Burbridge's advance came from a group of huts that Rebel sharpshooters were using as cover. A. J. Smith ordered the Twenty-third Wisconsin to charge the buildings, "which was done in the most gallant manner, thus forcing the enemy to abandon their stronghold and flee under a hot fire from our troops to their intrenchments." As the Badger State soldiers approached the buildings, "four guns from the enemy opened on us and a thousand rifles from the pits," D. W. Hitchcock wrote in his diary. "Thirty of our men fell from the first fire." Again the fire from Garland's brigade and Hart's battery was heavy, with a soldier in the Ninety-sixth Ohio recording that the Federals advanced "under a galling fire of grape that mowed them down." Burbridge ordered a section of the Seventeenth Ohio Battery forward, and "in ten minutes [it] silenced the guns that did such execution on us." The First Brigade again advanced, this time with all six regiments moving forward, reinforced on their right by three regiments of Landram's Second Brigade. The Sixtieth Indiana, "now numbering 150 men, moved out again into the marshy field in front of the enemy's works, not as at first at double quick, with hideous yells, but slowly and calmly till within about 100 yards of the fort, where they continued loading + firing while laying down," a Hoosier infantryman reported, while a Wisconsin soldier wrote that "once we commenced [firing] I felt just as cool as though I was at work on the farm." The Eighty-third Ohio, however, would not move forward as "the balls came as thick as hail; they buzzed like bees," and the Seventy-seventh Illinois was compelled to advance through the demoralized Buckeyes. One of those Illinoisans, William Henry Willcox, recorded in his diary that he "marched up and over the 83 Ohio who would not stire [sic]. I saw there major strike and kick his men trying to urge them forward." Another Illinoisan recalled that "we were compelled to charge over [the Ohioans] in the face of a terrible fire from the fort. As we passed over them we made it a matter of necesity to tramp on as many as possible at which they threw a few old fashioned anathemas after us. This we considered very ungentlemanly, and especially so as it was Sunday." A historian of the Ninety-sixth Ohio recorded that "the gallant" Maj. S. S. L'Hommediu of the Eighty-third finally "rallied his retreating soldiers who came back with a will, too proud to leave their comrades, and with them now ready to die." Lt. Col. William Baldwin of the Eighty-third reported that his men advanced until "we were within point-blank musket range of the fort." But as on the Union right, Burbridge's troops "kept lying down all the time, only getting up to fire as soon as loaded, the enemy from behind their breastworks keeping up their deadly fire."[48]

Osterhaus's Second Division formed the extreme Union left of the general assault against the Rebel works. As the gunboats began their attack, Daniel Webster's First Wisconsin Battery opened fire on Fort Hindman's *en barbette* 9-inch Dahlgren. "After six shots the piece was silenced and the enemy's artillerists, who were exposed to the severe fire of the gunboat fleet, deserted the rampart," Osterhaus reported. Robert Chalk of the Sixth Texas remembered that as the Arkansas cannoneers huddled in the rifle pits, Captain Hart followed, and "I saw him curse them and tell them to come back to their post or he would run his sword through them." Around 2:00 P.M. Osterhaus ordered Capt. Charles G. Cooley's section of the Chicago Mercantile Battery to move up, supported on the right by the 118th Illinois and on the left by the 127th Ohio. The Yankees were met with "a galling fire of the enemy's musketry" as the guns opened up. "I tell you the balls came thick and fast as hail if we did not hug the earth it was a pitty," Illinois infantryman Tom Mix wrote in his journal. As his artillery fire began to tell on the defenders, Osterhaus ordered the 120th Ohio to charge the Rebel works, providing the Southerners an opportunity to fight back. "Finally we got to watch the infantry," Franz Coller of the Sixth Texas remembered. "Now our batteries began to spit out and make gaps in their ranks. We let them come until we thought our shots to be more accurate, then we fired at them." Ohioan Marcus Spiegel was on the receiving end of that fire, writing home afterward: "Oh, my God, such perfect hailing of bullets and busting of shells. Cannon balls tearing up the ground big enough to use the holes for graves of its unfortunate Victims." Another Buckeye, J. S. B. Matson, wrote: "I expected that Mary would be a widow before I got ten rods but thank God I got through. We run up to within 100 yds. of the fort and lay down in shelters as best we could under a murderous fire balls whizzing all around us." An Ohio diarist recorded that "the enemy seemed determined to 'Hold the fort.' The men in the ditches fought like so many tigers, and it was like running against a stone wall to attempt to drive them out." The Federals struggled to the "very ditch of the fort, but unfortunately the ditch opens here into a very deep gully, making a crossing impossible." As had happened all along the assaulting lines, the Ohioans dropped and hugged the ground under the intense fire. Dunnington, his Fort Hindman troops battered by gunboats and artillery, called for reinforcements from Garland, who detached two companies of the Sixth Texas for that purpose. "It was a perilous trip for the air was thick with flying missles of every description," Texan Jim Turner declared. "We found the fort badly battered and in a very dilapidated condition." Franz Coller recalled entering the fort: "[I]t cannot be described horribly enough how the splinters and shrapnel flew here. It was terrible to see how several poor men were smashed. . . . There was a terrible fire from the musketballs which whizzed around. However, they were like little birds compared to the bombshells."[49]

"Like a serpent decoying its prey, the Federal troops lay coiled around us," Lt. S. W. Bishop of Texas wrote. The big guns in Fort Hindman were now silent, as were all but one of Hart's fieldpieces. The Union artillery continued to pulverize the Confederate lines, however, backed by Porter's gunboats, all firing with impunity. Fred Davis on the *Baron De Kalb* wrote home that his ship was "firing broadside guns at the rebel troops who were fighting our troops in plain sight on the banks. After we had drove them from the Batteries, dismounted and bursted their guns, we turned and kept up the fight with the soldiers." Texan Samuel Foster tragically recalled two brothers hit by one shell, killing one and slicing the legs from the other. "The one that was left without any legs turned his body halfway around. He seemed to want to tell his brother something. He was unaware that his brother was gone. When he did realize that his brother was dead, he took his pistol, a six-shooter, and killed himself. There was excitement sure enough." Despite their desperate straits, Churchill reported, "the fire raged furiously along the entire line and that gallant band of Texans and Arkansians having nothing to rely upon now save muskets and bayonets, still disdained to yield to the overpowering foe." The Federals, now within two hundred yards of the Rebel lines, prepared to charge again. "Oh, what a grand sight FORTY THOUSAND men pressing forward as one man . . . on, on they come like an irresistible thunder bolt," W. W. Heartsill declared. "The earth was literally blue from one end of their line to the other," L. V. Caraway remembered. The spectacle also impressed the historian of the Fourth Indiana Cavalry, who wrote that "the lines extended about three miles and a person that has never witnessed the like can hardly imagine the grandeur of the sight." Improbably at this time, Col. Edward E. Portlock, Jr., of the Twenty-fourth Arkansas arrived with 190 soldiers to reinforce the Arkansas Post garrison, having "made the unprecedented march of 40 miles in twenty-four hours." Sidney Little of the 118th Illinois chortled, "they come just in time for us to bag them."[50]

Little was correct. As the Federal host massed for a final attack, Churchill reported, "several white flags were displayed in the Twenty-fourth Regiment Texas Dismounted Cavalry." Colonel Garland, who "could not conceive it possible that a white flag could be thus treacherously displayed in any part of our line with impunity," did not believe they were raised under Churchill's orders as the men of the regiment were shouting and "did not feel authorized to give any order on the subject." Captain Foster recorded that the calls to raise the white flag started on the regiment's left and conveyed by word of mouth to the right, which was "the system we had of passing commands down the line. Any word that came to us, from either direction, was passed along without waiting to inquire whether it was legitimate or not." Nor was Foster disappointed in the surrender "order": "It was the only intelligible thing we could do." The Sixth Texas and Dunnington's survivors, meanwhile, continued to fire at Morgan's jubilant Yankees, who had rushed into the open on seeing the white flags. "No sooner had we advanced within fifty yards of their rifle muzzles," an out-raged Owen Hopkins of the Forty-second Ohio wrote, than "we were greeted with a treacherous and deadly fire of infantry and a raking discharge of grape and canister." Another Ohioan declared: "Some of the regiment's kept up firing for a few minutes. The enemy sent a deadly volley among us. . . . That volley did more damage than all the previous firing." John Kehrwecker of the Ninety-sixth Ohio wrote that on seeing the white flags: "Our boys commenst hollering and then some of the rebels comensted fireing agan, so our boys go down and give it to them again. The white flags then came up all along the line and then we went in." A. J. Smith said that General Burbridge "was handed a flag, with orders to be first in the fort and plant it," and he rushed forward to fulfill that order. Confederate guards blocked his way, refusing to acknowledge that they had surrendered until the Union general pointed out the white flags wagging along the line and ordered them to ground their arms. Burbridge was guided to Churchill but passed the honor of accepting the garrison's surrender to a jubilant McClernand, who arrived soon after. Dunnington, holding true to his naval roots, would not surrender until Admiral Porter was there to accept it; Porter recorded that the Confederate snarled, "You wouldn't have got us had it not been for your damned gun-boats." Sherman soon joined the brass in the fort, and a Kentucky soldier remembered his meeting with Churchill: "Both generals with their staffs were mounted, and the interview was in the center of the entrenched ground. 'Well, Sherman,' said Churchill, 'I have made the very best fight in my power.' 'And a very gallant fight you have made of it,' was Sherman's very prompt response. . . . Here for hours had they been hurling deadly missiles at each other, and yet under a little bit of white bunting they instantly became jolly good friends. The incident was a lesson for me."[51]

Farther down the Confederate line, the situation was tense and confused. Deshler saw the white flags waving over Garland's position but assumed they were small company flags of a dingy color. "Knowing that it was General Churchill's determination to fight to desperation, I did not think it possible that a surrender could be intended, and accord-ingly paid no attention to these flags," he reported. Yet Deshler ordered his men to stop shooting when a Federal officer carrying a flag of truce appeared in his front. As soon as the firing stopped, remembered Lt. R. M. Collins of the Fifteenth Texas, "the Yankees in front of us rose up as

An artist with *Frank Leslie's Illustrated Newspaper* embedded with Brig. Gen. Stephen Burbridge's Union troops captured the fall of Fort Hindman on January 11, 1863, not surprisingly including the general and his staff in the illustration. *Courtesy Butler Center for Arkansas Studies.*

if by magic." These were the men of Steele's brigade, massed "in three of four distinct and apparently parallel lines of battle," wrote Deshler, "and extending along my entire front and as far to the right and left as I could see." Steele and his staff rode forward and, pointing to the white flags now flying along the entire length of the Rebel lines, informed the Texan that Churchill had surrendered. Deshler still would not ground his arms without direct orders from his commander. Sherman, who was now inside Fort Hindman with several other generals, received news of the standoff and "advised General Churchill to send orders at once, because a single shot might bring the whole of Steele's division on Deshler's brigade, and I would not be responsible for the consequences." The two generals hurried down the line, Churchill pausing only to exchange angry words with Garland over the white flags. Reaching the irate Deshler, the Confederate commander said, "You see, sir, that we are in their power, and you may surrender." The Texan at last ordered his men to lay down their arms.[52]

The Union troops, braced for a final assault against the Confederate works, were jubilant. "You ought to have heard the cheering and seen the rest," wrote an officer of the Forty-second Ohio. "Infantry, artillery, cavalry, citizens, boatmen, nigers [sic], one and all set up a yell and rushed for the works." All along the lines the Federal troops streamed forward. Franz Coller of the Sixth Texas wrote: "[H]ardly had it been done [the white flag raised] when the Yankees were there. Thick as blackbirds . . . They came and joined hands with us as if we were old acquaintances." Illinoisan Henry Bear affirmed this: "[W]e shook hands after the fight. I was hungry and they gave me some bread and some meat that was good sure." A soldier of the Fifty-fifth Illinois told his wife, "our men bounded over the enemy works and received a hearty welcome from the . . . butternuts many of them taking our men by the hands to assist them over the breast works exclaiming you have made a good haul this time, our boys asking them where the *Blue Wing* was." Illinois artillerist Charles Kimbell remembered a grimmer sight as he entered the works: "Inside they saw a rebel soldier with both legs shot off, alive and holding the stumps in his hands and swearing like a trooper." At Fort Hindman, Sidney Little of the 118th Illinois wrote, "the white flag did not suit us we called for the Stars and Stripes and you ought to have seen them hoist it." The jubilation was shared by the sailors on the Union gunboats, with Fred Davis on the *Baron De Kalb* informing his parents: "All hands were *piped* on deck, to cheer . . . and we gave 9 hearty ones. . . . And the stars and stripes were seen floating from the Batteries." "It was a real splendid sight to see about 30,000 blue coats into the Rebels fortifications to the tune of Yankee Doodle," a soldier of the Twenty-ninth Missouri concluded. The rush of victory for many of the Union troops was tempered with respect for their vanquished foes. "They made a brave and stubborn resistance," George Marshall of the Forty-ninth Indiana acknowledged, while an Ohioan who had charged Fort Hindman allowed that the defenders "[s]urely defended their line nobly. But it was all for naught, because we had to firm a hold upon them."[53]

Looking back on the surrender of Arkansas Post years later, one Texan mused, "It has always seemed providential to surrender just at that time, as the next charge would have annihilated us." At the time, however, a comrade declared: "I shall never forget the scene of that hour. Strong men were weeping like whipped children. Others were enraged and were cursing." For the men of the W. P. Lane Rangers, "the humiliating part of a defeat [was] surrendering your trusty rifle and Navy six, to give up your noble steed." But Trooper Heartsill recorded, "there is one consolation for our boys . . . they got very few of the guns or pistols belonging to the 'Rangers,' for we have thrown them into a deep muddy Bayou." Texan Robert Chalk recalled that the order to "stack arms was humiliating indeed. Some threw their arms away while some of the officers rammed their swords into the ground and broke them off." An officer in the Fifty-fifth Illinois Infantry watched as "the rebels in front of Stuart's division gathered in a promiscuous crowd around a small pond of water, and commenced quietly tossing into it knives, revolvers and such like personal gear. This was soon discovered, and the icy, cold water explored by the victors, who splashed and dove until the last relic was discovered." For some of the Yankees, the capture of Arkansas Post was an opportunity to upgrade their weapons. Carlos Colby of the Ninety-seventh Illinois remembered that "our men threw away their old guns, and took Enfield rifles captured from the enemy. . . . When the ordnance officer found we had made the change he made a terrible kick, for he had no cartridges to fit the new guns . . . but the kick came too late, for we had the newer guns, and the old ones had been turned over as captured property." One Ohioan wrote home that he "found a Reb.

shot in the forehead. . . . [H]e had dropped a very nice Enfield rifle which I captured and have yet."[54]

Captain Foster recorded that in his company of the Twenty-fourth Texas, "my men stuck their Bowie knives into the breastwork and threw their guns and six-shooters into the dirt. A Yankee officer then ordered us to stack arms. No one had ever given us a command in that manner before. . . . We were affronted with the reality that we were prisoners." Not all of the Texans accepted that reality, for some drifted away singly or in groups to escape imprisonment. William Gates Hubert of the Sixth Texas remembered that his company commander, Henry Hancock, a Northerner, warned his men that "'it means death to many of you from the intense cold of that climate.' Drawing his sword, [he] said, 'If you will follow me, I will lead you out of this place or perish in the attempt.' With bayonets firmly fixed, they followed their captain through the very jaws of death and the Federals were considerate enough to give them room." John Faulk of the Seventeenth Texas wrote that he, "with four others of my company and my negro Jere got out when the Post surrendered." After wandering for a couple of days through south Arkansas, they encountered Hancock's company and Duncan Preston's Company F, Seventeenth Texas, which also had escaped capture. Marshall Pierson of the Seventeenth remembered that after hearing General Deshler state that they were surrounded, "[I] immediately . . . disengaged myself from a blanket which I had around my shoulders, shouldered my double barrel gun, and in a very careless and unconcerned manner walked off in the direction of the Bayou, the enemy's whole line having approached within fifty paces of us. . . . The effort was liberty, for I found the way clear in regard to the Federals, but very closely beset with Bayous, brush, etc." Pierson traveled with Preston's company at first, then "having lost everything in the way of baggage in making our escape rather than be a prisoner, I felt it not only my privilege but my duty to go home, which I was determined to do and did."[55]

The Federals now had their first close-up look at and chance to speak with their erstwhile foes. "They are a motley looking crew but they fight like Devills sure," was Illinoisan Henry Bear's assessment, while a Wisconsin soldier noted that "they were qurious looking Soldiers to us every one had his own Uniform to suit himself. You could hardly tell the Privates from the Officers." H. H. Helphrey of the Ninety-sixth Ohio saw the captured Rebels as "a hard set of looking fellows, all dressed in home spun butternut. They had splendid guns of all kinds, taken from the government." Hoosier George Wilkins was surprised to find "a number of Northern men among the prisoners, mostly belonging to Texas Regiments." A soldier of the Ninth Iowa admired the Confederate leadership, griping that "the fact of the business is their Officers fight to whip and ours are fighting for big pay." "They were all six feet high and regular tigers," Calvin Ainsworth of the Twenty-fifth Iowa wrote in his diary. "One of them told me that they were waiting and wishing that we would charge clear to their breast works, as they had double barrel shot guns in reserve." D. W. Hitchcock of the Twenty-third Wisconsin observed: "The prisoners are a fine set of fellows, well dressed in light brown and generally cheerful. They have or profess to have faith in the Confederacy; think that England will soon help them."[56]

Indeed, the Confederate prisoners remained confident and defiant despite their circumstances. Although he thought the Rebels "appeared to be the off-scouring of creation," Ohioan Owen Hopkins noted that "their convictions . . . were that we were fighting a war of extermination, and they expressed their determination of resisting bitterly to the end." George Pardee of the Forty-second Ohio spoke with Colonel Gillespie of the Twenty-fifth Texas, a Methodist preacher in civilian life, and learned: "[T]hey all felt it was their duty as Christians and they would fight as long as there was a man left. . . . I confess the thing looks hard, and will cause great loss of life and long suffering to whip the cusses." Asa Sample of the Fifty-fourth Indiana found the prisoners "*saucy* and impudent. Said they were determined to fight and fight for ever and their children that could but *lisp* were of the *same* sentiment." Illinoisan Sidney Little wrote to his mother that "they will lay down their arms as soon as we will[.] they think that we are trying to Over rule them and they say that they will fight us as long as they see well." Colonel Gillespie, despite the fact that his men were the first to show the white flag, thundered at another captor: "[the Federals] might by force of greater numbers kill off all the men, but . . . would then be confronted with an army of boys who were now growing up and learning the art of war; and when they were all killed [the Federals] would meet an army of women who would fight like men; in fact, [the North] could never whip the south." Such bombast impressed John Harrington of the Twenty-second Kentucky

Infantry, who wrote to his sister that "these men were over powered but not conquered. . . . On the word of a soldier these are *men*; and men of the order of '76 men who have their hearts enlisted in their cause who believe God is with them and ever willing to favor and defend them from the hand of oppression."[57]

The Yankees also had an opportunity to wander over the battlefield and examine the results of two days of concentrated destruction. Fort Hindman was a nightmarish scene, with a trooper of the Fourth Indiana Cavalry relating that upon entering the works, "the ground . . . was literally covered with Dead and wounded men and horses groaning and struggling for aid." "The Rebels best gunners were either killed or wounded," an Iowan wrote in his diary. "I saw eleven Dead horses laying close together all pierced through with bullets." An Illinois soldier, visiting the casemates, admiringly wrote that "the large guns on the fort were all knocked into a 'cocked up hat.' They are not worth anything except for old iron." His assessment was shared by an artillerist who noted that the defenders' "three heavy siege guns were all disabled—two of them were broken off a couple of feet back from the muzzles." No less an authority than Admiral Porter, who knew a thing or two about blasting fixed fortifications, later declared, "no fort ever received a worse battering, and I know of no instance where every gun in a fort was dismounted or destroyed."[58]

Hoosier George Marshall also entered Fort Hindman and remembered that "the sight was sickening, the gunners and their assistants were all shot and torn, their blood being splattered against the walls, some had their clothing burned almost all off of them. . . . But outside along the rifle pits and breast works it was worse. Men lay torn and bleeding and dying, the pits were full of dead and wounded." A. J. Withrow of the Twenty-fifth Iowa wrote: "[T]he Sight which met my eyes made me heart Sick. In one Spot I counted ten rebels who had been killed by one Shell. Some were cut in two, others had both legs Shot off, and blood, brains, and fragments of bodies lay all around, added to this dead horses, broken waggons, tents, clothing and indeed every thing that makes up the paraphernalia of a camp lay about in grand confusion." William Eddington of the Ninety-seventh Illinois found a Confederate who "was laying on his back, but his feet were standing up in front of him in a long pair of boots." Hoosier Asa Sample attested that "the fire of the gunboats was terribly destructive, mowing before it men, horses, breastworks, cannon and *everything*

but the hills and river banks. . . . I wonder how they held out so long."
The historian of the Forty-second Ohio made this grim notation: "the
large buildings at the rear, which had been used as hospitals . . . , stood
in the range of the gun-boat shells which over-shot the fort, they had
been riddled and many of the wounded unintentionally killed."[59]

Nor was all of the destruction on the Rebel side of the earthworks.
The battlefield was scattered with blueclad corpses and writhing
wounded, particularly on the two extreme flanks, where the troops of
Hovey and Burbridge had suffered more than half of the total Union
casualties. Indeed, a Texan noted that the Rebel musketry against
Hovey's men had left "the trees on their side . . . cut from the ground up
to twenty-five feet high; not a tree is left unscarred; some of them have
fifty balls in them." Rebel Lawson Jefferson Keener concluded with
satisfaction that "the Feds paid dear for their wrassle." Of the Union
dead, Iowan A. J. Withrow observed: "Some lay as if sleeping gently
as an infant, others as if even in death, they thought of vengeance,
the compressed lips and stern countenances Showed that they fell
as the brave do fall . . . they died fighting for the rights of men." A
fellow soldier of the Twenty-fifth Iowa "saw the dead and dying, some
places lying almost in heaps and some scattered round in almost all
kinds of shapes, limbs torn off and bodies mangled in almost every
manner." "In some places the dead lay very thick, not more than
3–5–10 feet apart," Calvin Ainsworth wrote, "some were shot in the
head, others in the breast and lungs, some through the neck, and I
saw 3 or 4 torn all to pieces by cannon balls; their innards lying by
their side, yet warm from their hearts blood." Many of the Federal
wounded were moved to transports to receive medical care, and
along the road to the river "were several fresh mounds where had
been buried soldiers who died under or after operation," an Ohioan
recalled. "On the bow of the lower deck was a stack of coffins ready
for use. . . . The long cabin was filled with wounded men lying in
rows on the floor with feet to center and an aisle along the center."
Nearly nine hundred Union soldiers were wounded in the struggle
for Arkansas Post.[60]

The magnitude of the Union victory began to sink in as the prisoners were gathered, the wounded tended, and the dead buried. "If the
blue wing had been left alone, we would not [have] gone to the Post,"
an Illinois soldier stated to his wife. "Our loss in killed I don't think is
more than that of the enemy. We have taken five thousand prisoners,

they none. So I think we are a little ahead, take the whole up one side and down the other." Churchill reported 60 killed and 80 wounded, with the Federals taking 4,791 prisoners, almost the entire Confederate force except for the few soldiers who managed to slip away in the initial confusion as the white flags first showed along the Rebel lines. McClernand's army suffered 134 killed, 898 wounded, and 29 missing in the one-sided but hard-fought victory. In addition, the politician-general bragged: "Seven stands of colors were captured, including the garrison flag. . . . Besides these, 5,000 prisoners; 17 pieces of cannon, large and small; 10 gun carriages and 11 limbers; 3,000 stand of small arms, exclusive of many lost or destroyed; 130 swords; 50 Colt's pistols; 40 cans of powder; 1,650 rounds of shot, shell, and canister for 10 and 20 pounder Parrott guns; 375 shells, grape-stands, and canister; 46,000 rounds of ammunition for small-arms; 563 animals, together with a considerable quantity of quartermaster's and commissary stores, fell into our hands." Samuel Gordon of the 118th Illinois proudly wrote home that "the amount of property taken from the rebels while we were up the Arkansas is estimated at a million dollars worth. . . . We were obliged to burn over one hundred wagons which could not be taken away there was a mill and several other manufacturing establishments of great importance to the rebels destroyed."[61]

Admiral Porter had the added satisfaction of having devised a successful innovation to protect his ships, ordering that the pilot houses and casemates of attacking vessels be coated with slush to make enemy fire glance away. He reported the results: "The *Rattler* was struck fair on her iron covering . . . by two IX-inch shells, which flew upward without scratching the iron. The *Cincinnati* was struck eight times on her pilot house with IX-in shell[s], which glanced off like peas against glass." Lt. Cmdr. John G. Walker acknowledged that his *Baron de Kalb* was damaged by shells entering his gunports but that the areas he had covered with slush were "repeatedly struck by 8 and 9 inch shot at very short range, and the iron in no case penetrated." Porter concluded: "I am perfectly convinced that a coating of tallow on ironclad gunboats is a perfect protection against shot if fired at an angle. The experiment is worth being tried." In the weeks that followed, slushing vessels before combat would become standard procedure for the ships of the Mississippi Squadron.[62]

For all the captured Confederates and materiel, perhaps the greatest benefit for the soldiers of McClernand's Army of the Mississippi was one of morale. "Our victory has hardly a parallel since the war commenced," George F. Chittenden of the Sixteenth Indiana informed his wife. "Our loss so small & the results so great make our army justly proud." A fellow Hoosier, Ralph Muncy, remembered: "[W]e Politely saluted [the Rebels] for two days, with out gloves on, when they kindly asked us to pull on our gloves and handle them more carefully, which we did. This revived our Sad Spirits a little." Ohioan J. S. B. Matson noted that the Federals "whaled hell out of them at Arkansas post and the boys felt better than before." A Kentuckian was satisfied that "by this capture we secure five thousand prisoners with General Churchill and staff at their head; possession of a commanding position on the river with an open road and open navigation to the capital of the state, and best of all, the moral prestige of returning victories by the national troops." In the Sixteenth Indiana one soldier noted a special satisfaction for his comrades, noting that the Rebel equipment included "wagons, arms, etc., captured from our Regiment at Richmond, Ky. General Churchill who commanded the enemy here was among our captors at that disastrous battle. It is quite a satisfaction to capture him in turn. Such is the fate of war."[63]

"I walked over the battlefield on the day after the fight and the same scenes met the eye . . . [as] on the scene of our disaster [at Chickasaw Bluffs] with the difference being that it was the enemy's dead you would see here, while at Vicksburg it was our own men," wrote a soldier of the Twenty-ninth Missouri Infantry. Indeed, for the veterans of the slaughter on the Yazoo River, there was grim satisfaction. "We got our revenge at Arkansas Post," William G. Dilts remembered. "The result was forgone and the slaughter of Confederates was simply hideous." Virgil Moats, a veteran of the Forty-eighth Ohio, told the folks at home, "[o]ur success was all that could be desired, and in part atoned for our ill success at Vicksburg," adding that "while it [the fighting at Arkansas Post] lasted Shiloh was nowhere." The historian of the Eighty-third Indiana concluded, "we felt greatly encouraged with our victory, though we had not succeed in our first (that of Chickasaw Bayou)." An Iowan noted simply, "Arkansas Post wiped out Chickasaw Bayou."[64]

The loss electrified and terrified the people of Arkansas, who expected the Union juggernaut that had reduced Fort Hindman to continue upriver, devastating everything in its path. A Texas soldier among those hastening to Churchill's relief wrote: "I could not describe, if I wished, the panic which struck the citizens of the Ark. Valley from the first news of the attack on the post. On our march down, large droves of Negroes were continually passing families moving, stock driving, splendid plantations deserted, fine mansions untenanted—everything looked like the besom [broom] of destruction had passed over the very best country in the world, for really some portions of the Ark. Valley is unsurpassed for fine lands and splendid plantations." Nor was the panic confined to civilians. Texan Elijah Petty fretted: "[S]o soon as the river rises their boats will ascend and we cant offer them any resistance. The Post is the key to all Arkansas and they now have a bill of sale to it. It is to Arkansas what Fort Donaldson was to Tennessee." Perhaps the most significant aspect of the disaster at Arkansas Post for Confederate Arkansas was the loss of some 5,000 men, which historians William Shea and Terrence Winschell maintain was "roughly one-fourth of the total Confederate strength in Arkansas, Missouri, and the Indian Territory," adding: "It removed the only potential threat to the Union line of communications on the Mississippi River, cost the Rebels men and supplies they could not afford to lose, and opened the Arkansas Valley to invasion. The defeat also extinguished any lingering hope that Jefferson Davis might work up the political courage to order Holmes to send reinforcements to Vicksburg."[65]

McClernand, flush with victory, was not necessarily finished with Arkansas. On the night of January 11, he asked Porter to take soundings of the Arkansas River up from Arkansas Post toward Little Rock.[66]

3

"WE MUST WHIP THEM OR SURRENDER"
Holmes Moves to the Offensive

McClernand was ecstatic over the success of his first independent command. But in a congratulatory order, he indicated that he had other ambitions in the Trans-Mississippi, writing that the victory at Arkansas Post "is an important step toward the restoration of our national jurisdiction and unity over the territory on the right bank of the Mississippi River. . . . Win for the Army of the Mississippi an imperishable renown. Surmount all obstacles, and relying on the God of Battles wrest from destiny and danger the homage of still more expressive acknowledgments of your unconquerable constancy and valor." The politician-general clearly had his eyes on the capital at Little Rock and further glory. Samuel Curtis's Army of the Southwest had threatened the city months before, but lack of supplies had forced it to abandon that goal and head for Helena. Perhaps McClernand could succeed where Curtis had failed and hand the political plum of a rebellious capital to President Lincoln. He wrote to Curtis on January 14, "if the river will allow within two or three days, I will ascend with my command to Little Rock, and reduce that place," though he acknowledged, "it is doubtful . . . whether the stage of water will allow it." Nonetheless, people in Little Rock were nervous about a possible campaign against the capital.[1]

In the meantime there was still work to do at Arkansas Post. Sherman reported that "the 12th [of January] was mostly consumed in collecting captured property . . . and in enrolling and embarking

the prisoners," who would be sent North. This decision was note-
worthy in that it ignored the Dix-Hill cartel, an 1862 agreement
under which the captured Rebels should have been exchanged with
Yankee troops. The cartel would collapse by mid-1863 as the Union
had less need for the manpower freed by prisoner exchange than did
the South and over disagreements on the treatment of black Union
soldiers. Capt. Samuel Foster of the Twenty-fourth Texas was almost
cheerful as he boarded a Federal transport, expecting that "the Yanks
are going to take us to Vicksburg to be exchanged. . . . We are going
to be free again, what is left of the Texas troops, and on the South's
side of the river too." That was not to be. The Confederate officers
were bound for the dreary prisoner of war camp at Johnson's Island
in Lake Erie, while the rank-and-file soldiers went to the harsh prison
at Camp Douglas outside of Chicago. As the Southerners filed on to
the transports, an Iowa observer noted, "they seemed to lack blankets
and I am inclined to think [they] will suffer some to-day, as it snows
hard today." As night fell and the transports began their long journey
north, "a cold rain, followed by sleet and snow, rendered our situation
more dreadful than the battle." The captives huddled on the decks
of the boats, shaking in the cold, and a Yankee artillerist observed
that "it was a terrible hardship for the men in grey on the upper
decks with no semblance of shelter." Confederate William J. Oliphant
remembered, "the eighteen days and nights which followed the capture
of Arkansas Post seem like a long, dark, horrible dream, such a one that
doubtless haunts the sleeping hours of the survivors of an Arctic expedition, as they dream of their frozen comrades and the ice and snow of
the Polar regions." The horror of the journey was shared by the men of
the Thirty-fourth Iowa Infantry, who were detailed as guards, as disease broke out on the crowded steamboats. "The floors of the cabin
were covered with the sick of our own regiment, and also sick rebels,
all lying closely together, some with fevers, some with pneumonia,
some with measles, some with small pox, all with chronic diarrheoa,"
one Iowan recalled. The regiment's colonel stated that "the human
suffering during the trip exceeded anything I have witnessed in the
same length of time."[2]

As the prisoners embarked on their hellish journey north, the
Army of the Mississippi continued the sad duty of burying its dead.
John Wilkins of the Sixteenth Indiana wrote: "[O]ur Regiment had
eleven killed and 64 wounded. A great many of the latter will die. Our

Regimental dead are all buried in one grave below the fort and near the river." As to the fallen defenders of Arkansas Post, an Illinoisan remembered that "the Confederate dead were pitched unceremoniously into the ditches, and the earth-works shoveled down upon them." McClernand ordered the fortifications destroyed, and Sherman noted with satisfaction, "we . . . proceeded to dismantle and level the forts, destroy or remove the stores, and we found in the magazine the very ammunition which had been sent for us in the *Blue Wing*, which was secured and afterward used in our twenty-pound Parrott guns." The Union men burned the Rebel camps, filled the trenches, flattened Fort Hindman, and threw the shattered enemy cannon into wells. A Texan visiting the site a month later noted the effectiveness of the destruction, writing that "only now and then may be seen a standing cabin—all burnt or charred. The timber is much torn by the terrible cannonading."[3]

General Gorman, commanding at Helena, sought to keep the Rebels off balance following the fall of Fort Hindman by advancing on their positions along the White River. On January 12 he sent a letter to Admiral Porter from the mouth of the White River, requesting a gunboat escort to move upriver. "I have 9000 Infantry, 20 pieces of light artillery; 2000 cavalry," he wrote. "The latter I sent by land to St. Charles, where they probably have arrived by this time." Porter accordingly ordered Lieutenant Commander Walker to take his *Baron De Kalb* and the *Cincinnati* to meet Gorman "and proceed in advance of him up the White River, cleaning out St. Charles." The combined force proceeded up the White in a steady rain that turned to snow by January 14—Daniel Kemp on the *Cincinnati* observed, "My! but it was cold and as the snow was several inches thick on our deck we poor wretches had to clean it off." Arriving at St. Charles, the Yankees found that the small garrison had loaded two 8-inch guns and a field battery on board the pesky *Blue Wing* and fled upriver to DeValls Bluff. "The fortifications here were very heavy and strong," the Ninth Illinois Cavalry's historian wrote. "Had the Confederate troops remained in their fortifications at St. Charles, they would undoubtedly have been able to give us a hard fight." Leaving the *Cincinnati*, a regiment of infantry, two companies of the Ninth Illinois, and a six-gun battery at St. Charles, the rest of the Union force continued its pursuit. The soldiers who stayed behind laid the hard hand of war on the small

White River town. Mary Patrick of St. Charles wrote in her diary: "[S]oon the steam mill was in flames, then several houses. . . . [T]hey commenced their burning—amid a storm of snow—I counted 17 houses on fire. . . . Piercing wind-driving snow—angry flames—fiendlike soldiers screaming their threats with angry oaths."[4]

On approaching DeValls Bluff, the *Baron De Kalb* took the lead and cleared for action, but, sailor Frederic Davis wrote, "as soon as they saw our *smoke* coming up the river they ran, leaving behind them two 8 inch guns, 200 muskets, 4 railroad cars, and several . . . prisoners." Gorman landed his cavalry to scout the area, moving about seven miles toward Little Rock "until the mud and water became utterly impassable." The next day, January 18, Walker proceeded up the White River with the light-draft vessels *Forest Rose* and *Romeo* and a transport carrying troops to Des Arc, where thirty-nine sick Confederates were captured and paroled and a quantity of ammunition and corn seized. The Yankees also captured a load of mail, Lt. George Brown of the *Forest Rose* remembered, and "from the contents of the letters we gathered much valuable information concerning the movements of the rebel troops, etc." The expedition turned back the next day, having been "as successful as could be desired, with the exception of the recapture of the *Blue Wing*." Gorman concluded, "I should have gone direct to Little Rock if it had been practicable to cross the sea of mud and water intervening between that place and Devall's Bluff, but this is impossible at present." Stopping at St. Charles, the Yankees blew up Rebel magazines using gunpowder captured at Des Arc. "I believe everything of use to the enemy at St. Charles that could be destroyed was destroyed by the army or ourselves," Walker reported. The destruction, however, was not limited to military supplies. Mary Patrick recorded the results of the Yankees' stay in St. Charles: "Our pretty town in ashes—Our Church and Sunday-school library burntd—our graveyard despoiled. Gen. G was heard to say 'My men are perfect devils.'"[5]

While Gorman's expedition rampaged up the White River, McClernand pondered his next move. The Illinoisan hoped that the Arkansas River would rise enough to allow him to move against Little Rock, crippling the rebellion in the state. The twin crises of Arkansas Post and Gorman's raid had led Governor Flanagin to issue a proclamation calling on volunteers to come to Little Rock and

under his command fight the Union invaders. Reflecting the shortage of materiel available, the proclamation stated: "Every man must
bring his own Blankets. It is urged upon every one to bring ARMS
and accoutrements if he has them." On January 13 McClernand
ordered Col. Warren Stewart to take his cavalry on a reconnaissance
mission toward the White and St. Charles, which brought the intelligence that the bottomlands through which an army would pass
could handle infantry and cavalry but were too soggy for artillery or
wagons. That night the weather took a turn for the worse, pelting
the Union troops with freezing rain and snow. Asa Sample of the
Fifty-fourth Indiana recorded that "when night came oh! horrors,
our place to sleep! A respectable *Hoosier hog bed* would have been a
luxury. . . . While memory lasts I will never forget last night's rest."
On the fourteenth, having learned of a large cache of corn at South
Bend on the Arkansas, McClernand sent ten men from each company of the Twenty-third Wisconsin Infantry aboard the transport
Luzerne to seize the supply. The Badger State troops disembarked at
South Bend, where "they saw about 50 men on horseback galloping
away," John Jones told his parents. "They expected trouble, and after
setting the corn on fire they got back to the boat which was then
riddled with bullets." As the *Luzerne* hurried away, the Wisconsin
troops realized that they were "leaving five men who had gone back
after chickens against the orders of the officer in charge; they were
taken prisoner, of course." But Thomas Townsend of the Twenty-third
reported that the erstwhile chicken thieves "escaped and . . . got back
safe and sound."[6]

McClernand was enraged by the attack on his raiding party, and
on the fifteenth he sent Colonel Stewart out to retaliate. Stewart
took the Fifty-seventh Ohio Infantry aboard the steamer *Omaha* and,
accompanied by a gunboat, steamed upriver. Arriving at South Bend
at 3:00 P.M., they burned 7,800 bushels of corn. The Ohioans spread
out, finding another supply cache two miles away and burning another
22,500 bushels of corn along with fifty hides. But Stewart wanted
to warn the locals that it was dangerous to attack U.S. vessels. He
continued to the plantation of a secessionist named Clay where, after
capturing "50 sheep, 6 mules, 50 hides, 1 bell, and other property contraband of war," he put the place to the torch. He posted a warning
against guerrilla attacks, writing that "all engaged in this infamous
practice are recognized by both sides as assassins. . . . To-day I have

burned one of your mansions. If you repeat your useless assassin-like attacks I will devastate this entire country." The raiders were back at Fort Hindman by 10:00 P.M.[7]

Time was running out for McClernand's Arkansas adventure, in part a result of Van Dorn's raid on Holly Springs, which had seriously disrupted Union communications. McClernand had written Grant on January 8 of his plans to attack Arkansas Post, but the commanding general did not receive the letter until the eleventh. Fearing that the newly styled Army of the Mississippi could get mired in a worthless campaign in Arkansas, he immediately ordered McClernand to return to the Mississippi River. Grant also wired Halleck that "McClernand has . . . gone on a wild-goose chase to the Post of Arkansas." The general in chief quickly ordered Grant to "relieve General McClernand from command of the expedition against Vicksburg, giving it to the next in rank or taking it yourself." Grant wrestled with the problems of army politics, recognizing that McClernand was the senior general and politically connected. "I would have been glad to put Sherman in command, to give him an opportunity to accomplish what had failed [at Chickasaw Bayou]; but there seemed no other way out of the difficulty, because he was junior to McClernand," Grant wrote in his memoirs, "nothing was left but to assume the command myself." McClernand was furious and scrawled in a letter to President Lincoln, "I believe my success here is gall and wormwood to the clique of West Pointers who have been persecuting me for months," arguing that his "should be an independent command, as both you and the Secretary of War, I believe, originally intended." Lincoln declined to get involved in the intraservice squabble, responding, "I have too many *family* controversies (so to speak) already on my hands, to voluntarily . . . take up another." A dejected McClernand ordered his army to board transports and return to the Mississippi.[8]

Sherman's XV Corps climbed aboard their boats on January 16 and Morgan's XIII Corps joined them the next day, leaving the ruins of Fort Hindman and the graves of both victors and vanquished behind them. They met at the river town of Napoleon, where, a soldier of the Thirteenth Illinois remembered, they were told "to go on shore and make ourselves as comfortable as possible in the vacant houses around town," noting that "we found some molasses and made some excellent candy." William Kennedy of the Fifty-fifth Illinois wrote home that the first time he had an opportunity to enter a

Catholic church since joining the army was at Napoleon, "but the joke is the Preast and all the fine fixins runaway before we got there." William Winters of the Sixty-seventh Indiana took "a stroll through the streets of this much begrimed place of misery, saw some of the troops enjoying themselves in the deserted domiciles of their enemies." As at St. Charles, some of that enjoyment took a bad turn, and much of Napoleon was burned to the ground. Grant arrived there on January 17 and took command of Union forces. Two days later he and his army descended the Mississippi to Milliken's Bend to continue their efforts to reduce Vicksburg.[9]

As mentioned previously, Arkansas Post did wonders for the Union soldiers, providing a balming victory following the bitter defeat at Chickasaw Bayou. Indeed, for the entire North, which was stunned by the recent slaughter at Fredericksburg, Virginia, and the heavy casualties at Stones River, Tennessee, the one-sided victory brought welcome relief. Ultimately, even Grant had to admit that McClernand's "wild-goose chase" had value, acknowledging that "five thousand Confederate troops left in the rear might have caused us much trouble and loss of property while navigating the Mississippi" and could have hindered future operations against Vicksburg. Even Sherman was happy, writing to his wife that "this relieves our Vicksburg trip of all appearances of a reverse, as by this move we open the Arkansas and compel all organized masses of the enemy to pass below the Arkansas River, and it will also secure this flank when we renew our attack on Vicksburg." But McClernand's hopes to parlay his win at Fort Hindman into an attack on Little Rock did not hold up as well. Continued operations would have mired 32,000 veteran Yankee troops in the interior of Arkansas, far from the vital effort against Vicksburg. The rapidly fluctuating Arkansas River, perhaps more importantly, could easily have trapped Porter's gunboats, keeping them from operations on the Mississippi. As historian Edwin C. Bearss has concluded, "it was fortunate for the Union cause that McClernand's scheme was nipped in the bud." Ultimately the Illinois general's fate was cemented by his political machinations following Arkansas Post. The antagonism between McClernand and the West Point generals became exacerbated, and Grant soon sent him back to Illinois, never to enjoy an independent command again.[10]

Alf Johnson's Spy Company and E. E. Portlock's unfortunate Arkansians were not the only Confederate troops who rushed to help the defenders of Fort Hindman, though the others would soon learn of the bastion's fall. Theophilus Holmes, on learning of the Federal advance on Arkansas Post, had ordered all available troops to speed to the garrison's assistance. For the Texans of the Seventeenth Infantry, "the news of the prospect of a fight was received . . . with cheers," E. P. Petty remembered; "all are making active preparations to give the Yankees a warm reception on Arkansas soil." On the night of January 10, the Twelfth Texas Cavalry cooked two days' rations and headed for Arkansas Post, the rest of Col. William H. Parsons's brigade following the next morning. Texan Finas Stone remembered, "it was cold and raining, and we got orders about 3 o-clock to saddle up, and with nothing to eat we started for Arkansas Post . . . and traveled all day through rain, mud and sleet." It was for naught; when the horsemen reached the Arkansas on the thirteenth, they learned that Churchill had surrendered. W. E. Stoker of the Eighteenth Texas Infantry wrote home that "the fight ended before we got there, about 48 hours too late," wryly adding that the victors were the "same forces that attacked Vixburg and got whipped. They wouldn't stay whipped." The infantrymen halted on hearing of the surrender, then fell back to "a place called Three Levies," John Porter of the Eighteenth Texas wrote, where they "threw up some entrenchments, and felled the timber around our fortifications and awaited the enemy. For several days, during our stay here, we were drenched by the heaviest rain I ever saw." It grew even worse for the men of the Seventeenth Texas as they turned back to the Arkansas. J. H. Pillow recalled: "[W]e were ordered to fold our tents and put them and our knapsacks on a boat for Pine Bluff. It was the last time we saw either. What went with them I never knew."[11]

For a week the Texans huddled miserably on the banks of the Arkansas River awaiting an attack that never came. On the night of January 12, it began to snow, which continued unabated. A troop of Parsons's horsemen discovered a supply of whiskey, and its commanders issued it to warm the men. Unfortunately, one officer remembered, "there was either a little to much of it, or long abstinence made them susceptible to its influences for when we started you would have thought we were driving a herd of wild cattle." The cavalrymen came upon a plantation, where they sheltered ten men at a time inside slave cabins, but "the thirty outside froze faster than the ten inside could thaw and so we passed a miserable night."

The men of Maj. Gen. John G. Walker's infantry division, their tents having been sent back to Pine Bluff, built works from mud, snow, and ice in what they would remember bitterly as "Camp Freeze Out." They were heartened a bit by the sight of six Yankee prisoners from Arkansas Post, "captured while foraging for some delicacies that Uncle Sam didn't furnish them with," who passed through the camp on the fourteenth; the Texans learned from them that the surrendered Southerners were being sent north on transports. It snowed hard on January 16, froze during the night, and began raining the next morning. Parsons's cavalry replaced the chilled infantrymen on picket duty on the seventeenth, enduring more rain that reduced the accumulated snow to slush. The Texans learned that night that McClernand had fallen back to the Mississippi, and the chilled, miserable men finally received orders to return to Pine Bluff the next day. Their suffering continued on this march as "the roads [were] from shoe mouth to knee deep in mud and water, some snow still on the ground, the ground still frozen underneath in places." The exhausted men were, one foot soldier remembered, "more lively than could reasonably have been expected under the circumstances," having suffered "almost beyond endurance." Many Southerners faulted Holmes for failing to send reinforcements in time, contending that Walker's Division would have been able to strengthen the garrison enough to withstand McClernand's horde. Capt. Elijah Petty was likely more accurate, however, when he wrote, "I expect it is well for us that we did not reach the fort for I expect they had force enough to have captured all of us."[12]

Walker's exhausted troops pitched their tents at Camp Mills (named for one of the Texas colonels captured at Arkansas Post) from January 20 to February 9, then moved to Camp Wright on the Arkansas River, of which Joseph Blessington wrote, "our situation here was a good one and for the first time since we had been in the State, the troops were comfortably situated." The Texans were bolstered by troops from Thomas Hindman's battered army as they filtered into central and southeast Arkansas following their defeat at Prairie Grove. Although McClernand's ambition to capture Little Rock was thwarted by low water, the Confederate high command began thinking about how to defend the capital from a Union riverine offensive. They immediately began fortifying the next two high spots along the Arkansas River above the shattered Fort Hindman: White

Bluff, about sixty-five river miles from Little Rock, and Day's Bluff, fifteen miles below that. The jittery public began to regain its composure as the Yankee threat lessened with McClernand's withdrawal toward Vicksburg and as Union troops in northwest Arkansas withdrew from the river valley. The *True Democrat* in Little Rock was soon cockily touting the defensive capabilities of the Arkansas River itself: "The navigation of the river itself, with its narrow channel, rapid current, and thousands of snags, would alone present many dangers and difficulties, but lined as its banks have been, since the fall of the Post, by General Walker's whole army, he will have a sheet of fire to pass through that will be neither safe nor comfortable."[13]

The main fortification at Day's Bluff was a massive earthwork, which around 150 slaves impressed from local plantations labored through the early months of 1863 to complete. Confederate commander Daniel Frost requested that if any of the heavy cannon from Arkansas Post were recovered, "they should be sent to Day's Bluff. With them, a force of 10,000 ought to stop 30,000 at that point." Originally dubbed Fort Weightman in memory of a Missouri colonel killed at Wilson's Creek, Holmes ordered its named changed to Fort Pleasants in March in honor of an Arkansas colonel who was mortally wounded at Prairie Grove. The works extended for hundreds of yards on each side and were flanked by bayous that were to be dammed to make the approaches impassable to attacking infantry. Most of the fort was earthen, but the sides that faced a likely assault were to have "heavy earthworks palisades with cypress timbers, calculated to resist heavy artillery. In the north west corner of the fort, there is being thrown up heavy embankments for siege artillery on the most commanding ground from which position heavy artillery can command the river for one thousand yards." A Missouri officer deemed "the position for defense . . . a good one," but Confederate engineer Henry Merrell wrote that Fort Pleasants was located "at a place so much out of the way as to suggest the inference that it had been built more to interest the men & keep them employed than for any use against the enemy." In any event, the works were never tested by Union assault.[14]

Another potential threat facing the Federals was the gunboat *Pontchartrain*. The side-wheel steamer, known as the *Lizzie Simmons* prior to her purchase at New Orleans by the Confederate navy in early 1862, was now the sole Rebel warship in Arkansas, the *Maurepas* having been sunk to block the White River at St. Charles the previous

June. Although her big guns had been lost at Arkansas Post, the *Pontchartrain* was still a comforting symbol for the soldiers manning the Arkansas River line, one Texas cavalryman writing in February that "our gunboat must be brought down from the Rock" to support their forces. The vessel was on the mind of Lt. Cmdr. Thomas Selfridge of the U.S. Navy as he roamed near the mouth of the White River in February. He wrote on February 6 that while the *Pontchartrain* "has not had steam up for some time" and "requires a good deal of pumping to keep her free," reports indicated that she was being outfitted as a ram and armored "with 30 inches of wood and railroad iron abaft of her wheels." He proposed a "sudden movement upon Little Rock" up the Arkansas to "capture or destroy the ram." The proposed raid never happened, doomed probably by the same low water that had stymied McClernand's plans. Two months later Selfridge asked for reinforcements based on reports from contrabands that an attack was planned on his ship, the *Conestoga*. He reported that steamboats *Cheney*, *St. Francis No. 3*, *Golden Age*, and *Bracelet* had been armored with cotton bales and manned with 2,000 soldiers, adding that "the fitting out of the *Pontchartrain* had been talked of at Little Rock." Four gunboats were sent to his aid, but low water on the Arkansas again prevented a Rebel naval sortie. Ultimately the *Pontchartrain*, facing the same lack of materials that hindered all Confederate shipbuilding in the Trans-Mississippi, would never sally forth against Union shipping.[15]

While the military situation in the Arkansas River Valley stabilized somewhat, conditions in the state were deteriorating. Confidence in the Confederacy was reflected economically as prices soared; in Little Rock, what flour was available went for $200 per barrel, boots sold for $106 a pair, and tea cost $10 a pound. A Rebel soldier complained to his sweetheart about high food prices, writing, "I will give you the prices of some articles at this city viz: Butter $2.50 per lb., Eggs $2. per dozen, chickens $2. each, Pepper $10.00 per lb., Flour 60 cents per lb. &c &c." The Confederate government's unpaid debts, secured by "abominable certificates of indebtedness . . . [that] carried not even the dignity of a promissory note," made merchants and citizens in the state reluctant to trade with the military. Texan William Physick Zuber noted the disdain for Confederate currency after returning to Pine Bluff following the failed attempt to reach Arkansas Post: "My landlady was a widow whose patriotism had died while I was gone down the river. On my former visit she had professed delight in entertaining Confederate soldiers. But now she received me and others with reluctance, saying she did not want to entertain us any more because we paid her in depreciated currency— Confederate bills. But, she continued, when the Federals capture the town, she would take pleasure in entertaining them, because they would pay her in specie." For Rebel soldiers in Arkansas, though, even depreciated currency was unavailable; it would be September 1863 before most of them would be paid for their hard service in the Confederate army during 1862.[16]

Conditions in rural areas of the state were in chaos. Most of the countryside north of the river valley was now the domain of guerrilla bands. Formed initially under Hindman's direction, they now disdained Confederate orders to disband and instead preyed on hapless civilians, who received no protection from Rebel soldiers and precious little from the few Federal outposts in the region. The situation south of the river was also deteriorating, and Confederate authorities were pressed to address the problems of civilians. In April forty-four women from Ouachita County sent a petition to General Holmes begging him to conscript the keeper of the Tate's Bluff Ferry, wailing that "he goes from house to house Keeping up disturbances in our neighborhood and trying to disgrace us in every sense of the word. Our husbands are in the Army & no one to protect us & it is to you the officers of the Confederate States that we look too for protection." Conversely, twenty-one women from Caddo Township in Clark County begged Holmes that James Golden, "who has recently established a mill for the purpose of grinding corn for volunteers wives . . . , be exempted and left at home, in order to grind corn for said families."[17]

Holmes also faced an acute shortage of manpower, particularly following the twin disasters of Prairie Grove and Arkansas Post. In February 1863 he reported 16,990 men on the army's muster rolls but only 8,475 available for duty. To replenish his supply of soldiers, the general issued wholesale pardons to deserters and sent enrollment officers into the countryside to enforce conscription laws. Enthusiastic recruiters brought Confederate military power to 22,264 men on active duty by May, with an additional 12,287 absent. While this was good for the army, it created a serious shortage of men available to do the work needed to keep farms and towns running, as was the case with miller James Golden; this shortage was exacerbated in eastern Arkansas as slaves fled the region's plantations to join the teeming contraband camps around Helena. By June Confederate authorities acknowledged that the state's supply of manpower was used up and all that was left were "old men, or [men who] have furnished substitutes, are lukewarm, or are wrapped up in speculations and money-making. It will be difficult to develop any force from such material."[18]

The pressure of dealing with both military and civilian affairs was too much for Holmes. A Texan wrote of the general: "[H]e looks to be about seventy years old, though he is said to be only fifty-seven. He is getting frail and looks more like an old farmer who has lived about long enough than the General of the Trans-Mississippi District." Holmes became a terror to his staff, whom he would "bawl out" and "cuss and roar." Finally, even Jefferson Davis had to concur that his friend was not up to the task of administering the sprawling area west of the Mississippi River. On January 14, 1863, Lt. Gen. Edmund Kirby Smith was given command of the Districts of West Louisiana and Texas; Holmes, with his myopic attention to Arkansas, wrote: "I thank you, dear sir, for sending General Smith to Louisiana and Texas. I was unable to do much there." Smith's command was expanded to leadership of the entire Trans-Mississippi Department on February 9, and on March 18 Holmes was given command of the District of Arkansas, which included Missouri and Indian Territory. One gleeful Rebel wrote that "this will indeed be gratifying news as every body solder and citizen are tired of the Old *Granny Genl.* as General Holmes is universally styled. Nobody expects any thing from him & nobody has any respect for him." A few months later, events would show that Holmes should not have kept even this circumscribed authority.[19]

The new commander of the Trans-Mississippi had impeccable credentials. An 1845 graduate of West Point, Edmund Kirby Smith had won brevet promotions for valor during the Mexican War and was a veteran Indian fighter on the Texas frontier. After Texas seceded, he refused to surrender a fort in that state to Ben McCulloch's troops, but after Florida left the Union, the St. Augustine native resigned his commission as a major in the U.S. Army. He joined the Confederate army as a lieutenant colonel but was quickly promoted to brigadier general. After being seriously wounded in the fighting at First Manassas, Smith commanded troops during Bragg's invasion of Kentucky, including Brig. Gen. Patrick Cleburne's Arkansans, who fought in the victory at Richmond. Historian Robert L. Kerby noted that Smith was uniquely qualified for command west of the Mississippi: "Besides his good fortune on the battlefield, Smith had other qualifications for the post: President Davis liked him, General Braxton Bragg . . . did not; and the Arkansas delegation to the Confederate Congress had explicitly asked for him." Although he felt that "my responsibilities are great and that my troubles will soon commence," the general vowed to "cheerfully and manfully discharge my duty despite the abuse and fault finding which I . . . expect to attend my efforts." Before long the entire Trans-Mississippi region would be known as "Kirby Smith's Confederacy."[20]

Two other command changes with significant consequences for Confederate Arkansas took place at this time. The first was the removal of the hated Hindman to a post east of the Mississippi River. Following the defeat at Prairie Grove, Hindman's First Corps, after shedding conscripts to desertion along the way, went into camp in central Arkansas. The general had sent J. O. Shelby and 2,370 Missourians on a raid into their home state that led Federal authorities to withdraw most of their troops out of Arkansas. This allowed Confederate troops to slink back into Fort Smith, but that was not enough to blot the stain of Prairie Grove and Hindman's draconic policies, which the state legislature had deemed "illegal, oppressive, and unconstitutional." On January 29 Arkansas's congressional delegation unanimously insisted that President Davis transfer Hindman to the Cis-Mississippi, a request granted the next day. On March 13 Hindman and his family left Little Rock.[21]

The second change was the return of Sterling Price. Following the debacle at Pea Ridge, the porcine Missourian had received a major general's commission in the Confederate army east of the Mississippi. There the team of Van Dorn and Price proved as ineffective as it had been in Arkansas, leading an offensive into northern Mississippi that resulted in little more than heavy Confederate casualties in vicious fighting at Iuka and Corinth. Following this campaign, Price, with half of the Missourians he had led east of the river dead, wounded, or down with disease, requested that he and his men be transferred back to the Trans-Mississippi. After bitter wrangling with Davis and the Richmond bureaucracy, Price was given leave to return to the West; his men, however, would stay in Mississippi (only four hundred of the eight thousand men who went east would survive to return to Missouri). Price, his staff, and a cavalry bodyguard snuck back across the Mississippi on March 18, arriving in Little Rock a week later. On April 1 he took command of a division of infantry containing Missourians under Brig. Gen. Mosby M. Parsons and Arkansians led by Brig. Gen. Dandridge McRae. The popular Missouri general was welcomed by the troops, including one Arkansian who had predicted that if "Gen'l. Price should come to the Department [of Arkansas] the joy of the troops would be incapable of restraint. Cheers loud and long, & salutes from artillery would be the inevitable result." That popularity would be sorely tested before the end of 1863.[22]

Changes in the Union high command in the Trans-Mississippi were also underway. Since late 1862 the Department of the Missouri contained Arkansas, Missouri, Kansas, Indian Territory, and Nebraska and Colorado territories. Samuel Curtis, the hero of Pea Ridge and the ranking officer in the region, initially commanded the department but soon became embroiled in the festering political intrigues of the region. By May Curtis was ousted to be replaced by Maj. Gen. John M. Schofield, who was recalled from a division command with the Army of the Tennessee to again serve in the Trans-Mississippi. President Lincoln wrote Schofield on May 27 that Curtis was not replaced because "he had done wrong by commission or omission. I did it because of a conviction in my mind that the Union men of Missouri, constituting, when united a vast memory of the whole people, have entered into a pestilent quarrel among themselves[,] General Curtis . . . being the head of one faction. . . . *If both factions, or either, shall abuse you, you will, probably, be about right. Beware of being assailed by one and praised by the other.*" Schofield made two decisions that would soon affect the fate of the Arkansas River Valley. The first was to create the Southeastern District of Missouri and a cavalry division to defend it, both under the command of veteran Brig. Gen. John Davidson. The second was to reorganize his western command and establish the District of the Frontier, consisting of southern Kansas, Indian Territory, western Arkansas, and nine southwestern Missouri counties. This command went to the combative abolitionist James Blunt. Schofield also sent troops to assist in the siege of Vicksburg with the understanding that once the Mississippi bastion fell, troops would be assigned to attack Little Rock and allay some of the pressure faced in southern Missouri.[23]

Perhaps the most important change to occur in the Trans-Mississippi—and in the American Civil War itself—was the recruitment of black soldiers, bringing the promise of Lincoln's Emancipation Proclamation to fruition. Early 1863 was the perfect time to begin this revolutionary activity, for heavy combat losses in the battles of 1862 had both reduced the number of soldiers in the Union armies and caused a sharp decline in recruitment and reenlistment. As the casualty lists lengthened, war-weary Northerners increasingly supported the idea that Southern blacks should fight for their freedom. In the spring of 1863, Brig. Gen. Lorenzo Thomas was dispatched to the West to begin recruiting black units. An administrative officer who had served as adjutant general of the army since 1861, Thomas accepted his new duties enthusiastically, and as one historian put it, "the old bureaucrat took to the stump like a born-again preacher." On April 6 Thomas arrived at Helena, where a large refugee camp provided shelter and food for the hundreds of former slaves who had flocked to the town after its occupation in 1862. The adjutant general spoke to 7,000 Union troops, who received him "with rapturous applause." Thomas shouted: "I am here to say that I am authorized to raise as many regiments of blacks as I can. I am authorized to give commissions from the highest to the lowest; and I desire those persons who are earnest in this work to take hold of it. I desire only those whose hearts are in it, and to them alone will I give commissions."[24]

The gathering took on the appearance of a tent revival as an Indiana congressman and officers of the Helena garrison stepped forward to proclaim their support for Thomas's mission. But it was Maj. Gen. Benjamin M. Prentiss who stole the show, turning to the adjutant general and saying, "tell the President for me, I will receive them [contrabands] into the lines; I will beg them to come in; *I will make them come in!* and if any officer in my command, high or low, *neglects to receive them friendly, and treat them kindly, I will put them outside the lines.*" As Minos Miller of the Thirty-sixth Iowa recounted, Prentiss then called for everyone in favor of arming the African Americans to remove their hats. "In a second evry [sic] head (that I could see and I was where I could see most of the crowd) was bare. He then told them that if there was any opposed to it to pull off their hats but not a man dared to raise his hat." Kansan George Flanders recorded the event somewhat differently, writing to his mother that "Gen. P told the soldiers when they go out on a scout to bring in all the niggers they can find 'and if you can get a good horse or mule fetch it along and if any officer says ought to you report him to me and I will jerk his straps off so quick it will make his head swim, I don't care how big he is."[25]

The next day recruiting began, and Thomas reported, "I authorized a regiment this morning and at noon three companies of 100 each were ready for muster." He also was sanctioned to appoint white officers for the black units, and in Special Orders No. 13 promoted seven sergeants, one first lieutenant, and two privates to captain; two corporals and two privates to first lieutenant; and two sergeants, two corporals, and six privates to second lieutenant. Thomas then continued downriver, raising additional regiments of African American troops. The old bureaucrat had a profound effect on Union manpower in the last two years of the war. By the end of 1863, twenty black regiments had been raised through his efforts, including 2,348 men serving in four Arkansas regiments. The total number of regiments for which Thomas could take credit would rise to fifty by December 1864. In all, around 76,000 black soldiers—some 41 percent of the total who served in the Union army—were enlisted through his efforts. In Arkansas a total of 5,526 black men would serve in the Union army, though some did so reluctantly. After the initial enthusiasm passed, Prentiss ordered all able-bodied black men in the region to be enrolled in the army. Newly minted second lieutenant Minos Miller, now of the Second Arkansas Volunteer Infantry Regiment (African Descent), led patrols in search of likely conscripts, noting, "they hide from us like chickens from a chicken hawk." Still, those new soldiers would soon show their courage under fire.[26]

For the South, the situation was looking increasingly bleak as Grant tightened his stranglehold on Vicksburg and Nathaniel Banks invested a second Confederate bastion at Port Hudson, Louisiana. The Confederate War Department, desperately seeking a means to ease the pressure on these Mississippi River strongholds, suggested in May that the seizure of Helena would "secure a great advantage to the Confederacy." Indeed, Helena had been problematic for the Rebels since Curtis's army had occupied it in 1862. The riverport provided a staging area for Federal troops for actions up and down the Mississippi and for raids into the Arkansas interior, a haven for runaway slaves, and a means of controlling trade in the eastern part of the state. In addition to removing this looming Yankee threat to Confederate operations, the capture of Helena could provide a strategic stronghold on the Mississippi if the Federals captured Vicksburg. But Holmes—typically—had doubts about his ability to take the town. He received little guidance from Kirby Smith in Louisiana, who ordered the old general in early May to "attack the enemy, should the opportunity offer for doing so with hope of success. You can expect no assistance from this quarter." Holmes's effective force at this point consisted of cavalry divisions under Marmaduke and Brig. Gen. Lucius Marsh Walker and about 4,500 infantry troops in Price's division, composed of James F. Fagan's Arkansas brigade in Little Rock and Mosby Parsons's Missouri brigade and Dandridge McRae's Arkansas brigade at Jacksonport. He also commanded Daniel Frost's Missouri division of some 2,700 men, most of whom languished around Pine Bluff combating boredom, desertions, and drunkenness.[27]

The cavalry, which would be Confederate Arkansas's main combat arm during most of 1863, was in turmoil. Marmaduke had led 5,000 cavalrymen on a raid into eastern Missouri in late April in pursuit of the expatriate Missourians' enduring myth that their fellow secessionists would mob the Rebel flag once it was shown. His column made it as far as Cape Girardeau, at which point they realized that they were attracting Yankee soldiers instead of recruits, and as one cavalryman put it, "[we ran] back a good deal faster than we went." Although the Rebels made it safely back to Arkansas, crossing the St. Francis River at Chalk Bluff on an improvised bridge held together by ropes and grapevines, reports of depredations during the raid followed them. Holmes responded by taking half of Marmaduke's division and placing it under the command of Walker, a Tennessean who had been shuffled to the Trans-Mississippi after Braxton Bragg deemed him unfit "to intrust with any command." The hot-headed Marmaduke was enraged, and his enmity toward Walker would have tragic results later that summer.[28]

On May 27 Holmes appointed Price commander of all Confederate forces in northern Arkansas and Missouri and allowed him to move his division to Jacksonport, from where the rotund general hoped to move to liberate his home state. But events along the Mississippi soon forced the Rebel generals to shift their focus east. The siege of Vicksburg was becoming critical, with Union artillery pounding the town every day and starving civilians abandoning their homes to live in hillside caves. In early June Holmes asked Smith whether he should focus his operations toward east Arkansas; the Trans-Mississippi commander replied that Holmes should not attack Helena unless he was sure he could take it. Holmes left Little Rock on June 8 for a formal conference with Price, but his wagon broke down and forced him to return to the capital. He instead sent a note asking the Missourian if his troops were in shape to attack Helena. Price replied that his men were "fully rested and in excellent spirits," that Marmaduke's scouts reported no more than four or five thousand Yankees in Helena, and that if an attack was carried out "with celerity and secrecy . . . I entertain no doubt of your being able to crush the foe at that point." Holmes dithered for a week, actually ordering Price on June 15 to "have everything in readiness for a move on Missouri" but later that same day telegraphing Smith in Shreveport: "I believe we can take Helena. Please let me attack it." Smith responded the next day, "Most certainly do it." So Holmes began working on his battle plan.[29]

Helena had been a Union base since its occupation by the Army of the Southwest on July 12, 1862. While it provided a strategic strong-point on the Mississippi and enabled the Federals to strangle crop production in what was perhaps the most fertile land in Confederate Arkansas, it also was a pestilential nightmare of disease and misery for the troops stationed there. Blistering heat, poor water, and improper sanitation led to epidemics of typhoid, malaria, and the soldiers' worst enemy, dysentery, during the first six months of occupation. One Kansas cavalryman confided to his mother, "I have no fear of being hit by the bullets, but I can't help dreading spending the summer in this sickly locality." A captain of the Twenty-eighth Wisconsin forbade his wife from joining him in Helena, writing, "it is almost sure death to at least 1 out of 3 of all unacclimated persons who come here, except late in fall or in winter." Another Badger State soldier, suffering from the "Helena Quickstep," made the best of it with a homemade cure, noting: "[A] bottle of quinine and pain-killer got broken in my medicine chest; the quinine soaking up the pain-killer, so I put them in another bottle and filled up with whiskey. A more villainous com-pound has never passed a man's lips. I have given [it to] several boys out of the same bottle and it has always cured them without fail. I think that I shall apply for a patent on it as a cure for all the ills the flesh is heir to from colic to cholera." Charles Musser of the Twenty-ninth Iowa summed up the feelings of most of Helena's Yankees when he called the town "this miserable grave yard of Soldiers. . . . I hope when we leave this place it will . . . Sink down and the Waters of the Old Mississippi cover it so deep that no lead can Sound the bottom."[30]

Union occupation was hard on Helena's citizens, many of whom were unabashed secessionists who received little sympathy from the troops. From the moment Curtis's army captured the town, the Federals scoured the region for supplies, a Helena preacher complaining: "[T]he surrounding country is, for miles around, swept by foraging parties. Farmers have both negroes and all kinds of stock stolen from them." Slaves escaping their masters for the contraband camps around Helena would often take horses, mules, and livestock with them, increasing the strain on the area's white population. In late 1863 a local woman lamented that the Federals "have shut us in on all sides . . . have taken from us the means of supporting ourselves and refuse to let us have anything unless we lie or smuggle."[31]

Despite the town's many drawbacks, the Federals made themselves at home, establishing camps, attending church services, and keeping their martial skills honed through constant drilling. Confederate horsemen, sometimes guerillas but often veteran cavalrymen from Arkansas and Texas, were a constant threat to pickets and isolated patrols, and Union troops spent much of their time beating the bushes in the countryside in search of these foes. These rural encounters were often deadly. A patrol in force of the Third Iowa Cavalry in early May, for instance, was attacked by three hundred Confederate cavalrymen at a cost of forty-one Union casualties. A raid by troops under Col. Powell Clayton between May 6 and 11 resulted in the destruction of as much as 100,000 pounds of corn, 50,000 pounds of meat, voluminous hay and fodder, the burning of a steam mill used to make flour for local Confederate troops, and wanton destruction of the personal property of the area's pro-secession landowners. The Confederates retaliated with a May 25 attack on a column of troopers from the Fifth Kansas and Third Iowa Cavalry at the Allen Polk plantation six miles from Helena; the Federals suffered as many as five killed and forty captured before the Rebels retreated before approaching infantry reinforcements. The back-and-forth raiding and fighting was devastating to the civilian population. Edward Redington of the Twenty-eighth Wisconsin wrote after a march through the countryside: "[Y]ou cannot conceive of the desolation of the country through which we passed. . . . I do not think there is 100 acres that is under

The sharpshooting Twenty-ninth Iowa Infantry Regiment held the line around Battery A at Helena. This photograph of the regiment's camp shows the towering loess ridges that surrounded the Mississippi River port. *Courtesy Butler Center for Arkansas Studies.*

crop. . . . It is hard to see old men and women that are worth three or four years ago from $100,000 to $500,000 reduced to beggars, living on corn meal ground in coffee mills." As the hot summer of 1863 ground on, Federal horsemen continued to prowl a fifteen-mile perimeter around Helena in search of Rebel troops.[32]

Once they realized that they were there to stay, the Federals began to fortify the city against attack. Helena is nestled on the banks of the Mississippi at the base of Crowley's Ridge, a line of ravine-riddled loess hills that tower above the flat delta landscape running south from southeastern Missouri. High ground surrounds it on all sides, providing the potential opportunity to command the town with artillery fire. Construction on a fort began in late August 1862. Indiana infantryman Gilbert Denny noted on August 24: "[T]here is 6 pieces of artillery here for it from 32 to 64 pounders. The Negrows is doing the work while we lay in the shade an drill." This fortification would become Fort Curtis, a square earthen bastion located north of town that would be able to bombard any point on the high ground around the city that might come under attack. The formidable stronghold was completed by October 29, when S. C. Bishop of the Eleventh Indiana Infantry wrote, "this has been a gay day with us, a grand review of all the troops and a general salute fired by all the Artillery and Gunboats in honor of the 'Fort' which is now finished."[33]

While Fort Curtis was complete, it did not solve the tactical problem of the surrounding high ground. Commanders began addressing the issue even during the fort's construction, with one Kansan writing in September 1862 that "entrenchments are being thrown up on the high ground north of Helena[.] Contraband darkeys employed on the works." By April work was underway on two additional forts, with one described as being "built partly of logs and part earth works a steep hill in front, and a moat on the flanks and rear. When completed [it] will be a strong little fort, capable of resisting anything but heavy artillery." Other Federal troops took part in the construction work; George Flanders of the Fifth Kansas Cavalry wrote on April 30 that "they put us to work on the fort and rifle pits in process of construction. . . . [W]hen done [they] will be a strong rallying point for the pickets in case of attack." But as often was the case, the African American soldiers did the bulk of the physical labor. Capt. Thomas Stevens approvingly noted on May 2: "The negro brigade is being made useful with the spade & pickaxe . . . building forts &c &c. 'Long may they wave' *while they help us.*" By early June one Iowan noted with satisfaction: "[E]very avenue to the town is so commanded as to make it impossible for a rebel army to get in here. I don't know how the generals feel about it, but there is no excitement among the men." Another Hawkeye bragged, "the town is now [so] strongly fortifyed . . . fifty thousand men could not take this town by attacking it."[34]

Even as they built formidable defenses around Helena, the Union officers kept their men on the drill grounds every day, honing their skills in preparation of an attack. The Federals practiced working together at everything from brigade-level maneuvers to skirmish-line actions. "There was an excellent drill-ground near camp, and we did not let weeds grow on it," one Iowan remembered. Benjamin Pearson of the Thirty-sixth Iowa took advantage of time on picket duty to set up a target 130 yards from his position and hold a target-shooting competition. He noted with satisfaction that "Benjm. F. Clark of Our Co made the best shot which was within 1 1/4 inches of the center, & it intitles him to a credit of one time from standing picket." Perhaps the most extreme example of drill occurred on June 22, when the Fifth Kansas Cavalry staged a sham battle against the Third Iowa Battery. The fierce Kansans may have taken the drill too seriously, one observer noting, "there was two men mortally wounded & one horse killed." The troops also occasionally passed in grand review before the general staff and visiting dignitaries. The Twenty-ninth Iowa in particular excelled in review: Benjamin Palmer of that regiment proudly reported that the unit was recognized as "being the cleanest and most Solderly appearing Reg. on the Ground. It has Since got the name of the Band Box Regiment."[35]

The Yankees would soon get an opportunity to put their drill to work. On June 18 Holmes went to Jacksonport to meet with Price and Marmaduke and develop a plan to bring their widely dispersed forces to Helena. The district commander remained nervous about the attack, telling Price, "I risk much in this expedition; you have a great reputation with the public, and if I am blamed for it, I expect you to sustain the propriety of it." The Missourian agreed to do so. With that aside, the generals turned their attention to the approaches to the town. They decided that Price's 3,095-man infantry division and Marmaduke's 1,750 cavalrymen would leave Jacksonport four days later, heading for Cotton Plant. The 1,339 Arkansians in Fagan's infantry division would leave Little Rock and take the train to DeValls Bluff, then march to Clarendon. Walker's cavalry, 1,462 men, would maintain their positions around Helena, screening the Confederate advance and keeping Union forces bottled up inside town. For better or worse, Holmes would leave his headquarters in Little Rock to personally lead what would be the signature military mission of his career.[36]

The march began pleasantly enough for Price's men as they left Jacksonport under pleasant skies through a verdant landscape, though ignorant of their destination. Capt. John Duncan wrote on June 23: "[W]e are traveling down white River on the Bank[.] it is the opinion we are going near Hellena to give the Feds a little Fight. I hardly think we will have a fight . . . yet we left our Baggage at Jacksonport which puts us in a good condition if they whip us too hard." A harbinger of things to come arrived that night in the form of rain. But the soldiers' spirits were still high as they marched through Augusta on the twenty-fourth and were cheered by the town's secessionist women. "The ladies who assembled by the road-side, from the town and the surrounding plantations, were most lovely, and the most accomplished, I have see since I left the State of Missouri," Surgeon R. J. Bell gushed. "If I be wounded in the impending battle, I wish to be placed in the care of the Ladies of Augusta." Bell was feeling considerably less romantic the next day, after a night of sleeping outside under the cold rain. As the Rebels arrived at the Cache River—"a wide, filthy river"—the Missourian stated, "I have never undergone a more disagreeable time." Ominously, he also noted that the privations of the march had begun to take a toll on the troops—"it became necessary to establish a hospital at Augusta, and to leave our sick." Missourian William Bull was among those falling ill during the march, writing that "living in swamps and drinking swamp water made a great many of our men sick. I had camp sickness for a week and could eat nothing."[37]

Price's division ferried its supply wagons across the swollen Cache as engineer Lt. John Mhoon forged ahead and built crude bridges across Bayou DeView and Caney Creek. By the time the miserable foot soldiers slogged across the sodden landscape to these bridges, the spans had already been swept away. Mhoon improvised a ferry boat, and the Confederates spent two days crossing the streams. Many of the men stripped almost naked to struggle through the two- to five-foot-deep water, Dr. Bell noted in his diary, adding: "While in this condition, several of the planters' daughters appeared on the road.

Seeing the soldiers partial state of nudity, they quietly retired." Price's soldiers finally reaching the vicinity of the village of Oakland on June 29, three days behind schedule. J. C. Dyer, a veteran who had survived Hindman's freezing retreat from northwest Arkansas the previous winter, glumly remembered: "[O]f all the marches that was the worst that I ever had. For days and nights we waded in water from shoe mouth to waist deep and lots of nights it was hard to find enough dry land to camp on." The dogged foot soldiers carried on, arriving at Big Creek to find the stream swollen to a mile and a half wide and three to five feet deep. They finally reached Phillips County on July 1, having taken ten days to march a mere sixty-five miles, and a relieved Surgeon Bell noted that "for the first time in a long while, I observed dust in the road." A later Missouri historian can scarcely be accused of hyperbole for writing, "Napoleon's passage of the Alps was hardly more arduous than the march of this army from Jacksonport to Helena."[38]

Compared to the ordeal of Price's troops, the rest of Holmes's army had a relatively smooth march. Marmaduke's mounted soldiers followed the same route as Price for the most part, but being on horseback, they had an easier time of it, hampered primarily by a lack of forage. Fagan's Arkansas division rode trains to DeValls Bluff and steamboats to Clarendon, then made a brisk thirty-four mile march across dry land to Trenton on June 28. The command staff caught up with them by the twenty-ninth, with Arkansian J. W. Paup observing: "General Holmes and staff are here. Poor old creature—I wish he was some where else for I do not think him a fit subject to command an army." Over the next several days, the various Rebel forces converged on Lick Creek, while J. O. Shelby's Missouri cavalry took over covering the northwest approaches to Helena. On the morning of July 3, the infantry began its final march toward Helena. Holmes summoned Price, Walker, Fagan, and Marmaduke to meet with him at the Alan Polk House, located six miles west of Helena, to make their final plans for the attack.[39]

Robert Kerby has described Holmes's plan of attack as "a model of brutal irresponsibility," an assessment with which it is hard to argue. Holmes proposed a synchronized assault from three directions on what he admitted were much stronger defenses than originally believed. The principal attack would be made by Price's division against the Union center, with Parsons's Missourians and McRae's Arkansians assigned to carry Battery C atop Graveyard Hill and hold it against any counterattack. Fagan's Arkansas troops were to assault the southernmost bastion, Battery D on Hindman Hill. Marmaduke's dismounted horsemen would strike from the north, hitting Battery A on Rightor Hill. Walker's horsemen were to support Marmaduke's left against counterattack as the Missourian placed his artillery atop Rightor Hill and blasted the Federals at Battery B and Fort Curtis. This convergent attack, a difficult operation under the best of circumstances, was further complicated by Holmes declaring that it would begin at "daylight," a term that would prove far too ambiguous for some of his generals. He ended the meeting by stating: "General Price, I intend to attack Helena immediately, and capture the place, if possible. This is my fight. If I succeed, I want the glory; and if I fail, I am willing to bear the odium. At twelve o'clock, tonight, we move toward Helena."[40]

The best chance for Holmes to take the town would require a strong element of surprise, but Benjamin Prentiss, commander of the District of Eastern Arkansas, would have none of that. Prentiss had commanded the Sixth Division at Shiloh the previous April, where his dogged defense of a sunken road (immortalized as the "Hornets' Nest") may have saved Grant's army from being pushed into the Tennessee River. The Virginia-born officer had languished for months in Southern prisons before being exchanged, and he continued to defend himself against accusations that he had been caught off guard at Shiloh. There would be no chance of that happening at Helena.[41]

As early as June 4 Ammi Hawks of the Twenty-eighth Wisconsin was excitedly writing home: "Marmaduke is but 7 miles from here with 7,000 men, and Price is 18 miles further behind, an attack is expected by morning. I mention this to let you know how we are kept in a state of anxiety." Two days later he dejectedly followed up: "The anticipated fight is over and we still hold Helena. The fact is the *fight* amounted only to a *scare*, as I expected at first." In light of such scares, Prentiss and his officers kept improving their defenses throughout the month. Iowan Charles Musser noted on the twelfth that "all the roads are blocked up by the falling of heavy timber." August Bondi of the Fifth Kansas wrote on June 15, "Lines closed—no more intercourse with citizens." Four days later George Cook of Wisconsin reported being "on fatigue today diging holes to prevent cavalry coming in on our soldiers if they should attack this place. they are called wolf holes." On June 16 a soldier in the Forty-third

Indiana recorded that the officers "have us up in line every morning at daylight looking for Rebs but they do not come," while Captain Youngs of the Fifth Kansas groused: "Our Pickets were instructed & *reinstructed* to be on the alert[.] we did som[e] splendid watching & a little cautious scouting but to no purpose." Yet fellow Kansan August Bondi wrote on June 18 that a "1st Indiana picket detail [was] on the Little Rock road when moving out to their post very early in the morning capture[d] four Confederate pickets enjoying a good nap by the roadside with their horses and arms." As the month drew to a close, Edmund Holt of the Twenty-eighth Wisconsin recorded a flurry of activity: On June 26, "Small forts are being made on the hills back of town. There is fort A.B.C.D. There is one upon every hill"; June 27, "Riflepits are being thrown up between the forts. There is some talk of our being attacked"; June 28, "There is a level piece of land between the river and the hills. Across this ditches have been cut out rather big holes so that cavalry cannot cross."[42]

July 3 dawned and quickly became "so hot that it is Realy Suffocating to move about." Ephraim Gaston of the Thirty-third Iowa dourly recorded that he was "on picket to day very warm looking for rebs was not disappointed in the least." Union officer W. A. Jenkins remembered that "for several days no citizens from the country had been allowed to come near our lines, while those already on the inside were quiet, reserved, and extremely reticent." The timberclad gunboat *Tyler*, which two days earlier had been at the Memphis Naval Yard with "her boiler in a dangerous condition," stood offshore in the Mississippi River. At 9:30 she "went to general quarters, exercised crew at broadside guns and Marines at small arms." Prentiss, convinced that an attack was imminent and that it would occur on Independence Day, cancelled plans to celebrate the Fourth of July, moved reveille up to 2:00 A.M., and announced that a single shot from one of Fort Curtis's cannon would be the alarm that Helena was being attacked. Edward Reddington of the Twenty-eighth Wisconsin concluded: "There is one thing sure that we cannot run. There is not a boat here except a ferry boat and one gun-boat, so we must whip them or surrender."[43]

At 2:00 A.M. on July 4, sleepy Union soldiers dressed, grabbed their weapons, and fell into line. At the four hilltop fortifications standing sentinel over the town, men peered into the foggy darkness.

At about three o'clock scattered fire erupted from the picket line, and blue-coated fugitives were seen falling back toward the main lines, even as faint shouts were heard from the contraband camps on the outskirts of Helena. At 3:30 A.M. a cannon at Fort Curtis roared its warning shot.

4

"A Grivous Calamity"
The Battle of Helena

Holmes's army would enjoy little sleep on the evening of July 3 as the Southerners moved to the areas from which they would attack the Union defenses. As the sun faded in the west, General Fagan sent a combat team under Col. William H. Brooks out of his brigade's camp to occupy the junction of the upper and lower Little Rock roads, along which his men would march on their way to attack Battery D. At around 11:00 P.M. Fagan set out with the rest of his division, which consisted of Col. James P. King's Thirty-fifth Arkansas Infantry, Col. Samuel S. Bell's Thirty-seventh Arkansas Infantry, and Col. Alexander T. Hawthorn's Arkansas Infantry Regiment. "The night was a beautiful one," one young officer remembered, but the march became nightmarish soon after the troops caught up with Brooks's command.[1]

At 1:30 A.M. Fagan ordered Brooks to continue along the lower Little Rock road with his regiment—the Thirty-fourth Arkansas Infantry—three companies of horsemen, and a section of light artillery under Lt. John C. Arnett of Etter's Arkansas Battery to make a demonstration against troops guarding the road and keep them from attacking Fagan's flank. He ordered Hawthorn's regiment to take the lead on the upper Little Rock road as the brigade moved into attack position. Stumbling in the dark through the tortured landscape of Crowley's Ridge, Hawthorn moved "not without considerable difficulty and

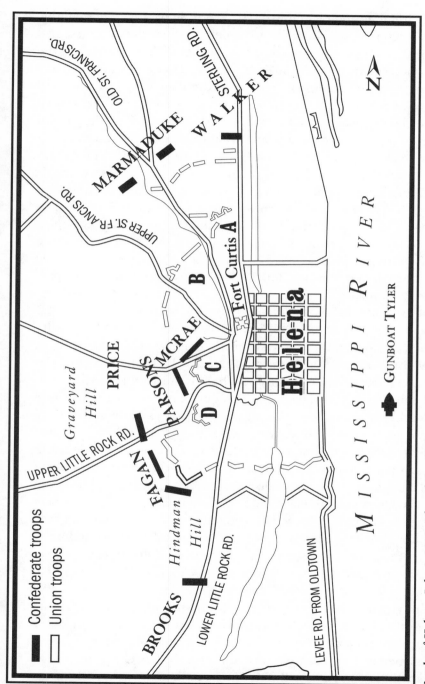

Battle of Helena, July 4, 1863. Theophilus Holmes's three-pronged attack was blunted by the strong fortifications of Helena's Union garrison. *Map by Kirk Montgomery.*

117

great fatigue to the men" until within a mile of the Federal works. There they ran into the first of the defensive barriers Prentiss had established: "the road was completely filled with felled timber, the largest forest growth intermingling and overlapping its whole length." Helena's natural defenses augmented the timber barrier, the land on either side of the road falling into steep ravines. A frustrated Fagan determined that his ammunition wagons and artillery could not continue from there and, after telling his officers to leave their horses behind, grimly ordered his division to continue. The Arkansians, "after crawling through the interstices of the closely jutting limbs and boughs, and climbing over the thickly matted timber for 1 mile," discovered the first line of Union works at 4:05 A.M. To his dismay Fagan "could plainly see that the enemy was on the alert, and evidently expecting and awaiting an assault." Nonetheless, and painfully aware of his orders to attack at daylight, the general ordered Hawthorn to move his men into line of battle to the right of the upper Little Rock road.[2]

It was Brooks's detachment, however, that would draw first blood. As they drew nearer to Helena, the colonel ordered his cavalry to the rear and sent infantry skirmishers forward. There, as W. C. Braly of the Thirty-fourth Arkansas recorded, "we had a little fight with the pickets about a mile and a half from town[.] we killed 2 or 3 wounded several and took 8 of them prisoner together with 7 or 8 negroes[.] it was just dusky dawn when we attacked them. . . . They did not discover us until we were rite on them." That fighting alerted a twenty-eight-man advance guard from Company G, Twenty-eighth Wisconsin Infantry, which had been sent out the night before to picket the Little Rock road. The Badger State troops gamely took position along an Osage-orange hedge and waited "until [the Rebels] were near enough to warrant them to fire with effect." Their volley had "the effect of emptying at least 5 or 6 saddles, besides the wounding or killing of several horses. . . . [A]s soon as we delivered our fire we turned and fled to the beech woods in our rear every one for himself at the hight [sic] of his speed," James Loughney recorded. (The Wisconsin guard would spend the rest of the morning in the rifle pits before Battery D.) Brooks, meanwhile, continued forward, placing skirmishers on both sides of the road "extending nearly to the river." As his men took up positions on a hill at the Widow Clements House, the artillerists of Battery K, First Missouri Light Artillery, loosed a

Brig. Gen. James Fagan's Arkansians
fought their way through several lines
of Yankee rifle pits, but exhaustion and
Union firepower stopped them from
their goal of conquering Battery D at
Helena. *Courtesy Civil War Museum,
Wilson's Creek National Battlefield.*

few shells from their rifled 10-pounders. The *Tyler,* having weighed
anchor at 5:00 A.M., fired from its 32-pounder stern gun, the first of
more than four hundred shells she would shoot that day, wounding
three men and killing three horses of Capt. William Denson's Louisiana
cavalry squadron. Brooks called his artillery forward, but the terrain
allowed only one gun, commanded by Lieutenant Arnett, to take
position. The artillerists gamely opened fire, but after thirteen rounds
they were forced to retire under the concentrated barrage from Battery
K and the *Tyler.* Brooks and his men would be little more than spectators for the rest of the day, though Braly noted that he "had a very
fair view of some parts of the field, especialy the gun boat."[3]

Fagan, meanwhile, brought the rest of his division into line
among the deep ravines and gullies south of Battery D. As Bell's regiment struggled forth from the timber barrier, the men were "double-
quicked into line on the left of the road." The two regiments advanced
against the first of five successive lines of Union rifle pits blocking
the way to Hindman Hill and began to take casualties. King's
Thirty-fifth Arkansas finally arrived on the battlefield and went into

The timberclad USS *Tyler* (left) provided massive firepower for the outnumbered Union defenders of Helena on July 4, 1863. *Courtesy Butler Center for Arkansas Studies.*

line on Hawthorn's right. As the Arkansians took position about 150 yards from the first Union line, Fagan ordered them to charge. "After scrambling over and under fallen timber, across a ravine that I would at any other time or under any other circumstances have considered impossible to make my way through, and at last up the side of a hill that was so steep the men had to pull themselves up by the bushes, we reached the first line of breastworks and drove the enemy back," King reported, expressing the frustration of all the men who contended with Helena's rugged landscape. As the exhausted Rebels fell into the captured trenches, they began taking heavy fire from Batteries C and D. Hawthorn's men also attacked the first line of rifle pits, climbing "step by step over vast piles of fallen timber up the rugged sides of almost perpendicular hills, and finally, after unheard-of toil and fatigue," forcing the Yankees from their works.[4]

On the opposite side of Helena, Marmaduke's division entered the action only minutes after Fagan's opening shots at Battery D. The cavalry's arrival on schedule after a difficult approach is not surprising, considering the man who led them. Marmaduke, a thirty-year-old West Point graduate who resigned his commission in the U.S. Army to join the Missouri State Guard, had helped rout a Federal brigade at Shiloh before being wounded. In the winter of 1862, he had led his cavalry skillfully in the fighting retreat at Cane Hill and in the bitter combat at and retreat from Prairie Grove; his abilities in these actions led to his promotion to brigadier general. Marmaduke led two audacious raids deep into Missouri, the first lasting nearly a month and the second resulting in a failed attack on Cape Girardeau. A soldier described him as "a small man of singular appearance. His hair was yellow and his complexion yellowish; he wore a yellow cap, a yellow coat, and a yellow vest and pants; he rode a yellowish bay or sorrel horse."[5]

Marmaduke's command, consisting of the 1,100 men of Shelby's Iron Brigade and Col. Colton Greene's 650 Missouri horsemen, left their camps around 10:00 P.M. on July 3 to work their way into position to attack Battery A from the north. When about three miles from the Union defenses, the cavalrymen dismounted, leaving every fourth man to hold the horses as the remainder continued forward on foot. The approach soon grew more difficult as the Rebels, as did Fagan's men to the south, "found the road and country thoroughly obstructed, the enemy having chopped down the trees and rendered almost impassible the approach to the fort and town." The Missourians grimly forced their way through the obstruction, manhandling four of Capt. Joseph Bledsoe's cannon along with them. As they worked their way forward in the pitch darkness, Marmaduke's guides, who had claimed knowledge of trails that would allow them to bypass the heaviest obstructions, soon became hopelessly disoriented. The frustrated commander ordered his troops to stop until dawn would allow them to see their way. Shelby's advance ran into Federal pickets about three-quarters of a mile from Battery A, and firing began as the Yankees were driven back, losing several dead and five captured as they fled to within 150 yards of the Union works. The Federals also drew blood. A captain of the Thirty-sixth Iowa wrote home that "Corpl. Matt Walker was on picket duty where the line was attacked. He exchanged 20 odd shots with 1 rebel but did not get him. He killed 1 other certain and the boys say 2." The Confederates began peppering the Federals with rifle fire as Bledsoe brought two guns into position on high ground about 400 yards opposite Battery A. Then, one Missourian wrote, "at daylight on the morning of the 4th, the old steel parrot guns of Shelby's Brigade exclaimed the anniversary of American Independence by several rounds of shell on the forts of the Federals."[6]

The 4,129 men of Prentiss's garrison knew what to do when the signal shot roared from Fort Curtis at 3:30 A.M. "Everything had been anticipated, and all was orderly and without confusion" as the troops took their positions, an officer of the Fifth Kansas Cavalry recalled. Prussian native Friedrich Salomon, commander of the Thirteenth Division of the XIII Corps (to which the Helena units belonged), held operational command of the troops and ordered them into line. On the Union right Powell Clayton's cavalry, the hard-bitten Fifth Kansas and First Indiana, would hold the line of the levee, controlling the approach to town along the Sterling Road with a pair of 2-pounder steel Woodruff guns and a section of the Third Iowa (Dubuque) Battery's 12-pounder howitzers. Col. Samuel Rice, a former Iowa attorney general, commanded the Twenty-ninth and Thirty-sixth Iowa Infantry, which would support the cross-trained gunners of the Thirty-third Missouri at Battery A, and the soldiers of the Twenty-eighth Wisconsin Infantry, who filed into place on either side of Battery B. More of the make-do artillerists of the Thirty-third Missouri manned the guns at Battery C, supported by four companies of the Thirty-third Iowa Infantry and comforted by the interlocking fields of fire that would allow the other hilltop forts and Fort Curtis to wheel to their defense if attacked. Col. William McLean's Forty-third Indiana held the five rows of rifle pits south of Battery D, which also was manned by the cross-trained artillerymen of the Thirty-third Missouri. Newly minted second lieutenant Adam B. Smith of the Thirty-third quickly scrawled in his diary that his officers "came up and told us to be in perfect readiness as the rebels were 4000 strong out . . . on the road which are stationed and 19000 strong on the Upper Little Rock Road." McLean also commanded the troops on the extreme Union left, consisting of the Thirty-fifth Missouri and the Second Arkansas Infantry (African Descent), supported by Battery K, First Missouri Light Artillery. Salomon held the Thirty-third Iowa, part of the Thirty-fifth Missouri, and a section of the Dubuque Battery back as a strategic reserve. As the excited Yankees took their positions, Salomon recalled, "a phenomenon, perhaps known only on the Mississippi, threatened to frustrate all our hopes. A fog rose from the bottom of the valley, white, thick. It rose so quick, covering everything from view. No one could see the approach of the enemy." But the fog, which the chaplain of the Twenty-eighth Wisconsin "feared . . . might be detrimental to us . . . , soon cleared away," and the fighting began in earnest as the sun rose over the Mississippi River.[7]

In the rifle pits before Battery D, McLean's Hoosiers fell back before the grim advance of Fagan's Arkansians. "Our pickets were drove in and a general assalt was made on our entire line comeing with a yell driveing our line back," one Indiana soldier wrote, "for 3 long hours the battle raged hotly contesting every foot of ground. They pound in upon us 5 to 1 but we stood undaunted." The Rebels doggedly advanced, Hawthorn reporting that "the three regiments now moved forward with a shout, and notwithstanding the perfect hail-storm of bullets that assailed us at every step, we soon drove the enemy out of his third line of defense." The exhausted troops reformed and caught their breath, then lurched forward and took the fourth line of works before Battery D. There they collapsed. Hawthorn noted that it was about 7:00 A.M., and his men had been fighting constantly for three hours. "The men were completely exhausted," he wrote. "Numbers had fainted from excessive heat and fatigue. Many had been killed and wounded, and a large majority of each of our three regiments were utterly unable to fight any longer." The Arkansians' morale was not helped by the perception that they were the only Confederates engaged. "Up to this time there had been no attack on any other point," Fagan angrily wrote in his official report. "Daybreak had come and gone, and still the guns of my brigade, and those of the enemy, were the only ones that interrupted the stillness of morning."[8]

Fagan was mistaken, of course, and it may have been the volume of fire around Battery D and the distance between it and Battery A that kept him from hearing the clamor of Marmaduke's assault. But Colonel Rice wasted no time in reacting to the Missourians' attack. The former Iowa politician had first ordered the Thirty-third Iowa into the earthworks that had been dug between Batteries C and D on the Union left, holding a small group back as a reserve. He then took care of business at Battery A, placing three companies of the Thirty-sixth Iowa into rifle pits on the fortification's left and the Twenty-ninth Iowa to its right and front. The men were ordered to "drive the enemy from the crests of the hills which they already had occupied." As the Iowans opened fire, the intrepid J. O. Shelby "received a dreadful wound that shattered his wrist, plowed through his arm, and caused intolerable agony. Faint from loss of blood and reeling in his saddle, he was forced from the field." Col. Thomas Hart Benton of the Twenty-ninth Iowa ordered two companies of skirmishers forward to drive the Missourians from the high ground north of Battery A, feeding six more companies into the attack as Marmaduke's men "fell back, resolutely contesting every inch of ground as they retired." One Iowan recalled, "We went into the fight alaughing and as mary as School Boys" as "the Balls fell around me as thick as hale." The determined advance of the Twenty-ninth, soon supported by troops of the Thirty-sixth Iowa, forced the Rebel cavalrymen from their positions. To make matters worse, Marmaduke discovered that Union troops had taken position to his left and rear, from which they "poured upon me a deadly fire."[9]

This new threat to the Missourians' tenuous position came from Powell Clayton's Fifth Kansas and First Indiana Cavalry. The Confederate battle plan called for Walker's Arkansas cavalrymen to race up the Sterling Road east of Battery A and attack the Yankee horsemen, occupying Helena after Marmaduke overran Rightor Hill. As with the other Confederate advances, Walker found the road blocked by felled timber as he moved toward town. He ordered three hundred of Col. Archibald Dobbins's Arkansans to dismount and move forward as skirmishers but held the remainder of his troops north of the barricaded road to move the felled trees "for the passage of artillery." Dobbins's men formed a thin line that "extended . . . from the hills to the Mississippi River" and waited.[10]

As couriers rushed back from the picket line in the initial moments of the Confederate attack, they found the First Indiana Cavalry in their camps outside of the Federal lines. Lt. Col. Thomas N. Pace quickly ordered his men to move their tents and baggage back within the lines. "All was bussel till we got in line," trooper Floyd Thurman wrote. "We got orders to fall back within the fortifications as we were nearly a mile below and our force being small made no pretension to fight out of the works." The bulk of the Hoosiers were soon ordered to the Union right, where Clayton's Fifth Kansas was already in position behind the levee guarding the Sterling Road. The First Indiana's two steel Woodruff guns were wheeled into position on the Kansans' right as a section of the Dubuque Battery took position between Clayton's left and the right of Rice's infantry flanking Battery A. The Kansans were "drawn up in line across the low grounds at the base of the hills, in plain view of the rebel batteries, that had been planted in the heights above town in the early grey of the morning," William Creitz wrote in his diary. "Our batteries were thundering close to our right, and for an hour we sat as passive spectators to this artillery duel between our batteries and the rebel artillerists some four hundred yards away." As Walker dithered behind the barricades, the Kansans took positions to snipe at Marmaduke's troops. "Without orders, we deploy[ed] as skirmishers, every man hunting cover, it was open timber. . . . [W]ithin five minutes every horse (nearly forty-five) of [Marmaduke's] battery was killed," August Bondi observed. Captain Youngs of the Fifth Kansas gleefully wrote after the fight, "in the woods we had a regular old bush fight just such a fight as our Kansas boyes glorey in we fought from behind trees under trees & some of our boys even climbed trees but we proved to much for Marmaduke."[11]

As Clayton's fire enfiladed Marmaduke's Missourians, Walker lingered north on the Sterling Road, and Fagan's exhausted Arkansans caught their breath in the rifle pits below Battery D, one question must have been foremost in every Confederate's mind: Where was

Price? The general and his men had left their camps around midnight, with Parsons's troops in the lead followed by McRae's Arkansians. Price's division was in line behind Fagan's soldiers for about two miles, then cut left up a trail that local guides said would lead them to the Federal works at Battery C. As the Southerners began ascending the tortured network of ravines, Old Pap found it "utterly impracticable to move my artillery during the darkness [so] I ordered the pieces to be left behind until daybreak"; this decision led one Missouri artillerist to observe, "all cannoneers put into the infantry with muskets on there shoulders—somebody is going to be hirt." Volunteer artillery-men were sought to man the guns that were expected to be captured when the Rebels took the fort on Graveyard Hill. Sgt. William Bull recounted proudly, "I was one of the thirty-two volunteers, and under the command of 1st Lieutenant A. A. Leseur we marched with the infantry five miles to the position from which we were to attack." The troops struggled forward, with one Missourian recalling that "for two miles or more we had to climb over logs from two to five feet thick." Then, when within a mile and a half of the Union works as the faint glow of first light broke from the east, Price ordered his men to halt, having determined "that my division would arrive upon the ground prematurely." While the roar of cannon on his right told of Fagan's determined assault, the booming of the *Tyler*'s guns stunted Brooks's advance, and the rattle of musketry to the left signaled Marmaduke's attack, Sterling Price idly waited for dawn.[12]

The soldiers made the best of it while they waited. Their time "was spent by most . . . in speculations and jests as to the results of the coming battle and by others in giving messages for loved ones in the event of accidents," William Bull wrote, adding that he himself took a nice long nap. General Holmes rode up to learn the reason for Price's delay. Given Holmes's irascible reputation, he must have shared some sharp words with the Missourian. Price had already sent McRae's regiments forward to fall upon Battery C from the north; after his tongue-lashing from Holmes, Price sent a courier scurrying ahead to move Parsons forward. After determining that both commands were in position, though shielded by a high ridge that blocked them from seeing each other, the Missourians and Arkansians advanced toward Graveyard Hill. Maj. Lebbeus A. Pindall's Ninth Mis-souri Sharpshooters, accompanied by Capt. C. N. Biscoe's company of Helena-area Arkansians, led the way, striking the Federal picket line about a half mile west of Battery C and sending the Yankees streaming back toward the hilltop fortification. "I was in the first plattoon," James C. Wallace of the Ninth Missouri wrote. "On we went in line over hills and hollows too steep to be climbed on other occasions which we went over in a run now. . . . The work now began . . . in good earnest. We however soon drove the enemys skirmishers inside of their works."[13]

The attacking troops now formed into column of divisions, creating a human battering ram intended to slam the thin Yankee line from its fortifications. As the Rebels began taking fire, the five civilian guides who had led Parsons and McRae slipped away even as the sun rose over the Mississippi River. The Missourians moved forward, and the cannon at Battery C opened up, causing the first twenty of hundreds of casualties the brigade would suffer that day. Pindall's marksmen advanced, with Sergeant Bull noting that "the hills in front of [the Federals'] works had been covered in heavy timber, this had been cut and the trees with their branching limbs allowed to lie where they fell. This made an excellent abatis." The sharpshooters took advantage of this cover, creeping to within musket range of Graveyard Hill "and from behind stumps and logs and the branches of felled trees were delivering an effective fire upon the gunners of the enemy's artillery." Parsons' men marched to within three hundred yards of Battery C's thundering guns and paused to allow McRae's brigade, which was following, to take position on their left. As McRae moved up, his men began taking casualties from the sharpshooters of Company B, Twenty-eighth Wisconsin Infantry, who had clambered into a ravine between Batteries B and C. One of the marksmen, J. D. Cummings, wrote: "We had the prettiest chance you could imagine. We just picked them off like sheep as they marched up the hill. We lay behind stumps and logs, and could see them fall eight or nine at a time." A soldier of McRae's Thirtieth Arkansas noted that as his regiment moved forward, "we were so near the guns that they had no range on us, and our Regiment huddled on a little point of the ridge, like so many sheep. The enemies infantry on our right could see our condition, and poured all the mini balls toward us they could." The Arkansians finally formed for the attack."[M]ore than an hour after the time named in the order," Holmes reported, Price's division charged.[14]

Colonel Rice's adjutant, John Lacy, had just ascended to Battery A as Price's attack began, giving him a clear view of the Rebel

Brig. Gen. Dandridge McRae commanded an Arkansas regiment in Price's division during the doomed attack on Battery C at Helena. A court-martial cleared him of charges leveled by General Holmes of "misbehavior before the enemy" during the battle. *Courtesy Anthony Rushing.*

assault. "It was a splendid spectacle, those dense and gallant lines of gray, as they rushed forward to meet the lines of blue lying in wait for them in the batteries and trenches," Lacy recalled. "Great masses of Price's bravest soldiers followed their battleflags with a daring that excited the admiration of the foe." From the lines on the Union right, a young officer of the Second Arkansas (African Descent) also observed the attack. "[W]e could see colum after colum pouring over the hills toward battery C," Minos Miller wrote. "[A]s soon as they come in sight[,] Ft. Curtis the gunboat and every battery that could get range of them let into them with a vengeance[.] the air was full of shell and we could see the rebels lines open and see them falling in all directions[.] directly they began to give back." Price's men paid the full toll for their tardiness. Because the Rebel attacks on Batteries A and D had failed by this time, the artillerists manning those forts were able to turn their cannon toward Graveyard Hill, joining their fire with that of the gunners at Battery C. Artillerists in Fort Curtis and gunners from the Dubuque Battery and First Missouri Light Artillery began pounding Price's men, and the *Tyler*, prowling offshore, started to hurl her terrible 8-inch shells at the howling Missourians and Arkansians approaching the Federal lines. "We came under the enemie's fire one mile from the fort," Sgt. William C. Morrow of the Thirty-sixth Arkansas grimly recounted. "Our men fell fast from shell and grape."[15]

The Rebels recoiled from the firestorm, reformed, and charged again, only to be repulsed a second time. Then, as Prentiss reported, "exhibiting a courage and desperation rarely equaled," Price's division roared forward again. "The bayonets of the three [sic] distinct regiments moving on [Battery C] glistened in the sun, as the troops moved across the low ridges," a historian of the Thirty-third Iowa wrote. "As they approached the work, they came up in neither line nor column, but in a dense mass, and were thus fired into by artillery and infantry, doing fearful execution. But their progress was not even checked. They came on, shouting like demons." As the Confederates drew within twenty feet of the works, the amateur artillerists of the Thirty-third Missouri unleashed one last blast from their cannon; one Confederate later honored these novice cannoneers by saying, "the way they handled the pieces made us wish we had met another kind." As their infantry support fell back toward Helena, Capt. Thomas M. Gibson ordered the cannon spiked, and the Union Missourians shoved a dry shot in one piece and fled with the friction primers and priming wires, rendering the guns useless. The grayclad horde swarmed over Graveyard Hill and, as a captain of the Twenty-eighth Wisconsin observed, "hauled down our flag and raised in its place the emblem of their treason. That was an exciting and terribly interesting scene."[16]

The cannonless Rebel artillerymen rushed forward, eager to turn Battery C's guns on the Union troops in Helena, only to find them inoperative. As six men clustered around a cannon, a Hoosier soldier observed: "[T]he *Tyler* threw a ten inch Shell and it lit under the gun. They were thrown a rod or two into the air." One Confederate desperately tried to drill the dry shot out of a spiked cannon, only to have both arms blown off at the elbows by a shell from the gunboat. "My hands were together in a line, and all at once I wondered why I could not twist the worm I had held a second before," he remembered years later. "Men who saw me say I stared and grinned like a madman, not knowing what had happened." Newton Scott, from his position with the Second Arkansas (African Descent) on the Union left, watched as the Confederates "Carried the Rifle Pits & Come a Head on the Battery & took the Battery[.] the Rebels was now in Fare View & our Artillery just mowed them & our Infty Had a Cross fire on them & they could not Stand it." Holmes and Price entered the chaotic scene and, finding the guns useless, sent orders to rush Tilden's and Marshall's batteries to the front. Unfortunately for the Southerners, the day at Helena would be decided long before the Rebel cannon could be manhandled into position.[17]

Wounded Confederates began streaming away from Graveyard Hill. Surgeon William McPheeters, who had accompanied Price to Battery C for fear the general would be wounded in the attack, was ordered to establish a field hospital. Union artillery fire forced the Rebel doctors to move back several times as they began treating an increasing number of injured soldiers. "After this, I saw but little of the fight," McPheeters wrote. "There was enough for all of us to do as the wounded were being rapidly brought back. . . . The first limb that I amputated was the left arm of a young man from Little Rock. . . . And thus I was engaged while the battle lasted." Federal shells continued to rain throughout the area. Surgeon R. J. Bell wrote that "the bombs from the gun-boat . . . were falling thickly in our midst, exploding with terrible noise, covering, in many cases, our faces with dust. In this condition, we continued the dressing of wounds."[18]

The roar of gunfire on Graveyard Hill brought hope to the dog-tired Rebels before Battery D. Fagan ordered a charge against the fifth and final line of rifle pits lying before the battery, and his "men, though thoroughly exhausted and worn, answered with a shout and sprang forward." The men of the Forty-third Indiana and Thirty-third Iowa fought desperately as the grim Confederates struggled across the uneven ground but broke before the assault and clambered to the high ground on which the battery sat. John G. Hudson of the Thirty-third Missouri watched from the fortification as "Bells Regmt charged over the Rifle Pits down in a deep Ravine and advanced within 30 yds of the Battery [until] they was checked by canister and Rifle." Hawthorn and King also succeeded in occupying the final line of Yankee works. "Of all the many obstacles and threatening fortifications that opposed our advance that morn, there remained only the fort," Fagan reported. "Rugged and almost impassable ravines, the steepest and most broken hill-sides, abatis, and line after line of breastworks, had been passed and left behind. . . . Notwithstanding the reduced condition of my command and the exhaustion of those yet remaining, I ordered a charge upon the fort." It was simply too much for the Arkansians to accomplish. "The men were so exhausted that most of them were unfit for further service," King reported, and Hawthorn concurred, writing, "our men were too much exhausted, and our numbers too few." The Rebels dug in beneath a "terrible, withering fire that continued to thin our ranks."[19]

Things went from bad to worse at Battery C with the arrival of Holmes and Price among the milling Confederates. Holmes ordered Parsons to take his Missourians and attack Battery D from the rear, easing the pressure on Fagan's Arkansians. But, Holmes reported, "everything was in confusion, regiments and brigades mixed up indiscriminately, and the order was not attended to." He then encountered McRae and ordered him to Fagan's relief. The Arkansian gathered two hundred men and gamely charged downhill to attack Battery D from the flank but was soon pinned down by heavy rifle and artillery fire. "I therefore deployed my men and commenced firing upon the rifle-pits and works . . . aiming to make as great a diversion as possible," he reported. Price now chimed in and ordered Parsons to attack Battery D, only to be told that McRae was already doing so. Holmes then issued the most disastrous order since his poorly considered command to attack "at daylight": he issued a direct order to one of Parsons's colonels to attack Fort Curtis. The officer, not questioning a direct command from a lieutenant general, immediately headed toward Helena from Graveyard Hill, and Parsons reported, "the other

Maj. Gen. Sterling Price's delay at Helena had disastrous results for the Confederates, but his decision to abandon his fortifications near Little Rock in September 1863 saved his army to fight another day. *Courtesy Civil War Museum, Wilson's Creek National Battlefield.*

commandants understanding it to be a general movement toward the town, advanced in that direction." All of the organized Confederate troops were now streaming away from Battery C.[20]

Unfortunately for the Rebels, Friedrich Salomon had not been idle as the multiple columns assailed Helena's defenses. Seeing the breakthrough at Battery C and cognizant of Walker's tepid movements against the Union right, the German-born colonel ordered Lieutenant

Colonel Pace and the First Indiana to leave the line along the Sterling Road to Clayton's Kansans and hurry to Fort Curtis. The Hoosiers, along with a section of the Dubuque Battery, rushed toward Battery C and dismounted, forming a line of battle along a small ridge to the left of the fort. Half of the troops of the Thirty-fifth Missouri were sent from the works along the levee on the Federal right to form alongside Pace's troopers, and the fugitive troops of the Thirty-third Missouri who had fled Graveyard Hill regrouped and took place beside them. Five companies of the Thirty-third Iowa detached from supporting Battery D to complete the Union line. At the same time, the cannon of Batteries A, B, and D and Fort Curtis continued to hammer Graveyard Hill, as did the big guns of the *Tyler*. "They seemed to think they had gained the day but they were woefully mistaken," gunner Henry Carroll observed from Fort Curtis. "While they were forming, we were throwing shot and shell into them that told fearfully."[21]

Parsons's doomed troops rushed shouting from Battery C, desperately trying to cross seven hundred yards of open ground between Graveyard Hill and Fort Curtis. "They charged down the hill toward the town in a very brave manner but were met by a most destructive fire of grape & canister as well as by volleys of musketry," the chaplain of the Twenty-eighth Wisconsin wrote. As the Missourians closed to within three hundred yards of Fort Curtis, "they were so close, the day seemed lost in spite of all we could do," gunner Carroll observed. "At this distance, we poured in a double charge of grape that made them reel and stagger. Their officers waved their swords and tried to urge the men forward, but it was of no use. It was not human to stand it."[22]

As the Missourians began their charge from Battery C, "for a moment, our hearts almost ceased to beat as those ranks of daring desperate men came over the hill, and we thought all was lost," a Wisconsin Yankee reported. Floyd Thurman of the First Indiana Cavalry noted that the women of Helena sensed victory, writing that "at the time the rebs were running over the hights the ladies waved their handkerchiefs and were very saucy." Parsons wrote that his men charged "all the way from Graveyard Hill to the town, and through it, [and] these devoted troops were exposed to a fatal cross-fire from the enemy's artillery and musketry. It was here that my loss was heaviest." From the Union left, C. H. Glines of the Second Arkansas (African Descent) watched as the Missourians "kept coming until they were almost under the cover of the fort when it got so hot that it made

[them] halt which gave us a good chance and *oh* what a slaughter we made among there Ranks as they turned to retreat."[23]

Reeling back from the intense fire from Fort Curtis and Salomon's counterattacking soldiers, Parsons's survivors fell back to the ravines below Graveyard Hill. "Some two hundred came to a hollow on our side, and crept into a ravine and commenced to fire on the gunners but unluckily for them, they were not covered next to us," Captain Redington of the Twenty-eighth Wisconsin wrote. "Our first fire killed fifteen, and wounded half the rest of them. They ran for the cover of the hill, but not one in ten reached any place of safety." Still, many of the Missourians took positions behind stumps and logs and began sniping at their enemies. "We were compelled to keep close to the ground as there was a brigade of sharpshooters to contend against[.] if a man would show his hed and shoulders half a minute he would be very apt to be carried off," a trooper in the First Indiana recounted. The artillerymen at Fort Curtis concentrated their fire on Parsons's troops, with Sergeant Carroll of the Thirty-third Missouri reporting that "dead, dying, and wounded were strewn thickly on the ground. . . . [T]he way we did slaughter them was something." A squad of Hoosiers rushed forward and opened fire on the Missourians, replacing their own carbines, which had been "condemned by a United States inspecting officer some time since," with captured Enfield rifles before falling back. Lieutenant Colonel Pace organized his reaction force and moved forward to retake Battery C. They were joined by at least one volunteer, Union gunner David Massey observed from Fort Curtis, writing, "there was a negro worker who left his spot and came up in the fort and got a gun and went over on the hill where the rebs was and took a prisoner and marched him over to the fort." Indeed, many of the Missouri Rebels gave up rather than face the firestorm of shells from Fort Curtis and the *Tyler.* Iowan John Lacy, while reporting to General Prentiss, watched as "the disarmed Confederates began to file past. . . . The splendid array of life and bravery that I had seen from Battery A had become a dejected and harmless body of unarmed prisoners. A large steamboat was just landing, bound for Cairo, and in a very brief time these men were steaming up the Mississippi as prisoners of war."[24]

Theophilus Holmes stood atop Graveyard Hill, watching his army dissolve and doubtless remembering his prebattle pledge to bear the odium should the attack on Helena fail. Price's division was mauled, Fagan's Arkansians were pinned down in the rifle pits below Battery D, and the Rebel cavalrymen to the north had been stopped cold. "Under these circumstances," Holmes reported, "at 10:30 A.M. I ordered the troops to be withdrawn." Texan Buck Walton observed the Confederate commander, writing that "it was in this fall back—though still under fire, that Genl. Holmes exposed himself recklessly and sought death—but it would not come—and half crazy because of his defeat, he commenced the retreat to Little Rock." The battered Rebels at Battery C were more than happy to hear the retreat order, and erstwhile gunner William Bull reported that "there was a rush made by the entire force we had left in front of the fort. We were thrown down and then learned that Gen'l Price had sent in orders for the men to get out as quickly as possible to avoid capture." Artillery fire continued to rain on the Rebels, Missourian Jeremiah Baker remembered, "O, but it was a warm day, and as we retreated over the hills they poured shells into us." Pindall's Sharpshooters continued firing, "holding the enemy in check covering the retreat, which was rather precipitate," James Wallace wrote. "The Yankees emboldened by our retreat followed us a short distance and firing with their artillery made it rather warm for comfort to us untill we were out of range of their guns which was done as soon as our weary legs could do it, urged on by the dread of being shot in the *Back* which we felt as brodd as a barn-door." As Pace's dismounted Hoosiers and midwestern infantry ascended Graveyard Hill, he reported that "the enemy did not receive us, but left their works." The Yankees followed suit, dropping back "in consequence of the shells from the gunboat *Tyler* dropping in all around us."[25]

As Price's division fell back from Graveyard Hill, Fagan's Arkansians hung on grimly, "the guns of the enemy (not more than 100 or 150 yards distant) . . . telling sadly against us, while the heat, the want of water, and the toil were no mean auxiliaries." With the drama at Battery C over, the combined Union fire again turned toward Fagan's division. "This latter was now most terrific," Colonel Hawthorn wrote, "and the whole force of the enemy now seemed to be directed against our little band." Between 10:30 and 11:00 A.M., Fagan received orders to fall back six miles to the Alan Polk plantation, from which they had left fewer than twelve hours earlier. Most of the men of King's Thirty-seventh Arkansas were trapped in a ravine to the left of

Battery D, and as Hawthorn and Bell retreated, the Yankees pounced. A force containing men from the Forty-third Indiana, Thirty-third Iowa, and Thirty-third Missouri closed on the position even as the twin 10-pounder Parrotts of the First Missouri Light Artillery's Battery K concentrated their attention on the ravine. Capt. John G. Hudson, commanding Battery D, climbed atop his works and shouted to the Rebels, demanding their surrender. "By what authority," a Confederate officer replied. "By authority of my twelve pound howitzer," the captain answered. The Arkansians had had enough and surrendered en masse. It was a proud moment for the Forty-third Indiana, and Colonel McLean remembered years later that "the Arkansas Regiment became the prey of our forces, and owing to the position of the 43d it reaped the harvest. . . . I have seen no historic allusions, in any of the engagements of the War, of any regiment having been captured by a regiment not larger than the captured." A major, the ranking officer of the Thirty-seventh after the fighting, glumly reported that "the regiment entered the fight with an aggregate of 432. The entire loss was 217." Hawthorn called for volunteers to cover his regiment's retreat but received no takers. The colonel himself took position to fire on the Yankee lines, and nine men joined him. They peppered the Federals for another twenty minutes before retreating—losing three men in the process—and concluding the fighting at Battery D.[26]

As the firing petered out at Battery D, William Brooks ordered a 6-pounder back up on Clements House hill south of town. Lt. E. T. Deloney fired only eight shells before the guns of Battery K, First Missouri Light Artillery, and the *Tyler's* stern gun convinced them to again pull back. Brooks, a prewar lawyer in Fayetteville who was the only Michigan native to serve the Confederacy as a colonel, finally received orders to fall back and serve as the rear guard for the retreating Rebels. Although the Thirty-fourth Arkansas had not seen much action during the morning, its colonel was satisfied that his command had kept the Yankees on the levee in place, preventing them from reinforcing the batteries, and "by the use of a 6-pounder . . . divert[ing] as much as possible the fire of the battery and gunboat from the attacking columns." As the regiment fell back, Denson's Louisiana horsemen burned a contraband camp, along with five thousand pounds of bacon, fifteen hundred bushels of corn, and other supplies.[27]

At Battery A Marmaduke was stalemated by Marsh Walker's inactivity on his left flank. "I twice dispatched to Brigadier-General

Walker to advance and assist me in dislodging them," he reported. "It was not done." The sharpshooting infantrymen of the Twenty-ninth Iowa continued to fire on the Missouri horsemen, with one Iowan writing, "it was a Sharp contest, but our boys drove the rebels before them and made many a poor rebel bite the dust." Much of the fighting centered around Shelby's cannon. The division's quartermaster, Maj. Robert Smith, worked the guns with the other Missourians. After being ordered to leave that post, Smith shouted, "One more shot, General, one more shot," then was killed by a bullet through the heart. The Rebels desperately sought to remove their cannon from the field, cutting dead horses from their traces and pulling the guns away by hand. "We heard one man's voice hollowing 'Now boys altogether,'" a Kansas cavalryman remembered. "It was . . . [Capt. Joseph] Bledsoe with his foghorn voice encouraging his men to drag the pieces out of harm's way." "Everyone worked for dear life and dear honor," John Newman Edwards wrote. "Over the matted barricade they were dragged and hurried. Back came the guns, but not all the young heroes sent to rescue them."[28]

With his cannon safe (though one caisson was left on the field), Marmaduke ordered his men to join the rest of Holmes's army in retreat. Angered over Walker's tepid attack, the Missourian did not bother to tell his fellow officer to fall back. Colonel Dobbins's Arkansas troopers remained in position opposite Powell Clayton's Kansans, the two forces sniping at each other. William Creitz wrote that the "Kansas men were at home bushwhacking—and could not be taken at disadvantage. . . . For at least three hours we held at bay an entire rebel Brigade, that were attempting to flank us with two pieces of cannon." Three hours after Marmaduke's men had retreated from Battery A, Walker fell back under pressure from Sam Rice's Iowans. "At about 2 o'clock I was informed by General Marmaduke that he had already withdrawn his command," Walker wrote. "I had hard fighting to protect my left flank, and when my right became exposed I commenced to get loose from the enemy and retired." With the withdrawal of the Arkansas horsemen, the Battle of Helena ended.[29]

The retreating Confederates left behind hundreds of wounded, and Missouri physician Aurelius Bartlett noted that "when the din of battle ceased and the smoke was lifted from the scene, one had only to look around to be convinced that uncommon opportunities [were] offered for mitigating the human suffering and for the exercise of the surgeon's art." Captain Stevens of the Twenty-eighth Wisconsin wrote that "under every bush, alongside every log & stump were the wounded." A comrade in the Twenty-eighth recorded: "[I]t is an awful sight to see and hear the rebels that are wounded. They are groaning, and call for their mothers, wives and sisters, and keep hollering." Parties of soldiers transported the wounded to houses throughout Helena, many of them belonging to the women who had "saucily" observed the beginning of the attack a few hours earlier. Confederate and Union surgeons worked together to care for the battered Rebels; Surgeon McPheeters wrote that "all the surgeons who were left in Helena . . . speak in high terms of their attention to our wounded."[30]

In addition to the wounded, the Federals also held hundreds of prisoners, including many of Parsons's Missourians who had been trapped in the ravines below Battery C and Fagan's Arkansians captured at Battery D. "They are a dirty, rough looking set of fellows," Edward Walden of the Twenty-eighth Wisconsin observed, "but who would not look both rough and dirty after a long march and a hard fight whipped and prisoners. They are to be excused for the mean appearance." Adjutant Savage of the Twenty-eighth wrote: "I escorted nearly fifty butternuts. I met Gen. Salomon as I was marching my secesh brethren down to the levee & received a compliment for my 'level head' in not taking a guard away from the rifle pits but went alone with them. It was a long walk & I went afoot & enjoyed some jovial conversation with the captured Secesh." River traffic on the Mississippi was soon busy transporting the captured men to Northern prisons. A report from Helena in the *St. Louis Daily Missouri Democrat* proudly stated: "The Tycoon took up North 612 prisoners, including 63 commissioned officers; the R. C. Wood 212 including 20 commissioned officers; and the Silver Moon 114, including five commissioned officers; and 75 prisoners are here now."[31]

And then there were the dead. Wisconsinite John Savage observed: "[T]here they lay in all shapes, postures & positions, under this blazing sun with the flies crawling in and out of their wounds. What a work for the anniversary of American Independence, American against American." Around Graveyard Hill William Creitz of the Fifth Kansas found "their dead were mangled by our shells in every conceivable shape—and some could only be recognized as belonging to humanity, by their clothing. . . . There lay in a confused mass, twelve, as they had been stricken down by the explosion of a shell, most of them dead, and others expiring; here a mutilated trunk, less a head; here a body rent assunder with hands extended—clutching apparently at vacancy—and eyes protruding with that peculiar stony stare, death's most repulsive cygnet." Capt. Thomas Stevens of the Twenty-eighth Wisconsin walked the ground around Batteries C and D and wrote that "it was a sickening sight. The ridges & ravines were thickly strewn with ghastly corpses covered with gore—heads, arms, legs shot away—mutilated in almost every manner by the shot & shell. . . . On one spot of ground less than a rod square lay *nine* dead bodies." An Iowa infantryman recorded that "the rebels turned black almost immediately after death. Some supposed this was caused by whisky and gunpowder mixture which was furnished them to drink, as remains of it were found in many of their canteens." The belief that the Confederates were drunk on whisky and gunpowder was widespread. James Loughney mentioned: "I have heard that the canteens and some bottles belonging to the rebs. contained powder & whiskey by which the poor wretches were wrought to the highest pitch of madness, and wreckless exposure." Wisconsite J. D. Cummings declared that the "Rebels were fed on gunpowder and whiskey, and they were just crazy."[32]

As the smoke of battle cleared, the armies' commanders were able to count their casualties. Benjamin Prentiss wrote that Helena's defenders sustained "a loss . . . so small almost to seem miraculous." Of the 4,129 men garrisoning the town, 57 were killed, 127 wounded, and 36 were reported missing—a total of 220 casualties. Prentiss's heaviest casualties were among the Thirty-third Iowa and Thirty-third Missouri, but the Second Arkansas Infantry (African Descent) suffered a milestone by recording what were among the first combat wounds sustained by black troops in battle in Arkansas. Theophilus Holmes, noting that "I write this report with deep pain," stated that of his attacking force of 7,646 men, 173 were killed, 687 wounded, and 776 missing, a total of 1,636 men. The heaviest casualties were among Price's division, victims of the slaughter pen at Graveyard Hill, and Fagan's Arkansians at Battery D. Walker's division suffered the slightest number of losses, a mere 12, reflecting the feebleness of his attack on the Sterling Road. A jubilant Iowan concluded, "We gave them one of the most Signal Thrashings that they Ever got from the Yankees."[33]

He was correct. Holmes planned what would have been an extremely difficult assault under the best of circumstances: a simultaneous converging attack from three points. He failed to adequately scout the routes in advance, being taken completely by surprise when his men ran into the felled timber that blocked the roads into Helena. Perhaps most importantly, he gave the order to attack "at daylight," which Price fatally interpreted to mean dawn even as he listened to the heavy firing from the attacks of Fagan and Marmaduke, officers who correctly deduced their commander's intent. Holmes's after-battle report blamed the loss "on the men not being well in hand after success. Most of my loss in prisoners resulted from not restraining the men after the capture of Graveyard Hill from advancing into the town, where many were taken without resistance." He conveniently left out his role in the confusion, riding into Battery C and issuing attack orders without going through the chain of command. The weak attack on Battery A, much of which can be blamed on Walker's almost complete failure to press the Union cavalry defending the Sterling Road, allowed Federal attention to concentrate on the valiant infantry attacks on their left and center. James Wallace of Pindall's Sharpshooters summed up the assessment of many Confederate survivors when he wrote, "it was a sad thought to think how many brave noble solders had been fruitlessly sacrificed we may say needlessly or foolishly done by a *dupe*."[34]

On the Federal side, Prentiss's army had fought a textbook defensive battle. On learning that Holmes was on the move with a much larger force, the Federals coolly strengthened the natural defenses of the town by building strong earthworks designed for mutual defense. Friedrich Salomon and his subordinates used their interior lines to rush troops to crisis points during the battle, ably utilizing their much smaller force to its greatest defensive potential. The Union artillery also played a significant role in the victory, switching their targets at the appropriate times during the disjointed Confederate attacks. They also did not spare the ammunition: John Hudson of the Thirty-third Missouri reported that his guns at Battery D fired "324 rounds during the entire engagement." Finally, the big guns of the USS *Tyler* dropped their shells wherever the fighting was heaviest, breaking up Brooks's attacks from the south and crushing the Confederates at Battery C. Its commander reported firing 433 shells, "most of which were 8 inch 15-second and 10-second shells." So impressive was the naval firepower that one Rebel cavalryman concluded, "if we had taken [Helena] we couldn't hold it on account of the gunboats, there was three of them there throwing their shells at us." Another Confederate horseman made a wide-eyed claim that "they had 9 gun boats to play against us."[35]

The Federals in Helena now faced the considerable task of burying the Confederate dead scattered throughout the area. Benjamin Pearson of the Thirty-sixth Iowa wrote on July 5 of performing "one of the most disagreeable & sickening jobs of my life" as he led a burial detail. "The stench was almost unindurable. In our burying partys we put from one I guess to 40 in one large grave according to how thick they ware piled together as we could not move them far, from the dreadful condition they ware in to handle." For days afterward around Helena, Rebel casualties were found in the undergrowth, where wounded men had crawled for shelter and died from their injuries. John Wright of the Twenty-ninth Iowa noted on July 7, "we find several squads of the enemy dead back of the picket line today and bury them." Two days later Kansan George Flanders wrote, "every day some dead rebel is found in the woods unburied." Gazing at the new graves, William Creitz of the Fifth Kansas mused that "the rebels wanted to make the day memorable, and judging from the fresh mounds of earth dotting the hill sides, I am afraid they have."[36]

Despite the magnitude of the Union victory, Prentiss remained jittery and kept his men on high alert all day July 5. A. F. Sperry of the Thirty-third Iowa noted, "we lay in the trenches until noon, but no attack came." Rebel surgeon R. J. Bell, still in Helena to tend Confederate wounded, wrote that the sound of gunfire along the picket lines during the afternoon of July 5 "caused intense excitement among the Federals. General Prentiss sprang to his feet, mounted his horse, and rode to and fro in the street, in a frantic manner. . . . Artillery flew precipitately to the anticipated battle-field; negro women, in great numbers, ran to the wharf-boats, carrying cooking utensils, bed-clothes, negro babies, etc.; and southern ladies in large groups, assembled in their yards, talking low and smiling." Despite occasional alarms throughout the day, there were no serious sorties against the Union lines. With the arrival of reinforcements—the 117th Illinois Infantry from Memphis—Prentiss felt secure enough on July 6 to send Clayton's cavalry out to patrol the area.[37]

In fact the one place where Prentiss can be criticized for his handling of the army at Helena was, as historian Edwin Bearss has noted, for "a common failure of the Civil War commander. He failed to follow up and harvest the full fruits of his victory." In his defense, however, Prentiss was aware that Holmes still commanded a force that dwarfed his Helena garrison. Capt. Edward Redington of the Twenty-eighth Wisconsin wrote in a letter to his wife: "[I]f we had had 2000 men more so that we could have followed them with what we had, we could have crushed them fine. As it was we dare not leave the town unprotected and follow them, for we knew that Genl. Frost was a few miles down the river with 8000 men, and if we marched out, he could march in, so we had to let them go in peace." Although Frost, manning the works at Fort Pleasants near Pine Bluff, was not the imminent danger Redington perceived, Prentiss was wise to be cautious.[38]

Clayton's July 6 patrol encountered little action—one trooper reported that they "found the retreating Confederates near Lick Creek and harassed their rear"—but instead discovered "only those left wounded at every house we passed." The biggest Confederate hospital was set up at the Polk Plantation, from which the doomed attack had set out two days earlier. Surgeon McPheeters had worked tirelessly since July 4 treating the 168 wounded men there. Federal doctors at Helena cooperated with McPheeters, providing medical supplies and such things as "a hogshead of ice, which is very acceptable as the weather is very hot." The Rebel doctor maintained the hospital until August 4, recording a depressing series of amputations and deaths as the fighting at Helena continued to exact its toll.[39]

The Yankee troops in Helena, meanwhile, were further cheered by the news of the fall of Vicksburg. Some 29,000 Rebels surrendered there on July 4, joined four days later by 7,000 more at Port Hudson, Louisiana. Word of Robert E. Lee's defeat at Gettysburg and retreat from Pennsylvania brought additional hope to the Helena garrison. A joyful Prentiss ordered a celebration to be held on July 8. The Federal commander announced that "Vicksburg and Port Hudson is ours and the River is once more cleared of Rebels from its origin to its mouth," one soldier wrote. "Bully for that. Bully for us. Bully for the western army and bully for our side. We have whipped the Devils and can do it again." Kansan George Flanders wrote to his mother that "three times three rousing cheers were given for Maj. Gen. U. S. Grant the *Hero of the War*. The cannon in Fort Curtis commenced when the cheering stopped then Battery's A.B.C. & D. and the gunboats, and we had a pretty noisy time of it." If there was any dark side for the hard-fighting Helena soldiers, it was that their battle was eclipsed by the news from the Cis-Mississippi: A. F. Sperry noted, "we had won a glorious victory; but it was obscured from public view by the still more glorious news from Vicksburg and the east, as moon-light is dimmed by the sun."[40]

Their enemies had a harder time accepting the news of Vicksburg's capitulation. Surgeon McPheeters first noted in his diary on July 6 that Federal officers told him of the defeat, but "I did not fully credit it— the Federals being such enormous liars"; it was a full week later that "several parolled persons from Vicksburg called by on their way home thus confirming the sad news of the fall of that city." An Iowa officer meeting with Archibald Dobbins, whose regiment continued to patrol the area around Helena, told him "that we had taken vicksburgh and the Colonel Replied yes you have taken vicksburgh about like we took Helena." By late July, however, even the most optimistic Rebel was aware of the fall of their Mississippi River bastions and what it meant. "Our own defeat [at Helena] could have been more cheerfully borne had it not been so closely followed by the news that Vicksburg had fallen. 'Oh what a fall was there,'" one Arkansian lamented. "This Department is now fully cut off from the Eastern portion of the government, and we must stand or fall alone."[41]

The battered Rebels straggled back to positions in the interior of Arkansas. "We are arrived here [Searcy] yesterday and are resting for a few days at any rate after a continued march of more than a month thro heat and rain and swamp and logs the [likes of] which I have never before seen anything to compare with," W. C. Braley of the Thirty-fourth Arkansas wrote to his relieved mother. "We have been compelled to do some hard marching, we have fought one battle, and lost, in every way, about half our army," an outraged Surgeon Bell wrote in his diary. "The battle of Helena was a grivous calamity. If it had been possible to capture Helena, it could not have been possible to hold one day." As in the aftermath of Arkansas Post, dispirited men deserted from the army in droves, particularly from the brigades of Fagan and McRae. The Confederate infantry would play little role in the subsequent actions that would decide the fate of the Arkansas River Valley.[42]

Indeed, the successful defense of Helena emboldened the Federals, and the sudden freeing of thousands of Union troops following the capture of Vicksburg did not bode well for Confederate Arkansas. As one Rebel engineer concluded, "Little Rock was lost at the Battle of Helena."[43]

5

"WE ARE AN ARMY OF PRISONERS"

The Campaign to Capture Little Rock

The Union garrison at Helena remained on high alert as rumors raced through town about the return of a Rebel army. "It has been rumored about in camp that Old Price calculates to try us on again but we stand as ready for him as ever and I think he will meet with a much warmer reception than he did on the fourth," Iowan Milton Chambers confidently stated on July 17. A week later another soldier wrote, "The report is that Price has a force of 30,000 men and is bound to take Helena." The next day Benjamin Pearson of the Thirty-sixth Iowa wrote in his diary: "[T]here is another attack expected almost hourly now. Men from the different Regts laid in the rifle pitts & at the brestworks last night."[1]

Even commanders were susceptible to the rumor mill, especially after the capture of a Rebel lieutenant in Missouri in early July who reported an impending invasion of that state by 19,000 troops under Price. Brig. Gen. John Wynn Davidson, commanding Union cavalry in eastern Missouri, took the bait, reporting to General Schofield that "Price crossed from Jacksonport to Crowley's Ridge, by a good road, 40 miles," with the intent to attack Davidson's division at Bloomfield, Missouri. Schofield duly reported this phantom movement to General in Chief Halleck, who saw an opportunity to crush the troublesome Missourian and his Rebels. In a terse note to Prentiss in Helena, Halleck reported Price's northern movement and ordered that "all available forces should immediately move on his rear so as to cut off his retreat. The forces in Missouri will prevent his pene-trating very far into that State and, if he is cut off in his rear, his forces must disperse or surrender."[2]

Far from considering an invasion of Missouri, Holmes's army was in terrible condition following the Helena fiasco and scattered in camps across central and northeast Arkansas. A visiting officer reported that "a great number of desertions . . . have occurred and are daily taking place, particularly in the case of Fagan's and McRae's brigades," two units composed primarily of Arkansians that had taken some of the heaviest casualties at Helena. Even General Shelby's crack Iron Brigade suffered "general dissatisfaction" after the attack on Battery A, with its wounded commander fearing that "there will in all probability be numerous desertions. The only remedy which I at present see is to detach the regiments from each other." As James Wallace of Pindall's Sharpshooters noted in his diary, "the fall of Vicksburg on the 4th Port Hudson surrendered on the 9th of July all this and what we had experienced was rather hard to bear and was the most discouraging time I have ever seen." The failure of Lee's invasion of the North in the hills of Gettysburg, Pennsylvania, brought further gloom to the western Rebels. Edmund Kirby Smith succinctly summed up the strategic situation in a letter to the Con-federate governors of the Trans-Mississippi states: "Vicksburg has fallen. The enemy posses[es] the key to this department."[3]

If there was a positive result of the Battle of Helena for the Trans-Mississippi Confederacy, it was the loss of Theophilus Holmes as head of the District of Arkansas. The dithering general—hard of hearing, irresolute, and possibly suffering from arteriosclerosis—was "confined to his bed by illness" following the battle. He would formally hand command of the District of Arkansas to Sterling Price on July 23.[4]

Despite their knowledge of the Rebels' poor condition after Helena, the Yankees took the threatened invasion of Missouri seriously. "Price, I believe, is on the [Crowley's] Ridge," Davidson informed Schofield on July 15. "If you will give me some infantry I will be glad to go down on the Ridge or on Batesville." Schofield, however, urged prudence, responding that any new troops would come from the now-idle captors of Vicksburg, who would have to travel via the White or Arkansas River to threaten the Confederate host: "The most you can do at present is to be ready to move in concert with them." Davidson told his commander that his supply train was loading "with all haste," and "the division will leave Bloomfield on the 17th and . . . will make good time." The Union buildup was sufficient to lead Col. Solomon G. Kitchen of the Tenth Missouri Cavalry (C.S.) to bring most of his forces back to Gainesville, Arkansas, observing that the Federals "are looking for Price to come into Missouri." U. S. Grant, with his characteristic overview of the region's strategic situation, pledged to immediately send a division of troops to Helena to release the garrison to pursue Price, but he bluntly told Maj. Gen. Stephen Hurlbut in Memphis, "I cannot believe any portion of your command is in any danger from anything more than a cavalry raid."[5]

The renewed Union offensive in Arkansas began on July 19, when a reconnaissance force of fifty Missouri horsemen swam the St. Francis River at Chalk Bluff, crossing at the instep of the Missouri bootheel. The Yankee cavalrymen captured a pair of Rebels and occupied the high ground as Col. Lewis Merrill's First Brigade of Davidson's First Cavalry Division laid a pontoon bridge to facilitate the remaining troopers' crossing. Merrill, an 1855 graduate of West Point and a veteran Indian fighter, sent the First Missouri Cavalry (U.S.) to Gainesville (farther down Crowley's Ridge) on July 20, with plans to move the rest of his command in their support the next day. Kitchen retreated before them, reporting to Col. John Q. Burbridge that the Federals' "entire force is estimated at 12,000, with some twenty pieces of artillery and 800 infantry."[6]

The Union command actually numbered around 6,000 horsemen, and the men were not fond of their commander. A Virginia-born 1845 West Point graduate, John Davidson was a Mexican War veteran and seasoned Indian fighter whose strict discipline did not play well with his volunteer troopers. After Davidson took command of the Union troops in southeastern Missourian, one Iowan wrote, "our Gen. is a stranger to us—don't like him very well though he may prove himself good in a fight." The general's popularity did not improve in late June, when "he ordered us out of our pleasant camp and . . . into an open field, one mile from any water that was fit for a man to drink," the Third Missouri Cavalry's historian remembered. "The boys cursed him continually." A day later Davidson "put the lieutenant commanding the camp guard under arrest for failing to salute him in the proper manner." Another Missourian wrote home, "our men are very much put out with Gen. Davidson and some of them are trying to kill him, in which undertaking I hope they will be successful."[7]

Regular-army colonel John Wynn Davidson's stern treatment of his voluntary cavalrymen bred schemes to murder him, but he won them over after leading them in the campaign to capture Little Rock. *Courtesy Don Hamilton.*

The cavalry was accompanied by Maj. G. A. Eberhardt's battalion of the Thirty-second Iowa Infantry, which Davidson reported was "attached to my division as the guard to my batteries." The general did not like the Iowans, who had burned several houses of Missourians they suspected of harboring bushwhackers, and the Thirty-second's colonel long suspected that Davidson brought them along on the Arkansas expedition as punishment. "It would be hard to pursuade many of the men who suffered, and whose comrades died under the hardships of a long campaign in which a small body of infantry was compelled to follow a cavalry expedition, that the act was not one of brutality rather than idiocy!" The hardy Iowans eventually would march beside their mounted comrades all the way to Little Rock.[8]

As the Yankee horsemen began descending Crowley's Ridge, Sterling Price assumed command of Confederate forces in Arkansas. While of questionable value as a tactician, Price still enjoyed immense popularity with the troops, as summed up by one infantryman of the Twenty-seventh Arkansas: "[T]here was hardly a man in our regiment but what loved General Price. He was always courteous and kind hearted." An officer on Holmes's staff assessed the Missourian's military acumen: "He was great on retreat. This rear-guard fighting was, they say, magnificent, & he was personally as brave as Julius Caesar, but for defensive and active offensive operations he had no genius." The new Confederate commander, fearing that the activity on Crowley's Ridge presaged a move on Little Rock, immediately began shifting his limited forces. Price ordered General Frost to bring his artillery to Little Rock from Pine Bluff, General Fagan to move his infantry division from Searcy and Des Arc to Bayou Meto east of the capital, Marmaduke to set up base at Jacksonport and harass Davidson's column, and Marsh Walker to set up a screen of cavalry scouts outside of Helena. He also commenced construction of strong earthworks on the north side of the Arkansas River about two and a half miles east of Little Rock but reported, "while I should attempt to defend Little Rock, as the capital of the state and the key to the important valley of the Arkansas, I did not believe it would be possible for me to hold it with the forces then under my command."[9]

By late July the Confederate horsemen in northeast Arkansas were certain that the Union incursion was no mere feint. A paroled Rebel cavalryman of Burbridge's command took advantage of his captive tour of Bloomfield, Missouri, and Chalk Bluff to count "not less than 10,000 Federals this side of Saint Francis, and about 2,000 infantry . . . 250 wagons and eighteen large field pieces . . . [with] 8 horses, and not under 24-pounders." Davidson's troops were in force at Gainesville by that time, leaving Burbridge "satisfied that this is no raid of the enemy, but that it is their intention this time to march to Little Rock." Burbridge was correct. The Union command was now aware that Price was no longer an invasion threat to his home state as he struggled to place troops over half of Arkansas to at least observe the Yankee forces at Helena and on Crowley's Ridge. The Northern strategy had turned from defense to an opportunistic bid to seize the Arkansas capital and split the Trans-Mississippi Confederacy in half.[10]

By evening of July 24, a Union regiment had driven as far down the ridge as Jonesboro, and Davidson's horde was "destroying all the corn and wheat, feeding it to their horses." The troopers also were suffering from hunger, with one Missourian noting that the "weather [was] very warm, blackberries very scarce, and Union folks quite as much so." The column moved swiftly down Crowley's Ridge for one reason, an Ohio artillerist observed: "Our fast marching was for *grub*."[11]

Much of Davidson's division was encamped at Wittsburg on the St. Francis River by July 29. While there, "scouts reported that Price and Marmaduke were between us and Jacksonport preparing to give us battle. Preparations were made to receive them, fortifying the approaches to Wittsburg," an Iowan noted. As the Federals fortified the bluffs commanding the small river town to guard against Rebel incursions, a Missouri trooper wrote that "it was the intension of the Gen. when he executed the defenses of this place to leave a garrison but when the march was resumed the idea was abandoned and none was left." On July 30 the hungry cavalrymen finally received supplies as a small steamer from Helena pulled in at Wittsburg. Davidson left Wittsburg on August 1, and his advance elements arrived at the L'Anguille River near present-day Marianna on August 3, though troopers continued to straggle in until the sixth. He then sent his wagons on into Helena in search of supplies. The troopers apparently shared their opinions of the West Pointer with some of the garrison soldiers in Helena, for one Iowa captain noted in a letter home that "General Davidson's troops hate him very much." As the wagons loaded up with provender, the rest of the division headed west for Clarendon.[12]

The road to Clarendon took the Union horsemen through "some very bad swamps," which were unpleasant in more ways then one. One lieutenant remembered, "there is a stench that can be smelt in those marshes which is very offensive," and "water . . . [being] very scarce we was forced to drink swamp water after takeing a stick and pushing of[f] the thick green scum." It is not surprising that the Federal army would suffer heavily from illness during the drive toward Little Rock.[13]

Davidson was also aware of the continuing danger posed by the Rebel cavalry standing between his troops and the capital. A company of Missouri cavalrymen on August 3 "burned a house . . . on account of the bushwhacking of one of our men and killing of him. He was Chief of Scouts. His name was Glenn from Texas." On August 6 the Third Missouri Cavalry (U.S.) was detached with the Tenth Illinois under Col. Dudley Wickersham to "cut up" Marsh Walker's Confederate cavalry brigade, which was reported to be at Cotton Plant north of Clarendon on the White River. The Yankees found, however, that Walker had already crossed the White in search of more defensible ground. Davidson's force then approached the White River south of Clarendon, where he "established a ferry for crossing the Troops, corduroying two miles of bottom and laying down the frontier bridges across Rock Roe Bayou. Meanwhile, "the enemy had constructed rifle pits in a commanding position fronting the crossing on Rock Roe Bayou but on the approach of Davidson's division had fallen back, leaving only a picket. This position could easily have been turned."[14]

On August 9 the division arrived at Clarendon, where the Federals met a small flotilla under Lt. George M. Bache, U.S. Navy, who reported, "the river is bank full, and entirely clear of guerillas as far as we have been." Bache steamed upriver to DeValls Bluff the next day with a detachment of cavalry, intending to capture rolling stock of the Memphis and Little Rock Railroad, the only railroad in the state. While the train was not there, he did startle a twelve-man picket detachment, "who went off bare-backed, showing only the tails of their horses. We captured saddles, clothes, one horse, and a shotgun." Following this raid, Davidson and Bache decided to mount an amphibious expedition "to gain information about Price's army, to destroy the telegraph at Des Arc and capture the operator, and catch the steamboats *Kaskaskia* and *Thos. Sugg.*" The Federals would end up sparring with some of Marmaduke's best cavalry on the Little Red River.[15]

Bache led three gunboats, the *Cricket, Marmora,* and *Lexington,* along with Eberhardt's contingent of the Thirty-second Iowa Infantry up the White River on August 12 to ascertain the whereabouts of "the ubiquitous Marmaduke" and his horsemen. At 3:00 A.M. the expedition moved out, pausing at Des Arc, where the Yankees "took some citizens, and burned a large warehouse containing a quantity of Confederate States Army property." At the mouth of the Little Red River, the flotilla divided, with the *Cricket,* under acting volunteer lieutenant A. R. Langthorne, heading up the Little Red in search of the two Confederate steamers, while the *Lexington* and *Marmora* continued up the White. The latter boats arrived at Augusta around noon, lingered for a half hour or so, then headed back downriver. Leaving the *Marmora* at the mouth of the Little Red at 3:00 P.M., Bache and the *Lexington* steamed upriver in search of the *Cricket,* which had not yet returned.[16]

The *Cricket* had been busy. After leaving the Augusta-bound troops, its skipper learned that one of the Rebel steamers had lain near

Pvt. George Fox of the Thirty-second Iowa Infantry marched from southeast Missouri with John Davidson's cavalry division only to be mortally wounded fighting aboard a gunboat on the Little Red River during the campaign to capture Little Rock. *Courtesy Butler Center for Arkansas Studies.*

the shore of the Little Red the night before and was about an hour and a half ahead of the pursuing bluecoats. Moving upriver forty miles, they "came in sight of the town of Searcy, the two boats, and a good pontoon bridge across the river," over which much of Marmaduke's force had crossed to the western bank. The Union infantrymen "piled up the bridge and burned it, leaving part of Marmaduke's force yet on the east side of the river." The Yankees seized the *Tom Sugg* and *Kaskaskia,* and the infantrymen joined prize crews aboard the steamers for a triumphant journey back down the Little Red. "Before returning," Sgt. J. M. Boyd of the Thirty-second Iowa remembered, "cotton bales were taken on board and a line of bullet-proof breast-works built around the boats composing the little fleet."[17]

Marmaduke's horsemen at Searcy, however, were not willing to let such Yankee audacity go unpunished. The Rebels were part of Shelby's Iron Brigade, now under the command of Col. Gideon W. Thompson following Shelby's wounding at Helena. The plan was for Thompson's troops and Capt. Richard A. Collins's battery to use a mixture of artillery and sharpshooter fire to bring the invaders to justice. The "horrible condition" of the roads, however, kept Collins from reaching the ambush point, leaving the assault in the hands of the cavalrymen. About ten miles below Searcy near the West Point community, Thompson's men intercepted the flotilla. The lead Confederate regiment under Lt. Col. Charles Gilkey rushed up to the riverbank and opened fire. A Mr. Morehead, piloting the *Kaskaskia,* "stood at the wheel nobly until disabled; he received two shots and fell," leaving the vessel swinging uncontrolled in the current. "At times the *Kaskaskia,* the stream being very narrow, the limbs on both sides would brush the boats and swing them against the bank, and the enemy only prevented from boarding her at the point of the bayonet," Sergeant Boyd wrote. "Had it not been for the protection of the cotton bales as breast-works hardly a man could have escaped." As the Missouri horsemen and Iowa infantry fired at each other from "a distance of about 30 yards," the *Cricket* succeeded in taking the *Kaskaskia* under tow while the cavalry was driven back. Six Iowans of Company D were wounded, one mortally, but the Yankees reported that their attackers "had a great many more hurt, for they were seen to fall in a peculiar manner." Thompson reported "7 or 8 men wounded" and sourly noted, "we were unable to get our battery up. . . . If we had good horses in our battery we could have captured them easily." Some of the Iron Brigade continued downriver another fifteen miles and again attacked the little fleet, reunited now with the *Lexington.* "The *Cricket* opened with her howitzers; the old *Lexington* with her 8-inch guns, which must have given them such a scare as never before, for they left very suddenly," Eberhardt reported.[18]

Davidson was "tickled wonderfully at the unexpected success of the expedition." The veteran cavalryman wrote a gleeful report to Maj. Gen. Frederick Steele in which he told not only of the capture of the steamers but also of intelligence gathered by the expedition. He reported erroneously that Kirby Smith was at Little Rock but correctly noted that the Rebels were concentrating at Bayou Meto twelve miles north of the city, with their left anchored at the hamlet of Brownsville on the prairies east of the capital. The Yankees now knew that Marmaduke was on the south side of the Little Red River. "I think, my dear general, every hour is precious to us now, and that you should have another brigade, at least, of infantry," Davidson

Maj. Gen. Frederick Steele, fresh from the victory at Vicksburg, led his disease-plagued Federal troops in a campaign that saw more maneuver than combat and resulted in the capture of the Arkansas capital. *Courtesy Civil War Museum, Wilson's Creek National Battlefield.*

advised. Steele agreed, writing on August 16 that "the rebels know exactly what force I have, and if they make a stand, they will be well prepared for it."[19]

Eberhardt's infantrymen, meanwhile, suffered for the results of their success. Davidson "now thinks a great deal of the detachment, but gives us, in consequence, plenty to do," the Iowan wrote. Instead of waiting in the relative comfort of Clarendon for Steele and the bulk of the army, the Thirty-second Iowa was sent on August 16 with a detachment of Maj. Lothar Lippert's Thirteenth Illinois Cavalry to Harrison's Landing, some eight miles below Clarendon. The next day eight companies of Illinois horsemen surprised 250 men of Robert Newton's Arkansas cavalry and captured "50 stand of arms, any number of saddles, some horses, and a half dozen prisoners. . . . The rebels left in such haste that they forgot to pick up their haversacks with cornbread and love letters, which were discovered by some of the men." W. W. Garner of Newton's command wrote that "some of our boys could not stand it and gave way, while the others retreated. So did the Fed. . . . Not a man of ours was touched by a ball." Davidson issued a special order in which he took "pride in expressing his satisfaction at the gallant conduct of the 13th Illinois Cavalry . . . in charging and completely routing the rebels . . . at Grand Prairie, Ark."[20]

As Davidson's cavalry tarried at Clarendon, the infantry prepared to join the horsemen. Grant requested Frederick Steele, then under Sherman's command in Mississippi, to lead operations in Arkansas. Steele, a West Point classmate of Grant, was no stranger to the Trans-Mississippi, having commanded troops at Wilson's Creek, Pea Ridge, and Arkansas Post. Grant considered Steele "a first rate commander of troops in battle"—an assessment that would be supported by the coming campaign—and "a splendid officer . . . fully capable of the management of the Army of the Potomac or any of the Departments." One Union officer described Steele as "a small-spare man, with light hair, deep blue eyes, and a very quiet manner"; Minos Miller of the Second Arkansas Infantry (African Descent) sourly noted that the general "has too much Copper mixed in him to suit the most of soldiers."[21]

For Benjamin Prentiss, Steele's appointment to lead the Little Rock expedition was an affront, especially in light of the July 4 victory at Helena. He offered his resignation to General Hurlbut in Memphis, who urged Grant to accept it: "He thinks he is undervalued, and in all such cases it is well to relieve the army and make way for men who are not plagued in that way." Steele himself was less than pleased with his new assignment. He wrote Davidson on August 9: "I did not seek this command and would rather it had been given to you. Not but that I would like to have the honor of being present at the taking of Little Rock, but . . . Genl. Grant informed me that he had recommended me for the command of the 16 Army Corps, which would suit me very well. . . . By this new honor which has been heaped upon me, my chances for an army corps are very much diminished." Despite Steele's protestations, Davidson was rankled at being superseded in command, and his relationship with Steele would remain strained.[22]

Steele reviewed his infantry on the morning of August 10, "and I must confess I was disappointed in regard to their numbers and general appearance. The Regiments were much smaller than their official Return shows. . . . The five first that I inspected would not if consolidated make more than one full one. Those that reported a few days ago 500 & 300 did not turn out on inspection more than 150 & 125. Regts. were [commanded] by Capts. and Companies by Sergts." A historian of the Twenty-seventh Wisconsin Infantry noted that the regiment "had 150 men in line when [they] started on the march, the rest . . . being sick in Helena." Steele also was appalled by the lack of transport, writing, "it is very tedious fitting up here. Transportation is deficient. I shall be obliged to leave one section of a Battery for want of horses & harness. Rations are also short."[23]

That same day the Union infantry prepared for the long march ahead. Milton Chambers of the Twenty-ninth Iowa Infantry wrote to his brother, "my knapSack weights 8 pounds beside my gun and cartridge box which will weigh about the same then two days rations on top of that I think will be as much as I want to pack." While one Hoosier cavalryman wrote home that "it appears like leaving home to pull up stakes after being here so long," most of the Yankees were glad to depart Helena. "So at last we are agoing to leave this miserable place," Kansan George Flanders wrote. "We may find a worse place, but I have my doubts about it." An Iowa officer reasoned, "I would rather risk my chances on that trip [to Little Rock] than here in this sickly place," and a newcomer from Ohio sourly described the town as "a hard hole which should be spelled with a double 'l.'"[24]

Steele started his column of 6,000 infantrymen and sixteen artillery pieces westward on the evening of the tenth. Charles Musser of the Twenty-ninth Iowa expressed the confidence of many of the troops, writing, "we will find no enemy on our march worthy of notice, only the myriads of Nats and Musquitoes," and "we are all in good spirits and are ready for the tramp." A fellow Iowan declared: A "fight is what we are after until the Confederacy is completely Squelched. . . . We here there are 25,000 Rebels out about Little Rock but they will be there to run before our men get out there if they (Price, Marmaduke & co.) do as they are in the habit of doing as they seldom ever stand their ground and fight." The Yankees would soon discover that eastern Arkansas held foes deadlier than gnats, mosquitoes, or even Confederates as they faced the blistering heat of an Arkansas August and the debilitating malarial diseases of the region's miasmic swamps.[25]

The wretchedness of the march soon became apparent. On August 11 Capt. Thomas Stevens of the Twenty-eighth Wisconsin wrote that the regiment "got in motion . . . about dark. It was black as pitch & raining before we had gone a mile. . . . Marched a little further by the light of the candle—laid down in our wet clothes and tried to rest a little in the rain." The difficult conditions soon took their toll on the soldiers. After marching fifteen to eighteen miles, Stevens reported seven men sick. A day later, after a march of fifteen miles, he recorded, "this has been a terrible day for us who go on foot—the dust, the hot sun & sweltering heat—it was rough. The men fell out by scores. We are marched too far for men in our condition, & at this time of year in Arkansas, half the time without water." The next day was no better, with the Twenty-eighth trudging another fifteen or sixteen miles "in the hot sun & blinding, choking dust." William Dinsmore Hale of the Third Minnesota echoed Stevens's assessment of the march, writing on August 19 that "the *heat* and the *dust* added to the debilitated state of the system in this climate is quite as much as humanity can stand." The Northerners suffered not only from the heat on the march—Iowan John Talbut wrote to his sister, "Esther [if] you was down heare you would think that it was hot you would want to ware knothing but hoops"—but especially from a lack of decent water. William Hale of the Third Minnesota admitted, "I was glad of a sip of coffee made from filthier water than I had ever thought to drink," while a fellow Minnesotan observed, "during the march we got very poor water to drink—most of the time nothing but Bayou water." The unsanitary water, coupled with the rigors of marching in an Arkansas summer and the fact that many of the Union units were unhealthy before they even started, caused an appalling rate of illness. Confederate delaying actions added to the Yankees' misery. The Twenty-ninth Iowa's Musser noted that on arriving at Big Creek some twelve miles from Helena, "we found the bridge burned and had to build a new one. . . . [T]he Guerrillas shot one of the ambulance drivers while crossing the river or creek. it was eight at night when we got into camp and had to be up and going before light again." Kansan August Bondi wrote: "Bushwhackers molest troops, one soldier killed while filling his canteen at a well, one wagon master wounded. . . . Every company on grand guard." Still, some of the Yankees took advantage of the region's relative bounty to make the best of the difficult situation. William Storrs of the Seventy-seventh Ohio Infantry bragged in his diary that "this day the boys gobbled chickens Ducks Turkeys geese apples and Peaches in a way to make a man stare—not to mention green corn and cabbage."[26]

The infantrymen began arriving at Clarendon on August 15, with George Cook of the Twenty-eighth Wisconsin noting, "we got to Clarendon at Sundown all the citizens have left it looks quite lonely." A historian of the Third Minnesota wrote that the town "at that time had only about fifty buildings, scarcely one of which appeared occupied. Windows had been broken and the ashes here and there told the

tale of previous destruction." The Yankees began ferrying across the
White River, a process that took several days. Five days after arriving,
Edward Redington of Wisconsin observed: "[T]he ferry runs every
twenty minutes with four teams and a steamer crosses nearly as
often with horses. They have been running day and night for days
and still the Cavalry are not yet over." The delay did offer the weary
foot soldiers a chance to relax. "Today we are resting from our toils,"
one Hoosier wrote. "And will stay here a few days to rest. We have a
nice shady camp but the weather is so extremely hot we can't rest
much." It also provided many of the Union cavalrymen their first
look at their new commander, who arrived on the eighteenth. One
Iowa horseman wrote: "Gen. Steel came in today will have command
his name certainly sounds better to me than Davidson—although
Davidson is better than we expected." Apparently the volunteers were
beginning to warm to the veteran regular.[27]

For the debilitated Yankees, this low-lying location on the White
River was not the best place to camp. As A. F. Sperry of the Thirty-
third Iowa Infantry explained: "Clarendon was the very home and
head-quarters of ague in bulk and quantity. The very air was thick
with it. We could almost hew out blocks of it and splash them in the
river." In fact, Sperry wrote, the area set the malarial standard for the
men of the Thirty-third: "Comparatively speaking, the real genuine
'Clarendon shake' is to ordinary chills and fever, about as a big bull-
dog is to a pet poodle. We experienced it in all varieties and degrees;
and the worst any ague can ever do now for us, is to make us think of
Clarendon." The artillerymen in the expedition also suffered heavily.
The Twenty-fifth Ohio Battery recorded a grim milestone: "At Clarendon, the battery lost its first man by death since its organization [on
August 27, 1862]. Pvt. Thomas Scott, of Chagrin Falls, Ohio, died of
chronic diarrhea, aged sixty-two." The Fifth Ohio Battery lost fourteen
men to disease on the road to Little Rock and at Clarendon "had not
enough men able to water their horses and care for the sick." The
losses among the cannoneers was so great that Henry Hunt of the
126th Illinois Infantry wrote: "[O]ur Company was detailed into the
11th Ohio Battery artillerists. As they were short of men, we had to
learn the artillery drill in addition to our infantry tactics. It is hard
work in hot weather."[28]

As when the Federal army occupied Helena, slaves escaped from
their masters wholesale and flocked to Clarendon. William Gulick

of the First Iowa Cavalry wrote that the Yankees "have brought in negros by the hundred [and] have them do all our dirty work & they are well satisfied at that but some of the women & children look pitiful. They have had a hard row to hoe for a long time, have been hid out in swamps with mules & cattle some times." The Twenty-eighth Wisconsin's Captain Redington wrote on August 20: "[T]he niggers are coming in by hundreds now. . . . There are several hundred waiting for a boat to take them to Helena. Since we have been at Helena, some three thousand have been sent north, and these will follow. They are all women and children. The men are put in the army." In fact Steele had anticipated a crop of new recruits for the army's new black regiments and had detailed officers to accompany his expedition to enlist them; Minos Miller of the Second Arkansas (African Descent) had written as the army left Helena, "our business is to take charge of all contrabands that comes to our lines that will make soldiers." Capt. Madison Bowler of the Third Minnesota Infantry Regiment brought in one fugitive slave while on a foraging mission. The party hit the Redmon plantation at Lawrenceville and took "a short time to empty Redmon's corn crib and depopulate his poultry yard." As the bulk of the 160-man contingent returned to Clarendon, Bowler took five men and the contraband guide on a ride through the area. The escaped slave "knew the country to perfection . . . so we followed bye-paths and visited everybody in the neighborhood." The visits included the home of the man's former owner, whom he chastised for planning to "run him off to Texas." On returning to Clarendon, the contraband, Alfred Gales, enlisted in the Third Minnesota as a cook and served with the regiment throughout the war, moving to Minnesota afterward.[29]

Already battered, Clarendon suffered greatly during its occupation by the sick, frustrated Yankees. Franklin Denny of the First Missouri Cavalry wrote on August 16: "[T]his evening about nine Oclock some one set fire to a block of wooden buildings on the leve[e] which our men had been fit[t]ing up for a hospital. They all soon burnt down." A fellow Missouri horseman attributed the blaze to "some reckless fellows." The destruction continued after the Union infantry arrived. Soldiers of the Forty-third Indiana rushed into the White River for a cool swim after completing their march and were fired on by guerrillas. Their colonel recorded: "[T]he residents of Clarendon paid dearly for the acts of their bushwhacking friends. . . . It was the only time I ever saw the 43d engage in ransacking a town. Furniture of every description was brought into camp. Mahogany bedsteads with canopy tops, lounges, sofas, rocking chairs, large plate glass mirrors, dining tables, dishes, and may other articles were there. These luxuries were enjoyed one night, and split up and used in cooking breakfasts next morning. . . . I have called it 'Retaliation.'"[30]

General Steele, seeing a thousand of his troops ill, by August 22 turned Davidson's horsemen toward Little Rock while moving his foot soldiers to the higher and presumably healthier ground at DeValls Bluff. He reported to Hurlbut on August 23 that "the sick list is frightful, including many officers. One brigade is commanded by a lieutenant-colonel, two colonels having given up in the last three days. If you do not send re-enforcements I shall likely meet with disaster. This is the poorest command that I have ever seen, except the cavalry." Despite Steele's assertion, the historian of the Thirteenth Illinois Cavalry noted that "of Davidson's Cavalry Division, 1,500 had fallen sick or were disabled by wounds or were killed before the attack on Little Rock was made." Hundreds of Union soldiers were too sick to be moved and were left behind as their healthier comrades marched to DeValls Bluff. "No doubt some will find their last resting place on earth," Thomas Stevens of the Twenty-eighth Wisconsin mused. "How sad it seems that they must die so far from home and friend—here in the wilds of Arkansas."[31]

On arriving at DeValls Bluff, the marching troops found that their stricken comrades had been transported to the new location by boat. James Lockney wrote on August 24: "[T]his morning we found the sick of our Co. that we left at Clarendon had come up on the boats & they had to lie on the bank of the River. Very many of them are very weak exhausted & dispirited. There were many sick belonging to all the different Regts. And for some reason no preparation was made for them, and all is hurry and bustle yet they are left to do the best they can for themselves, or go untended[.]" Captain Stevens of the Twenty-eighth Wisconsin noted: "[W]e have 700 or 800 sick men here & very inadquate provisions for their comfort. It seems hard to see such misery which we can't relieve." Although DeValls Bluff had seen the hard hand of war—one Iowan wrote, "not a house to bee seen[.] it is Like all the southern towns when you get to them they arnt there"— the location was impressive to Redington. He declared: "[T]his is a splendid sight for a town, and if in any of the Northern states, in as fine a country with a railroad connecting it with the interior, and the best river for navigation in the United States, of its size running past it, would have been a city of 25,000 inhabitants."[32]

Steele made a good choice in selecting DeValls Bluff as a base of operations, for the fast-moving White River kept a clear channel scoured for most of the year, giving the town regular access to steamers and gunboats. Taking advantage of the White at his back, Steele brought up two gunboats to protect the river side of town while "an intrenchment can be thrown up in rear that will make the place tolerably secure against any force that will be likely to annoy us while we are pushing the enemy to the front." He also found the Memphis and Little Rock Railroad in good shape and immediately requested rolling stock from Memphis.[33]

As the Federal infantry moved to their new base, Davidson's horsemen began to advance toward Little Rock across the flat, arid Grand Prairie. As they set out, Samuel Baird of the Second Missouri Cavalry wrote, "we had a dress parade. All the cavalry, artillery and wagons drew up into the line, with banners and flags flying, and I tell you it was as fine and beautiful a display as I ever saw." The historian of the Third Missouri concurred: "[W]e were formed and marched in line of battle as follows: The 1st brigade on the left, the 2d brigade on the right, and the 3d brigade in the centre, the train following in the rear in four columns. The scene was a beautiful one, and will be remembered a long time no doubt by every one who witnessed it." Although they did not know it at the time, the Union cavalry would bear the brunt of nearly all the combat to come in the campaign to capture Arkansas's capital.[34]

The infantry also soon headed west toward its prize, moving through the flat, waterless prairies that separated DeValls Bluff and Little Rock. As with the march from Helena, the trek across the prairie would be a wretched experience for the Union troops. "This country is as famous for the fever and ague as the White River ever was and Rattle Snakes, Lizards, ticks and Chiggers are beyond calculation so that rest is next thing to impossible," a miserable Indiana infantryman confided in a letter home. Nor were mounted troops immune from the rigors of the march, as three Illinois cavalrymen were left "dropping suddenly from their horses as if shot. . . . All three had been repeatedly warned to abstain from drinking the water out of the bayous, but would quench their thirst with the greenish-looking fluid. They were put in ambulances, when congestive chills set in, of which they died within a few days." Another Union horseman wrote, "we drank water that I thought a dry ox would not touch."[35]

As Steele's men decamped for DeValls Bluff on August 23, Price consolidated the Confederate cavalry opposing them, placing Marmaduke under Walker's command. This created a situation that would exacerbate, with tragic results, the bad blood that had existed between Marmaduke and Walker since the Battle of Helena. Price also received desperately needed reinforcements as Lieutenant General Smith released Brig. Gen. James C. Tappan's brigade of infantry from Louisiana. Price placed Daniel Frost in command of all infantry north of the river, keeping Tappan's brigade on the south side in reserve. "Seeing that the position at Bayou Meto could be easily turned, and that it was otherwise untenable," Price "ordered General Frost . . . to withdraw his entire command within the line of defenses" being prepared near Little Rock. The Rebel cavalry would face the Union host alone. One observer astutely summed up the tactical situation: "The prospect is very good for a fight or foot race sometime this fall." But morale remained low among the Confederates. W. W. Garner of the Fifth Arkansas Cavalry confided to his wife: "[T]he men are deserting from this regiment. . . . They have not been paid and the fall of Vicksburg and Port Hudson seems to weigh very heavily on the men and those that are deserting are rather weak on the cause." Nor were the Rebels immune from the illnesses that bedeviled Steele's troops. Garner noted, "the health of our Regiment is not good and some 20 men in our camp are either sick or on the puny list." Still, Davidson's troops began encountering Confederate skirmishers with increasing frequency. For the first time since leaving Missouri, Rebel bullets became a hazard to rival thirst, dust, and disease for the Union horsemen.[36]

The first sizable encounter between the two armies occurred on August 25 near the hamlet of Brownsville, "a small town situated on a broad, flat and extensive prairie, about thirty miles distance in an easterly direction from Little Rock." It was here that the Rebel rear guard under Marmaduke, outnumbered four-to-one in men and eight-to-one in artillery, attempted to slow the Union advance. Lt. Col. B. Frank Gordon, a private and bugler in the Mexican War who prospected for gold in California before returning to more mundane pursuits as a Missouri grocer, commanded around seven hundred men of Shelby's Iron Brigade. On the morning of the twenty-fifth, "ere the men had partaken of their scanty meal," an order came to form line of battle at

Bayou Two Prairie and block the Little Rock road. One section of Bledsoe's Battery was placed on the road while Maj. Benjamin Elliott's battalion moved a mile and a half ahead on the prairie to act as the advance and skirmish line. Marmaduke's six hundred men under Col. William L. Jeffers formed on the edge of Brownsville, with Charlie Bell's battery in place on the right and elements of Burbridge's and Jeffers's regiments and Young's battalion on the left.[37]

"The enemy's lines, extending across the prairie, could be plainly seen advancing, supported by a large body of cavalry with artillery, and when within about 200 yards of our lines Major Elliott, from his entire line, opened fire upon them, which was immediately returned, and the charge sounded by the bugles of the enemy brought their columns sweeping across the prairie and down upon our retiring column like a whirlwind," Gordon reported. Bledsoe's cannon opened on the Yankee horsemen "as soon as our men had approached sufficiently near to distinguish them from the enemy." A Union Missourian remembered, "our brave boys flinched not but moved slowly on and preasantly a few shots were exchanged between small arms and the enemy fell back and abought the same time one of our batteries opened up on them and then comenced a great Skedadle and we followed and gave them Shell to their satisfaction." Trooper Petty of the Third Missouri Cavalry (U.S.) remembered the encounter in less grandiose terms, dismissing the entire action with one sentence: "When getting within two miles of Brownsville we encountered rebel pickets; they were charged and driven in; we soon shelled the rebs out of the place and occupied it." Gordon's troops lost one man killed and four captured "by their horses and mules falling with them" in this first contact with Davidson's troopers. As the Rebels fell back, Pvt. John Scott of the Seventh Missouri Cavalry (U.S.) made a significant contribution to the Little Rock campaign by capturing "the notorious guerrilla leader" Colonel Burbridge, whose Fourth Missouri Cavalry had been hindering Davidson's approach ever since the Yankees had crossed the St. Francis River. The former infantry commander would cool his heels in Federal prisons until the following spring.[38]

The Rebels retreated through Brownsville to a position on a second prairie some six miles west of their original position. The Yankees approached cautiously, pausing to shell the initial Confederate position and then a band of timber on the eastern border of the prairie, where the Southern horsemen reformed. Captain DeMuth of the

Eighth Missouri Cavalry (U.S.) remembered: "[W]e shelled him for an hour probably, when our regiment prepared to fight on foot. We went into the brush and searched all round for him, but could not find him, he gave us the slip." The Missourian added: "This is a part of the business that I do not like. We had to go into the brush, into places a rabbit could hardly squeeze through." On seeing the Rebel cavalry, the Union troops again moved to the attack. "'Here they come!' is again passed up the lines, and, as one column filed right and another left, in the most perfect order, with their banners gaily streaming in the wind, we could but admire their perfect discipline and soldierly bearing," Colonel Gordon wrote. When the Union cavalry was about halfway across the two-mile-wide prairie, Bell's battery "mischievously ambushed" the Second Missouri Cavalry (U.S.), also known as the Merrill Horse, a regiment mounted on white horses. This "was the signal for Captain Bledsoe, who sent crushing through their lines shell after shell, throwing them into the most beautiful confusion." John Newman Edwards colorfully recorded: "Merrill's White Horse brigade, that had acquired much fame in chasing citizens over the country in Missouri, proved itself very expert at this bastard kind of Cossack warfare. They advanced with wonderful impetuosity, and retreated with an impetuosity even superior to that of their advance whenever a shell exploded near them." Davidson ordered up a pair of batteries that then proceeded to throw "a shower of shells" into the Rebel lines, which Gordon claimed "fell harmless." DeMuth remembers this action thus: "We proceeded some farther, shelled him again, but cannot catch him." This ended the fighting at Brownsville, with the Rebels falling back to their works at Bayou Meto and the Yankees holding the battlefield, "very well satisfied with our days work." Nevertheless, Marmaduke's delaying action succeeded in slowing the Union advance as Davidson decided to wait on the infantry column.[39]

The initial Confederate plan had called for Marsh Walker to arrange his troops in a wooded area west of Brownsville, where Marmaduke would lure Davidson's horsemen into an ambush. Instead, Edwards wrote, "the main body of the command, under General Walker, was not disturbed by these small affairs of the rear-guard, but held its leisurely line of march during the day." Thomas Barb, who served in Dobbins's cavalry under Walker, wrote in his diary on August 25: "this morning we heard Marmaduke fireing on the feds with artillery. we saddled up and struck out across the Pararie and came very near being cut off. . . . went to within six miles of the Bridge on Bayou Meto and there formed and waited on Marmaduke to fall back." Marmaduke's perception that Walker had failed to support him in the skirmishing further fueled the anger that had been building in him since the failure of the attack on Battery A at Helena.[40]

The next morning the Confederates sent out scouts to watch for Union thrusts against their lines at Bayou Meto. Robert Newton's Fifth Arkansas Cavalry was ordered to Shallow Ford south of the Rebel cavalry's main lines, from which he "sent out small scouts upon all the roads on the east side of the bayou leading to the ford." One party, consisting of Lt. J. C. Barnes and eight men of Company A, some two miles past the bayou on the Wire Road encountered a Federal patrol, "who fled precipitously at his approach. He pursued them some distance, but was unable to overtake them." Beyond this encounter, none of Newton's parties located any curious Yankees and spent the rest of the twenty-sixth picketing the area around Brownsville. Colonel Jeffers also reported skirmishing with Union scouts along the Confederate right as Davidson probed the Rebel positions.[41]

While Newton was chasing Yankee patrols to the south, a force of the First Iowa Cavalry, Third Missouri Cavalry, and sections of Lovejoy's and Clarkson's batteries pressed up the Little Rock road to feel out the Rebels at Bayou Meto. "The enemy were found posted in force at a position about 9 miles beyond Brownsville, estimated by Colonel [J. M.] Glover, commanding, at 6,000 strong," Davidson reported. Glover's advance skirmishers made first contact, locating Rebel pickets about six miles from Brownsville and driving them back some two miles to entrenched positions about two miles east of Bayou Meto. "After a considerable artillery duel, I ordered Lovejoy to advance his section, in doing of which he had one cannoneer pierced through with solid shot and killed instantly, so well did the enemy have the range of the road," Glover reported. A swift reconnaissance led him to conclude that the Confederate position was more than he wanted to tackle with the force at hand, and the Yankees fell back to Brownsville. In addition to the unfortunate Union artilleryman, the engagement claimed the lives of three Confederates.[42]

On August 27 Davidson returned in force to confront the Confederate horsemen at Bayou Meto. John Edwards of Shelby's command succinctly described the bayou and its importance: "The Bayou Metre [*sic*] was a low, sluggish stream, with a miry bed, abrupt banks, and its sides fringed with a heavy growth of timber. It was difficult to cross, and presented the only water at which a command could conveniently camp after leaving Bayou Two Prairie." It was here that Marsh Walker's horsemen would make a stand and that Davidson's thirsty troops would face their first serious combat of the campaign.[43]

Glover's troops again had the advance, and with a battalion of the Tenth Illinois Cavalry leading as skirmishers, they began moving forward on the road to the Bayou Meto bridge. They first encountered Marmaduke's horsemen about five miles east of the span, and after "a brisk fire" the Rebels fell back about two miles. The Tenth Illinois again hit Confederate resistance at this new position, losing a lieutenant to Southern marksmen. Davidson then ordered Glover's entire brigade into action. The colonel placed his artillery in the center on the road. Two battalions of the Third Missouri Cavalry (U.S.) climbed from their horses to the right of the road to fight as infantry; six squadrons of the Tenth Illinois covered their right flank. A third battalion of the Third Missouri, joined by the hard-marching foot soldiers of the Thirty-second Iowa, comprised Glover's left. "In this order, with a heavy line of skirmishers in front, the brigade moved forward," the Union commander reported.[44]

Facing the approaching enemy cavalry, Marmaduke placed Shelby's Iron Brigade under B. Frank Gordon as his forward line above Reed's Bridge north of Bayou Meto. Marmaduke's own brigade, under Colonel Jeffers, formed below the bridge, along with Dobbins's regiment. The Confederates would contest the advancing Federals above the bridge but braced for a heated defense from behind the natural rampart of Bayou Meto. The Rebels' first line of defense consisted of some 125 dismounted troopers of Shelby's Brigade, detailed to Marmaduke that morning to serve as skirmishers and accompanied by the "little teaser" prairie guns of Bell's Battery. These troops watched the approaching Yankees as "they pushed forward their columns impetuously until, coming upon the main body of our skirmishers, a roar of musketry sent death crippling through their ranks, completely breaking up their lines for the time in dismay and confusion."[45]

This "dismay and confusion" did not last long. The advancing Yankees drove Gordon back to a fixed line of defenses north of Bayou Meto, which Glover described as "a very strong and elevated position, covered by extended rifle-pits on the left, where he made a more obstinate stand." A charge by the dismounted Third Missouri on Glover's right drove back the Rebels facing them and flanked the remaining Southerners out of their rifle pits, sending the entire force "in greatest disorder and confusion toward the Bayou Meto," pursued by additional Missouri troopers and the Iowa infantrymen. Davidson assisted them with a subterfuge by ordering drums beaten to convince the Confederates that they were facing concentrations of infantry in addition to cavalry. "The rebs made a charge on our battery and when this was done a regt. of Cav Stood ready with pistol and carbine," Francis Marion Emmons of the Seventh Missouri Cavalry (U.S.) wrote. "When they charged near enough these men with drums beat the charge and the rebs thought ten thousand infantry was on them when they turned and run our men fireing voley after voley and the Artillery using grape and canister pileing them in heaps After this the Genl Sat on his horse and laughed to see them run at the trick he played on them." Union troops on the left were "then thrown forward to the bayou, where we remained about three hours, getting an occasional shot at the enemy concealed on the other side." Thomas Barb of Dobbins's First Arkansas Cavalry wrote, "they come in such force that we had to leave on doble quick." The artillery was ordered up to shell the retreating Rebels, a bombardment that lasted around thirty minutes. Having foreseen the probability of falling back across Bayou Meto, Capt. John Mhoon, a Rebel engineer, had given Reed's Bridge "a thorough coating of tar and other inflammable material," John Edwards remembered, "and as the last of the rear-guard crossed it, the torch was applied."[46]

The Union horsemen suddenly noticed the smoke in the distance and realized that the Rebels were burning the only crossing of the steep-banked stream. Davidson ordered Lt. Col. Daniel Anderson and the First Iowa Cavalry, comprising Glover's reserve, to charge "in the face of a terrible fire of artillery and small-arms." The Iowans "went after them again, fighting in good earnest. 1st Batalion got in a very hot place," M. S. Andrews wrote with considerable understatement. Colonel Gordon watched as the Iowans, "perhaps thinking the 'frightened rebels in terror fled,' charged down the road in splendid style, as if to save the bridge; but it were better had many of them never been born. The dense cloud of smoke from the crackling, burning bridge, like sorrow's veil, hung between them and Bledsoe's battery, and when the head of their long lines had nearly reached the bridge, these noble old guns sent shell and shot, winged with fury, screaming and hissing up their lines, scattering the mangled fragments of men and horses like chaff before the wind." An Iowa historian recorded: "The charge was made with drawn sabers, in a most gallant manner, the troops rushing right up to the bridge under a heavy and destructive fire from the enemy's artillery and sharp-shooters." Thirty-seven of the horsemen fell dead or wounded. Lieutenant Colonel Anderson, whose horse was shot from under him, reported: "We reached the bridge, but not in time to save it; it was already enveloped in flames. . . . I then dismounted the command and went forward on foot. Never have I seen a greater coolness of courage displayed. Not a man flinched from performing his whole duty as a brave and loyal soldier. When I had ascertained the position of the enemy by severe skirmishing half an hour, I withdrew under cover of the hill and out of range of their guns." Davidson's dismounted troopers continued forward, forming a line along Bayou Meto to fire at the entrenched Rebels on the other side. Missourian Sam Baird, dodging Confederate artillery fire, took shelter in a log house. "The first thing I did was to search the house, but I found nobody in it," he remembered years later. "But, on the table were biscuit, applesauce and buttermilk. I soon found out what they tasted like, for I was very hungry."[47]

Glover's men would attempt several more advances against the entrenched Rebels at Bayou Meto, most likely in an effort to recover the dozens of wounded Iowans of Anderson's regiment, but the remainder of the day's fighting would be done primarily by the artillery. The colonel selected a position from which his guns could relieve the now-dismounted First Iowa. "They opened with twelve or sixteen guns," according to John Edwards. "Marmaduke's artillery, though inferior in strength, replied as promptly and as vigorously. For nearly an hour the ring of musketry along the line was incessant, and the deep-toned artillery lent its voice to swell the diapason of harmonious discord." The Yankee "shot and shell ripped and roared through the forest, tearing the trees around the battery into fragments, and plowing up the earth in the most approved demoniac style but all without avail," Gordon wrote. "The long, rakish-looking pirate rifles [of Bledsoe's Battery] seemed to shout in proud defiance, as with great precision they sent tearing through their ranks their iron missiles, driving them from position to position."[48]

Marmaduke ordered Lt. Charlie Bell's small battery of prairie guns to a position near the bridge, "in open view of the enemy, and in point-blank range of their guns." The Union artillery did not miss the opportunity, shattering the unit, killing Bell and seriously wounding one of Marmaduke's aides before the cannon were withdrawn to safety. In retaliation the general determined to punish the Yankee artillery "and for that purpose massed his six guns in a commanding position and opened a vigorous fire upon them." Lt. R. A. Collins, who commanded an artillery battery in Shelby's brigade, had "crossed the bayou and worked his way from point to point, despite the fire of their sharp-shooters, until he had thoroughly reconnoitered their position." As the Rebel guns opened fire, "by a natural impulse the men along the entire line on both sides, in a great measure, ceased operations, and employed themselves in watching the progress and results of the duel." The artillerists used Collins's reconnaissance to deadly effect, firing with precision on the more numerous Union guns. As the disconcerted Yankee cannoneers flinched under the accurate fire from Collins and Bledsoe, "they entirely lost their coolness and precision, and sent their shells recklessly through the tops of the trees, destroying much foliage and frightening the wild birds terribly." Illinois cavalryman Charles Field, who with his comrades was supporting the artillery, remembered that "the enemy's battery had pretty good range on us and we had to get on our feet and doge cannonballs. . . . We could see them and would run to the right or left and they would roll down to a rail fence some ten rods in the rear and knock the rails out. It was very lively for some time."[49]

Perhaps the best hope for a Union victory was on their left, where one hundred men of Young's Battalion of Marmaduke's brigade held the extreme right of the Confederate line, covering a crossing of Bayou Meto that "entirely turned the position." These men, under Maj. George W. C. Bennett, resisted repeated attempts by Companies D and F, First Iowa Cavalry to effect a crossing. Bennett "informed Marmaduke . . . that he was heavily pressed, and feared he could not hold his ground," John Edwards recalled. "Marmaduke replied that he could spare him no men, and that he must beat back the enemy and make good his position. Bennett replied that he would do it, and did do it." Had Davidson or Glover ordered some of the Iowans or Missourians idly sniping at Rebels across the bayou on the Union left to join in a concerted attack against Bennett's troops, they may have been able to turn Marmaduke's flank and drive the Rebels from the field. Yet this was not to be, and the best opportunity that day for a Union victory passed.[50]

As the combatant artillerists hammered away at each other, Glover discovered "a strong force of the enemy on this side of the bayou, on the right of our line." The Tenth Illinois was given the task of forcing this rump remnant of Marmaduke's force—inadvertently cut off when the rest of the Rebels fell back across Reed's Bridge—from their position, which they did, "putting them across the bayou after a very hot contest." After skirmishing until late in the evening, Glover's exhausted troops were ordered back to Brownsville, "getting into camp at midnight." "The sun went down smoke-begrimed, red-faced, and furious," Gordon concluded. Despite their tactical victory at Bayou Meto, the Confederates were ordered to retreat that night to within five miles of Little Rock, giving up the last substantial line of defenses east of the considerable works built northeast of the capital.[51]

Federal casualties totaled seven killed and thirty-eight wounded, most from the ill-fated charge of the First Iowa Cavalry. Confederate losses were undisclosed, but at least two officers were killed and numerous soldiers wounded.

The steady Yankee advance toward Little Rock left the Rebel defenders jittery. James Wallace of Missouri wrote on August 27, "the whole command [is] ordered into the ditches, our Battalion are deployed in front about 1/2 mile from the works ready to meet the enemy's advance which hourly we expect to see." Surgeon Junius Bragg noted on August 23 that many Little Rock citizens were preparing to flee to Texas, including former governor Henry Rector, who "doubtless . . . thinks the Yankees might handle him a little roughly if they were to catch him." Two days later Bragg reported: "[A]ll government property is being removed from town, and they are not stopping with it this side of Arkadelphia. . . . This is a precautionary measure, and I think a very wise one, because we are not in a condition to lose such things, and they would probably be lost if left at L.R."[52]

For several days after the action at Bayou Meto, the two armies restricted their activities primarily to scouting. On August 29 Davidson sent Col. Washington F. Geiger, commanding a battalion each of the Merrill Horse and Eighth Missouri Cavalry (U.S.) and a section of

Lovejoy's battery, on an uneventful trip down Shallow Ford Road to the left of the Union forces. The next day, August 30, John F. Ritter's brigade and Capt. Gustave Stange's mountain howitzers took the same road beyond Bayou Meto, encountering Colonel Newton's Fifth Arkansas Cavalry. After driving back the Union advance, about forty Rebels under Maj. John Bull encountered the bulk of Ritter's force concealed behind the embankment of the Memphis and Little Rock tracks. "In short time, being reinforced from Shallow Ford by cavalry and artillery, the enemy commenced advancing from his position behind the railroad," Newton reported. "Bull resisted his advance almost at every step, his men behaving with admirable courage and steadiness." Ordering all of his men with long-range rifles to snipe at the advancing Union cavalry, Newton began a fighting withdrawal in the face of Stange's cannon and Ritter's larger force. Around 2:00 P.M., after five hours of fighting, the colonel requested reinforcements from Marsh Walker. About one mile from Ashley's Mills and a river crossing at Terry's Ferry, he set an ambush with shotgun-wielding Southerners under Capt. P. J. Rollow. Advance Federal scouts obligingly rode into the trap, and "the enemy, not willing to run onto the ambuscade a second time, although my men had been withdrawn from there, commenced sending heavy bodies of dismounted cavalry to my right and left." Fearing envelopment, Newton fell back another three-quarters of a mile to Hicks's plantation to again contest Ritter's pursuit, "but he advanced upon me no further." The Federals fell back to Shallow Ford and established a heavy picket there. Davidson's report only briefly mentioned the day-long combat with the Fifth Arkansas. "They were driven, with sharp skirmishing, by Colonel Ritter, 8 miles, and until the ground became totally unsuitable for the action of cavalry; the enemy leaving 9 of their killed upon the field. Ritter's loss was 1 captain and 4 men wounded." Newton continued skirmishing and scouting between Shallow Ford and Hicks's plantation for several days, clashing with Federal scouts at Mrs. Ewell's place on August 31. On September 1 he was ordered to move his regiment to Ashley's Mills, which he did the next day, leaving a skeleton force at Hicks's. He remained at the mills for the next two days.[53]

Back at DeValls Bluff, the arrival of Col. James M. True's reserve brigade on August 30 allowed Steele to advance the rest of his infantry west in support of Davidson's horsemen two days later. The general reported that DeValls Bluff was left "in such a state of defense that the convalescents and a small detail left there were deemed sufficient to hold it against any force the enemy would be likely send against it." The soldiers continued to suffer from the hellish Arkansas summer. An Iowa chronicler wrote that "it was so hot that many were sun-struck on the march. There were not enough ambulances to carry those who gave out, so that they would load up, travel ahead, leave the sick by the road-side, and return for others. By repeating this operation, the men unable to walk were by turn conveyed in the ambulances and left to suffer in the broiling sun through the greater part of two days." As the tired foot soldiers joined their mounted comrades, Frank Emmons of the Seventh Missouri Cavalry noticed, "the Regts are very Small Some not numbering more than 150 & 200 There is one company of Seven men."[54]

The bulk of Steele's infantry arrived at Brownsville on September 2, and the commander of the Arkansas expedition began making his final plans for the capture of Little Rock. With True's reserve brigade, the Federals' aggregate strength stood at between 14,500 and 15,000 men with forty-nine cannon. Price's total effective command consisted of some 7,749 men, most of whom manned the trenches on the high ground north of the Arkansas River. The Yankees' approach panicked the slaveowning Confederate citizens of central Arkansas, who now fled wholesale to the southwest. Missouri's Confederate governor, Thomas C. Reynolds, noted on September 4, "the roads are crowded by fugitives both from the Washita & Arkansas rivers, and from N.E. Arkansas; on the road from N. Louisiana to Washington, I passed each day some five or six families with from 200 to 300 negroes on their way to Texas. The road from Arkadelphia to Washington presents a similar appearance."[55]

Steele spent the next two days scouting out the best approach to Little Rock. He quickly dismissed the road on the south side of Bayou Meto, which "passed through a section impracticable for any military operations—swamp, timber, and entanglements of vines and under-growth—and was commanded by the enemy's works." He ordered Davidson to swing around the Confederate left and explore the roads there, while Brigadier General Rice's Third Division diverted Confederate attention with a demonstration against Bayou Meto. The Union infantry passed through Marmaduke's advance positions of August 27; following the hellish march through eastern Arkansas, they were spoiling for a fight. But after spending the night in the former Confederate positions, they were ordered back to Brownsville. "Our men growled at having to come back," Capt. Thomas Stevens of the Twenty-eighth Wisconsin reported. "Nine out of ten would have rather gone forward to a fight—they hate to march so far for nothing, over these dusty prairies, half choked with thirst." Charles Musser observed that the Twenty-ninth Iowa was equally upset: "I never Saw a Set of men So mad in my life. it would make the blood run cold to hear some of them curse the Officer in command. when we arived at the picket lines, the men that were there would ask 'how far have you been out?' The first answer would be 'go to h—ll' or Some other like answer. I guess they thought our command was a crabbed set of men." Meanwhile, Davidson's scouts revealed that "the great length to which it would increase our line of communication with our base rendered it impracticable for us to attack the enemy on his left flank." The Yankee cavalry did capture a load of Confederate mail at Austin, Trooper Petty of the Third Missouri noted, writing that it included "letters of importance in regard to the movements of the enemy, besides many spicy love billets from rebel gallants in the army to their ducks at home." Steele ultimately decided to take the Shallow Ford Road via Ashley's Mills to the Arkansas River and Little Rock, attacking east of the Rebel fortifications.[56]

Price's Confederates, meanwhile, continued to strengthen the earthworks on the north side of the river. William Hoskins of the Third Missouri Artillery wrote, "Artillery men [are] hard at work all day to save their [own] lives—every man is working for his own intrust & this is the way to fortify." On September 4 he recorded, "Our First section crossed over & comenced preparing forts for themselves—we now have 26 pieces on our lines." An Arkansas soldier told his parents of "substantial earth works, being fronted by a ditch near ten feet deep and about the same width, and calculated to withstand artillery or anything else," adding, "it would be a source of great joy to us if we could give them an effectual repulse." The Rebels would learn, however, that Frederick Steele was less likely than Theophilus Holmes to obligingly dash his army against a well-entrenched enemy.[57]

As the Federal army crossed Bayou Meto at Shallow Ford on September 6, Confederate cavalry commanders Marsh Walker and John Marmaduke culminated their long-simmering feud with the last duel fought in Arkansas. The bad blood between the two generals originated during the July 4 attack on Helena, when Marmaduke contended that Walker's failure to support him adequately on his left caused the failure of his assault on Battery A. The Missourian's ire was exacerbated during the fighting at Brownsville on September 25, when he felt Walker again had failed to come to his support. Marmaduke's patience was exhausted during the combat at Bayou Meto, where he contended that his superior officer had ignored repeated requests to leave his headquarters in the rear of the Confederate positions for conferences on the firing line. Following the action at Reed's Bridge, Marmaduke asked either to be removed from under Walker's command or to have his resignation from the Confederate army accepted; Price approved the transfer. On hearing that his actions had been censured, Walker at first "only laughed." But that laughter turned to anger when he heard that his courage was called into question. A flurry of letters between the generals led on September 5 to a formal challenge. Around midnight on the fifth, Price learned of the impending duel and sent orders to both men "to remain closely at his headquarters for the next twenty-four hours." Walker never received the order; Marmaduke ignored it.[58]

They met at the Godfrey LeFevre plantation, about seven miles below Little Rock on the north side of the Arkansas River, arriving before dawn. Their seconds selected the location for the ritual combat, pacing off the distance and ensuring that neither general would have the advantage of the rising sun at his back. Each held a six-shot, regulation-model 1851 Navy Colt revolver. At the command to fire, both loosed a single shot with no effect. Marmaduke immediately fired again, striking Walker in the side. As the Tennessean fell backward, his pistol fired harmlessly. Using Marmaduke's wagon, they transported Walker to the Cates residence in Little Rock, where the general lingered until the next evening. As he lay dying, Walker asked an aide to "see General Marmaduke and tell him that before taking the sacrament I forgive him with all my heart, and I want my friends to forgive him and neither prosecute nor persecute him." Lucius Walker was buried in Little Rock's Mount Holly Cemetery with full military honors on September 8.[59]

On hearing that the duel had proceeded, an angry Price ordered Marmaduke placed under arrest. But on the appeal of Marmaduke and the generals of his division, and "feeling . . . the great inconvenience and danger of an entire change of cavalry commanders in the very presence of the enemy, and when a general engagement was imminent," he released his fellow Missourian and restored him to command of the Confederate cavalry. The duel did nothing to improve Confederate morale as Steele's host threatened the Arkansas capital. Silas Turnbo of the Twenty-seventh Arkansas Infantry condemned it, writing that "this was an unfortunate and lamentable affair, for we had neither officers nor men to spare in throwing away their lives in settling differences by fighting duels. . . . It was disheartening to our soldiers and gave encouragement to the enemy." Another memoirist wrote that "this act threw a gloom over the whole army, and threatened for a while to make a disruption in our forces inasmuch as the duelists had warm friends and adherents." A Federal officer concluded that "no doubt the envy and jealousy between Walker and Marmaduke gave us an easier victory at Little Rock."[60]

On September 6 Archibald Dobbins assumed command of Walker's cavalry division, consisting of Dobbins's Arkansas brigade (now under Colonel Newton and including Newton's Fifth Arkansas), Carter's Texas brigade, Alf Johnson's Spy Company, and Denson's squadron of Louisiana horsemen. The bulk of the Texans, however, were on picket duty and scattered across southeast Arkansas.[61]

Steele began his advance the next day, hitting Newton's cavalry at Ashley's Mills by way of Shallow Ford Road. Francis Emmons of the Seventh Missouri Cavalry laconically observed: "we march to the Ark River ten miles South of Little Rock with Some Skirmishing and considerable Shelling we Succeeded in driving them across the River." The Confederates gave ground stubbornly but were forced steadily back by the overwhelming numbers of Union horsemen. By 10:00 A.M. on September 7, the Rebel cavalry fled across the Arkansas River eight miles below Little Rock "without molestation from the enemy, who ceased the pursuit as soon as they reached the river." The Confederates lost one killed, three wounded, and two captured, including Dobbins's brigade adjutant, whose papers provided "some important information." Steele spent the next two days reconnoitering the area, repairing the road to Bayou Meto and consolidating his forces. He still suffered from a lengthy sick list, with more than seven hundred men and officers too ill to fight. Two brigades—True's infantry and Ritter's cavalry—were detailed to guard the supplies and the sick at Brownsville. Dobbins reported "continual skirmishing between my scouts and the enemy, and also constant firing across the river" during this period.[62]

By September 9 Steele had determined his strategy. Rather than go head to head with Price's strongly entrenched infantry on the high ground on the north side of the river, he would divide his army in the face of the enemy, sending Davidson's cavalry across the river to flank the Rebels out of their works while the Yankee infantry moved west on the north bank of the Arkansas. It was a bold plan by a clever general, and it hinged on a swift and successful crossing by Davidson's horsemen. Dobbins, holding the south bank of the Arkansas, was not in an enviable situation. His thin screen of horsemen was "very much scattered" in trying to cover the area between Little Rock and Buck's Ford, a twelve-mile stretch of river with a dozen fords. On the evening of the ninth, a local citizen reported to the Rebel cavalryman that he had seen the Union army "to be 30,000 strong," an inflated estimate to be sure but far outnumbering the approximately 1,200 Confederate horsemen holding the south bank. Another Rebel officer, having received similar intelligence from a sympathetic citizen, reported that "the ball opens tomorrow."[63]

Steele backed his force with guile. Although he intended to cross closer to Little Rock, he sent a force down to Buck's Ford "and built up camp-fires within sight of the ford." Dobbins hastily ordered some two hundred bales of cotton rushed to the area to create impromptu fortifications and planted J. H. Pratt's artillery battery to cover the crossing. The First Missouri Cavalry (U.S.) under John Ritter, supported by Lt. K. S. Clarkson's battery, saw the cotton bales "two deep, so as to have a raking fire of the ford," on the morning of the tenth and sent a company of horsemen out to draw Rebel fire and ascertain whether they faced infantry or cavalry. Charles Field of the Thirteenth Illinois Cavalry remembered that "there was a desperate cannonading for some time. The enemy got range of us first." As Pratt's cannon and Confederate sharpshooters hammered the Yankees, Field reported, several artilleryman were injured and one cannon was disabled, dragged out of range by the Illinois horsemen. Finally, he wrote, "I saw the Captain (Clarkson) sight all four of the guns and he said: 'Now fire all at once.'" This concentrated fire found the range of the cotton-bale fort, "setting the cotton on fire and driving the enemy from the place." Because of the losses from Rebel fire, Clarkson "had not enough men to man the guns," Field remembered. "Some of our boys had to help them. It was amusing to see green cavalrymen load those guns." This delaying action, which lasted about two hours, held up part of the thin gray line on the south side of the Arkansas as Steele effected his main crossing three miles upstream. The Union general had selected his true crossing point well. Although there were a dozen fordable locations below Little Rock, Steele chose to build a pontoon bridge at a point where the Arkansas River made a horseshoe bend, allowing him to place his batteries in positions that would enable them to concentrate converging fire on any Rebels who tried to contest the crossing.[64]

Late on the evening of September 9, Davidson gathered his cavalry commanders at his headquarters at Ashley's Mills and gave them their orders. "It was announced by him that early the next morning the whole available force of the army would move; the infantry, under General Steele, to assault the enemy's strong works on the north side of the river, while our cavalry division was to cross the Arkansas River 8 miles below, and move to the capture of Little Rock," Colonel Glover reported. "He stated that no ordinary obstacle was to be allowed to defeat the purpose of the division; that we were to make a dash upon the city and capture it, and either hold or destroy the enemy's bridges, though it cost us one of our regiments." As the meeting of Union officers broke up, elsewhere Confederate gunner William Hoskins recorded that the Rebels also were making preparations, writing in his diary that "troops [were] aroused at the hour of 3 this morning—horses harnessed and hitched up redy for action—all in rediness for the enemy at eny time—infantry pickets sent out—enemy reported to be advancing—great preparations are being made—some are fortifying—others are diging well."[65]

Infantry troops silently filed into positions on the north side of the Arkansas as engineers began to slap together a pontoon bridge across the river. The Fifth, Eleventh, and Twenty-fifth Ohio batteries and a section of the Second Missouri Light Artillery took up positions covering the laboring pioneers and the wooded salient south of the Arkansas. Yankee horsemen under Glover and Merrill massed out of sight, ready to rush across the river and exploit the bridgehead once established. Col. Christopher C. Andrews of the Third Minnesota, emplaced to the right of the Eleventh Ohio Battery, ordered the best sharpshooters from each of his companies "to get into position under cover, and well secluded from the enemy. This arrangement met the cordial approval of the division commander."[66]

At 3:00 A.M. the harried Dobbins, "reports from scouts having been very unsatisfactory and conflicting," rode from Buck's Ford to "ascertain, if possible, what movement the enemy was making." On seeing construction of a pontoon bridge under way, the colonel ordered C. B. Etter's battery "to occupy the point opposite to where the enemy was engaged in cutting down the bank, and to open fire on it, which it did." Maj. John Bull and a party of sharpshooters were sent to support the artillery. Etter opened fire shortly after daylight, and "his second shot took effect, clearing the bridge of workmen." The Rebel guns were answered with a maelstrom of fire from the waiting Union batteries. "Before the smoke of the first discharge of their guns had scarcely reached the tops of the trees, which concealed their movements, twenty guns belched forth from their Conceal-ment on the north side of the river a stream of shell into the midst of their battery," Capt. Julius Hadley, commanding Davidson's artillery, reported. Second Division commander Col. Adolph Engelmann wrote with satisfaction that "after firing no more than 1/2 dozen Rounds the secesh had to withdraw, our Artillery being too numerous, and the Batteries of my Division in particular firing with great precision." One unit, the Eleventh Ohio, reported firing about one hundred rounds during the "short but decisive engagement." Dobbins ordered a piece of Pratt's Battery to assist Etter's hard-pressed cannoneers, "but the fire from the enemy's batteries was so terrific that they were unable to hold their position, and, after being engaged about two hours, were compelled to retire, leaving [behind] one piece of Etter's battery, which I had brought off afterwards by the cavalry."[67]

The pontoon bridge was completed about 10:00 A.M. As the For-tieth Iowa and the Forty-third Illinois Infantry regiments prepared to dash across the bridge and sandbar into the screen of trees across the river, Engelmann ordered the Eleventh Ohio Battery and two rifled pieces of the Fifth Ohio to shell the wooded area after "great masses of the enemy were seen moving on the opposite shore." With the Fortieth Iowa in the lead, the two regiments "advanced with alacrity across the half mile of sand" to the tree line. Willie Hale of the Third Minnesota watched breathlessly as "the 40th Iowa advanced a half mile to the wood most gallantly in perfect silence. Withholding our breath expecting to see the sheet of flame leap out of the woods that would send many a brave fellow to his long home—O! twas thrilling! *But* nary reb was there—they were *out-witted.*" Capt. Gustave Stange, with eight howitzers, including Lovejoy's battery, was next across the river, sent to support the infantry and afterward accompany Glover's horsemen on their advance up the south bank of the Arkansas. Glover sent two squadrons of the First Iowa Cavalry across the bridge as the infantry troops spread out along the levee, securing the Union beachhead. As the rest of Glover's Second Brigade clattered across, Colonel Merrill received permission to cross the First Brigade at a ford above the bridge.[68]

With the successful crossing of the Arkansas River, Davidson's division moved toward Little Rock from the river's southern side while Steele ordered his foot soldiers toward the formidable Rebel fortifications. At this point in the campaign, Price reported 7,749 men of all arms present for duty, but only about 1,250 faced the Yankee cavalry while the remaining 6,500 held the trenches against the Federal infantry. Steele fielded 10,477 men "present for duty" and fifty-seven pieces of artillery for the final assault on Little Rock. On hearing that Union troops were crossing the Arkansas, Price ordered James Tappan's infantry brigade to Dobbins's support and sent Marmaduke's division south of the river, with Marmaduke to take command of all cavalry forces. In the earthworks north of the river, Missouri Rebel William Hoskins recorded, "we are all redy now for the enemy with rifle-musket & pick in hand—redy to give another stand."[69]

Glover's Second Brigade, as in earlier actions, formed the van of the Union advance, fronted by skirmishers of the First Iowa. They were followed by more Iowans, Stange's battery of Missouri artillery, the Tenth Illinois Cavalry, and the Third Missouri Cavalry. At about noon "the enemy opened a heavy volley of musketry, soon repeated, accompanied with artillery." Dobbins's cavalry contested the Union advance but were driven back five miles, "fighting all the time." When within a mile of Bayou Fourche, Dobbins ordered Newton and about five hundred men of his brigade to form along the bayou, "while I remained and held the enemy in check." He also ordered the troops facing the Union feint at Buck's Ford to join him at Bayou Fourche in a last-ditch effort to defend the capital. Trooper Barb of the First Arkansas Cavalry was among the grayclad defenders at Bayou Fourche, writing in his diary, "we started for little Rock about 11 o'clock stoped on Bayou and dismounted and succeeded in driving them back once captureing a good many horses and some prisoners." The ill-considered duel of September 6 now claimed yet another Confederate cavalry commander. When Marmaduke arrived to take command of the Rebel defenses, Dobbins refused to take orders from the man who had killed his commander, Marsh Walker. Marmaduke placed the Arkansian under arrest, making Col. Robert C. Newton the third officer to command Walker's division in four days. As with Marmaduke before him, Dobbins was soon released from arrest and returned to command of his troops.[70]

Glover continued to push forward, driving Major Bull's screen of Rebels before him until reaching the point where Fourche Bayou feeds into the Arkansas River, about six miles below Little Rock. The road forked there, with one branch going northwest and the other southwest, separated by the bayou. The area to the north was heavily wooded, while that to the south was planted in corn. The cornfield was bordered at its western terminus by a sharp southward turn of the bayou, with a levee located on the bayou's far bank through which the southern road passed. "The ground," Merrill reported, "was very difficult to reconnoiter." Rising dust clouds to the southwest indicated the presence of a heavy Rebel force, so Glover sent the First Iowa Cavalry with a section of howitzers to the left along the levee road while the Tenth Illinois with Lovejoy's battery deployed to the right. The colonel warned his Iowans to watch their left flank, which was unsupported; he held the Third Missouri Cavalry (U.S.) to support them. Forming against Glover was Marmaduke's division, commanded by Col. William Jeffers of the Eighth Missouri Cavalry (C.S.). Jeffers placed Colton Greene's regiment on his right, the Eighth Missouri and Burbridge's regiment in the center, and Young's battalion on the left, anchored on the Arkansas River.[71]

Meanwhile, Lewis Merrill, heading the First Brigade, proceeded up the bank of the Arkansas to Glover's right. As he heard firing from the troops ahead of him, Merrill sent the Seventh Missouri Cavalry (U.S.) in support of four pieces of the Twenty-fifth Ohio Battery, which was firing on the Rebels from the river's sandy beach; this effectively removed the Seventh Missouri from the remainder of the day's action. Merrill was ordered to take the southern road across Fourche Bayou. He dismounted the Eighth Missouri Cavalry (U.S.), supported by a

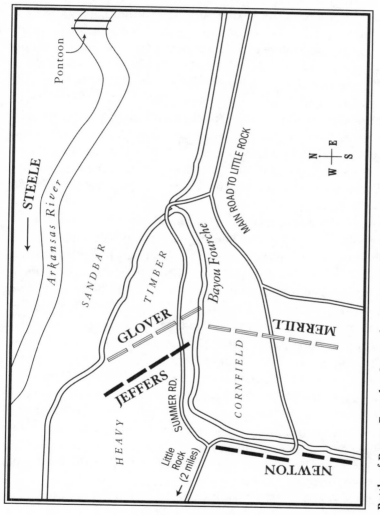

Battle of Bayou Fourche, September 10, 1863. Federal cavalrymen fought their way past Confederate horsemen at Bayou Fourche to capture Little Rock. *Map by Kirk Montgomery.*

section of the Twenty-fifth Ohio, and ordered them to feel out the
enemy on the road ahead. He held the Second Missouri Cavalry (U.S.),
his own Merrill Horse, in reserve. This road was the same taken by the
First Iowa, and the Eighth Missouri, under Col. W. F. Geiger, soon
found the Iowans skirmishing briskly with the enemy. Part of the First
Iowa, formed in line of battle in a cornfield to the right of the road,
had "one of their guidons . . . incautiously exposed near the road, and
a hot fire of shells and spherical case was drawn upon them from the
enemy's battery, posted at the dam across the bayou." Newton placed
most of his troops along the levee on the west side of the bayou to
oppose Merrill. The Confederate colonel placed Maj. Sam Corley's
regiment of dismounted Arkansas cavalry (Dobbins's regiment) and
Etter's Battery to the left of the levee road, with Pratt's Battery commanding the road and Bull's regiment, Denson's Louisiana squadron,
and Morgan's Texas cavalry on the right to protect the artillery and
guard against a flanking movement. They were later bolstered by the
arrival of Tappan's infantry.[72]

Glover was actively engaged on the Union right. The Tenth Illinois,
under Lt. Col. James Stuart, had barely entered the dense woods
along the northern road when they encountered Jeffers's mounted
Rebel skirmishers. His advance companies charged "to a point where
a deadly fire was poured in upon him from an overwhelming force of
the enemy, dismounted and in ambush." The Union horsemen fell
back in confusion, breaking up the balance of the regiment, which
was moving up in support. Glover had ordered Lovejoy's Missouri
battery to support the Tenth Illinois from its right but discovered the
guns had become the targets of the Rebels as the Illinois horsemen
tried to straighten their lines. "I repeatedly ordered them back, and,
by the assistance of Lieutenant-Colonel Stuart, who here received a
severe contusion on the top of the head by a bullet, held the cavalry
as long as possible to save the section, but in vain, as no one at the
howitzers would obey orders." Gustave Stange, who had arrived with
his battery, was ordered to fire on the Rebels threatening Lovejoy, but
"instead of obeying orders, he fell back, and even failed to fire from
where he was, which was an excellent range for grape and canister."
Stuart ordered the artillerists "to run [the guns] out by hand, but
they all got under the gun carriages and did not obey." Jeffers's and
Burbridge's horsemen rushed upon Lovejoy's hapless battery, "which
we captured, on the field." As the Rebels swarmed around their prize,

sixteen-year-old John Moore of the Third Missouri Cavalry (C.S.) "was the first man to reach the artillery, and jumped on it, waving his hat as the Yankees ran away."[73]

The loss of Lovejoy's Battery led Glover to change his tactics. "I now determined to fight [the enemy] in his own way, and brought up the Tenth Illinois and Third Missouri, and dismounted them to fight on foot, in three lines," with skirmishers fronting the Union line of battle, and a second line following in a solid row between the bayou and the river. Needing "to combine all my forces to vanquish a vaunting and defiant foe," Glover brought the First Iowa from its position with Merrill's troops to provide mounted support and to exploit any breaks in the enemy lines. Presently Glover thought he saw an opportunity to bag the entire Confederate force facing him. The colonel wrote in his after-action report that he met with Merrill and "explained . . . the nature and connections of the road, and suggested to him to send up his brigade . . . and fall on the rear of the enemy by way of the levee, and I would drive back and capture his whole force. The result seemed to me inevitable, if this movement on the left should be made." Merrill reported no such meeting, writing after the battle that he learned that the First Iowa had moved to the right only after sending for the horsemen and being "informed that they had been ordered out and had moved to the rear, by whose orders I could not learn, as the order was not given by me." In any case, the First Brigade's leader soon found himself far too busy to participate in any neat encirclement actions. After learning that the First Iowa was gone, Merrill was further confounded by a burst of artillery fire to his left rear. Fearing an enemy battery had slipped in behind him, the Missourian was relieved to discover "a section of Stange's howitzers, of whose presence on my line of attack I now learned for the first time."[74]

Merrill's thin line of skirmishers pushed forward. The colonel soon discovered Pratt's 12-pounder howitzers behind the levee across the bayou, commanding the road. An additional field piece was firing across the stream from his right. "These guns were supported by a strong line of skirmishers on the west side of the bayou, and a weak line in the same cornfield in which my line was advancing." Colonel Newton, whose men confronted Merrill, later reported: "The enemy in small parties came up in my front so as to be distinctly visible . . . but I directed Pratt to reserve his fire until they advanced in some force and came into easy range, when he was to ply them vigorously with grape and canister.". The Second Brigade also advanced, "and in a few moments a terrific and deadly fire prevailed along the whole line from friend and foe" as the Tenth Illinois and the Third Missouri (U.S.) moved forward on foot. Bayou Fourche meandered to the left ahead of the Federals, leading Glover to bring up part of the First Iowa to fill out his center and left and prevent a possible flanking movement. Merrill ordered up a section of the Twenty-fifth Ohio Battery to support Geiger's Eighth Missouri Cavalry (U.S.) to the left of the road, as two squadrons of the Merrill Horse filled out his line to the right. But Captain Hadley, Davidson's artillery chief, ordered the cannon withdrawn to the left and began a long-range fire on the Rebel battery behind the levee. "No apparent effect was produced by his fire except to explode one shell among our own skirmishers," Merrill reported later. The colonel ordered the cannon to the rear, "where I could use it in case what seemed to be an effort to turn my right flank should prove successful."[75]

Newton and his Rebels watched as the First Brigade advanced through the cornfield. "Pratt opened with his two guns and quickly drove them back," the colonel wrote. "Moving to our right, they attempted to force a crossing of the bayou, but were met and handsomely driven back by Bull's command, assisted by Pratt's trusty guns, which continued to rake them with canister and grape until Fletcher's field, which was immediately in my front, was cleared of them." Capt. Albert DeMuth of the Eighth Missouri Cavalry (U.S.) was on the receiving end of that fire. "We dismounted and proceeded about a quarter of a mile when the grape and canister came rattling among us like hail, one man belonging to company 'L' was shot in the stomach right in front of me. We then got into a corn field. Here they gave us *Hail Columby*—for a short time, we squatting down in the weeds and grass as close to mother earth as possible, but nevertheless the enemy's shells bursted immediately over us wounding several of our men."[76]

The terrain, marked by tall corn, heavy timber, and a deep bayou separating the two Union brigades, caused confusion for the Yankees. Knowing there was a heavy Confederate force facing Glover to his right, Merrill sent "all that I could spare of Merrill's Horse" to ascertain the location of the Second Division's left. He soon heard a heavy fire to his right-rear and was informed that his skirmishers were "flanked by the enemy on the right, and that they were pouring in a

Col. Robert C. Newton became the third officer to command Brig. Gen. L. Marsh Walker's cavalry division after Brig. Gen. John S. Marmaduke fatally wounded Walker in a duel and Col. Archibald Dobbins refused to serve under the Missourian's command. *Courtesy Arkansas History Commission.*

heavy discharge of grape and canister from the gun on his right and of musketry from his right rear." Simultaneously Geiger reported that the Rebel artillery had found the range of the Eighth Missouri (U.S.) and was bombarding them. The harried First Brigade commander ordered the last three squadrons of his reserve to the right to prevent a flanking maneuver. "Already [having sent] a staff officer and then an orderly, and having no staff left, I gave Colonel Geiger orders to hold everything as it was, and went myself to examine the bayou on the other side, and find, if possible, what Glover's position was with reference to mine." Merrill's personal reconnaissance was enlightening, but his report does not reflect whether he was angry or relieved by what he found. The colonel discovered that Bayou Fourche was full of water—not dry as he had been led to believe—thus eliminating much chance of a flanking movement from his right. He also found that "the left of Glover's line of skirmishers was very considerably in rear of my right, and was overshooting the enemy into my line." What he had feared was an effort to turn his right was actually friendly fire. With his flanks secured, Merrill "immediately sent an order to the whole of my line to move forward and drive the enemy from his position. . . . The line moved forward as directed, driving the enemy from the corn-field and across the bayou."⁷⁷

At about 1:00 P.M. Shelby's Iron Brigade, under Colonel Thompson, belatedly arrived on the field, and one of the benefits of Steele's risky plan to split his command was realized. Thompson "formed in line of battle in an open field [behind Jeffers's embattled Rebels on the Confederate left]; but the enemy, running up their batteries on the opposite side of the river, opened an enfilading fire, which swept up and through our lines in a most unsatisfactory manner, compelling us to change our positions every few moments, and without being able to go return the fire with any effect."⁷⁸

On the north side of the bayou, Glover's Second Brigade advanced steadily through the timber against stiff Confederate resistance. "We failed of any co-operation of Colonel Merrill's brigade on the north side of the bayou," Glover reported later. "With small-arms alone did we contend with an enemy four times our number, supported and encouraged by a battery of artillery, which sent a steady hail of solid shot, grape, and canister among our ranks." On reaching the point where the north and south roads met, Glover found no sign of Merrill's troops. He immediately sent three squadrons to the left through a cornfield, which "unmasked Colonel Merrill's brigade by driving the enemy in disorder and capturing a caisson filled with ammunition, and 6 mules." Like Glover, Union artillery chief Julius Hadley faulted Merrill's cautious approach. "I am of the firm conviction that had the advance of the left of our line been as vigorous as that of the right, this battery and a large portion of its support could not have escaped capture." Merrill blamed ignorance of the "topography of the battle-ground" for his failure to support Glover's advance, especially when the First Brigade could have poured a flanking fire into Jeffers's defenders. "The weakness of my force prevented me from learning earlier in the action that the bayou was impracticable below as well as above the dam, a knowledge that would have freed me from apprehension in regard to the heavy firing on my right rear, and left me free to push the right of the line boldly instead of with the caution with which it was advanced."[79]

But the stubborn Confederate resistance was for naught, for Price had decided to abandon Little Rock as soon as he learned that Davidson was south of the Arkansas. "On being informed that his flank was turned, he replied that the Yankees were not going to entrap him like they did Pemberton [at Vicksburg], and immediately gave the order to retreat," Steele reported later. The corpulent Missourian, in dispatching Marmaduke to face the blueclad cavalry, ordered him "to hold the enemy in check until I could withdraw my infantry and artillery from the north side of the river, and, when this had been accomplished, to cover the retreat, the orders for which were at once given. The infantry began to leave the intrenchments at about 11 o'clock in the morning." Sharpshooter James Wallace recorded: "by the time we reached the river we were almost suffocated with heat[.] the air was filled with smoke from the burning Boats & cars and other property." The Missourian added with singular understatement: "This seemed to indicate a retreat." After crossing the river around 3:00 P.M., cannoneer William Hoskins wrote that the Third Missouri Battery (C.S.) unlimbered "on the bluff in the Citty to cover the crossing of the remaining troops & waggons—while we sit on the bluff we can see the burning flames of the boats & [rail] cars—8 or 10 boats burned to ashes. . . . we comence retreating about 5 o'clock." Also guarding the south side of the river was one of the more unusual Confederate units. W. E. Woodruff commanded a volunteer battery, formed in early September, consisting of a bronze Napoleon and a bronze howitzer. Because of a shortage of horses, the battery was served by "oxen, of Texas brand." As the Rebel forces began an orderly retreat to the southwest, Woodruff's "bull battery" joined them with orders to "aid them if necessary, but above all, to save the guns." The cannon were safely turned over to Confederate ordnance officers in Arkadelphia, the bulls to commissary officers.[80]

All of the fighting took place south of the Arkansas River. With the exception of a few shells lobbed by Rebel cannon, the Union infantry faced no hostile fire as it marched west. Samuel Wells of the Fiftieth Indiana, watching his mounted colleagues engaged on the south side of the river, wrote, "we could not assist them only the artillery—which if it did not hurt the rebels any, it scared them terribly—for we used it freely." The only Union casualties on the north bank occurred when two men of Vaughn's Illinois Battery were "dangerously wounded by a premature explosion of a howitzer shell from a battery in action near by."[81]

Meanwhile, the scene in Little Rock was chaotic. Price ordered pontoon bridges, railroad cars, and the once-feared ironclad gunboat *Pontchartrain* burned to keep them out of Union hands. "I saw the hopeless, but unflinching remnant of Price's army in full retreat, while close upon their heels the blue coats came," one Little Rock woman remembered later. "I strained my eyes following the gray men, in retreating, on firing lines. Watched as our colors trail the dust till the sound of a drum corps or regimental band in another part of the city, aroused me to the consciousness that Little Rock was evacuated and we were in the hands of the enemy."[82]

Davidson sent Glover's brigade in pursuit of the Rebels retreating from Bayou Fourche, but the tired Yankee cavalrymen and their horses played out two miles short of the city. The general then ordered up his reserve brigade under Colonel Ritter, who sauntered toward the city against only light skirmishing. The brigade, accompanied by some of Stange's howitzers and troopers from the ubiquitous First Iowa, charged into Little Rock, meeting no opposition until the First Missouri Cavalry (U.S.) approached the U.S. arsenal, "when a sharp fire was opened from the enemy's batteries in the timber, doing no damage, however, except the killing of 1 horse." Trooper James Rogers of the Third Iowa Cavalry captured the thrill of the final rush into the capital: "The 3d Iowa with Col. Caldwell at the head were the first to charge into the city, and as they passed town they were met by women old and young waving handkerchiefs and clapping their hands. Company M rushed forward to the Capitol and hoisted their guidon on top of the steeple. Companies F & G proceeded to the

The Third Minnesota Infantry Regiment chose its triumphant entry into Little Rock as the subject of its official painting for the Minnesota capitol building. *Courtesy Minnesota Historical Society.*

Arsenal and hoisted their guidons there while the other three companies busied themselves running out two or three regts of rebels that wer trying to blow up the Arsenal and fire the town."[83]

The Twenty-seventh Arkansas Infantry was the last Confederate unit to leave Little Rock, its men sweeping the city for stragglers as they headed south. "It did not take us long to find out that we were giving up Little Rock and that our entire army was on the retreat," infantryman Silas Turnbo recalled. "The men grumbled and protested at giving up the town. It was our last hope for Arkansas and it would soon be in the hands of the Federals." The hard-fighting Rebel cavalry also was discouraged by the decision to abandon the capital, an officer recorded, writing, "never did men fight better and never were more hurt at the giving up of a place, for they felt that it would be a long retreat." Thomas Barb of Dobbins's First Arkansas Cavalry recorded in his diary, "we come through little Rock about 4 o'clock this evening and there found the whole army under a full retreat without ever giving them a general fight so the big expected fight for our capitol is come and gone and wasent nothing but a skirmish."[84]

The Confederates formed defensive lines at the fairgrounds on the southern outskirts of the city, John Edwards reported, "but the enemy's cavalry did not deem it advisable to accept the challenge that was thus offered. They might well be content with the capital of the State and the rich valley of the Arkansas, gained so cheaply and with such inconsiderable loss." By 5:00 P.M. the last Confederate defenders were out of town, and General Davidson reported, "at 7 P.M. the capital of Arkansas was formally surrendered by the acting civil authorities, and the United States arsenal, uninjured, with what stores remained in it, was repossessed." A captain in the Sixty-first Illinois Infantry proudly wrote to his wife: "We planted the Stars and Stripes on the capitol of the state before the setting of the sun." "This was more than we expected," an Indiana soldier reported with relief, "old Price could not help running." At the arsenal, which Price had ordered destroyed, Union forces captured three thousand pounds of gunpowder and "a considerable quantity of cartridges" as well as several siege guns the Rebels had salvaged from the destruction of Arkansas Post. Two burning locomotives were rescued by Union troops. Indeed, "most of the ordnance, quartermaster, and commissary stores housed in the capital were left for the enemy." The Rebels did succeed in damaging the bridges across the Arkansas, as Colonel Engelmann noted: "[W]hen we drove the Secesh out, they had 3 pontoon Bridges across the river. But as they left, they set fire to them and burned them so badly that of the 3 bridges hardly enough remains, to now constitute one good bridge across the river."[85]

On the north side of the river, the Union infantry explored the earthworks they would have had to take had Steele's bold gamble not succeeded. Sgt. William Bull, a Confederate Missourian, described the works as "well-constructed, with an extensive open space cleared in front, and it would have been difficult, if not impossible, for an enemy to have crossed this open space and capture the works." His counterparts agreed. Samuel Baird of the Merrill Horse wrote that Price "had slashed down two hundred acres of heavy timber on the north side, blocking every pass but the main road, giving him a large sweep with his artillery." Private Sperry of the Thirty-third Iowa noted: "[T]he road [leading to the works] was well obstructed, and the earth-works strong enough to command the passage. Here was where the rebels were prepared for us; and had not General Steele so surprised them by the Bayou Metoe feint, and the present flanking-movement, we should certainly have had some difficulty with them here. As it was, the pans and kettles, with victuals yet cooking on the fire, showed how unexpectedly they had discovered the position to be no longer tenable." Colonel Andrews of the Third Minnesota found the fortifications "well-built and formidable," noting too that his troops "found the Confederate kitchen fires still burning and their corn cakes yet warm." The Federals also got an opportunity to view the remains of the once-feared gunboat *Pontchartrain,* one of the few things the Confederates did succeed in destroying during their hasty retreat. A Wisconsin soldier wrote on September 11: "[T]he ruins of a vast gun boat is yet burning. Here is a good lot of rail Road Iron lying as if it had been used for coating [the vessel] many shot & shell lie about her guns were removed." Edward Rolfe of the Twenty-seventh Iowa visited the *Pontchartrain*'s wreckage on the twentieth, writing that "it had a pair of the most powerful Cilenders I ever saw and the stoutest wheel shafts that I ever [saw] but there lays a perfect wreck. . . . the iron is all spoiled Except the Rail Road iron and that is good yet."[86]

The roads south out of Little Rock were chaotic as the Rebels retreated. John P. Quesenberry of the Eleventh Missouri Infantry wrote that "the road was crowded with horsemen ox wagons Buggys and all Kinds of vehickles—Men Women children Negros & Dogs. The Heat & Dust was . . . oppressive." As the Twenty-seventh Arkansas joined the fugitives, Silas Turnbo remembered: "General Price road up near our line and some of the boys said, 'General, ain't we going to fight the Yankees?' The good commander shook his head and said, 'No, boys, they are too many for us.' He looked like he was almost crying." Old "Granny" Holmes, riding out of Little Rock with Marmaduke, summed up Rebel prospects: "we are an army of prisoners, and self-supporting at that."[87]

The next morning Merrill took up the pursuit of Price's retreating army, leaving Little Rock with a makeshift cavalry division consisting of the Second, Seventh, and Eighth Missouri (U.S.); the Fifth Kansas; the First Indiana; and the Tenth and Thirteenth Illinois, supported by six mountain howitzers of Stange's Second Missouri Artillery (U.S.) and Lovejoy's Merrill Horse artillery, the First Indiana's 6-pounder rifled guns, and two 3-inch rifles and two 12-pounder howitzers of

Clarkson's Second Missouri Artillery (U.S.). By 6:00 A.M. the column was heading down the Arkadelphia Road after the beaten Confederates. "We had scarcely left the suburbs of the town before we began to find the debris of a retreating and demoralized army—broken wagons, arms and equipment, partly destroyed, ammunition upset into small streams and mud-holes, and deserters and fagged-out soldiers in numbers continually brought in by our advance and flankers."[88]

About four miles into the pursuit, the advance Union elements ran into Confederate pickets, and two miles farther the Eighth Missouri dismounted to fight the Rebel rear guard. The Eighth, under Colonel Geiger, then engaged in a running skirmish with the slowly retreating Southerners. The Rebels, Colton Greene's regiment under Maj. Leonidas A. Campbell, retreated slowly "by company, making successive formations, for 7 miles." Merrill ordered up the Merrill Horse and Stange's howitzers, which engaged a Rebel battery posted up the road. The Confederate defenders consisted of Thompson's Sixth Missouri Cavalry (C.S.) and Jeans's regiment of Shelby's brigade, accompanied by Ruffner's four-gun battery. "Captain Ruffner . . . in quick succession sent shot, shell, and grape roaring and whizzing through the woods in such a demoralizing manner as to drive the enemy out of sight and hearing for the time." Bayou Fourche meanders through the area, and a civilian told Merrill that he had been shooed from his house by the Confederates because "their determined stand would be made at that point." Pushing cautiously forward and making a wrong turn he blamed on his guide, the colonel moved the Seventh Missouri and Tenth Illinois to the front, with the Thirteenth Illinois serving as flankers. Clarkson received permission to do some long-range shelling of the dust cloud marking the Rebel retreat. "The day was now well worn away, and my troops, weary from the previous day, were worn out with 16 miles of skirmishing through thickets and heavy timber," Merrill reported, but he sent Powell Clayton and the First Indiana Cavalry and its field guns forward as the main Union column stopped for the night. The pugnacious Clayton rushed forward two miles and engaged the Confederates, leading Merrill to send the Merrill Horse and Clarkson's rifled guns to his support and help drive off the Rebel defenders. The Union commander then ordered Clayton's troops to rejoin their comrades at Bayou Fourche.[89]

The retreat from Little Rock was miserable. A Confederate soldier wrote to his wife, "it is impossible for you to imagine how much the

Col. Lewis Merrill led his Second Missouri Cavalry Regiment in battle at Brownsville and Bayou Fourche but was roundly criticized for his timid pursuit of the retreating Confederates after the fall of Little Rock. *Courtesy Civil War Museum, Wilson's Creek National Battlefield.*

men suffered on account of the heat, dust, and scarcity of water." As the Rebels fell back through Benton, many of the hungry soldiers had their first food in days. On the evening of September 11, Turnbo's regiment stopped at General Fagan's Saline River plantation, where "the general had plenty of fine hogs and he gave the soldiers permission to kill all they could eat, and for once, we fared sumptuously. He said if the Confederates would not get them, the Federals would, and he would much rather his own men make use of them than the enemy." Missouri sharpshooter James Wallace wrote in his diary that on arriving at Benton, "we found that Waggons . . . and the details that cooked our grubb for us and again we had plenty to eat something we had not got for some time. . . . We dined sumptuously on hoe cakes Bacon Beef molasses Sugar and meal coffee and slept sound all night." With full bellies and a good night's sleep, Price's men continued their march toward Arkadelphia.[90]

Clayton again took up the pursuit on the morning of September 12 but found that the Rebel rear guard had rejoined their main column. "He had been ordered to return when he found pursuit useless, and accordingly returned about 12 o'clock." Thus ended the Little Rock campaign, with Steele characterizing Merrill's pursuit of Price as "not as vigorous as it should have been." The historian of the Thirteenth

Illinois was not as politic, writing that "the pursuit of Price & Marmaduke . . . was a mere farce; a useless promenade, that took the last wind out of our poor horses." Davidson suggested an official inquiry into Merrill's performance, but it apparently never transpired.[91]

As the Federals settled into Little Rock, old grudges were forgotten. Davidson issued general orders praising his cavalrymen, now that "your long, weary march is at length terminated by victory. . . . For you, may there be continuous success wherever it may be our lot to go. For me, I have no higher aim and ask no greater honor than to lead such men." Frank Emmons reciprocated, writing that "the men have forgoten all the hatred they had for Genl. Davidson and like him more than they could hate him and the Genl. says he has got the best Cavalry that ever was out."[92]

For the Yankees, the relatively bloodless campaign was a major morale booster, delivering a Confederate state capital into Union hands and setting the stage for installation of a loyal government. More importantly to the men, health conditions improved almost at once. The Third Missouri Cavalry's Petty noted in his diary on September 15: "[W]e found about 1400 sick rebels in different hospitals. Our boys were placed in St. John's while the rebs occupied the other part. . . . We were informed by the post surgeon that the health of the troops greatly improved after the arrival of the army in Little Rock." He added the next day, "our sick boys are now getting well very fast and returning to the camp for duty." Captain Bowler of the Third Minnesota also observed that "the health of the troops is improving since we arrived here where we can get good water and high ground to camp upon. During the march we got very poor water to drink—most of the time nothing but bayou water."[93]

Official reports give total Union battle losses for the Little Rock campaign as 137 men: 18 killed, 118 wounded, and 1 missing. Incomplete Confederate reports show 64 casualties: 12 killed, 34 wounded, and 18 captured or missing. Rebel casualties were almost certainly higher, and neither total accounts for the widespread deaths from disease that occurred during the campaign. Confederate desertions following the campaign numbered in the hundreds as Arkansas and Missouri troops left the ranks in disgust.[94]

Desertions were so high, in fact, that Arkansas's Confederate governor, Harris Flanagin, remarked that a pitched battle would have been less costly. Albert DeMuth of the Eighth Missouri Cavalry

(U.S.) noted that Merrill's pursuit on September 11 "captured some two or three hundred prisoners, generally conscripts. Myself, with two of my men, captured eight, but I reckon they were tolerable well satisfied with the change. Indeed, all the Arkansians are leaving the army." A Missouri Confederate agreed with DeMuth, writing: "nothing that can be said will influence them to Rally when they have been forced in[.] they have done no good they were not reliable in a Fight and nearly all that was conscripted have deserted." A soldier of the Twenty-seventh Iowa noted that the victorious Yankees "took a thousand prisoners and lots Deserted the Rebble army and came to ours and keep coming in yet." Silas Turnbo wrote of the desertions of Arkansas troops: "They did not sneak off to keep any one [from] seeing them go. They left publicly in squads of four or five. They were neither ashamed nor afraid. . . . It looked for a while [that] they would all go but enough men remained to keep the company officers a few men to command. I well recollect some of the officers in command of their companies when the few men would straggle would give the command, 'Boys, all three of you close up in ranks' or 'All four of you keep near together' or 'All five of you must not separate,' as the case may be." Missouri gunner William Hoskins also noticed this, writing in his diary on September 14 that "there has bin many dissirtions on this retreat—they have disirted almost by Compeneys." Historian Carl Moneyhon has assessed Confederate losses to desertion following the fall of the capital at 1,900 men in addition to 650 sick and wounded men who had been abandoned in Little Rock. To counteract this huge loss of manpower, Governor Flanagin issued proclamations on September 16 calling the militias of Clark, Hempstead, Sevier, Pike, Polk, Montgomery, Lafayette, Ouachita, Union, and Columbia counties into active service, exempting only "six Physicians, one Druggist, millers to supply the wants of the country, Clerks, Sheriffs, Posters and persons in the employ of the Confederate states."[95]

Despite the crushing blow to Confederate morale, Price acted correctly in abandoning his works north of the Arkansas and giving Little Rock to the Federals. Had he fought it out, his infantry would almost certainly have been encircled and forced to surrender. Trans-Mississippi commander Edmund Kirby Smith agreed, writing a letter to Price in which he said: "[Y]ou have acted wisely in saving and keeping together your little army. Unfortunate as the loss of the

Arkansas [River Valley] is, it would have been infinitely more disastrous had the little army upon which all our hopes in that area are concentrated been lost."[96]

Frederick Steele achieved a remarkable victory with few casualties, a tribute to the abilities of a clever, resourceful, and methodical professional. Yet as with the fighting at Helena, the Trans-Mississippi action was overshadowed by events east of the Mississippi. An Iowa historian observed that "the campaign was highly creditable to General Steele and the troops under his command, but sandwiched between that against Vicksburg and that which drove the rebels whirling out of Tennessee, it did not receive the *éclat* which it otherwise would have received." General Schofield, however, praised Steele, writing that his "operations have been conducted with marked skill and good judgment, and the importance of his success can hardly be overestimated. . . . All Arkansas and the Indian Territory west of it are virtually in our possession." Historian Shelby Foote has placed the victory into perspective: "the loss of Little Rock—fourth on the list of fallen capitals, immediately following Jackson, which had been preceded the previous year by Baton Rouge and Nashville—extended the Union occupation to include three-fourths of Arkansas, a gain which the victors presumably would have been willing to pay ten or even one hundred times the actual cost." The soldiers who marched with Steele appreciated what had been achieved. An Iowa captain declared: "Steele must have out generaled Price. At least all the prisoners and deserters agree that they intended fighting us until we effected a crossing from below." The sole criticism that can be lodged against the Federal commander is that he, like Prentiss after Helena, did not vigorously pursue his beaten enemy.[97]

One Rebel who did not desert nevertheless felt despair at the loss of the Arkansas capital. W. W. Garner, a soldier from Quitman, Arkansas, perhaps expressed Confederate morale best in a letter to his wife two months after the city's capture: "In bygone days I thought that I felt the sting of being deprived of my family; but I acknowledge that I have never until the fall of Little Rock felt the sting of being an exile."[98]

6

"If They Take Fort Smith, the Indian Country Is Gone"

The Western Arkansas River Valley

As Frederick Steele's Union horde closed on Little Rock to the east, control of the western reaches of the Arkansas River came under Federal sway as a hard-driving Yankee column under the combative James G. Blunt quietly slipped into Fort Smith. The capture of that storied bastion, coupled with the seizure of Fort Gibson the year before, ended any serious Confederate ambitions for western Arkansas and Indian Territory north of the river.

The return of the forts to Union garrisons ended nearly two years of campaigning for dominance of the river valley in the West. In the months since Opotholeyahola's mixed band of Creeks, Cherokees, and other Indians had made its bitter flight to Kansas, the predominant loyalties in Indian Territory had careened wildly from pro-Confederate to a pragmatic leaning toward the Federals. The lukewarm enthusiasm that marked the initial recruitment of Indian troops for Confederate service waned considerably in the weeks following Pea Ridge. Col. John Drew's First Regiment of Cherokee Mounted Riflemen was partially furloughed, with the remaining active-duty troops scattered at guard posts from Tahlequah to Webbers Falls. Col. Stand Watie's First Regiment of Cherokee Mounted Rifles prowled northern Indian Territory, cooperating with white Rebel units for raids into Missouri,

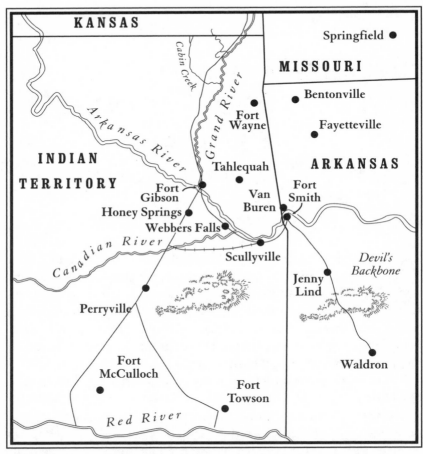

Western Arkansas and Indian Territory, 1863. Native American and African American troops played prominent roles in the struggle to control western Arkansas and Indian Territory. *Map by Kirk Montgomery.*

Kansas, and Arkansas. Brig. Gen. Albert Pike withdrew with most of the other Indian troops to Fort McCulloch, located in the Choctaw Nation north of the Red River. This placed them in position to defend the Texas border but provided scant protection for the Indian home-lands, a situation that did not sit well with many of Pike's troops. In addition, most of the supplies promised for the Confederate Indians— including clothing, weapons, and tents—were appropriated by Earl Van Dorn in the chaos following Pea Ridge.[1]

Federal forces in Kansas and Missouri, meanwhile, saw an oppor-tunity to recruit Indians into the Union army and return some of the thousands of refugees from Indian Territory to their homes. As Blunt received his brigadier's star and command of the Department of Kansas, Col. Charles Doubleday of the Second Ohio Cavalry recruited and began training two regiments of Unionist Indians. The First Indian Home Guard was raised from loyalists of the Creek and Seminole nations, while Cherokees, Creeks, Osages, Choctaws, and Chickasaws formed the Second Indian Home Guard. Blunt also began planning an invasion of Indian Territory. He assembled the Tenth Kansas Infantry, Ninth Wisconsin Infantry, Second Ohio Cavalry, Sixth and Ninth Kansas Cavalry, Rabb's Second Indiana Battery, and the First Kansas Battery near Baxter Springs in southern Kansas. These units, with the two Indian Home Guard regiments, would seek to drive the Rebels from Indian Territory and hopefully be the vanguard of a sea of refugees who would return to their tribal homelands.[2]

The opening move came on June 1, 1862, when Doubleday led about one thousand men of the Second Ohio and Sixth Kansas Cavalry, the Ninth Wisconsin and Tenth Kansas Infantry, and Rabb's Indiana battery south. Their goal was to hit Watie's Confederate Cherokees and Col. John T. Coffee's Rebel Missourians at their camp on Cowskin Prairie near the Arkansas border and stop them from preying on Fed-eral supply and communication lines. The Yankee column slipped up to Cowskin Prairie around sundown on June 6 and formed into line of battle, with four of Rabb's cannon unlimbering and opening fire on the enemy camp. The Rebels fled after the Hoosier cannoneers fired only six shots, but one Ohio cavalryman noted with satisfaction that "the shelling was splendid. The shells would bound from tree to tree and burst with a thundering noise." While the Federals "captured a large amount of stock, equipage and munitions of war" in the brief engage-ment, no casualties were reported on either side. But the skirmish did give notice to Confederate forces that the Yankees were assuming an aggressive posture toward Indian Territory.[3]

Blunt had gone to Fort Leavenworth to make arrangements for supplies, leaving Col. William M. Weer in command of Federal forces in southwest Kansas. The colonel called Doubleday back from Cowskin Prairie. The veteran Jayhawker replaced Doubleday, who soon after resigned from the service because he was "so enraged at the intrigue and rascality of the Kansas officers and politicians who made Wier rank him." Weer, who Kansan Wiley Britton said "would have been an efficient officer except for the fact that he was addicted to the liquor habit, which was frequently so pronounced as to unfit him for having command of troops in the field," continued training the Indian regiments to prepare them for the occupation of Indian Territory. Union patrols prowled through the region and in late June determined that Col. James Clarkson's Fifth Missouri Militia (C.S.) was at Locust Grove while Watie's troops were camped along Spavinaw Creek. Clarkson, with a tiny force of a few hundred men, had been sent to bolster the Confederate Indians after Watie begged Thomas Hindman for reinforcements following Cowskin Prairie, reflecting perhaps that general's views on the importance of Indian Territory. On June 28 Weer set out on the offensive with six thousand men. One Ohio cavalryman dryly noted of the Kansan, "I do not know what he had to eat, but I know he had a ten-gallon keg strapped on a mule, and of course that means he did not lack for drink."[4]

Weer split the Union column, sending troops under Col. Lewis Jewell down the east side of the Grand River to take on Watie's force while he led the remaining Yankees down the Verdigris River to attack Clarkson's command. Watie, fearing an attack, put out orders for his supply train to fall back toward Fort Gibson. As Weer's column approached the Confederate camp early on the evening of July 2, Theodore Gardner of the First Kansas Battery wrote that "the doughboys and cannoneers were piled promiscuously into wagons"—this method of transporting infantry would be used frequently in campaigns in Indian Territory, where relatively few troops had to cover long distances quickly under threat of attack by Confederate raiders. "With the first blush of dawn," Gardner continued, "our cavalry took the enemy pickets and rushed pell-mell upon the unsuspecting Rebs who were just starting campfires for their morning meal." The surprise was complete, and Clarkson and one hundred men were quickly taken prisoner while thirty men were killed. Unfortunately for the Confederates, Watie's order to move the train had not been followed, and Weer gleefully reported that the Yankees captured "their entire baggage wagons, mules, guns, ammunition, tents, etc." Federal losses were one corporal of the Ninth Kansas Cavalry and the doctor of the First Indian Home Guard (who a Kansan shot by accident) and four wounded. Watie's troops, surprised at Spavinaw Creek, quickly fell back toward Tahlequah, where they and fugitives from Clarkson's command alarmed civilians with their reports of the approaching Federals. A Rebel missionary with the Creek agency summed up the results of the actions at Locust Grove and Spavinaw Creek: "Pike's forces being at Red River, they rather caught us with our breeches down. You ought to have seen the stampede and how our women and children skedaddled toward Dixie."[5]

The victorious Yankees gathered the next day at Cabin Creek and celebrated the anniversary of the nation's independence by splitting the spoils of the previous day's battles. Wiley Britton remembered that "the Indians who took part in the expedition were allowed to help themselves to the captured loot except as to army supplies; but the Indians got most of it, for the clothing was nearly all citizens' clothing and of no use to the white soldiers." The military supplies were turned over to quartermasters for distribution. The Rebels may have missed a good opportunity for a counterattack as the Yankees, reflecting Weer's affection for the bottle, proceeded to have what Luman Tenney of the Second Ohio Cavalry caustically called a "great day": "So many drunk. Officers gave the freest license to the men. Both caroused. I was disgusted."[6]

The Federals then made what was the most momentous act of the first invasion of Indian Territory. As Weer moved the bulk of his force to Flat Rock, he ordered Capt. Harris S. Greeno to take the Sixth Kansas Cavalry and two companies of Indian soldiers to the Cherokee capital at Tahlequah. It was a timely move. The recent defeats had demoralized a people who were never fervent in their support of the Confederacy from the beginning. Chief John Ross had long felt that Southern leaders had ignored the needs of the people of Indian Territory, failing to provide adequate defense against the "white men roaming through the Indian country" and saddling the region with a poor commander in Albert Pike. Weer confidently boasted, "Ross is undoubtedly with us, and will come out openly when we reach there." But Ross remained a politician and keeping his options open had declined a July 7 request from Weer to confer about conditions in the Cherokee Nation. The old chief glibly responded, "there is no nation of Indians, I venture to say, that has ever been more scrupulous in the faithful observance of their treaty obligations than the Cherokee."[7]

Greeno's flying column rode into Tahlequah late in the afternoon of July 14 and found it virtually deserted, most of its pro-Confederate population having scurried south after hearing the panicky reports of Clarkson's survivors. The next morning the Yankees rode to Chief Ross's home at Park Hill. There they found two hundred men and officers of John Drew's regiment, who had just been ordered to join Confederate forces at Fort Davis, and Ross, who had received instructions to conscript every Cherokee between the ages of eighteen and thirty-five to resist the Union invasion. Greeno sensed the ambivalence of the Cherokees and addressed the crowd. The former doctor spoke at length of the many Union victories in the western theater and along the Mississippi River as well as at nearby Pea Ridge, stressing that these successes would free Union troops for more-aggressive operations in the Trans-Mississippi. He overcame the hesitation of Ross and the Cherokee officers to abandon their allegiance to their treaties with the Confederacy by making them prisoners of war, then paroling them. Most of Drew's erstwhile Rebels went straight to the Union camp and became the core of the Third Indian Home Guard. Chief Ross, his family, and most of the Cherokee Nation's treasury and archives went north to Kansas. As historian Clarissa Confer has observed, "The Cherokee Nation was officially divided."[8]

While Greeno was in Tahlequah, Weer advanced toward Fort Gibson, which commanded the confluence of the Grand and Arkansas rivers. The Yankees encountered Confederate pickets around 2:00 A.M., and Lt. Col. Albert Ellithorpe of the First Indian Home Guard reported, "the men moved at the double-quick. Upon the first volley [the Rebels] fled in great consternation leaving behind, ten killed and thirty wounded. Most of the guns were left on the ground with all the camp fixtures." The small Confederate force scattered, and according to Wiley Britton, the Federals "raised the Stars and Stripes to the top of the flag pole, the first time its graceful folds had waved from that place for a year and a half." Weer advanced to the Arkansas, and scattered firing broke out between his men and Rebel troops manning a works dubbed Fort Davis on the south side of the river. Then, Weer reported, "reconnaissance being accomplished we returned to camp" at Flat Rock.[9]

Once there, the colonel apparently tapped into the whiskey keg that Trooper Gause had earlier noted. As his men suffered from the searing heat baking the prairie, the Kansan stayed in his tent and went on a bender. The troops, hungry after having been put on half rations, anxiously awaited an expected supply train from Kansas and worried that Confederate raiders might slip between them and their line of retreat. Finally, with no communications from Kansas for twelve days and the rank-and-file soldiers growing increasingly restive, Col. Friedrich Salomon of the Ninth Wisconsin Infantry (who would command the Federal defense of Helena so masterfully a year later) acted. Citing the lack of supplies and communications and contending that Weer's "grossly intemperate habits . . . had produced idiocy or monomania," the German sent his adjutant with one hundred men to place their commander under arrest on July 18. An angry Weer was escorted at bayonet point to Salomon's tent, where officers from most of the regiments had gathered. Luman Tenney wrote that when Weer noticed that Capt. Norman Allen of the First Kansas Battery was among the group, "he said, 'And you are here?' and burst into tears. I never saw so much excitement. All were glad." Salomon ordered all of the white troops in the Yankee force to fall back toward Kansas the next day; defense of Indian Territory would be left in the hands of the three newly recruited Indian regiments and a single section of the First Kansas Battery.[10]

Salomon turned toward Kansas on July 19 after receiving word that the missing supply convoy was sitting seventy-five miles away awaiting an escort. Col. Robert W. Furnas then began the difficult task of determining how his Indian Brigade could best defend the territory so recently taken and abandoned by Weer's command. Furnas consolidated the three regiments on the Verdigris River, but some of his troops, feeling abandoned by their Northern comrades, began to slip away toward their homes. Furnas ordered Maj. William A. Phillips to move the Third Indian Home Guard to Pryor Creek to keep them from being infected with the dissatisfaction creeping through the other regiments, then withdrew the rest to a camp at Horse Creek, where they could block Confederates advancing up the Military Road into the Cherokee Nation.[11]

It was Phillips and the Third Indian Home Guard who would fight the last action of any consequence in this first Federal invasion of Indian Territory. Emboldened by the Union withdrawal, Confederate troops had crossed the Arkansas at Fort Gibson to harass the Indian Brigade and to wreak vengeance on Unionists in the area. On July 27 Phillips sent his command forward along three roads that would converge at Bayou Menard, some seven miles northeast of Fort Gibson. Four hundred Confederate Indians under Lt. Col. Thomas Fox Taylor hit the Federals on the westernmost road, forcing them into a desperate delaying action. As Taylor concentrated on Lt. John Haneway's Union column, the rest of Phillips's regiment swept down the other two roads and hit the Confederates hard in the flank. Pvt. Edward Folsom of the First Choctaw and Chickasaw Cavalry (C.S.) wrote: "[T]hey charged and ran over [us]. They killed our Col. and Captain and 15 privates. I got away, we scattered every man for his self." Phillips proudly reported that the Rebels "were utterly routed and fled precipitately in great confusion to Gibson." At least thirty-two Confederates lay dead on the field, among them Taylor. "The enemy's loss in killed wounded and missing cannot be short of 100 men," Phillips reported. "We took 25 prisoners." In the aftermath of Bayou Menard, Stand Watie moved his regiment east into Arkansas, while the remainder of the Confederates fell back south of the Arkansas River to reorganize. Furnas, concerned about Rebel buildups in Arkansas and southern Indian Territory, ultimately decided to move his brigade north, placing the First Indian Home Guard at Baxter Springs, Kansas; the Second near Carthage, Missouri; and the Third at Neosho, Missouri. Indian Territory was again left to Confederate control.[12]

Conditions there deteriorated quickly. The Federal withdrawal caused panic among the Unionist Indians who had returned from exile as well as those who had just switched allegiance to the Stars and Stripes. Those who had sought revenge against their secessionist neighbors now found the tables turned; others acted on feuds that reached back to the time of the southeastern removals of the 1830s. Bushwhackers roamed the countryside preying on any and all. Some 1,500 Indians who had followed Weer back to their old homes now made the long march back to Kansas.

The chaos of the summer of 1862 was exacerbated by turmoil within the Confederate high command. Thomas Hindman had assumed command of the Trans-Mississippi District following Van Dorn's

Brig. Gen. Douglas Cooper led his Native American Confederates to defeat in several battles but remained popular with his troops because of his longstanding efforts on behalf of the Choctaw and Chickasaw tribes. *Courtesy Library of Congress.*

move east of the Mississippi, where he took most of the men and materiel in Arkansas. As he tried to rebuild an army, Hindman turned his attention west and ordered Albert Pike to send all of his white troops and artillery to Arkansas "without the least delay." The two generals' relationship soured quickly, with Pike attacking Hindman's declaration of martial law in Arkansas with vitriolic letters to President Davis and Hindman continuing to pilfer white troops from Pike's command. On July 31 Pike published a screed to the chiefs of the Five Civilized Tribes in which he excoriated Van Dorn and Hindman for their cavalier treatment of Indian Territory, incidentally resigning from his position as chief Confederate officer in the region. Col. Douglas H. Cooper, field commander of troops in Indian Territory during the July campaign, replaced Pike, who would spend the rest of the war impotently defending his reputation. Cooper enjoyed solid regard in the region, having served as U.S. agent to the Choctaw Nation in the 1850s and being adopted as a member of the Chickasaw Nation in 1861. But this militia veteran of the Mexican War had a taste for the bottle that rivaled that of Weer, and his tenure would be tempestuous.[13]

With the Rebels again ascendant in Indian Territory, Hindman moved to take control of northwest Arkansas and southwest Missouri. The Arkansian ordered all Confederate troops in the region, including Cooper's Indians, to gather at Newtonia with an eye toward taking Springfield. James Blunt and his department commander, John Schofield, moved to stop them. The first blow came from Salomon, who had been rewarded for his abandonment of Indian Territory with a brigadier's star. Learning that Cooper had around 4,000 men at Newtonia, the new general sent a strong reconnaissance force south from Sarcoxie. Confederate Choctaws and Chickasaws hit the Yankees hard on September 30, sending them reeling back six miles to join the rest of Salomon's troops. Cooper then attacked with his entire command, driving the Federals back to Sarcoxie. Heavy skirmishing continued in the region for several days as Blunt prepared his newly reorganized Army of the Frontier for a counterattack. The Yankees moved forward on October 4, surrounding Newtonia on three sides. Cooper, who area citizens claimed was "drunk as a lord," quickly abandoned the Missouri town and fell back into Indian Territory, while the rest of the Confederate troops there withdrew to Huntsville, Arkansas.[14]

Schofield ordered Blunt to take the fight to Cooper, who was regrouping his troops at Old Fort Wayne, just west of Maysville in northwest Arkansas, in preparation for an advance into southern Kansas. Leaving Salomon to protect his supply wagons, Blunt moved forward with around 3,500 men of the Second, Sixth, Tenth, and Eleventh Kansas; the First and Third Indian Home Guards; and the First Kansas and Second Indiana Batteries. On October 21 they set out on a grueling thirty-mile night march to attack a force Blunt estimated at 5,000–7,000 men. The Union advance stopped around 2:00 A.M. to let the rest of the column catch up, Blunt reporting, "the men were weary and exhausted, and no sooner were they halted than they dropped down in the brush by the road-side and were soon fast asleep." The general moved forward to Maysville to personally reconnoiter Cooper's position. Posing as a Rebel soldier, he stopped at a home on the edge of the prairie and fooled a Confederate soldier's wife into telling him where Cooper's pickets were stationed and where the main Rebel camp was located. The general then encountered a slave who, when promised his freedom, agreed to serve the Yankees as a guide and lead them to Cooper's camp, where his master was stationed.[15]

Blunt sent two companies of the Second Kansas to capture Cooper's pickets, but the Rebels fell back to their main camp, leading the always combative Kansan to engage with his single regiment and two mountain howitzers while sending a messenger back for the rest of his troops, seven miles away. As dawn broke, the Yankees found

Cooper's troops extended in line of battle across the prairie. Blunt pitched right in with his little force; Pvt. Vincent Osborn of the Second Kansas summed up their tactics: "we run our horses over the fence and attacked them." Capt. Samuel Crawford of the Second Kansas and his company were opposite the Confederate artillery in Cooper's center. The battery opened fire and at first "seemed to be shooting at the stars." But the Rebels soon lowered their sights, and "the shells came closer and closer to our heads as they passed over us with that peculiar warning well remembered by old soldiers." Crawford's men advanced, delivering a devastating volley on the artillerists. Capt. Sylvanus Howell, commanding the Rebel guns, reported that "nearly all the Batteries horses were shot in consequence of which we were unable to remove the battery from the field and the 4 guns, 3 six pounders and one 12 pound howitzer and 2 caissons were captured by the enemy"; only two caissons escaped the field. As Crawford drove in the center, the Sixth Kansas and Third Indian Home Guard regiments roared onto the field, hitting the Rebels on their right and left flanks. Cooper's men broke before the Federal onslaught, falling back to the Arkansas River, with the Confederate colonel reporting, "we barely escaped the entire destruction of the whole command, including a valuable train, in which was some 10,000 or 12,000 pounds of powder." Blunt reported one killed and nine wounded, four mortally; Confederate reports showed their losses as sixty-three killed, wounded, or missing. The fight at Old Fort Wayne effectively put Indian Territory north of the Arkansas under Union control, raising again the possibility of refugee Indians returning to their homes.[16]

With Cooper's Rebels out of the picture, Blunt turned his attention toward Confederate forces in northwest Arkansas. Placing his Indian troops along the Arkansas border and in southwest Missouri to protect his flanks, the Kansan embarked on the campaign that culminated in the battle of Prairie Grove and the brief occupation of Van Buren, sending Hindman's army streaming in disarray toward Little Rock. In early December Blunt ordered Col. William Phillips back into Indian Territory with the three Home Guard regiments, a contingent of the Sixth Kansas Cavalry, and an artillery battery. The brigade skirmished with Watie's Rebels and spent Christmas Day in Tahlequah. On December 27 Phillips advanced to Fort Gibson, finding it abandoned but spying the Confederate flag still flying above

Cantonment Davis on the south side of the Arkansas. The Yankees stormed across the river and "took and burned Fort Davis, reducing all the barrack and commissary buildings and the whole establishment to ashes." Satisfied with the day's work, Phillips fell back to Tahlequah, while Cooper's Rebels fell back to winter at Scullyville in the Choctaw Nation.[17]

As Cooper made excuses for the disaster at Old Fort Wayne and many of his troops simply went home, Confederate leaders in Richmond moved to stabilize the situation in Indian Territory. In December they tapped Brig. Gen. William Steele to take command of Rebel forces in the territory as superintendent of Indian affairs. The New York–born Steele was an 1840 graduate of West Point, a Mexican War veteran, and a seasoned fighter from campaigns against the Apache and the Sioux. Arriving at Fort Smith in January 1863, he found Indian Territory in disarray, with supplies "utterly exhausted," its soldiers ragged and undisciplined, and its leadership incapable. "Thus impressed, I ordered the main body of the troops in the Territory to encamp as near Red River as was convenient," he wrote. Cooper would retain brigade command, and Watie still led his regiment.[18]

Steele received considerable assistance in February 1863 when Brig. Gen. William L. Cabell, recovering from wounds received at Corinth, Mississippi, was placed under his command. "Old Tige" Cabell, who had graduated from West Point ten years after Steele, had an impressive resume east of the Mississippi, having served on the staff of Joseph E. Johnston, been quartermaster under P. G. T. Beauregard, and functioned as Albert Sidney Johnston's chief quartermaster. (He also was credited with helping Beauregard and A. S. Johnston design the Confederate battle flag, with its distinctive St. Andrew's cross.) Cabell was given the task of cobbling together a force from the shattered remnants of Hindman's army. As historian Robert Kerby has observed, Cabell's brigade was "never more than a thousand strong, was made up of neighborhood guerrilla bands, local partisan rangers, conscript Arkansans—many of whom would have preferred to enlist in the Union army—and some homesick Texans. With this host, Cabell was expected to defend the western third of the state of Arkansas."[19]

Following the Rebel reverses of 1862, the Cherokee Council met at Cowskin Prairie in February 1863 and formally repealed the tribe's

1861 treaty with the Confederacy. The Cherokees voted to negotiate a new treaty with the United States, to repeal slavery and free all slaves in their nation, and to outlaw all Confederate Cherokees, which made it legal to seize their land and belongings. Steele responded to this political development by sending Watie and two regiments north to harass Federal communications and supply lines. Theophilus Holmes, smarting from the defeat of his garrison at Arkansas Post and fretting over developments in Indian Territory, began to worry about his west-ernmost bastion in Arkansas, writing on February 13, "If they take Fort Smith, the Indian country is gone."[20]

Despite General Holmes's concern about Fort Smith, Federal attention was focused farther west in the spring of 1863. In April Colonel Phillips's Indian Brigade, numbering some 3,000 troops, drove deep into Indian Territory, sweeping aside what little resistance was offered. On the thirteenth he occupied Fort Gibson, which would be the key Federal post in Indian Territory for the rest of the war. Kansan Wiley Britton noted that "the position was naturally a strong one with even temporary earthworks thrown up. There was no point as high as the bluff that overlooked Grand River that flowed at its foot, within a mile or so, from which an enemy could use artillery to advantage." Phillips ordered the construction of bake ovens, which convinced local Indians that he was there to stay, and renamed the post Fort Blunt.[21]

While Phillips set up camp at Fort Gibson, pro-Southern Cherokees decided to gather at Webbers Falls to hold their own council. Meeting on April 24, the secessionist Indians elected Stand Watie as principal chief of the Confederate Cherokees. They were rudely awakened at daybreak the next morning when six hundred of Phillips's Indians and Kansans, who had made a thirty-mile night march from Fort Gibson, rushed into their camp, from which they "routed and broke them up killing a number and taking prisoners; took equipage and etc." The Fed-erals suffered two killed, including Dr. Rufus Gilpatrick, who was shot as he tended the wounds of an injured Confederate Indian. Gilpatrick was James Blunt's uncle and was married to the general's sister-in-law. The enraged Yankees burned several houses in retaliation.[22]

Phillips and his men returned to Fort Gibson and for the next several weeks lived anxious lives. Douglas Cooper moved north with his Indian and Texas troops, while Watie's soldiers nipped at

Col. Stand Watie and his Confederate Indians were a constant threat to the Union armies that sought to gain control of the western end of the Arkansas River Valley in Indian Territory. *Courtesy Civil War Museum, Wilson's Creek National Battlefield.*

the Federals' flanks and Missouri partisans remained a threat to their tenuous supply line with Fort Scott. Union patrols and Confederate raiders skirmished almost every day. Pvt. Robert Elder Horn of the Fifth Texas Partisan Rangers recalled a typical confrontation in mid-May: "[W]e tried to capture a train of men and wagons near the fort. After we had destroyed some wagons and captured some mules and horses, the reinforced army came out and we had to skedaddle." Cabell's Arkansas brigade further threatened Fort Gibson. The Arkansians controlled Fort Smith and held sway over western Arkansas, despite the repulse of a mid-April attack on Fayetteville (from which the Federal garrison there was withdrawn to Missouri on April 25). As Britton observed: "There being no Federal force holding a position in Western Arkansas, or in the larger area of the Cherokee Nation east of Grand River and north of Fort Gibson, . . . made it a region over which the Confederate forces could march almost at will and a constant menace to the supply trains of the Indian command coming down from Fort Scott."[23]

Cooper's Rebels kept picking away at Phillips's troops, focusing on their supply lines and raiding their livestock, which had to be taken farther and farther away from the Federal works in order to find decent grazing land. A particularly destructive sortie on May 20 cost the Yankees around twenty-five fatalities and the loss of hundreds of horses and mules. As Pvt. Black Fox of the First Cherokee Mounted Rifles (C.S.) remembered:"[A] number of our cowboys with the best horses were selected and made a dash across the prairie, taking the herders by surprise and shooting at every man in sight. They ran the heard together and when they got them started in our direction, our command covered the retreat." Phillips, anticipating the arrival of a supply train from Kansas, took a risky gamble four days later, taking part of his force out of Fort Gibson and heading south of the Arkansas River to draw Cooper's attention away from the caravan. The Yankees reached mid-river when the Rebels opened fire. "The rattle of grape and musketry was rapid and sharp," Col. Charles DeMorse, whose Texans occupied the south bank, reported. "On our side it was well answered, but from short range weapons. The bed of the river was so thoroughly enveloped in smoke, that the effect produced by us could not be seen; but some horses without riders were seen to go up the opposite bank." While Confederate attention focused on Phillips's assault, other Federal troops moved out to escort the supply train.[24]

The reinforcement of the wagon train was fortunate. With Phillips's sham attack out of the way, Cooper again turned his attention to the wagons from Fort Scott, detaching two Creek regiments and a Texas regiment under the command of Col. Daniel N. McIntosh north of the Arkansas to capture the prize. They caught up with the train near the Verdigris River on May 28 and attacked, capturing several wagons. At least two men were captured with the train, with Pvt. John Howard of the Fifth Texas Partisan Rangers remarking: "[S]ome of our straggling Indians found these men and stripped them of their clothing and as we came up we found the Indians murdering one of the men and we got there in time to save the other. And after he was dead they 'gobbled' over him." The troops in Fort Gibson reacted quickly. Edward Butler of the First Cherokee Mounted Rifles observed, "the Federals were reinforced [and] immediately recaptured [the wagons] so that made an entire failure" of the attack. The Confederates again retreated to the south side of the Arkansas.[25]

The hungry Yankee garrison was grateful for the supplies, but these were quickly consumed as the men skirmished with Watie's troops throughout June. Phillips beseeched Blunt for supplies and reinforcements for his besieged stronghold, and the general ordered another wagon train assembled for Fort Gibson's relief. As an escort he sent elements of the Second Colorado Infantry; the Third Wisconsin, Ninth Kansas, and Fourteenth Kansas Cavalry regiments; and the Second Kansas Artillery. At Baxter Springs the First Kansas Colored Infantry Regiment joined the escort, anticipating a baptism by fire for this unit composed of former slaves from Arkansas, Missouri, and Indian Territory. Part of the Third Indian Home Guard from Fort Gibson also joined the train at Baxter Springs; the entire column moved forward under the command of Col. James Williams of the First Kansas. On arriving at Cabin Creek on July 1, the Yankees found Watie firmly established on the south side of the creek with the First Cherokee Mounted Rifles, First Creek Mounted Volunteers, and elements of the Twenty-ninth Texas Cavalry and Martin's Partisan Rangers. William Cabell and 1,500 Arkansians lurked ominously on the east side of the Grand River, held there only by high water. After an unsuccessful attempt to force a crossing, Williams's men went into camp on the high ground on the north side of Cabin Creek.[26]

The next morning Williams determined to make a second attempt at crossing the creek before Cabell's column could cross the Grand and reinforce Watie's troops. He ordered his artillery to open fire, and "Forman's battery commenced throwing grape and canister into the timber opposite," Capt. George West of the Second Colorado wrote, "and rebels were returning the compliment sharply with musketry." As the artillery thundered, Williams directed the First Kansas and Second Colorado to cross the stream and drive the Rebels from their positions. "The boys rushed in, waist deep, with a yell that sounded like the shout of a thousand bull whackers," West reported. "They got across with little loss, and charged on the rebel position," Pvt. Christopher Kimball of the Ninth Kansas Cavalry wrote. The Confederates "fled from the center precipitously when the Negroes and Colorado boys charged, leaving arms and accouterments scattered as they went." While declaring, "I am proud of my men they stood cannonade as well," Watie lamented: "I had to fight under great disadvantage. . . . I fought them about six hours at the crossing of Cabin Creek. . . . [I]f the Creeks had stood I would have fought them longer but they would not do it." Britton estimated the Union losses at nine killed and thirty wounded, noting that Watie lost fifty killed and nine captured. The Federal wagon train proceeded unhindered to Fort Gibson, while Watie retreated to Honey Springs and Cabell's men retired to the vicinity of Fort Smith.[27]

Following the Union victory at Cabin Creek, General Blunt left Fort Scott, escorted by elements of the Sixth Kansas and Third Wisconsin Cavalry, two sections of the Second Kansas Battery, and a pair of 12-pounder howitzers. He arrived at Fort Gibson on July 11 and, at a reception that night, brought word of the stunning Union victories at Vicksburg, Gettysburg, and Helena. The general, ever on the offensive, began making plans to take the battle to Cooper. The Confederate commander, learning of his adversary's arrival and mindful of the trouncing he had received at the Kansan's hands at Old Fort Wayne, sent word to Cabell in Fort Smith to join him as soon as possible and placed pickets along the Arkansas to warn of any Federal movements. Blunt's arrival signaled the end of the siege of Fort Gibson. That same day William Steele confided in a letter, "I have neither the Artillery, nor the kind of forces necessary to take a place of the strength of Fort Gibson."[28]

Blunt began moving to secure Indian Territory on July 15, when he built flatboats and began ferrying troops across the Arkansas River, while Cooper concentrated his command at the supply depot at Honey Springs. The Kansan moved forward with about 3,000 men and twelve artillery pieces on a night-long march, driving Rebel pickets back to join their main line of battle south of Elk Creek. Blunt halted to give his soldiers "a couple of hours of rest and eat a lunch from their haversacks," then moved to the attack at about 10:00 A.M. The Federal artillery commenced hammering the Confederate lines as the Yankee infantry moved forward. Despite being hindered by ineffective gunpowder and a three-to-one disadvantage in artillery, the Rebels fought for two hours before their lines began to crumble. "I discovered our men in small parties giving way," Cooper reported. "These increased until the retreat became general." The jubilant Yankees followed the fleeing Rebels for about three miles before returning to Honey Springs, where they found five thousand pounds of flour, a sizable store of salt, meat, and sugar, two cannon, and five hundred small arms. The men of the First Kansas Colored Infantry, who had helped break the Confederate center, were perhaps amused by the discovery of five hundred sets of shackles with which the Rebels had confidently intended to return them to slavery. Cooper reported losing 134 killed and wounded and 47 captured, while Blunt's

Maj. Gen. James G. Blunt, pugnacious by nature, attacked his Confederate enemies in Indian Territory at every opportunity. He marched into Fort Smith unopposed on September 1, 1863. *Courtesy Civil War Museum, Wilson's Creek National Battlefield.*

forces lost 13 killed and 62 wounded in the victory at Elk Creek. The defeat badly demoralized the Confederate Indians and Texans, as evidenced by Dallas Bowman of the First Choctaw and Chickasaw Mounted Rifles, who wrote, "I am rather low spirited since our army have been defeated here lately. . . . [W]e were all to sure of whipping them but no." Cooper's troops fell back below the Canadian River, while Blunt returned his forces to Fort Gibson.[29]

With Blunt ascendant in Indian Territory and Frederick Steele's army closing on Little Rock, Union strategy in the region began to crystallize. Department commander John Schofield wrote that to control Arkansas, "the natural line of operation during the season of high water is the Arkansas River, and its possession and use is of the greatest importance as a means of securing Missouri and Northern Arkansas against future rebel inroads. . . . It is my desire to get possession of the whole length of the Arkansas River to Fort Smith and open communications by that line with the troops now under General Blunt in the Indian Territory." His opponent in Indian Territory, William Steele, feared such an outcome: "[T]he instant that the Indian Country is over run, most of the tribes, now friends, will be against us. They are most of them of but little value as soldiers, but they are better as friends than enemies."[30]

In light of Cooper's unbroken string of disasters, General Steele joined the battered and demoralized Confederate army at the Canadian River and took personal command. This move did nothing to improve morale, for Cooper, with his long record of service to the Indian nations, remained popular with his American Indian troops, who did not trust the Northern-born Steele. The Rebels were further disheartened by poor discipline, not having been paid in eight months, and being armed with gunpowder that Steele reported was "scarcely more than sufficient to drive the ball from the piece." Nevertheless, the Rebel commander assembled some 6,500 men at the Canadian and sent to Texas for reinforcements, a column led by Brig. Gen. Smith P. Bankhead that also brought ample quantities of fresh powder. When Bankhead arrived, Steele could commence offensive operations against Blunt. In the meantime he moved his troops to a threatening position within twenty miles of Fort Gibson.[31]

Steele would never have his opportunity to strike. Blunt learned that a sizeable Federal force had moved into the Fayetteville area and ordered them to join him at Fort Gibson. The brigade, under the command of Col. William F. Cloud, consisted of the Second Kansas Cavalry, the First Arkansas Infantry, two sections of Rabb's Second Indiana Battery, the Sixth Missouri State Militia Cavalry, and part of the Eighth Missouri State Militia Cavalry. The troops received orders to move quickly. The First Arkansas reported that they were to receive "one-half rations, without tents and with one-half blanket to the man"; the Sixth Missouri complained that they were "in the field without tents, clothing, or cooking utensils." General Steele, learning of this new development, elected to split his command. On August 19 he ordered Cabell's brigade, which was bleeding deserters by the score, back to Fort Smith, also sending Cooper's troops south to the supply depot at Perryville in the Choctaw Nation and Col. Chilly McIntosh's Creeks west to the headwaters of the Canadian River. Cloud's column reached Fort Gibson on August 20; the garrison was further strengthened by the Thirteenth Kansas Cavalry, which arrived as escort to a supply train. As Britton described it, "General Blunt was in fighting mood again and determined to immediately cross the Arkansas, advance south and attack the Confederates, and if possible make their result more decisive than the battle at Elk Creek." A Federal army of some 4,500 men crossed the Arkansas on August 22, determined to crush Steele's 9,000 Confederates.[32]

With characteristic drive, Blunt hurried his army forward, marching sixty miles in forty-eight hours. Steele fell back before the Federal pressure, a skirmisher from the Thirteenth Kansas Cavalry writing, "we could only get near enough to skirmish with their rear guard a couple of days." The Yankees found few Confederates as they moved down the Texas Road but encountered many refugee families hurrying south. Chaplain Francis Springer recorded: "On our march today we fell in with fifteen or twenty Indian families numerously supplied with children whom the fleeing rebels had lured from their cabins by the most flagrant & unscrupulous misrepresentations regarding the spirit & intentions of the General government. To the inquiry, 'Where are you going?' the answer was, 'I do not know where; I am trying to get out of the way of the Abolitionists.'" On August 25 Union advance troops skirmished with a company of Choctaws on reconnaissance for Steele, killing four and capturing a captain. The prisoner told Blunt that his men were from a new regiment of eight hundred Choctaws who had just joined Steele's army. But this report did nothing to slow the Federals, who continued down the Texas Road.[33]

Steele determined to make a rear-guard stand at Perryville, a major depot from which he was trying to remove desperately needed supplies. The Confederates threw together some barricades and placed their artillery where it would hammer any Yankees approaching town. Blunt's advance encountered Steele's artillery around 8:00 P.M., suffering four wounded from Confederate canister. The Sixth Kansas Cavalry was dismounted and ordered forward, some dragging their howitzers through the timber while the rest deployed on both sides of the road. Wiley Britton reported that the Kansans "advanced up to within two hundred and fifty yards of the barricades . . . and opened fire upon them with their Sharps' carbines by moonlight." The Federal artillery thundered into action, hurling a dozen shells into the Confederate works. The Rebels quickly fell back, joining the rest of Steele's army in retreat toward the Red River. Blunt reported: "[W]e had made a march of 40 miles with stock in bad condition and completely exhausted. I therefore considered farther pursuit through a rough and timbered country in the night entirely futile." But Samuel Crawford recalled, "I followed [the Rebels] with the Second Kansas for quite a distance on the road to Red River." The Federals captured quite a prize at Perryville, finding every building full of Confederate supplies. Blunt had the entire place burned. Historian Whit Edwards has declared that the destruction of Perryville and subsequent obliteration of a supply depot at North Fork Town "would cripple the Confederate forces in Indian Territory as much as if General Cooper's army had been destroyed."[34]

With Steele and Cooper in headlong flight to the Red River, Blunt moved his focus toward "Old Tige" Cabell's Arkansians and the key to control of Indian Territory, Fort Smith. The Confederate general commanded a conglomerate of cavalry outfits, Col. Asa Morgan's infantry regiment, four iron 6-pounder cannon, "and several little independent companies of Partisan Rangers." The overall quality of his command was poor, to put it charitably. "Hill's regiment, and Woosley's and Cawford's battalions were raised from deserters and jayhawkers who had been lying in the mountains, and forced into service," Cabell reported. "The aggregate of the whole amounted to over 3,000, yet, notwithstanding, I could never get into the field at any time over 1,600 men and never more than 1,200 of them for duty." By mid-August "nearly all of Hill's regiment, a large number of Thomson's regiment, and nearly all of Crawford's battalion [had] deserted." Nonetheless, on August 22 he doggedly established a line at McLean's Crossing on the Poteau River, nine miles southwest of Fort Smith and eight miles east of Scullyville, where J. M. Oneill's cavalry company—the "Rawhides"—reported that they "lay in line of battle for half a day." Cabell, remembering his quartermaster duties in the eastern theaters, "made preparations to protect and send off the public property of every description at Fort Smith. I had

Bleeding deserters from his command of reluctant conscripts, Brig. Gen. William L. Cabell managed to save his supply train from a determined Federal attack on Devil's Backbone ridge after the Confederates abandoned Fort Smith. *Courtesy Arkansas History Commission.*

all the ordnance of every description that I could find or hear of loaded up and placed in a position of safety," ready to be moved south toward Waldron.[35]

Meanwhile, Blunt had split his forces, sending William R. Judson's troops west to deal with Chilly McIntosh's two regiments of Creek fighters, who had been conspicuously absent from the fight at Perry-ville. Blunt headed toward Fort Smith with the remainder of his troops, marching a punishing one hundred miles in four days. Resistance was virtually nonexistent during his advance, though Chaplain Springer recorded an ambush by a bushwhacker on August 29: "The Indian fired from a concealment by the wayside, the fatal ball taking effect in the young man's head. It is perhaps needless to say that the sneaking bushwhacker was not long permitted to remain among us, nor was he treated as a prisoner of war. His death saves the life of many a man loyal to the Federal Nationality. The body lies unburied in an adjacent copse. He was half Spanish & Choctaw."[36]

Colonel Cloud's advance troopers ran into Cabell's scouts two miles west of the San Bois Mountains on August 30, the latter falling back to the Poteau line, where the Rebels had obstructed the road with felled timber. The remainder of the Union column arrived the next day, camping within three miles of the Confederates. Cloud's men crept to within a quarter mile of the Rebel lines, "receiving a volley of artillery, as well as musketry." But, one Southerner recorded, "the powder used by the Confederate pickets would knock up the dust in the road, only 60 or 70 feet ahead when it was aimed to strike 100 yards ahead." Blunt marshaled his troops to attack the next morning but found the enemy line deserted. Cabell, "knowing that [he] could rely on but little more than one-half of the small number of men [he] had to fight," had decided to abandon Fort Smith.[37]

Cabell started his long wagon train south on the evening of the thirty-first, heading for Waldron by way of Jenny Lind. The next day Blunt again split his force, sending Cloud after the retreating Rebels with 1,500 cavalrymen, six cannon, and forty wagonloads of infantry. The general then continued on to claim his prize, accompanied only by his staff and bodyguard and the hard-marching First Arkansas Infantry. "I quietly entered the town of Fort Smith, September 1st, and lowered the rebel flag that had been left floating in this garrison, and raised upon the same staff the 'stars and stripes,'" Blunt reported. An officer of the First Arkansas recorded that "the regiment entered Fort Smith in advance of the Federal forces. The entire distance traveled 400 miles on scanty rations and poor water." Chaplain Springer exulted: "Joyous delivery from the land of Indians & glad to be in Fort Smith." The reoccupation of Fort Smith was virtually unopposed, one resident noted, writing that "there were but few

Confederate soldiers in the town when Cloud arrived & these either skedaddled instanter or were captured."[38]

Cabell, meanwhile, his quartermaster's instincts prevailing, established a line on a jagged ridge southeast of Fort Smith called Devil's Backbone to hold Cloud in check while the supply train moved out of harm's way. He placed J. C. Monroe's dismounted cavalry at the base of the ridge, then positioned the rest of his regiments en echelon along the road up to the top. William F. Hughey's battery of iron guns was placed on the slope behind the rest of the troops "so as to command the whole field of operations." Maj. Americus V. Rieff of Oneill's Rawhides (in Monroe's regiment), watching Cloud's approach, "discovered in peeping through skirts of timber, that he had no flankers out to avoid an ambuscade." Rieff moved his men west of the road and ordered them to lay down in a field behind a fence. As the advance element of the Second Kansas Cavalry "came dashing up, yelling and shouting, confident of success," the Arkansians opened fire, killing Capt. C. D. Lines and four men while wounding several others. Cloud quickly halted his headlong approach and placed his troops in line of battle.[39]

Cloud placed Rabb's Hoosier artillery in the center, the Sixth Missouri Cavalry filed out on the right, and the Second Kansas Cavalry deployed on the left, then they began moving forward. Hughey, who a fellow Confederate officer said "was one of the best artillerists and handled his gun more effectively than any one I served with, except Capt. Collins of Shelby's Brigade," opened fire on the approaching Yankees. Samuel Crawford of the Second Kansas noted that "the enemy, firing down-grade, overshot with both their small arms and artillery. Rabb, in using shell at an elevation, made the same mistake; but when he changed to canister, there was something doing." The Federals drove off the skirmishers and pushed toward the crest of Devil's Backbone.[40]

For hours the adversaries pelted each other with rifle and artillery fire, "Rabb double-charging his guns part of the time." The Rebels held their own, Crawford recalled, until "I discovered that Cabell's right flank was unprotected and I immediately threw forward the two mounted companies on my left, and with a sudden dash put that part of his line out of business." Confederate John C. Wright reported that "Cabell's leading regiment . . . stampeded without firing a shot and running into and through the two regiments in its rear, stampeded them and the whole combined mass ran through the left wing of Morgan's regiment and swept them off the field." Cabell agreed, writing that "eight companies of Morgan's infantry regiment, Hill's and Thomson's regiments, and Woosley's battalion of cavalry ran in the most shameful manner." As the mob cleared the top of Devil's Backbone and streamed down the back of the ridge, they swept through Cabell's provost guard, holding eighty men "under sentence for treason and desertion"; the grateful prisoners fled with the rest.[41]

Incredibly, the remaining Confederates held, with Cabell directing the fire of Hughey's cannon as Morgan's right wing and part of Monroe's cavalry formed alongside, allowing the precious supply train to escape south. Cloud reported that "during a suspense of my fire, the enemy suddenly withdrew, leaving his dead and wounded, together with arms, baggage, &c." Federal losses totaled fourteen, while Cabell reported five killed and twelve wounded. His greatest loss, however, was in the flood of men who had fled from Devil's Backbone, who Cabell bitterly described as "either deserters from other regiments or conscripts or jayhawkers forced into service . . . worthless as troops to defend a country." In fact men continued to drift away following the fighting; by the time Cabell reached Waldron, his brigade had dwindled from 1,250 to 900. Wiley Britton had a different view, however, writing that "probably no one believed it was because the men of these regiments were frightened that they ran, but because they were Union men and did not wish to fire upon their friends, or be placed in a position to be shot by them." Subsequent events would prove the Kansan correct.[42]

Cloud returned to Fort Smith the next morning, finding Blunt sick in bed, perhaps already suffering from the chronic syphilis that eventually would kill him. The first priority was to calm the panicky populace. As the Federal advance had approached Fort Smith, the scene in town had been chaotic, with "women praying, children screaming, donkeys braying, dogs yelping—every quadruped that could navigate being . . . attached to some unwieldy vehicle . . . rank disorder claiming the hour." Samuel Crawford wrote that "many intelligent, educated, refined ladies looked upon Federal officers and soldiers as rough, uncouth barbarians, without any regard for truth, integrity, or virtue. . . . They were afraid to venture out of their houses and afraid to stay at home without a guard." Eventually, he added, "by proper treatment, [they] began to see that, after all, the

Federal troops were not as bad as they had been represented." With the departure of Confederate forces, Fort Smith also became a magnet for area Unionists. Cloud wrote, "my office as been constantly thronged by Mountain 'Feds,' deserters from the rebel army, who deliver themselves up, and citizens from the country, to the distance of 80 miles, who come in with joyful countenances and cheering words, to assume the relation of citizens of the United States."[43]

After a week in Fort Smith, Blunt was well enough to resume command, and Cloud led two hundred men of the Second Kansas Cavalry and a section of the Second Indiana Battery on an expedition to Dardanelle, held by Col. Ras. Stirman with a sizeable force of Rebels, according to deserters. As the Yankees marched west, "we were joined by six companies of Union men, about 300 all told, with the Stars and Stripes flying, and cheers for the Union," Cloud reported. This throng included "three officers and about 100 men, who had fought me at Backbone, under Cabell, and it was a novel sight to see men with the regular gray uniform and Confederate State belt-plate fighting side by side with the blue of the army." The augmented Union column reached Dardanelle on September 12 and pitched forward against Stirman, who had taken command of the town only two days earlier. The two forces fought for two to three hours before the bluecoats and erstwhile Rebels drove the Confederates from town. The Yankees were delighted to find that they had captured considerable commissary stores "upon which," Cloud noted, "I subsisted my command, having no rations with me, and obliged to depend on the country."[44]

After securing Dardanelle, Cloud picked one hundred men and "started to explore the river," heading to Little Rock to make Frederick Steele aware that Fort Smith was firmly in Union hands and that the Arkansas River line was anchored there and at Fort Gibson. The colonel reported, "the people come to me by hundreds, and beg of me to stand by them and keep them from being taken by the conscript officers or from being taken back to the rebel army, from which they have deserted, and to show their earnestness they came in with their old guns and joined us." Steele, flushed with his nearly bloodless victory at Little Rock, ordered Cloud "to organize the Union men and use them until something new is developed."[45]

The Confederates would not make a serious effort to retake Fort Smith. Cabell, receiving conflicting orders from generals William

Steele and Sterling Price, elected to follow the command of the latter and joined the refugees from Little Rock at Arkadelphia. Steele's Confederates were effectively held to the Red River line, and Rebel tactics in the western Arkansas River Valley shifted from conventional offensive operations against the Federals to guerrilla activities, with few exceptions, for the rest of the war.[46]

With the return of Fort Smith to Federal control, the town became a haven for Unionists, who quickly organized politically. On October 3 they adopted a series of resolutions supporting the Lincoln administration's policies, abolishing slavery, and barring all but "Unconditional Union" men from voting in elections. Despite the relative safety of the post, conditions would remain difficult for the civilians and refugees who would crowd into Fort Smith over the next two years seeking protection from the guerrillas who infested the region. Both bushwhackers and organized Confederate cavalrymen constantly interfered with efforts to supply the post; by early 1865 the town's citizens were reduced to directly petitioning President Lincoln for both food and seed to plant spring crops, writing, "thousands are awaiting your decision with the greatest anxiety, and will have to leave and abandon their all if not succored in time."[47]

Despite the continued difficulties at Fort Smith, with its capture Union forces held nominal control of everything north of the Arkansas River in western Arkansas and Indian Territory. Refugee Indians were able to return to their homes, regiments of "Mountain Feds" were organized to combat the guerrillas infesting the Boston and Ozark mountains, and Unionists in the region had a place where they could seek refuge. The western end of the Arkansas River line was, for all intents and purposes, secure.[48]

7

"THE FEDERALS FOUGHT LIKE DEVILS"

The Battle of Pine Bluff

Following the capture of Little Rock on September 10, Frederick Steele's Federal army settled into camps and assessed a capital city that had spent two years under Confederate rule. The city itself received favorable reviews—one Ohioan wrote that he "found Little Rock a very pretty place with many fine residences Arsenal State House," while a Minnesotan described it as "one of the prettiest towns I have seen down South"—but the stress of the war was apparent in the lack of available supplies. Col. Adolph Engelmann of the Forty-third Illinois wrote: "[T]here is not a Yard of any kind of cloth left in the stores, no coffee, no tea, no spice, no spoon, nor knife nor fork, not even a sixpenny nail was to be bought in Little Rock. The crops and beef cattle were to a great extent eaten up by the Secesh Army."[1]

One thing that was not in short supply was Rebel deserters. As late as the first of October, a Kansas officer wrote that dissatisfied Southerners "are comeing to lines by 10s 20s & 30s. The arm[y] west of the Mississippi is virtually *played out.*" A captain in the Fifth Arkansas Cavalry (C.S.) dejectedly observed: "I believe we have seventeen men in our company and about 250 or 275 in the regiment, all told. Last April we had 900 men in the regiment." An Arkansas infantryman, noting, "our men have deserted dreadfully since we left L. Rock . . . and some of them the best soldiers we had," nevertheless pledged: "I shall stick to them till the army 'goes up.' That may not be long." A Rebel Missouri soldier predicted, "we will have to cross

Red River this winter." For the time being, it looked like Union control of the Arkansas River Valley was secure.[2]

The conquering Federals also found Little Rock residents more than ready to profess a long-suppressed loyalty to the Stars and Stripes. "This town is full of union people and . . . [a] good many deserted and took the oath of alleigeans," Olof Liljegren of the Third Minnesota reported. This was confirmed by Iowan Edward Rolfe, who wrote, "there is the Most union people here of any town . . . and hundreds are coming in to take the *Oath* every day." Wisconsinite Edward Redington confided to his wife: "[T]he inhabitants here seem more loyal than any that I have seen South. Many of them seem almost wild with joy." Missourian F. M. Emmons perhaps explained this happiness, stating that Little Rock "has always been called by the Rebs an Abolition hole."[3]

Conditions improved rapidly for the citizens, who were used to straitened circumstances under Confederate rule. As one historian has noted: "[B]usiness picked up, more goods were available . . . , and empty homes and public buildings were pre-empted for military use. Many activities suspended by war, such as racing and the theatre, returned; on book shelves could be found once again copies of *Leslie's, Harper's, Atlantic,* and *Godey's* magazines." Federal authorities encouraged Little Rock's people to sign oaths of allegiance to the U.S. government, with one woman reporting that after doing so, she was given "$175 for supplies, mostly dry goods."[4]

Little Rock was not the only town willing to return to Federal allegiance—or at least to enjoy the protection afforded by a Union garrison. One officer wrote that after the fall of the capital, "immediately a deputation of citizens were sent from Pine Bluff to request Genl. Steele to occupy Pine Bluff by his forces, and prevent the destruction of property and the conscription of unwilling Citizens into the Confederate Army." The general, seeing both the strategic value of holding another strong point on the Arkansas River and the political value of addressing the needs of Pine Bluff's Unionists and businessmen, dispatched part of the Fifth Kansas Cavalry. "All able men ordered on three days scout," August Bondi noted on September 14. William Creitz reported that "the regiment took possession of the place . . . without meeting with the slightest resistance, the citizens generally giving our soldiers a friendly reception, throwing open their larders and inviting them to partake of the best their larders contain."

Three days later, Bondi recorded, "all the balance of the Regiment for Pine Bluff."[5]

The Kansans made themselves at home in Pine Bluff. Bondi recorded on September 19, "by about eleven A.M. . . . the Regiment is quartered in deserted frame buildings"; a regimental historian added that "a few days later, the other regiment of Clayton's brigade (the First Indiana) joined us." For some of the residents, the arrival of the battle-hardened horsemen was frightening. One woman remembered that "the Yankees arrived . . . with flashing sabers and big oaths." Another sniffed: "They have not *forced* anyone to take the *oath*— though numbers have done so voluntarily. There are more union people here and in L. R. than anyone ever thought." For the next month or so, this little band of around 550 horsemen would hold this anchor in the line of the Arkansas.[6]

Pine Bluff was an attractive location that had drawn superlatives from visiting soldiers since early in the war. A Texan in the W. P. Lane Rangers noted in late 1862 that the city "can boast of several thousand inhabitants and several magnificent buildings; nice clean streets." Another Rebel declared, "Delightful gardens, tasteful lawns, and spacious streets, give the whole place an air of comfort and elegance." He also noted a fact that made Pine Bluff strategically important: "The river was navigable to this place at all seasons of the year." A visiting Iowan agreed with these assessments, writing of Pine Bluff: "[T]he town is pleasantly situated on a high bluff. . . . It is one of the most important posts on the river, and necessary to be held to insure uninterrupted navigation of the river." By the fall of 1863, however, the city had lost some of its luster. A Kansas cavalryman sourly wrote: "[T]here are not a dozen tasty buildings in town, and their churches—of which they have a superabundance— . . . are wretched affairs, almost totally destitute of beauty or inside decorations. . . . A graveyard almost in the center of town, with brokendown fences, marred tomb-stones and neglected shrubbery, speak eloquently of the refinement and taste of the more wealthy citizens of Pine Bluff."[7]

Although small in number, the new Union garrison was manned by some of the toughest cavalrymen west of the Mississippi. Veterans of the hit-and-run raids that had defined the military situation in Arkansas in 1863, the Fifth Kansas had a reputation as a hard-fighting outfit and for ruthlessness in dealing with civilians who collaborated with Confederate troops. An Iowan of the Helena garrison found them "tough and hardy looking fellows," while a pro-Southern Pine Bluff youth grudgingly described them as "well equiped and a fine looking specimen of hardy Kansas men." The Fifth, with their constant comrades, the First Indiana, had held the extreme Union right at Helena, thwarting Marmaduke's attack on Battery A.[8]

The rough-and-tumble attitude of the Kansans did not endear them to the citizens, though. Mrs. Arabella Lanktree Wilson wrote that the Union horsemen "were going around stealing horses . . . hunting up firearms, & taking everything they thought proper." Bondi admitted on September 21 that he had to "assist two Jehudins to their horses taken by Company F men," adding that his aid led to an invitation to "rash hashona dinner with Mr. Kohn." After a few weeks, however, the men fell into the routine of garrison life, leading Captain Youngs to muse to his brother, "don't know what the 5th will do for Excitement[.] guess we will take to the union girls of the Country[.] they are affectionate in the extreem feast us on *butter milk & corn dodgers* which by the way is the climax of Arkansaw hospitality."[9]

Regardless of the rowdy reputation of the men of the Fifth Kansas, their commander was held in high esteem by friend and foe alike. Powell Clayton was a native Pennsylvanian who had attended the Partridge Military Academy in Bristol, Pennsylvania, before moving to Kansas in 1855 to find work as a civil engineer. Although there is no evidence that he took part in the bitter cross-border raiding in the 1850s, his biographer observed that "the type of vicious warfare that he saw in Kansas and Missouri . . . helped to prepare him for the guerrilla warfare he would contend with in Arkansas during the Civil War." Idolized by many of his men—one gushed, "He is considered the best cavalry officer in this latitude"—he also was respected by his enemies. A secessionist Pine Bluff woman allowed that Clayton was "a very gentlemanly man and by his humane and obliging manners has quite won the people." John Edwards of J. O. Shelby's command wrote: "Colonel Clayton was an officer of activity and enterprise, clear-headed, quick to conceive, and bold and rapid to execute. His success in the field had caused him . . . to be considered the ablest Federal commander of cavalry west of the Mississippi." These qualities would be put to the test soon after arriving in Pine Bluff.[10]

With Federal occupation, the city became a magnet for runaway slaves, who flocked there by the hundreds. The Yankees established camps for them to the east and west of town. Boston Blackwell and a

Col. Powell Clayton's fierce defense of Pine Bluff led his Confederate opponent to simply comment that "the Federals fought like devils." He would later serve as Arkansas's Reconstruction governor. *Courtesy Civil War Museum, Wilson's Creek National Battlefield.*

fellow slave fled from their plantation after their owner threatened them with a whipping. "It was cold frosty weather," Blackwell remembered. "When we gets to the Yankee camp all our troubles was over. We gets all the contraband we could eat. . . . The Yankees feeds all the refugees on contraband." Mary Harris, another Jefferson County slave, mentioned: "I remember the Yankee soldiers come and took the colored folk away if they wanted to go. . . . They carried us to the 'county band' and fed us." Pine Bluff resident Arabella Lanktree Wilson noted the "stampede" of fleeing slaves, writing that "for 30 miles round, they came pouring in by 100's—every ones servant ran off to P. Bluff, there is scarcely a house here that has a servant left."[11]

As Clayton's brigade established itself at Pine Bluff, its colonel considered offensive operations. Following the fall of Little Rock, the bulk of Sterling Price's Confederate army had fallen back to Arkadelphia, leaving John Marmaduke's cavalry to keep a watchful eye for any Federal activity. Archibald Dobbins's Arkansas horse-men covered the Rebel right from a base at Rockport, while Col. John C. Monroe, commanding Cabell's brigade after that general went on leave, held the left from Caddo Gap. Marmaduke estab-lished his headquarters at Rockport on the Ouachita River. Some of Price's best horsemen, the bulk of Shelby's Missouri cavalry, left Arkansas on September 23 on a raid into Missouri that would last until early November.[12]

The aggressive Clayton decided to bring the battle to the Con-federates. Picking three hundred men and four mountain howitzers, he set out for Tulip. Around 4:00 A.M. on October 11, the Federal cannon opened fire on Dobbins's sleeping Arkansians. "The Fifth Kansas . . . made a furious charge through their lines. . . . The entire rebel force, six hundred (600) strong, fled in dismay, leaving nearly everything behind them; their tents, wagons, arms sabers, pistols, and one battle flag," a final report of the action stated. Dobbins fell back on the lower Arkadelphia road with about two hundred men, rejoining Col. Robert C. Newton's division. The victorious Yankees returned to Pine Bluff around sunrise, with their one casualty, Colonel Clayton, nursing a slight injury from a glancing bullet.[13]

Following the raid, Price moved deeper into southwest Arkansas, pulling his infantry back to Arkadelphia while Marmaduke gathered the cavalry at Princeton. This repositioning signaled a general skittish-ness regarding Frederick Steele's intentions—the Rebels already had taken their telegraph facilities from Arkadelphia and relocated their military stores all the way to Shreveport, Louisiana. Clayton also looked toward improving his capabilities, both offensive and defen-sive. August Bondi of the Fifth Kansas wrote in his diary on October 14 that a detachment "started . . . for Little Rock . . . to bring back a

Brig. Gen. John Sappington Marmaduke tried to salvage the dismal Confederate fortunes along the Arkansas River by attacking Pine Bluff on October 25, 1863, but a spirited Federal defense denied him a victory. *Courtesy Civil War Museum, Wilson's Creek National Battlefield.*

battery of four small rifled cannon which the boys called howitzers." Three days later he recorded that "by noon [they] returned to Pine Bluff with Battery of four howitzers." A week later Clayton's foresight would be rewarded.[14]

Marmaduke in the meantime was gathering intelligence on the defenses of Pine Bluff. Texan Buck Walton, a veteran foe of the Union cavalry around Helena, remembered that he "sent in two of my men . . . as countrymen hauling wood. They went, acted well their part, got what information I wanted and reported to me—which consisted of the number of cannon—where planted—the number of troops—and where camped—where headquarters were—etc. This information was sent by courier to Genl. Marmaduke." Young Benjamin Riggs of Pine Bluff declared, "my blood boiled with hatred and enmity at the sight of them" after the Federals occupied his town, and made careful observations of Yankee positions before stealing away from the city. The youth rode sixty miles to Princeton, avoiding both Union patrols and bushwhacker bands, and presented himself to Colton Greene. "I explained every thing I Knew about the Federals in Pine Bluff," he wrote. "The number of troops, where the Battery was parked. I told him that the place could be easily taken and surprised. I suspected that they were aiming to attack Pine Bluff, though the General gave me no intimation."[15]

Riggs was correct: Marmaduke was formulating a plan to attack his old enemy at Pine Bluff. The thirty-year-old veteran raider—perhaps the best-educated Confederate general in the Trans-Mississippi, having attended Yale and Harvard before graduating from the U.S. Military Academy—was still under a cloud from his fatal duel with Marsh Walker. A successful assault on Pine Bluff would erase the memories of the failure of his division at Helena and the series of retrograde movements during the Little Rock campaign. Marmaduke met with his commanders at Princeton on the evening of October 23 and ordered them to be ready to move out the next morning. Each man was to carry rations for three days and, because of a shortage of ammunition, twenty-five rounds each instead of the usual forty. The attacking party would consist of 2,300 horsemen and twelve cannon.[16]

Marmaduke inspected his two divisions of cavalry on the morning of October 24, then set forth toward Pine Bluff, halting at the Saline River after a hard ride of six hours. As his men rested and their horses foraged, the Rebel general gathered his commanders and issued orders. Marmaduke would continue up the Princeton Road with Colton Greene's Missouri Brigade and John Monroe's Arkansians, approaching Pine Bluff from the west. Robert Newton, leading Maj. John Bull's Arkansas troopers, Maj. B. D. Chenoweth's Texas brigade, and Maj. Robert C. Wood's battalion of Missourians, would split off at Cantrell's Springs and attack Pine Bluff from the southeast. The two columns would trap Clayton's small command within the city and crush them there or force them across the Arkansas River.[17]

The Rebels crossed the Saline but found it slow going as their artillery bogged down in soggy bottomland that had been "cut up by the passage over it of thousands of horses." Afternoon turned to night, and Colonel Thompson wrote, "the intense coldness drove many of the thinly clad soldiers to building fires by the roadside whenever a halt in front admitted the delay." The Confederates continued their march, "tedious and irksome in the extreme," throughout the night, but morning already had broken when Newton's column arrived at Cantrell's Springs, the designated point for them to peel off to their attack positions.[18]

On arrival, Newton's men cut off on back roads to gain the Bayou Bartholomew Road, aiming to hit Pine Bluff from the southeast. Monroe led his Arkansas troops on the Little Rock Road to strike Pine Bluff from the northwest, while Greene's Missourians would proceed up the center on the Sulphur Springs Road. When in position, the Rebel forces would await a cannon shot from Greene's column, their signal to swarm the city and overwhelm the little Federal garrison.[19]

In Pine Bluff, meanwhile, the Yankees were stirring on a sleepy Sunday morning. Lt. Col. Thomas N. Pace had his troopers of the First Indiana Cavalry out early in full fig, undergoing an inspection of arms, while Colonel Clayton sent a company of the Fifth Kansas under Lt. Milton F. Clark on a routine scout toward Princeton. Clark had not moved much beyond the picket lines when, to their mutual surprise, the Kansans ran into the lead elements of Greene's column. The startled troops fired on each other, and Clark quickly positioned his men on either side of the road. As the tense Kansas men braced themselves, an armed group of Confederates rode forward under a flag of truce, and as A. D. Brown of the Fifth Kansas reported it, "after relieving themselves of a surplus of gas and empty bravado, they informed the Lieutenant that they were bearers of dispatches from Marmaduke." Clark chastised the Southerners for first firing on him before coming forth with the flag of truce, then requested thirty minutes to send a man back to ask Clayton if he would accept the Rebel delegation. The Confederates refused the request, implying that their dispatches included a surrender demand. Clark coolly replied, "Colonel Clayton never surrenders, but is always anxious for you to come and take him, and you must get back to your command immediately, or I will order my men to fire on you." Skirmishing began in earnest as Clark sent a courier racing back to Pine Bluff, and Marmaduke, slowed by the passage of his artillery through the Saline bottoms the day before, lost the essential element of his planned attack—surprise.[20]

In Pine Bluff Powell Clayton heard the crackle of gunfire and, realizing an attack was imminent, assessed his situation. His command consisted of the veteran Fifth Kansas and First Indiana Cavalry regiments, a small home-guard company of around fifty men under the command of Capt. R. Murphy, six mountain howitzers, and three rifled steel cannon. The city, as Kansan A. D. Brown noted, was

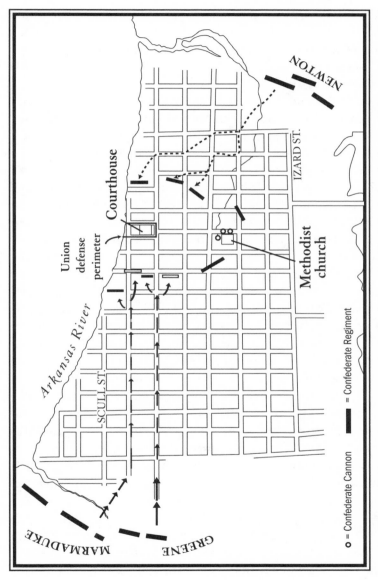

Battle of Pine Bluff, October 25, 1863. Powell Clayton fortified the Pine Bluff courthouse square to fend off John Marmaduke's Confederate attackers. *Map by Kirk Montgomery.*

"built, as near as practicable, on the Southern plan for rural villages, namely: a court house and square form the center, and the town grouped all around in picturesque confusion, except on the north side where the river forms the boundary." This arrangement would work well for defense, especially because the local businessmen had the town's warehouses bursting with heavy bales of cotton. Also the Federals could make use of the hundreds of contrabands from the camps on the outskirts.[21]

Pace had his bugler sound "Boots and Saddles" as Lieutenant Clark's courier warned him of the approaching Confederates, and the First Indiana clattered into town, where, August Bondi recorded, "the public square was made the center of our position." Clayton ordered the Hoosiers to deploy, with Companies A and H to ride out and "feel the enemy and notice his movements," Companies D and F to occupy the courthouse and cover the streets approaching the square, and Companies B and G to move forward and act as skirmishers. All of the troopers sent to the front had orders to fall back if pressed, use the houses fronting the square as strong points, "and to hold them at all hazards." Maj. Thomas W. Scudder, commanding the Fifth Kansas, put his men into position, with two companies sent out to the skirmish line and the rest deployed within town. As the Yankees raced to their positions, Clayton ordered Capt. James B. Talbot of the First Indiana, who had charge of the contraband camps, to bring freedmen in to fortify the square. About three hundred black men were soon rolling heavy cotton bales into position. "In less than half an hour I had all the streets leading into court square completely and very formidably fortified with cotton-bales, and my artillery—six mountain howitzers and three small steel-rifled guns—planted as to command every street leading into the square; my sharpshooters posted in all of the houses and other buildings on the square, so that the enemy could in no way approach the works only through the open spaces"; Clayton was ready.[22]

Scudder rushed the Fifth Kansas into position to support Clayton's artillery. Companies A and I deployed next to a section of the Fifth Kansas Battery on the northwest edge of the square; Company K was sent to the southwest side with the three steel guns of the First Indiana Battery; Companies C and F supported a single howitzer directly south of the courthouse with Companies B, D, and E occupying their left; Company H formed on the southeast with two Kansas howitzers; and

Company G supported the final Kansas gun at the northeast angle of the square. Some men were ordered to collect the brigade's horses in the courthouse lot, and as Bondi reported, "all horses were gathered and tied just as such work could be done in a hurry, [but] some 100 of them ran off during the battle and were captured." Realizing he could be in for a siege, Clayton sent two hundred contraband to "commence carrying water from the river up to the square, and fill all the barrels they could find, so that, if necessary, I could hold out two days."[23]

The Confederates, unaware of Clayton's preparations, continued their advance. On the Princeton Road Col. Robert Lawther, commanding Greene's brigade, charged forward, driving back Lieutenant Clark's skirmishers, killing two men and wounding four others. When within a mile of the courthouse, Lawther ordered his men to dismount and advance on foot, with Col. Merritt L. Young's battalion on the left and Greene's regiment, under Maj. Leonidas A. Campbell, on their right, all forming to the left of the road; Solomon G. Kitchen's regiment remained in the saddle, ready to dash in if an opportunity presented itself. The Rebels moved forward, forcing the skirmishers of the Fifth Kansas behind their cotton-bale fortifications. Lawther reported "a portion of the command being deployed as skirmishers and doing good execution whenever the enemy dared to show themselves above their works."[24]

Newton, meanwhile, moved his men into position at a brickyard a half mile from town. He ordered Chenoweth's Texans, Wood's Missourians, and the bulk of Bull's Arkansians to dismount and form along the Bayou Bartholomew Road. One hundred of Bull's men under Capt. W. B. Anderson remained on their horses, ready to drive back the Yankee pickets and watch for any attempt by the Northerners to retreat across the Arkansas. Newton heard Greene's signal gun fire at 9:00 A.M. and moved forward, with Wood advancing up the road and the Texans on their right. They drove the Yankee skirmishers steadily backward in house-to-house fighting, halting to reform as they came in sight of the barricades around the courthouse. J. H. Pratt's battery moved up with them and soon opened fire on the sharpshooters in the building.[25]

On the Confederate left Monroe dismounted his Arkansas cavalry while Thompson formed on his left with the remnants of Shelby's brigade, remaining mounted. Thompson's left rested on the river; he sent a company of the Sixth Missouri Cavalry to Monroe's right to guard that flank. On hearing Greene's signal gun, the Rebels moved forward. Thompson's troops soon encountered one of the contraband camps, which was "taken possession of, containing tents, various articles of clothing, &c., with horses, mules, and wagons; also many negroes." Skirmishers from the Fifth Kansas opened fire on the Missourians but "were hastily dislodged by our sharpshooters, and steadily driven behind their cotton-bale fortifications." The Missouri Rebels dismounted to fight on foot, their right linking with Monroe's left. Monroe reported that his Arkansians "steadily drove them back until within a short distance of their fortifications, when a destructive fire was poured into my ranks from the buildings and fortifications." Thompson too was stymied in his advance as he reached the outskirts of Pine Bluff, writing, "being in the rear of a row of large buildings, we could effect nothing more than to keep up a running fire from our sharpshooters." Monroe ordered Hughey's Battery forward to shell the Yankee positions, but his "dismounted men were not engaged again during the day." Marmaduke's encirclement of Pine Bluff was complete, but he would see no aggressive moves from the troops on the left.[26]

As the Rebel noose tightened, the citizens of Pine Bluff sought what cover they could find. "Many of them fled to the river and concealed themselves under the bank, while others remained in their dwellings, half frantic with fear throughout the day," A. D. Brown observed. An officer remembered that "it was a Cold raw October day, and many suffered extremely from Cold as well as fear." As Confederate sharpshooters on both flanks started sniping at contrabands passing water up the bank, "it [became] necessary to place the women and children as far as possible in the small ravines formed by water running down the steep and caving banks of the river," he wrote.[27]

By mid-morning, a Union officer remembered, "the cannonading and musket firing had become constant on all sides. . . . All men were at work, the Artillery men at their guns, the Cavalry men with their Carbines, the negroes passing water to extinguish the fires in cotton breastworks as they caught from recoils of guns." The Federals began taking casualties from the relentless fire of the Confederate sharpshooters and artillery. A soldier of the Fifth Kansas saw a First Indiana trooper "prostrated by a spent round shot, which struck him in the face and neck; after lying a few minutes, to all appearances dead, he rose deliberately and resumed his gun." Others were not so lucky. The same soldier reported that Rebel artillery "carried away a leg each of two men; another carried away a man's head; a third killed a man after glancing from a tree; and a fourth passed through an opening in the barricades, exploded in our midst, killing three and severely wounding several others." August Bondi reported that "Company K lost one man, Pat McMahan, killed (hit by a shell in back part of skull) and one wounded" as they took up their positions on the firing line.[28]

Company K, Fifth Kansas fell back as its cotton-bale barricade caught fire, erecting another one 150 feet farther back. Colonel Clayton ordered "all bales at the old barricade removed and fired at several places for quick consumption, else the Confederate sharp shooters would profit by them." That duty fell to Bondi:

> The reb Hotchkiss shells and the bullets of small arms came amongst us like hail. I pulled my hat over my eyes, laid down my carbine, pulled my pistol and cocking it called on some twenty contrabands behind us to come up, which they did, explained to them what was to be done and how, picked up some lariat ropes which happened [to be] handy and organized three bands out of them and at the word "forward," we fairly flew towards the bales left at the old barricade. Seven negroes were shot down around me, one right by me, three dead, four died before night, the balance with me at the barricade tied the ropes to three bales respectively and pulled them by main strength in three directions, the bales sheltering the pulling crews, set fire to them and to all remaining bales, the smoke hiding us from sharp shooters more or less and so without the loss of another man I succeeded.[29]

With the element of surprise lost and the determined Yankee defenders in an obviously strong position, Marmaduke decided to try to blast them from their barricades. After careful reconnaissance, the Confederates determined that artillery placed on the grounds of the wood-frame Methodist church and its adjacent graveyard would have an advantageous field of fire on the Union center. Greene ordered Samuel T. Ruffner's three-gun Missouri battery to unlimber at the church and Daniel B. Griswold's light battery to open fire from their left. Ruffner's guns soon "played upon the court-house and adjoining buildings with effect, while Griswold's battery . . . drove the enemy's sharpshooters from their shelter." Yankee Horace Allis remembered that the Confederate cannon "sent its solid shot and shell crashing through the Courthouse and . . . buildings in their range and into the open square among the corrall'd Cavalry horses." Lieutenant Colonel Pace of the First Indiana reported that the Rebel James and Hotchkiss shells slammed into the courthouse, "compelling our men to vacate on the double-quick." A. D. Brown wrote that "our men labored persistently to silence these . . . guns, but to no purpose; to reach them we were compelled to fire across the grave-yard and through the church." The Kansan was scandalized that the Confederates would place their cannon at a house of worship on a Sunday morning, writing that "such people would botanize over their own mother's grave, and canonize Judas Iscariot or C. L. Vallandigham."[30]

On the Confederate right Pratt's Battery had "silenced such of them as were firing from the cupola of the court-house and those in Rodgers' store-house, but the shots seemed not to do other very great good," according to Colonel Newton. The Texans were ordered to limber up and join the Rebel cannon at the more advantageous position by the Methodist church. As Pratt left his position, Marmaduke's aide William Price raced up and warned Major Bull, whose Arkansians had been positioned in support of the Texas cannoneers, that the Pine Bluff garrison was trying to flee across the river and escape the Rebel trap. Bull ordered his men to charge toward the river. As they raced across one of the streets commanded by Clayton's troops, "the enemy opened on me with grape, and their sharpshooters poured a perfect shower of bullets into my ranks," Bull reported, though only one man was slightly wounded.[31]

As the Arkansians reached the riverbank, they discovered not a fleeing garrison but Pine Bluff's contraband men, forming a bucket brigade to pass water to dowse the burning cotton barricades. Spotting the approaching Confederates, the black men abandoned their buckets, grabbed bales of cotton, and man-handled them into a breastwork to block any advances along the riverbank. Fifteen of the laborers were armed, and they quickly began blazing away at the Rebel cavalrymen. Bull reported that his troops held their position for forty minutes, "the enemy keeping up a severe fire," before pulling all of his men save forty sharpshooters to a safer position to the rear. Captain Talbot praised the men on the riverbank for "firing as many as 30 rounds, . . . one actually ventured out and captured a prisoner. None of them had ever before seen a battle, and the facility with which they labored and the manly efforts put forth to aid in holding the place excelled my highest expectations."[32]

As the clock crawled past noon, Marmaduke became frustrated. His surprise attack having been discovered by Clark's patrol, the assault on Pine Bluff had settled into a stalemate, with an artillery duel in the center of town and sharpshooters taking pot shots at each other around the perimeter. Clayton's cannon effectively commanded all of the approaches to the courthouse square; direct assault would be suicidal. The Southerner decided to burn the Yankees out of Pine Bluff.

An indignant A. D. Brown wrote that "the town was fired in several . . . places at the same time, and their programme began to develop itself. Failing to drive us from our position, they proposed to burn us out, even if they were compelled to sacrifice the whole town to their insatiable lust." Arkansian Capt. J. Ten Rieff was among those who set the fire, and a Union officer reported that he "was pierced by three balls simultaneously either of which was mortal with his torch in his hand he met his death which continued burning until the hand that held it was blackened by the smoke and fire." Rieff was not the only Rebel who died in the flames, the officer continued, writing that several wounded Confederates had crawled into the quarters of the Fifth Kansas, which were soon ablaze. They "were unable to extricate themselves from the flames kindled by their friends. In an attempt to rescue them by some of the 5th Kansas they were fired upon and wounded and forced to leave them to their fate to be burned up by friends." Clayton confirmed the deaths, accusing Marmaduke of a "gross and barbarous deed," that "several of his own men, who were wounded, were burned to death, and almost entirely consumed by the flames that he kindled."[33]

Clayton quickly ordered the contraband bucket brigade to begin "carrying water and throwing it on the buildings immediately joining the square, and thus prevented the fire from doing me any damage." Sgt. Jacob D. Orcutt of Company A, Fifth Kansas Cavalry, also fought the fires, a comrade wrote: "Amid the fire of rebel sharpshooters, he climbed upon the jail roof and drenched it with water to prevent that from catching; he then made his way on top of a large two story and a half house, and by his diligence he preserved that. To him we are indebted for the preservation of one whole side of the courthouse square." As the fires encroached on a building holding the regiment's mule herd, the Kansans opened the doors, and A. D. Brown noted indignantly, "we were obliged to cut them loose to prevent their burning up and they sloped with the graybacks much to our disgust."[34]

As the fires died down by midafternoon and the Union garrison still stood fast, Marmaduke faced a tough decision: should he charge the courthouse square or call it a day? "The Federals could only be captured by storming their works, which would have cost me the loss of at least 500 men," he reported. "I did not think it would pay." The general ordered his men to disengage. The Confederates affected an orderly withdrawal, pausing to take everything they could carry from the camps of the First Indiana and the contrabands. What they could not take, they burned. Marmaduke claimed that "much more would have been captured and brought off but the order to prevent pillaging and straggling during the battle was strictly observed, and in withdrawing, the men did not have time to collect the valuables." Yankee Horace Allis, however, reported widespread looting, claiming that the Rebels "were feasting and frolicking among Eatables and drinkables in the houses of those who had taken shelter under the river. . . . Blankets, bed quilts and Every description of house hold comforts and necessities were gone, not a horse mule bridle or saddle remained outside the courthouse square to any citizen."[35]

Realizing that the Confederates were retreating, Clayton ordered a pursuit. Major Scudder quickly mounted Companies A, E, F, and part of G and thundered down the Princeton Road. About a half mile from town, they were greeted with a volley from Colonel Lawther's rear guard, comprised of Greene's regiment and Young's battalion. A sharp firefight commenced for the next fifteen minutes, after which the Kansans fell back. Regrouping, Scudder moved forward again, but after receiving a volley from Kitchen's Missourians, he decided to break off and return to Pine Bluff.[36]

As Pine Bluff's tired but victorious garrison settled in for the night and Marmaduke's defeated troopers rode hard for Princeton, news of the attack reached Frederick Steele's headquarters in Little Rock. He quickly ordered Col. Henry C. Caldwell, commander of the cavalry in Benton, to hurry to Clayton's relief. A section of the Twenty-fifth

Ohio Light Artillery set out at midnight, escorted by troopers of the Third Missouri and First Iowa Cavalry regiments. The remainder of Caldwell's cavalry set out the next morning, catching up with their advance contingent, which had made camp about twelve miles from Pine Bluff, at about midnight of October 26. Caldwell's force was swelled by troopers of the First Missouri and Third Iowa Cavalry regiments, part of the Little Rock garrison under Colonel Glover, who Steele had dispatched as well.[37]

At about 7:00 A.M. the next morning, the column proceeded toward Pine Bluff, less hurried after learning the night before that "Colonel Clayton had repulsed the enemy, and stood in no need of re-enforcements." The troops arrived in Pine Bluff that afternoon, and the historian of the First Iowa Cavalry gleefully recorded that Marmaduke "had met with a hot reception and a most disastrous repulse, and was now on a retrograde march to a more temperate climate." Caldwell received word that Steele had ordered men from Benton and Little Rock, along with cavalry from Brownsville, to pursue the Rebels, assisted by a regiment of infantry from General Rice that would meet them at Arkadelphia. Clayton was to command the cavalry column, but pleading illness, he left it under Caldwell's control. Caldwell left the Twenty-fifth Ohio Battery, its horses "completely broken down," at Pine Bluff, borrowing a pair of the garrison's mountain howitzers for the pursuit. The colonel tarried until 5:00 P.M., waiting for the troops from Brownsville, then set out, riding thirty miles to the Saline River, where they halted at 4:00 A.M. for a brief rest.[38]

The Yankees galloped on toward Tulip, arriving at 3:00 P.M. and capturing a Rebel lieutenant but learning that Marmaduke was at Princeton, having sent his baggage and loot ahead to Camden. Caldwell camped at Tulip, then moved on Princeton the next morning, only to find that the elusive Confederates had again slipped away. The colonel concluded that because Marmaduke had no supply train to slow him down, "I was satisfied farther pursuit would be fruitless of any satisfactory result," so he turned his column toward Arkadelphia. The Yankees thundered into that town at 2:00 A.M., capturing a pair of lieutenants and a handful of soldiers, $1,370 in Confederate cash raised by the sale of government salt, a large amount of mail, and several horses, mules, and wagons. They did not find Rice's infantry column. The Yankee foot soldiers had abandoned the chase after learning that Marmaduke was headed toward

Camden, placing the Rebels well beyond their ability to pursue on foot. Caldwell returned to Benton, arriving there on October 31.[39]

With Marmaduke safe in south Arkansas, the troops in Pine Bluff took time to assess the results of the October 25 fight. Clayton reported losing eleven soldiers killed, twenty-seven wounded, and one missing, in addition to five contrabands who died in the fighting and twelve others who were injured. Sixty-two of the mules that were cut loose to keep them from being burned alive were now Confederate property, and August Bondi wrote that of the cavalry horses corralled around the courthouse, "some 100 of them ran off during the battle and were captured, as well as the sixty army wagons and their mule teams." Fire had consumed many of the buildings in town, including the quarters of the Fifth Kansas, which held all of the regiment's records and camp equipment. Captain Youngs bemoaned: "I lost on the day of the fight all my company Books & records, all my private property Trunk clothes one gold watch &c &c. . . . [A]ll the Officers in Our Regt with a few exceptions lost their baggage & clothing, but all considered we were satisfied to get off as cheaply as we did."[40]

Despite the heavy fire, there were no civilian casualties reported, though A. D. Brown mentioned, "we hear of one woman having the knot of hair at the back of her head entirely cut away by a fugitive shot." Several people, however, did show their secessionist loyalties during the battle. Brown observed that "some ladies appeared upon the street parading their . . . handkerchiefs and shouting for the 'nigger' confederacy." Robert McMahan wrote that "many of the women shouted for Jeff Davis, and one in particular was clapping her hands and shouting for Jeff when suddenly slap comes some mans open hand clasp on her big traitorous mouth and she was silent for the rest of the day." He also noted that a civilian "took quite an active part in favor of the rebels. He cut loose a number of horses belonging to the Ks. boys and drove them back so the rebs could easily get them in their herd," adding that the man "lies now in the guard house and will probably hang or be shot."[41]

Pine Bluff itself was shattered. Arabella Wilson wailed that "the whole town [was] utterly spoiled" and the Confederates had "burned down the whole of front street." Clayton reported that the courthouse and several homes "were all nearly destroyed by the enemy's artillery. There is scarcely a house in town that does not show the effects of the battle." A Wisconsin officer who arrived two weeks later shared this conclusion, noting, "the town shows marks of a hard fight, many of the houses being riddled with shot." The Methodist church had suffered for sheltering Marmaduke's artillery, Ohioan Robert McMahan observed, writing that "the floor was strewn with small fine splinters, also with shot that had fallen on the inside not having had force to pass through only one wall. The old bible, however, lay untouched, though one of the lamps near was knocked to atoms and the end of the building behind the pulpit perforated by 2 or 3 large shot."[42]

The triumphant Yankees reveled in their victory. A. D. Brown declared, "our eagles have again been victorious after a sanguinary struggle of six hours, and the haughty foe is in full retreat for the Southern border, flatly whipped." Powell Clayton praised his troops in general orders issued on the first of November, writing: "*You* did it. To *you* belongs that reward, which is dearest to the heart of every true soldier—a Nation's gratitude and praise." The men who supported the veterans of the First Indiana and Fifth Kansas also garnered commendations. One soldier noted that "the Home Guards or militia under Capt. Murphy did well, though the rebs got nearly all their horses, their quarters and stables being on the lower side of town. The Guard after fighting a while as skirmishers on the East gradually fell back with the rest behind the barricade." And of the contrabands Brown observed that "they worked patiently and with an unselfish devotion to our cause that goes far to remove the jaundiced prejudice of color. Many of them displayed a heroism under fire highly gratifying, and not a few were found behind the breastworks, using the rifle."[43]

Marmaduke reported 101 casualties in his failed assault: 18 killed, including two officers; 67 wounded, and 16 missing. He tried to make the best of the situation, writing, "we burned 1,000 bales of cotton, all their quartermaster and commissary stores, and some ordnance stores, brought away 300 Federal horses and mules, killed and scattered 200 more, captured and brought off 100 Negroes, destroyed the Negro camps (bringing off many tents), and scattered the Negroes." The general praised all of the troops in the battle: "My troops behaved well. The Federals fought like devils."[44]

The loss at Pine Bluff dealt yet another blow to Southern morale. Theophilus Holmes fretted in a letter to Marmaduke, "your failure at Pine Bluff will make them feel perfectly secure there and [they] may mass their cavalry at Benton for a raid on Washington." Texan Buck

Walton observed that "the result was that eight hundred men whipped at least 2500 of as good men was we had . . . We took our defeat 'manfully' and marched back to camp at Camden." A Missouri cavalryman concluded that "the PB battle was a complete failure on our part. There was lots of grumbling among the men after the fight [who] didn't thing [sic] it was managed right. Our only thought was to capture the place but we were doomed to failure after surprising them at that." Confederate engineer Henry Merrill placed the blame squarely on Marmaduke's shoulders, writing that "he summoned the town to surrender, when he could have gone in without permission."[45]

Marmaduke's assault on Pine Bluff was doomed from the moment his central column was challenged by Lieutenant Clark's patrol on the Princeton Road. The loss of the element of surprise allowed a resourceful Union officer to create a practically invulnerable citadel manned by some of the toughest Yankee soldiers in Arkansas. The Rebel general ultimately made the best choice available by calling off the attack instead of trying to take the town by a frontal assault. As historian Edwin Bearss has observed, "considering that he had in the first place failed to capture the town by miscalculation on his part, he declined to retrieve the error he had made by sacrificing the blood of his men without any compensating advantages." The editor of the *Washington Telegraph* provided a conciliatory attitude and put the role of Marmaduke and his men into perspective in an editorial on November 11: "The services of cavalry are not to be estimated by victories. The very nature of the service implies defeats and retreats. They are used to protect the rear of armies against heavier forces, to harrass the foe, cut off details, destroy their trains, and cripple and retard their movements in every manner. This, Gen. Marmaduke has accomplished most effectively, and has gained many laurels for his command. He in the West, with Shelby and others, will form a gallaxy of cavalry officers, which will shine in history beside that composed of Morgan, Forrest, Wheeler and others in the middle department, and with that of the cavalry heroes in Virginia."[46]

Epilogue

"OLD YEAR, I BID YOU FAREWELL"

The Arkansas River Line, December 1863

The fighting at Pine Bluff marked the last combat of any consequence along the line of the Arkansas River in 1863. With Frederick Steele firmly in control of Little Rock and James Blunt's Yankees entrenched at Forts Smith and Gibson, those Confederate troops who still stood with the colors were encamped far south of the territory they had held at the beginning of 1863.

Sterling Price's army had retreated to Arkadelphia following the Little Rock debacle, demoralized and shedding deserters by the hundreds. Even after being joined by "Old Tige" Cabell's fugitives from Fort Smith, the Rebel army—once more under Theophilus Holmes's command after September 25—numbered less than 7,000 men, around 2,000 of whom were unarmed. In early November Powell Clayton's Fifth Kansas ventured south. August Bondi noted in his diary: "[A] scout to Arkadelphia finds works dismantled. Price and Marmaduke reported at Camden." A month later George Flanders of the Fifth wrote: "The rebs have concluded not to fight us since the fight [at Pine Bluff]. Scouts are out most of the time and find small squads of the rebels but they don't seem inclined to stand and fight."[1]

The dejected Confederates had moved even farther into southwest Arkansas, with their state government setting up shop in the small town of Washington and troops quartered at Camden, Murfreesboro, and Spring Hill. Edmund Kirby Smith, with Nathaniel Banks's Union army threatening a move toward Texas, considered ordering Holmes to abandon the state altogether, suggesting that the Arkansas army could retreat "by Monticello, along Bayou Bartholomew to Monroe [Louisiana], through a country abundant in supplies." As the Rebels settled into winter camps in late 1863, however, their situation began to improve. J. P. Johnson, the inspector general for the Trans-Mississippi Department, reported in early November that "the retreat from the valley of the Arkansas was very demoralizing to the army, and a great many desertions occurred; this has stopped now." Johnson even saw the potential for a counteroffensive, writing that "with 3,000 or 4,000 re-enforcements, the commander would be able to reoccupy the valley of the Arkansas, which is of the first importance to the Trans-Mississippi Department."[2]

Steele would not threaten the defeated Rebels, despite his boast soon after Little Rock fell that, "with 6,000 more infantry, I think I could drive Smith and Price into Mexico." Instead he followed orders from Maj. Gen. John Schofield for his army to begin "perfecting communications including repair of the railroad to Devall's Bluff, the fortification of Little Rock, and the occupation of points necessary to the security of the Arkansas River as a line of defense," with an eye toward future cooperation with Banks's army in Louisiana to threaten the Red River Valley. Union forces established themselves at Little Rock, Pine Bluff, Lewisburg, Clarksville, Fort Smith, Van Buren, and Fort Gibson, creating a line of vedettes that held nominal control of everything north of the Arkansas River. With Helena and Vicksburg in Union hands, historian Robert Kerby has observed, "a Federal steamboat could proceed all the way from Memphis to the eastern frontier of the Creek Nation without once encountering a Rebel patrol."[3]

That relative security had not come easily in the western part of the Arkansas River line. In the weeks following the abandonment of Fort Smith, William Steele determined to return to the offensive and drive Federal forces from their posts, forcing them back to Kansas for lack of forage for their animals. On October 23 he joined Texas troops under Smith P. Bankhead and Indian soldiers led by Douglas Cooper at a camp about twenty-five miles southwest of Fort Smith. He was disappointed to find that 500 of the 3,000 soldiers gathered there were unarmed, and half of the remainder were "Indians without drill or discipline and armed with all kinds of guns." Despite the quality of his troops, Steele gamely moved forward, only to be pummeled by a severe mixture of rain, sleet, and snow that caused much suffering among his poorly clad soldiers. To make matters worse, his scouts reported that Fort Smith had just been reinforced, giving the garrison an effective strength of around 3,800 officers and men. The Rebel general glumly decided to move his men back to defensive positions protecting the approaches to northern Texas.[4]

The Confederate Indians centered around Boggy Depot in the Choctaw Nation well south of the Arkansas River, launching occasional strikes to attack Federal patrols, raid the supply trains making the long trek from Fort Scott, or to harass Unionist refugees returning to their homes. Stand Watie's resilient troops actually managed to strike Park Hill in October, burning John Ross's mansion and the Cherokee council house; Yankee soldiers in turn torched the homes of Watie supporters at Webbers Falls. The American Indian families who remained loyal to the South moved to the Red River region, living as refugees in the Choctaw or Chickasaw nations or in northern Texas.[5]

The refugee Indians were relatively secure compared to civilians in Arkansas. By the end of 1863, many of Thomas Hindman's partisan bands had degenerated into gangs of brigands who were as likely to prey on civilians as on military targets. The area north of the Arkansas River Valley, with no organized Confederate forces and few Union outposts, was the preferred hunting grounds for these bushwhacker bands Nor was southern Arkansas safe from such depredations. After the fall of Little Rock, Rebel forces south of the Arkansas spent more time combating their erstwhile bushwhacking comrades than threatening Yankee forces. It was not until J. O. Shelby's grim Missourians were sent out to crush the outlaw gangs that some measure of control was gained, but for the duration of the war, the people who lived outside of the security of occupied towns were never truly safe.[6]

With the military situation relatively stabilized, Frederick Steele looked toward establishing a Unionist government in Arkansas. The general faced some of the same pressures as had his Confederate counterparts earlier in the war as he was ordered "to hold the line of the Arkansas and to send such troops to the Dept. of the Tenn. as can be spared." Confiding to William Tecumseh Sherman, Steele wrote that if he weakened his forces: "I should be thrown on the defensive all over and compelled to concentrate my forces. In such an event the Union men of Arkansas would lose their confidence in my ability to protect them, the advantages we have gained would be lost and the condition of Arkansas worse than when we came here." Steele stood his ground and began conciliatory efforts to bring Arkansas back into the Union, leading a Confederate officer to write to Jefferson Davis that Steele was "winning golden opinions by his forbearance, justice, and urbanity." Yet one Iowa observer disagreed: "[I]t was the policy he adopted in governing the people of a subjugated district—nearly all of them bitter rebels—which lost him much of his popularity. . . . He believed that the speediest way to bring a dissatisfied people back to a love of the Union was to treat them with kindness. He was right in principle: he only forgot that he was dealing with those who were rotten with treason, and totally destitute of principle."[7]

Unionists began holding meetings in Federal-controlled areas of the state in the fall of 1863, adopting resolutions to support the United States, cooperate with other Unionists, and abolish slavery. Some called for a convention to create a loyal government, while others advocated appointment of a provisional government under the leadership of Isaac Murphy, remembered for his refusal to vote in favor of secession. The mood was conducive, then, when Abraham Lincoln announced his plan for reconstruction on December 8, 1863. Under his program, once 10 percent of the voters who cast ballots in 1860 took the oath of allegiance, they could create a state government that U.S. authorities would recognize. Admission of representatives to Congress would remain within the purview of the Senate and House of Representatives.[8]

Delegates from twenty-four of Arkansas's fifty-seven counties convened at the statehouse in Little Rock on January 4, 1864. Historian Ruth Caroline Cowen has described these men as a rather motley group, "chosen by the so-called county conventions, by loyal state troops on duty outside their county, by self-appointment and by refugees residing in Little Rock." Despite the possibly questionable methods of their appointment, the delegates began the process of drafting a new state constitution, a document that largely retained the 1836 constitution with a few minor revisions, a preamble that nullified the 1861 secession act, and an article outlawing slavery. The convention established a provisional government led by Isaac Murphy and disbanded on January 20, having set a March 14 date for ratification of the proposed constitution.[9]

Elections held March 14–16 yielded 12,177 votes in favor of the constitution, with only 226 cast against it. Murphy's provisional status was superseded as 12,430 voters selected him to be the governor of Arkansas's new Unionist government; he would be escorted to his inauguration by a battalion of African American soldiers, a strong statement of the new government's repudiation of slavery. Voters also elected two senators and three congressmen to represent them in Washington, D.C. But Radical Republicans in Congress blocked their acceptance, and it would be 1868 before Arkansas would have representation in the U.S. government. While never recognized by Congress, the Murphy administration would continue to function throughout the war and stood ready to help organize the state at the cessation of hostilities.[10]

The year 1863, which Texan W. W. Heartsill had welcomed with the observation, "we can only hope that our journey through the coming year may be so bright and lovely as this its first day," ended, in the words of Iowan A. F. Sperry, "in cold and storms, and the new year came in, bright, clear and cold, like the eyes of a northern maiden." With Confederate forces consigned to the southwest corner of the state, Missouri surgeon William McPheeters glumly stated: "This is the last of '63. Many sad and solemn reflections crowd on me to which I cannot here give expression." The Confederacy had failed in its invasion of Pennsylvania, lost control of the Mississippi River, and failed to contain Federal troops at Chattanooga. These events overshadowed the unbroken string of Union successes in Arkansas and Indian Territory, where Federal forces now controlled the strategically crucial Arkansas River Valley. Although brigands ruled the countryside, no serious attempts would be made to challenge Union domination of the valley, and with the exception of Sterling Price's quixotic 1864 raid, a 1,400-mile failure resulting in the loss of most of the state's Rebel cavalry, Arkansas would never again serve as a base for a Confederate invasion of Missouri. Kansan Wiley Britton was justified in ending his chronicle of the war in the region in 1863 "firmly believing that we are near the dawn of a brighter day, when the noble sacrifices of our soldiers will be universally acknowledged not to have been in vain, I can simply say, Old Year, I bid you farewell!"[11]

Notes

PROLOGUE

1. W.J.K. to Dear Mother, Jan. 16, 1863, William J. Kennedy Papers, Abraham Lincoln Presidential Library; Samuel Gordon to My Dear Wife, Jan. 10, 1863, Samuel L. Gordon Papers, ibid.; Heartsill, *Fourteen Hundred and 91 Days*, 89; Estes Letters, Historical Research Center, Texas Heritage Museum, Hill College, 23.

2. Wise, "Letters of Lt. Flavius W. Perry," 29; James M. McPherson, *Battle Cry of Freedom: The Civil War Era* (New York: Oxford University Press, 1988), 502–505, 557; Joel M. Seymour, "The Vicksburg Campaign: From Chickasaw Bluffs to Perkins Plantation," in *Campaigns 42nd O.V.I.*, 2.

3. John B. Cummer to Dear Friend, Feb. 11, 1863, Arkansas Civil War Materials, Butler Center for Arkansas Studies, Central Arkansas Library System; Affectionate Brother John to Dear Sister, Jan. 19, 1863, John T. Harrington Letter, Kentucky Historical Society; David T. Massey to Dear Father, Jan. 11, 1863, David T. Massey Papers, Civil War Collection, Missouri Historical Society; Sidney Little to Sarah Durant, Jan. 11, 1863, Sidney O. Little Papers, Schoff Civil War Letters, William L. Clements Library; George Russell to Kind Friend, Jan. 27, 1863, George W. Russell Papers, Abraham Lincoln Presidential Library.

4. Minos Miller to Dear Mother, Jan. 9, 1863, Minos Miller Civil War Letters, Special Collections Division, University of Arkansas Libraries, Fayetteville; Prentice to Bro. Simon, Apr. 18, 1863, Arkansas Civil War Materials, Butler Center.

5. Estes Letters, 23; Cutrer, "'Experience of Soldier's Life,'" 125; Elisha Stoker to Mrs. Elizabeth Stoker, Feb. 4, 1863, W. E. Stoker Civil War Letters, 1861–65, Small Manuscripts Collection, Arkansas History Commission.

6. Federal troops had captured Nashville, Tennessee, and Baton Rouge, Louisiana, in 1862, and Jackson, Mississippi, would fall to the Union on May 14, 1863. Little Rock would be the fourth Confederate capital captured by Union forces.

7. U.S. House, *Survey of the Arkansas River*, 3–4.

8. "Albert Pike Describes the Arkansas: 'Singularly Winding,' Changing River," quoted in "Chronicles of Arkansas," ed. Margaret Ross, *Arkansas Gazette*, Nov. 30, 1958, 3E

9. U.S. House, *Survey of the Arkansas River*, 6–7.

10. Ibid., 7.

11. Ibid.; McConnell, "Up the Arkansas," 237; "Albert Pike Describes the Arkansas." For a concise description of the hydrology of the Arkansas and White rivers, see Bobby Roberts, "Rivers of No Return," in Christ, *Earth Reeled and Trees Trembled*, 74–76. Roberts includes the Ouachita and Red as other rivers worthy of note in Civil War Arkansas.

12. Your Brother Isaiah Harlan to Dear Alpheus, Dec. 18, 1862, Isaiah Harlan's Civil War Letters, Historical Research Center, Texas Heritage Museum, Hill College; DeBlack, *With Fire and* Sword, 121; Bolton, *Arkansas 1800–1860*, 20; U.S. House, *Survey of the Arkansas River*, 28. Because the slow-moving Arkansas could not keep a dependable channel clear, it saw relatively little action from warships, with the notable exception of the fighting at Arkansas Post. Bobby Roberts has concluded: "The physical characteristics of the White River meant it could accommodate deeper draft vessels better than slower-moving, silt-laden streams. . . . It is this favorable hydrology that kept the channels scoured, thus making the White River the most important Arkansas River during the Civil War." Roberts, "Rivers of No Return," 75.

13. C. Fred Williams, "Window on the Southwest: Arkansas's Role in the Mexican War," in Frazier and Christ, *Ready, Booted, and Spurred*, 29; Roberts, "Rivers of No Return," 75–78.

14. The twelve counties bordering the Arkansas River in 1860 were Arkansas, Conway, Crawford, Desha, Franklin, Jefferson, Johnson, Perry, Pope, Pulaski, Sebastian, and Yell. They held 395,943 acres of improved and 1,541,119 acres of unimproved farms. Production in 1860 included 159,403 bushels of wheat; 3,757,576 bushels of Indian corn; 88,557 400-pound bales of ginned cotton; 70,190 bushels of peas and beans; 118,055 bushels of Irish potatoes; 285,418 bushels of sweet potatoes; 959,063 pounds of butter; 4,554 pounds of cheese; 3,585 tons of hay (which could prove an important factor in the cavalry-heavy operations of 1863); and 211,826 pounds of honey. U.S. Bureau of the Census, *Agriculture of the United States in 1860*, 6–9; Cutrer, "'Experience of Soldier's Life,'" 123.

CHAPTER 1

1. DeBlack, *With Fire and Sword*, 19; Carl Moneyhon, "1861: 'The Die Is Cast,'" in Christ, *Rugged and Sublime*, 1–3.

2. Dougan, *Confederate Arkansas*, 41; Moneyhon, "1861," 3.

3. Dougan, *Confederate Arkansas*, 41–42.

4. DeBlack, *With Fire and Sword*, 21–22; Dougan, *Confederate Arkansas*, 41–42.

5. Based on the candidates elected to the secession convention, the February 18 voting resulted in 23,626 ballots for the Union and 17,927 for secession. Dougan, *Confederate Arkansas*, 43, 45; DeBlack, *With Fire and Sword*, 24–26.

6. DeBlack, *With Fire and Sword*, 26–27.

7. Scott, *Loyalty on the Frontier*, 21; Dougan, *Confederate Arkansas*, 62–63.

8. Moneyhon, "1861," 11–13; DeBlack, *With Fire and Sword*, 34; Christ, *Getting Used to Being Shot At*, 5.

9. DeBlack, *With Fire and Sword*, 30–31; Scott, *Loyalty on the Frontier*, 102.

10. The First Arkansas Infantry Regiment, serving under Brig. Gen. Theophilus Holmes, was present at the First Battle of Bull Run on July 21, 1861, but was not actively engaged in the fighting. Moneyhon, "1861," 14; Christ, *Getting Used to Being Shot At*, 22–25, 30; N. Bart Pearce, "Arkansas Troops in the Battle of Wilson's Creek," in Johnson and Buel, *Battles and Leaders*, 1:303.

11. DeBlack, *With Fire and* Sword, 42–43; Moneyhon, "1861," 17.

12. Edwards, *Prairie Was on Fire*, xii, 1; Josephy, *Civil War in the American West*, 323–24.

13. Edwards, *Prairie Was on Fire*, 2; DeBlack, *With Fire and Sword*, 37–39; Josephy, *Civil War in the American West*, 328–30.

14. Edwards, *Prairie Was on Fire*, 3–9.

15. Ibid., 10–14; Christ, *Getting Used to Being Shot At*, 26.

16. William L. Shea, "1862: 'A Continual Thunder,'" in Christ, *Rugged and Sublime*, 21–22; Warner, *Generals in Gray*, 314–15.

17. Shea, "1862," 22; Warner, *Generals in Blue*, 107–108.

18. Shea, "1862," 23–26; Shea and Hess, *Pea Ridge*, 32–35.

19. Shea, "1862," 27–28; Shea and Hess, *Pea Ridge*, 55–56.

20. Shea, "1862," 28–30.

21. Ibid., 31–33; Gaines, *Confederate Cherokees*, 80–82; Shea and Hess, *Pea Ridge*, 144.

22. Shea, "1862," 34–35; Shea and Hess, *Pea Ridge*, 217.

23. Shea, "1862," 35–37; Shea and Hess, *Pea Ridge*, 260.

24. Shea, "1862," 37–38; DeBlack, *With Fire and Sword*, 49–50; Gaines, *Confederate Cherokees*, 93; Christ, *Getting Used to Being Shot At*, 31.

25. Shea, "1862," 38, 41; Dougan, *Confederate Arkansas*, 90; DeBlack, *With Fire and Sword*, 53–54.

26. Neal and Kremm, *Lion of the South*, 117.

27. Ibid., 118; DeBlack, *With Fire and Sword*, 55; Shea, "1862," 39.

28. The best study to date of the guerrilla war and Union counter-measures in Arkansas is Mackey, *Uncivil War*. General Orders No. 17 is reprinted in ibid., 206–207.

29. Hubbs, "Rebel Shot Causes Torture," 46–50; *Official Records of the Union and Confederate Navies*, ser. 1, 23:200 [hereafter referred to as *ORN*; all references are to series 1 unless otherwise indicated].

30. Hubbs, "Rebel Shot Causes Torture," 50. Hubbs notes that the single shot at St. Charles was responsible for 7 percent of the U.S. Navy's total of 1,804 fatalities during the Civil War.

31. Shea and Hess, *Pea Ridge*, 301–303; Shea, "1862," 42–43.

32. Shea and Hess, *Pea Ridge*, 302–303; DeBlack, *With Fire and Sword*, 58–59.

33. DeBlack, *With Fire and Sword*, 59–61; Shea and Hess, *Pea Ridge*, 303–304; John B. Scott to Dear Brother, July 21, 1862, John B. Scott Letter, 1862, Special Collections, University of Arkansas Libraries. Scott described Helena as "a rite smart place and a nice place if the river did not over flow so mutch." Union troops there would soon have a distinctly different opinion of the riverport.

34. Dougan, *Confederate Arkansas*, 94–95; Christ, *Getting Used to Being Shot At*, 47.

35. Castel, "Theophilus Holmes," 11–17; Neal and Kremm, *Lion of the South*, 133; Geise, "Holmes Fails to Create a Department," 170.

36. Castel, "Theophilus Holmes," 14; Shea, "1862," 45–6; Geise, "Holmes Fails to Create a Department," 170–71.

37. Shea, "1862," 46–47; Neal and Kremm, *Lion of the South*, 140–41.

38. Allardice, *More Generals in Gray*, 190; Neal and Kremm, *Lion of the South*, 141–42; Shea, "1862," 47.

39. Geise, "Holmes, Arkansas, and the Defense of the Lower River," 231–32; Castel, "Theophilus Holmes," 14; S.C. to Lt. Gen. Holmes, Dec. 14, 1863, Theophilus Hunter Holmes Papers, Rare Books, Manuscripts, and Special Collections Library, Duke University.

40. Kremm and Neal, *Lion of the South*, 143–45; Shea, "1862," 48; Shea, "'Whipped and Routed,'" 26–39.

41. Shea, "1862," 50–51; Kremm and Neal, *Lion of the South*, 146; DeBlack, *With Fire and Sword*, 67.

42. Historian William Shea has noted that Herron's troops averaged thirty-five miles per day, with some making the last sixty-six miles in thirty hours, concluding that "the march was one of the extraordinary events of the war and an epic of human endurance." Shea, "1862," 51–52. See also Neal and Kremm, *Lion of the South*, 149–50.

43. Shea, "1862," 54–55; DeBlack, *With Fire and Sword*, 68–70.

44. Shea, "1862," 55–56; DeBlack, *With Fire and Sword*, 70–71.

45. DeBlack, *With Fire and Sword*, 71; Neal and Kremm, *Lion of the South*, 153; Shea, "1862," 56–57.

46. Shea, "1862," 57–58; Neal and Kremm, *Lion of the South*, 154; Robertson, "Civil War Letter," 82, 84; Bearss, "Federals Raid Van Buren," 131, 139–42.

47. Shea, "1862," 58; Mackey, *Uncivil War*, 37; DeBlack, *With Fire and Sword*, 73–74; Kerby, *Kirby Smith's Confederacy*, 37–43.

CHAPTER 2

1. Bearss, "Battle of the Post of Arkansas," 237. A Wisconsin soldier later recorded in his diary that construction of Fort Hindman "was done

entirely by negroes. Rebel account books of workmen furnished by slave holders were found showing that nearly five hundred negroes were employed." D. W. Hitchcock Journal, Arkansas Post National Memorial, 22.

2. For a succinct account of Arkansas Post's rich history, see Coleman, *Arkansas Post Story.*

3. Bearss, "Battle of the Post of Arkansas," 239, 248. The *Pontchartrain* itself was in a kind of bureaucratic limbo, lying in the Arkansas River near Arkansas Post. J. D. Caldwell, the vessel's chief engineer, reported on December 18, 1862, that the commissary officer at Arkansas Post refused to issue provisions to the *Pontchartrain's* skeleton crew, a situation that was not fully corrected until January 8, 1863. The correspondence regarding this issue indicates that the *Pontchartrain* may have lingered near Fort Hindman up to the day before the Federal flotilla arrived. Jno. D. Caldwell to Sir, Dec. 18, 1862, John W. Dunnington Papers, Miscellaneous American Manuscripts Unassigned, Pierpoint Morgan Library; Jno. W. Dunnington to Sir, Jan. 8, 1863, ibid.

4. R. Q. Mills to My Dearest Wife, Dec. 14, 1862, J. N. Heiskell Civil War Collection, University of Arkansas at Little Rock Archives; Turner, "Jim Turner, Co. G," 155; Your Brother Isaiah Harlan to Dear Alpheus, Dec. 18, 1862, Isaiah Harlan's Civil War Letters, Historical Research Center, Texas Heritage Museum, Hill College; Heartsill, *Fourteen Hundred and 91 Days,* 85; Oliphant, "Arkansas Post," 736.

5. *ORN,* 23:491–92; Cyrus Bussey Reminiscences, Iowa State University Library Special Collections Department, 24; Bearss, "Battle of the Post of Arkansas," 240–43.

6. Bearss, "Battle of the Post of Arkansas," 239, 243; *Handbook of Victoria County,* n.p.; Collins, *Unwritten History,* 63; "Confederate Letters of Bryan Marsh," *Chronicles of Texas* 14 (1975): 20; R. Q. Mills to My Dearest Wife, Dec. 14, 1862, Heiskell Civil War Collection.

7. N. D. Brown, *One of Cleburne's Command,* 192; Wise, "Letters of Lt. Flavius W. Perry," 28; Letter, Dec. 25, 1862, Isaiah Harlan's Civil War Letters; Caraway, "Battle of Arkansas Post," 127; John Arrington to Dear Mother and Brothers and Sisters, Dec. 21, 1862, John M. Arrington Letters, Company D, Fifteenth Texas Infantry, Historical Research Center, Texas Heritage Museum, Hill College.

8. Letters, Dec. 18, 25, 1862, Isaiah Harlan's Civil War Letters; Darst, "Robert Hodges," 33–34; Collins, *Unwritten History,* 65; Estes Letters, Historical Research Center, Texas Heritage Museum, Hill College, 22.

9. *War of the Rebellion,* ser. 1, 13:928 [hereafter referred to as *OR;* all references to series 1 unless otherwise noted]; Warner, *Generals in Gray,* 49–50; Collins, *Unwritten History,* 66.

10. Bearss, "Battle of the Post of Arkansas," 243–44; E. Paul Reichhelm Memorandum, 1862–63, Diaries, Thomas Ewing Family Papers, Library of Congress, 23; Simons, *In Their Words,* 27; Heartsill, *Fourteen Hundred and 91 Days,* 88; Wise, "Letters of Lt. Flavius W. Perry," 29–30, Anderson, *Campaigning with Parsons' Texas Cavalry,* 88; Turner, "Jim Turner, Co. G," 155.

11. Shea and Winschel, *Vicksburg Is the Key,* 41–45. For a detailed account of the Holly Springs raid, see Bearss, *Campaign for Vicksburg,* 1:287–347.

12. Shea and Winschell, *Vicksburg Is the Key*, 46–52.

13. Ibid., 53–55; Sherman, "Vicksburg by New Year's," 47.

14. Warner, *Generals in Blue*, 293; Sherman, "Vicksburg by New Year's," 48. For a sympathetic and balanced assessment of McClernand as politician and soldier, see Kiper, *McClernand*.

15. Kiper, *McClernand*, 132–34, 138–40, 149, 153; Webster, *First Wisconsin Battery*, 110; Byrne and Soman, *Your True Marcus*, 218–19; Jones, *My Dear Carrie*, 30; Cox, *Kiss Josey for Me*, 116–17.

16. Kiper, *McClernand*, 156–57; Thorndike, *Sherman Letters*, 182; Sherman, *Memoirs*, 445. Gorman had reported on December 15, 1862, that Sherman's levy on his troops left the Helena garrison with "less than 3,000 effective infantry and 2,000 effective cavalry and four miserable batteries, with 1,500 sick on my hands." *OR*, 17(1):701, 22(1):836–37.

17. Bearss, "Battle of the Post of Arkansas," 246–47; "Capture of the Post of Arkansas," *Harper's Weekly*, Feb. 7, 1863, *Abraham Lincoln and the Civil War*, http:www.lincolnandthecivilwar.com/asp/ViewArticleTextAR (accessed Dec. 22, 2005; site now discontinued), copy in author's files; Sherman, *Memoirs*, 319. Bearss concludes that "probably the thought of reducing the Southern bastion occurred to each of the generals at about the same time." Bearss, "Battle of the Post of Arkansas," 246. Porter recalled telling Sherman that McClernand "shall not treat you rudely in my cabin, and I was glad of the opportunity of letting him know my sentiments." Ibid. Richard L. Kiper gives an in-depth analysis of the incident and the three men's relationships in *McClernand*, 158–61.

18. C. W. Gerrard, *A Diary. The Eighty-Third Ohio Vol. Inf. in the War, 1862–1865* (1889), 27 (copy at Ohio Historical Society, Columbus); Bearss, "Battle of the Post of Arkansas," 247; Diaries of Thomas B. Marshall, Walter Havighurst Special Collections, Miami University, 50–51; Woodworth, *Musick of the Mocking Birds*, 19; Asa E. Sample Diary, Manuscripts Section, Indiana State Library; Reminiscences of John F. Roberts (L229), Ripley County Civil War Papers, ibid., 2; Heartsill, *Fourteen Hundred and 91 Days*, 90.

19. John A. McClernand to Admiral, Jan. 8, 1863, David D. Porter Papers, Bixby Collection, Missouri Historical Society; Robert S. Huffstot, "Battle of Arkansas Post," 4–5; *ORN*, ser. 2, 1:46; Sample Diary, 36; T. B. Marshall Diaries, 54; Reichhelm Memorandum, Ewing Family Papers, 24; R. B. Beck Diary, Jan. 9, 1863, Mrs. Douglas W. Clark Papers, Library of Congress.

20. *OR*, 17(1):780, 790; Cuthbertson, "Coller of the Sixth Texas," 133; "They Were There," 3.

21. *OR*, 17(1):783, 790; Oliphant, "Arkansas Post," 736; Heartsill, *Fourteen Hundred and 91 Days*, 91; Cuthbertson, "Coller of the Sixth Texas," 133.

22. Lucien B. Crooker, "From Chicago to Arkansas Post, October 1861–January 1863," in Committee of the Regiment, *Fifty-fifth Regiment Illinois Volunteer Infantry*, 199; *OR*, 17(1):702, 751; Hess, *German in the Yankee Fatherland*, 54; Bearss, "Battle of the Post of Arkansas," 249–50.

23. Bearss, "Battle of the Post of Arkansas," 250; *OR*, 17(1):702–703, 719, 754; W.J.K. to Dear Wife, Jan. 12, 1863, William J. Kennedy Letters, Abraham Lincoln Presidential Library.

24. *OR*, 17(1):702, 754, 765–66; L. Brown, *American Patriotism*, 353; Heartsill, *Fourteen Hundred and 91 Days*, 92; Larimer, *Love and Valor*, 101.

25. Bearss, "Battle of the Post of Arkansas," 253; Warner, *Generals in Blue*, 485; *OR*, 17(1):703, 772, 775, 777, 791; Kimbell, *Battery "A" First Illinois Light Artillery*, 60; Crooker, "Chicago to Arkansas Post," 200–201.

26. *OR*, 17(1):725–26, 746.

27. Ibid., 703–704; Justin W. Meacham, "Military and Naval Operations on the Mississippi," in *Military Order of the Loyal Legion of the United States*, 4:391; Bearss, "Battle of the Post of Arkansas," 256; *ORN*, 11:731, 23:400; Milligan, "Navy Life on the Mississippi River," 71.

28. Fred to Dear Mother and Father, Jan. 11, 1863, Frederic E. Davis Papers, 1860–63, Special Collections and Archives Division, Robert W. Woodruff Library, Emory University; [John Harper] to Dear Parents, Jan. 13, 1863, John Harper Letters, Abraham Lincoln Presidential Library; Samuel Gordon to My Dear Wife, Jan. 10, 1863, Samuel L. Gordon Papers, ibid.; Reid, *Fourth Indiana Cavalry*, 43; W.J.K. to Wife, Jan. 12, 1863, Kennedy Papers; Foster, "We Are Prisoners of War," 27; Collins, *Unwritten History*, 67; Turner, "Jim Turner, Co. G," 165; *OR*, 17(1):784. The Union bombardment of Arkansas Post was so loud that a resident of Spring Vale in Clark County reported: "When the Feds took the Post of Arkansas every body heard the cannon here one hundred miles [from the Post]." H. N. Miller to Sarah, My Dear Child, Mar. 5, 1863, Adams-Miller Family of Clark County, Ark., Letters: 1860–63, Arkansas History Commission.

29. Meacham, "Military and Naval Operations on the Mississippi," 391; Scharf, *Confederate States Navy*, 349; *ORN*, 23:400; Cuthbertson, "Coller of the Sixth Texas," 134; Milligan, *From the Freshwater Navy*, 71; Turner, "Jim Turner, Co. G," 156.

30. Clark, *Life in the Middle West*, 86; E. Paul Reichelm Diary, 1862–63, Diaries, Ewing Family Papers, 25–38; John T. Buegel Civil War Diary, Western Historical Manuscript Collection, University of Missouri–Columbia, 23; Miller, "Narrative of the Services of Brevet Major Charles Dana Miller," Tennessee State Library and Archives, 32; Calvin Ainsworth Diary, Bentley Historical Library, University of Michigan, 18–19; Beck Diary, January 10, 1863, Clark Papers; Latimer, *Love and Valor*, 101; David Palmer Diary, Jan. 10, 1863, David James Palmer Papers, Special Collections Department, University of Iowa Libraries.

31. Bearss, "Battle of the Post of Arkansas," 257; Collins, *Unwritten History*, 67; *OR*, 17(1):791; Simpson, *Bugle Softly Blows*, 31; Mason, *Forty-Second Ohio Infantry*, 173; Sherman, *Memoirs*, 320–21; Grecian, *Eighty-Third Regiment, Indiana Volunteer Infantry*, 20; George B. Marshall Reminiscences, Manuscripts Section, Indiana State Library, 34.

32. *OR* 17(1):781, 791; Bearss, "Battle of the Post of Arkansas," 257; Bailey, *Between the Enemy and Texas*, 102; Delaney, "Diary and Memoirs of Marshall Samuel Pierson," n.p.

33. Foster, "We Are Prisoners of War," 25. Sherman, *Memoirs*, 321; Diary of John E. Wilkins, Community Archives, Vigo County Public Library, 72.

34. Miller, "Narrative of the Services of Brevet Major Charles Dana Miller," 32; Mason, *Forty-Second Ohio Infantry*, 174; Bentley, *77th Illinois*

Volunteer Infantry, 115; Oliphant, "Arkansas Post," 787; Belser, "Military Operations in Missouri and Arkansas," 483.

35. Miller, "Narrative of the Services of Brevet Major Charles Dana Miller," 32; Ainsworth Diary, 19–20; *OR*, 17(1):792; Reichelm Memorandum, Ewing Family Papers, 29; Buegel Civil War Diary, 23.

36. Bearss, "Battle of the Post of Arkansas," 260–63; *OR*, 17(1):706, 765; Scott, *Sixty-Seventh Regiment Indiana Infantry*, 19.

37. Caraway, "Battle of Arkansas Post," 128; Collins, *Unwritten History*, 67–68; Bishop, "Battle of Arkansas Post," 152.

38. *ORN*, 24:104. "Slush" was a mixture of white lead and tallow used to coat wire rigging and machine parts. Traditionally, naval vessels kept a slush barrel to save grease and fat that then would be used to coat masts and rigging. McEwen and Lewis, *Encyclopedia of Nautical Knowledge*, 512.

39. Meacham, "Military and Naval Operations on the Mississippi," 393; *ORN*, 11:731, 23:400; Foster, "We Are Prisoners of War," 28; Hegarty, *Father Wore Gray*, 37–38; Fred to Dear Mother and Father, Jan. 11, 1863, Davis Papers; Milligan, "Navy Life on the Mississippi River," 71–72; Simms, "Union Volunteer with the Mississippi Ram Fleet," 189–90.

40. *OR*, 17(1):749, 751–52; Mason, *Forty-Second Ohio Infantry*, 176–77; Heartsill, *Fourteen Hundred and 91 Days*, 96–97; Caraway, "Battle of Arkansas Post," 128; Foster, "We Are Prisoners of War," 28. Jacob Foster also noted the effect of his fire on Samuel Foster's position: "While we were firing we saw the rebel flag fall at this point, and the body of a rebel soldier was found blown over the epaulement, the flag lying down not 20 feet distant." *OR*, 17(1):749.

41. *ORN*, 24:108, 119–20; Simms, "Union Volunteer with the Mississippi Ram Fleet," 190; *OR*, 17(1):752.

42. Bearss, "Battle of the Post of Arkansas," 265; Delaney, "Diary and Memoirs of Marshall Samuel Pierson," n.p.; Larimer, *Love and Valor*, 102; Buegel Diary, 23; Black, *Soldier's Recollections*, 33; *OR*, 17(1):756, 792.

43. Miller, "Narrative of the Services of Brevet Major Charles Dana Miller," 33; *OR*, 17(1):793; Collins, *Unwritten History*, 68; Buegel Diary, 24; Wilhelm to Dear Mina, Jan. 13, 1863, Johann Wilhelm Osterhorn Papers, Missouri Historical Society; Ainsworth Diary, 21–22; A. J. Withrow to Dear Lib, Jan. 12, 1863, Adoniram Judson Withrow Papers (3679), Southern Historical Collection, Wilson Library, University of North Carolina.

44. *OR*, 17(1):769–70, 793; *Rolla (Mo.) Express*, Feb. 7, 1863. A later assessment of the Twenty-sixth Iowa concluded, "In none of the numerous battles in which they were subsequently engaged did the men and officers show more fortitude than while advancing against the rebel stronghold at Arkansas Post." The regiment suffered 25 percent casualties in the attack, more than any other Union regiment engaged. Iowa Adjutant General's Office, *Roster and Record*, 3:1019; Clark, *Life in the Middle West*, 87; Ingersoll, *Iowa and the Rebellion*, 531.

45. Bearss, "Battle of the Post of Arkansas," 267–68; Smith, *Life and Letters of Thomas Kilby Smith*, 260; Woolworth, *Experiences in the Civil War*, 19; [Harper] to Dear Parents, Jan. 13, 1863, Harper Letters; *OR*, 17(1): 774, 776.

46. *OR*, 17(1):793; Hegarty, *Father Wore Gray*, 38.

47. Bearss, "Battle of the Post of Arkansas," 268–69; Hatch, *Dearest Susie*, 35; Diary of John E. Wilkins, 72; Eugene to ?, Jan. 29, 1863, Owen Mss., Lilly Library, Indiana University; T. B. Marshall Diaries, 58–59.

48. *OR*, 17(1):726, 731, 736; Hitchcock Journal, 22; Hezekiah K. Helphrey Letter, n.d., Arkansas Civil War Materials, Butler Center for Arkansas Studies, Central Arkansas Library System; Eugene to ?, Jan. 29, 1863, Owen Mss.; Puck, *Sacrifice at Vicksburg*, 43; T. B. Marshall Diaries, 57; Woods, *Services of the Ninety-Sixth Ohio*, 23; Perdue, "Wartime Diary of William Henry Willcox," 22; Bentley, *77th Illinois Volunteer Infantry*, 116; Hatch, *Dearest Susie*, 35. The historian of the Forty-eighth Ohio remembered: "Our batteries . . . soon exploded the enemies magazine and caissons, which sent the fragments flying to every part of their works." Bering and Montgomery, *Forty-Eighth Ohio Veteran Volunteer Infantry*, 67. The Eighty-third Ohio would suffer eighty-nine casualties at Arkansas Post, including eight killed. Edwin Bearss notes, "The desperate nature of this fight is seen in the fact that more than one-third of the loss sustained in McClernand's army in the battle for the Post occurred in Burbridge's brigade." Bearss, "Battle of the Post of Arkansas," 269.

49. *OR*, 17(1):747; Hegarty, *Father Wore Gray*, 37; Mix and Earley, *Journal of Thomas E. Mix*, 5; Cuthbertson, "Coller of the Sixth Texas," 134–35; Byrne and Soman, *Your True Marcus*, 221; J. S. B. Matson to Friend Lyman, [Jan. 1863], "Matson3," *They Were the 114th O.V.I.*, http://www.fortunecity.com/westwood/makeover/347/id192.htm (accessed Feb. 18, 2009); Gerard, *A Diary*, 28; Turner, "Jim Turner, Co. G," 157.

50. Bishop, "Battle of Arkansas Post," 152; Fred to Dear Father and Mother, Jan. 11, 1863, Davis Papers; Foster, "We Are Prisoners of War," 29; *OR*, 17(1):781; Heartsill, *Fourteen Hundred and 91 Days*, 95; Caraway, "Battle of Arkansas Post," 127; Reid, *Fourth Indiana Cavalry*, 43; Sidney Little to Sarah P. Durant, Jan. 13, 1863, Sidney O. Little Papers, Schoff Civil War Soldiers Letters, William L. Clements Library.

51. *OR*, 17(1):707, 726, 781, 785; Foster, "We Are Prisoners of War," 29; Bond, *Under the Flag of the Nation*, 48; Hatch, *Dearest Susie*, 36; John Kehrwecker letter, Jan. 13, 1863, Kehrwecker Family Papers, Center for Archival Collections, Bowling Green State University; Scharf, *Confederate States Navy*, 350; Hearn, "Admiral Porter and His 'Damned Gunboats,'" 42; Stevenson, *Letters from the Army*, 171. The iconic image of the final moments of the Federal assault emerged when *Frank Leslie's Illustrated Newspaper* depicted Burbridge rushing across the causeway into Fort Hindman bearing a streaming flag and urging his men on. The Union general had the advantage of having a sympathetic reporter embedded with his headquarters. "Battle of Arkansas Post and Capture of Fort Hindman," *Frank Leslie's Illustrated Newspaper*, Feb. 14, 1863.

52. *OR*, 17(1):794; Collins, *Unwritten History*, 69; Sherman, *Memoirs*, 323. For a detailed account of the effects of his brigade's surrender on Col. Robert Garland's career, see Woodworth, "Scapegoat of Arkansas Post."

53. Your aff. Brother Jo to Sister Crete, Jan. 12, 1863, Lucretia Rudolph Garfield Letters, Library of Congress; Cuthbertson, "Coller of the Sixth

Texas," 135; Temple, *Letters of Henry C. Bear*, 31; W.J.K. to Dear Wife, Jan. 8 [*sic*], 1863, Kennedy Papers; Kimbell, *Battery "A" First Illinois Light Artillery*, 61; Sidney Little to Dear Mother, Jan. 17, 1863, Little Papers; Fred to Dear Father and Mother, Jan. 11, 1863, Davis Papers; "Civil War Letter," *Grand Prairie Historical Bulletin*, 37; G. B. Marshall Reminiscences, 34; Frey, *Grandpa's Gone*, 23.

54. Caraway, "Battle of Arkansas Post," 128; Bishop, "Battle of Arkansas Post," 153; Heartsill, *Fourteen Hundred and 91 Days*, 97; Hegarty, *Father Wore Gray*, 36; Crooker, "Chicago to Arkansas Post," 203; Bilby, "Memoirs of Military Service, Carlos W. Colby," 25; J. S. B. Matson to Friend Lyman, [Jan. 1863], "Matson3," *They Were the 114th O.V.I.*

55. Foster, "We Are Prisoners of War," 30; William Gates Hubert, Civil War Reminiscences, Historical Research Center, Texas Heritage Museum, Hill College; John Faulk Memoir, ibid., 5; Delaney, "Diary and Memoirs of Marshall Samuel Pierson," n.p. Other Texans would seek their freedom while being transported up the Mississippi River to Northern prisons. A soldier of the Forty-second Ohio wrote that "many of them jumped overboard and swam ashore; that is, if they were lucky enough to escape the fire of the guards, and he judged that most of the balls went high." Rudolph, "Early Life and Civil War Reminiscences," 18.

56. Temple, *Letters of Henry C. Bear*, 29; Puck, *Sacrifice at Vicksburg*, 43–44; H. K. Helphrey to Dear Friends at Home, Jan. 17, 1863, Arkansas Civil War Materials, Butler Center; Diary of John E. Wilkins, 74; Matteson and Eckert, "Dear Sister," 17; Ainsworth Diary, 23; Hitchcock Journal, 23.

57. Bond, *Under the Flag of the Nation*, 49; Jones, *My Dear Carrie*, 32–33; Sample Diary, 21; Sidney Little to Dear Mother, Jan. 17, 1863, Little Papers; Clark, *Life in the Middle West*, 89; Affectionate Brother John to Dear Sister, Jan. 19, 1863, John T. Harrington Letter, Kentucky Historical Society.

58. Reid, *Fourth Indiana Cavalry*, 43; Diary of an Unidentified Soldier of the 31st Iowa Infantry, Civil War Collection, Missouri Historical Society, 28; W.J.K. to Dear Wife, Jan. 8 [*sic*], 1863, Kennedy Papers; S. P. Coe to Dear Friends, Jan. 29, 1863, Schuyler P. Coe Papers, 1863, Pearce Civil War Collection, Navarro College; Scharf, *Confederate States Navy*, 351.

59. G. B. Marshall Reminiscences, 35; A. J. Withrow to Dearest, Jan. 15, 1863, Withrow Papers; Frey, *Grandpa's Gone*, 20; Sample Diary, 20; Mason, *Forty-Second Ohio Infantry*, 178. Elijah Petty of Walker's Texas Division angrily wrote home, "the feds fired upon and burned the hospital though the Yellow flag was floating over it and burned up in it 4 sick men a barbarity that none but heathens and Scoundrels ever indulge in." N. D. Brown, *Journey to Pleasant Hill*, 129.

60. Bearss, "Battle of the Post of Arkansas," 275; Anderson, *Campaigning with Parsons' Texas Cavalry*, 92; Lacy, *Letters from Lawson Jefferson Keener*, n.p.; A. J. Withrow to Dearest, Jan. 15, 1863, Withrow Papers; Larimer, *Love and Valor*, 103; Ainsworth Diary, 23; Willison, *Reminiscences of a Boy's Service*, 41–42.

61. To Dear Wife, Jan. 19, 1863, Kennedy Papers; Bearss, "Battle of the Post of Arkansas," 275; *OR*, 17(1):708; Samuel Gordon to My Dear Wife,

Jan. 24, 1863, Samuel L. Gordon Letters, Abraham Lincoln Presidential Library. Most of the captured animals were transported to St. Louis, where, one Federal wrote, "I suppose they will be sold at public auction to the highest bidder as a great many are ponies and not fit for government service." S. S. Marrett to ?, Jan. 25, 1863, S. S. Marrett Papers, Rare Books, Manuscripts, and Special Collections Library, Duke University. The official Confederate assessment of equipment loss at Arkansas Post reported 5,000 muskets, Enfield rifles, and shotguns; 300,000 rounds of ammunition; 4,000 each of canteens, haversacks, and accouterments; three 6-pounder iron guns; one 12-pounder howitzer; four caissons with related gear; six 3-inch Parrott rifles; 800 pounds of artillery ammunition; two 8-inch and one 9-inch Dahlgren guns; and the weapons and ammunition that the Rebels had seized earlier from the *Blue Wing. OR*, 53:867–68.

62. *ORN*, 8:484, 24:109.

63. Geo to My Dear Wife, Jan. 17, 1863, George F. Chittenden Letters, Indiana Historical Society; Ralph Muncy Memoir, Bentley Historical Library, University of Michigan, 6; J. S. B. Matson to Friend Lyman, [Jan. 1863], "Matson3," *They Were the 114th O.V.I.*; Stevenson, *Letters from the Army*, 169; Diary of John E. Wilkins, 74. The men of the Sixteenth Indiana were among 4,303 green Federal troops captured by Edmund Kirby Smith's Confederate army at Richmond, Kentucky, on August 30, 1862. Christ, *Getting Used to Being Shot At*, 46.

64. "In Camp before Vicksburg," Phillip A. Reilly Collection, Western Historical Manuscript Collection, University of Missouri–Rolla, 92; Black, *Soldier's Recollections*, 110; V.H.M. to Dear Eliza & Family, Jan. 12, 1863, Virgil Moats Letters, Schoff Civil War Soldiers Letters, William L. Clements Library; Grecian, *Eighty-Third Regiment, Indiana Volunteer Infantry*, 21; Ingersoll, *Iowa and the Rebellion*, 532.

65. Cutrer, "'Experience of Soldier's Life,'" 123; N. D. Brown, *Journey to Pleasant Hill*, 129; Shea and Winschell, *Vicksburg Is the Key*, 58.

66. Kiper, *McClernand*, 178.

CHAPTER 3

1. *OR*, 17(1):710, 22(2):41; DeBlack, *With Fire and Sword*, 81.

2. *OR*, 17(1):1, 757; Surovic, "Union Assault on Arkansas Post," 39; Foster, "We Are Prisoners of War," 30; *Rolla (Mo.) Express*, Jan. 14, 1863; Woods, *Services of the Ninety-Sixth Ohio*, 23; Black, *Soldier's Recollections*, 35; Oliphant, "Arkansas Post," 789; Clark, *Life in the Middle West*, 88–89; Clark, *Thirty-Fourth Iowa Regiment*, 11.

3. Diary of John E. Wilkins, Community Archives, Vigo County Public Library, 73; Lucien B. Crooker, "From Chicago to Arkansas Post, October 1861–January 1863," in Committee of the Regiment, *Fifty-fifth Regiment Illinois Volunteer Infantry*, 204; Bearss, "Battle of the Post of Arkansas," 276; Sherman, *Memoirs*, 324–25; Anderson, *Campaigning with Parsons' Texas Cavalry*, 91. A Rebel engineer noted, "The cannon that had been disabled and thrown into the Well in the Fort by the Federals were afterwards recovered

and mounted for the defense of Little Rock; and so late as June in 1863, Government mules, arms, and other property were collected in that vicinity by officers detailed for that purpose." Skinner, *Autobiography of Henry Merrell*, 319.

4. W. A. Gorman to RAdm. D. D. Porter, Jan. 12, 1863, David D. Porter Papers, Bixby Collection, Missouri Historical Society; *ORN*, 24:153–54; Milligan, "Navy Life on the Mississippi River," 73; *OR*, 22(1):216; Davenport, *Ninth Regiment Illinois Cavalry*, 55; Mrs. Mary S. Patrick Diary, no. 9, box 14, Small Manuscripts Collection, Arkansas History Commission, 8.

5. Your Most Affectionate Boy Frederic to My Dear Mother, Jan. 19, 1863, Frederic E. Davis Papers, Special Collections and Archives Division, Robert W. Woodruff Library, Emory University; George W. Brown, "Service in the Mississippi Squadron, and its Connection with the Siege and Capture of Vicksburg," in *Personal Recollections of the War of the Rebellion: Addresses Delivered before the New York Commandery of the Loyal Legion of the United States, 1883–1991,* ed. James Grant Wilson and Titus Munson Coan (reprint, Wilmington, N.C.: Broadfoot, 1992), 306; *ORN*, 24:157–60; *OR*, 22(1):217–19; Patrick Diary, 7. The last reference to the elusive *Blue Wing* in the *Official Records* is dated April 10, 1863, when Col. William Weer reported that the steamboat had just delivered supplies to Rebel troops at Batesville. *OR*, 22(2):210. It is possible that the vessel was one of the steamboats that Sterling Price put to the torch when abandoning Little Rock on September 10, 1863.

6. Kiper, *McClernand*, 179; Bearss, "Battle of the Post of Arkansas," 276–77; Harris Flanagin Papers, Arkansas History Commission; Asa E. Sample Diary, Manuscripts Section, Indiana State Library, 42; John G. Jones to Dear Parents, Jan. 18, 1863, John Griffith Jones Papers, Library of Congress; D. W. Hitchcock Journal, Arkansas Post National Memorial, 23; Puck, *Sacrifice at Vicksburg*, 44.

7. Bearss, "Battle of the Post of Arkansas," 277; *OR*, 22(1):720–21.

8. Bearss, "Battle of the Post of Arkansas," 278–79; Kiper, *McClernand*, 180–82; Grant, *Memoirs*, 294.

9. Committee of the Regiment, *Fifty-fifth Regiment of Illinois Volunteer Infantry*, 294–95; Letter, Jan. 21, 1863, William J. Kennedy Papers, Abraham Lincoln Presidential Library; Woodworth, *Musick of the Mocking Birds*, 20.

10. Bearss, "Battle of the Post of Arkansas," 279; Grant, *Memoirs*, 293; Howe, *Home Letters of General Sherman*, 237. For a solid assessment of a possible conspiracy of West Pointers against McClernand, see Kiper, *McClernand*, 182–85.

11. Bailey, "Henry McCulloch's Texans," 57; Bailey, *Between the Enemy and Texas*, 103; Yeary, *Reminiscences of the Boys in Gray*, 610, 729; letter, Jan. 22, 1863, W. E. Stoker Civil War Letters, 1861–64, Small Manuscripts Collection, Arkansas History Commission; John Porter Memoir, Historical Research Center, Texas Heritage Museum, Hill College, 11. Another soldier of the Eighteenth Texas wrote, "We got in about fifteen miles of the place & stopped on the river & throwed up some breast works, expecting that they would come up the river & aim to go to little rock, but they turned back after they taken the post." Glover, "War Letters of a Texas Conscript," 378.

12. Bailey, *Between the Enemy and Texas*, 106–107; Blessington, *Campaigns of Walker's Texas Division*, 70–71; Lowe, *Walker's Texas Division*, 65; N. D. Brown, *Journey to Pleasant Hill*, 129.

13. Blessington, *Campaigns of Walker's Texas Division*, 75–78; Banasik, *Serving with Honor*, 53–55; *Little Rock True Democrat*, reprinted in *The Index*, Apr. 16, 1863, *Lincoln and the Civil War*, http://www.lincoln andthecivilwar.com/asp/ViewArticleText.asp?url=contents%3A%2 (accessed Dec. 22, 2005; site now discontinued), copy in author's files.

14. *OR*, 22(2):790; Banasik, *Serving with Honor*, 59–61; Skinner, *Autobiography of Henry Merrell*, 28. The earthworks apparently were completed by June, when the Confederate government was paying for the labor of the impressed slaves; Maj. J. N. Finks advertised, "Persons having claims . . . for the hire of negroes employed on the fortifications at Ft. Pleasant" were to present their claims at his office in Pine Bluff. *The War Bulletin*, June 2, 1863, Small Manuscripts Collection, Arkansas History Commission.

15. Sunken Civil War Vessels in Arkansas Waters, Subject File, Civil War, Arkansas History Commission; *ORN*, 24:242, 540, 549, ser. 2, 1:263; Anderson, *Campaigning with Parsons' Texas Cavalry*, 91. Confederate secretary of the navy Stephen R. Mallory looked into creating shipbuilding facilities in Texas and Arkansas but abandoned the notion after determining that "adequate quantities of timber and iron were not available and could not be shipped in." Confederate records do indicate, however, that John W. Dunnington commanded a "Little Rock Naval Station" in 1863, the primary purpose of which was to perform repairs on the *Pontchartrain*. Still, *Confederate Shipbuilding*, 46; Beers, *Guide to the Archives of the Confederate States of America*, 377.

16. Richards, *Story of a Rivertown*, 67; Waterman and Rothrock, "Earle-Buchanan Letters," 132; Scheiber, "Pay of Troops and Confederate Morale," 353, 357; Mayfield, *William Physick Zuber*, 158.

17. Mackey, *Uncivil War*, 38–39; petitions, Feb. 4, Apr. 4, 1863, Theophilus Hunter Holmes Papers, Rare Books, Manuscripts, and Special Collections Library, Duke University. Holmes on April 18, 1863, referred the Tate's Bluff matter to an officer "who will please cause the man to be conscripted unless he is clearly exempted by the law." The ferry keeper, John H. Cubage, joined Company D, 33rd Arkansas Infantry at Camden on May 2, a victory for the outraged wives of the Tate's Bluff area. National Archives and Records Administration, Compiled Service Records, roll 211. Golden was discharged from military service on March 30, 1863.

18. Moneyhon, *Impact of the Civil War*, 112–13.

19. Anderson, *Campaigning with Parsons' Texas Cavalry*, 90; Castel, "Theophilus Holmes," 14; Anne Bailey, "Theophilus Hunter Holmes," in Davis and Hoffman, *Confederate General*, 3:117.

20. Warner, *Generals in Gray*, 279–80; Kerby, *Kirby Smith's Confederacy*, 52–53.

21. Kerby, *Kirby Smith's Confederacy*, 36; Neal and Kremm, *Lion of the South*, 155–58. Hindman commanded troops at Chickamauga, Chattanooga, and various actions during the Atlanta Campaign until injuries forced him

to relinquish field command. Following the war, he fled to Mexico for a time, as did many Trans-Mississippi Confederate commanders, but returned to Arkansas in 1868. On September 27 of that year, an assassin fatally wounded Hindman as he relaxed with his family in the sitting room of his Helena home, a murder that many attributed to the former general's opposition to carpetbag rule in Arkansas. Warner, *Generals in Gray*, 138; Neal and Kremm, *Lion of the South*, 235–37.

22. Warner, *Generals in Gray*, 247. Following the Iuka-Corinth debacle, Jefferson Davis finally acknowledged that Van Dorn was unfit to command an army—Braxton Bragg wrote the president that the Mississippian was "self willed, rather weak minded and totally deficient in organization and system"—and assigned him a cavalry division. The result was the successful raid on Holly Springs that led to the Federal expedition against Arkansas Post. Castel, *General Sterling Price*, 126–27. For more on Price's dysfunctional relationship with Richmond politicians, see ibid., 128–39; and Thomas A. DeBlack, "1863: 'We Must Stand or Fall Alone,'" in Christ, *Rugged and Sublime*, 74.

23. Connelly, *Schofield and the Politics of Generalship*, 55, 66, 68–69. Connelly provides a good account of the political machinations raging in Missouri, and the difficulties of military command in the region. See ibid., 55–68.

24. Kaufman, "Fifty-Fourth U.S. Colored Infantry," 1–2; Trudeau, *Like Men of War*, 47; Quarles, *The Negro in the Civil War*, 195 Cornish, *Sable Arm*, 116; W. W. Brown, *The Negro in the American Rebellion*, 124.

25. "Arming the Negroes—What the Soldiers Say about It," *Douglass' Monthly*, June 1, 1863, *Abraham Lincoln and the Civil War*, http://lincolnandthecivilwar.com/asp/ (accessed Dec. 22, 2005; site now discontinued), copy in author's files; W. W. Brown, *The Negro in the American Rebellion*, 126; Philbeck, "A Union Soldier in Arkansas," 45; Geo. E. Flanders to My Dear Mother, Apr. 10, 1863, George E. Flanders Civil War Letters, Kansas State Historical Society.

26. Cornish, *Sable Arm*, 116, 205; Philbeck, "A Union Soldier in Arkansas," 44; McConnell, "Procurement of Negro Troops," 317; Ronnie A. Nichols, "The Changing Role of Blacks in the Civil War" in Christ, *All Cut to Pieces*, 71; Kaufman, "Fifty-Fourth U.S. Colored Infantry," 3.

27. Kerby, *Kirby Smith's Confederacy*, 128–31; DeBlack, "1863," 74–75.

28. Warner, *Generals in Gray*, 322. For succinct summaries of Marmaduke's Cape Girardeau raid, see DeBlack, "1863," 68–74; and Kerby, *Kirby Smith's Confederacy*, 127–28. One Missourian wrote: "The raid injured our cause in Missouri, and a few more such, and saltpeter will not save the State. . . . Every man sworn into my command is informed that we kill for stealing and deserting." *OR*, 22(2):841.

29. Castel, *General Sterling Price*, 142–44; Kerby, *Kirby Smith's Confederacy*, 129–31; DeBlack, "1863," 74–75.

30. Geo. E. Flanders to My Dear Mother, Apr. 10, 1863, Flanders Civil War Letters; Blackburn, *Dear Carrie*, 118; "28th Wisconsin Infantry Regiment at Helena: VI," 11; Popchock, *Soldier Boy*, 58. For an insightful analysis of

the health problems facing the Helena garrison, see Kohl, "'This Godforsaken Town,'" 109–44.

31. Moneyhon, "Civil War's Impact in Arkansas," 25–27; Baker, "This Old Book," 5.

32. *OR*, 22(1):316–17; *Military History of Kansas Regiments*, 113; "28th Wisconsin Infantry at Helena: IV," 27. For a detailed account of Clayton's raid, see Kohl, "Raising Thunder with the Secesh," 146–70. The Third Iowa reported five men wounded and two missing, while the Fifth Kansas acknowledged seven or eight dead and twenty-three prisoners in the affair at Polk's Plantation. *OR*, 22(1):340–41. The hand of war fell heavily on Phillips County. Carl Moneyhon has documented that 44 percent of the horses, 54 percent of cattle, and a devastating 78 percent of mules were gone by the end of the war compared to 1860, while 51 percent fewer men were listed on the county's rolls in 1865 than in 1860. Moneyhon, "Civil War's Impact in Arkansas," 28.

33. The first reference found on construction of fortifications at Helena was in the diary of a Hoosier cavalryman, who briefly noted, "Preparing to fortify Helena," in his entry for August 21, 1862. Denny's August 24 letter shows that actual construction was underway three days later. Curtis, *Civil War Diary of James H. Hougland*, 25; "Indiana Troops at Helena, Part II," 4; "Indiana Troops at Helena, Part IV," 34.

34. Capt. J. F. Youngs to Brother Thos., Sept. 29, 1862, John F. Youngs Civil War Collection, Missouri Historical Society; Geo. Flanders to Dear Brother, Apr. 24, 29, 1863, Flanders Civil War Letters; Blackburn, *Dear Carrie*, 94; W. F. Vermilion to My Darling, June 4, 1863, Civil War Letters of William F. Vermilya [Vermillion], Co. C, 36th Iowa Inf., U.S.A., 1863–64, Arkansas History Commission; Popchock, *Soldier Boy*, 51. E. G. Martin of the Twenty-ninth Iowa noted: "There is to be two more forts built here this summer. They have got one considerably on the way already so I understand." "Civil War Letters," *Phillips County Historical Quarterly*, 31. The strong fortification described, built under the supervision of Colonel Clayton of the Fifth Kansas Cavalry, was probably Battery A, the northernmost of Helena's hilltop fortifications.

35. Pearson, "War Diary," 204; Urwin and Urwin, *History of the 33d Iowa Infantry*, 32, 259n; Ben to Dear Wife, May 25, 1863, Benjamin Palmer Collection, Butler Center for Arkansas Studies, Central Arkansas Library System.

36. Castel, "Fiasco at Helena," 13; Bearss, "Battle of Helena," 259–60; Urwin, "A Very Disastrous Defeat," 29.

37. Ferguson, "Letters of John W. Duncan," 302; Fragment of the Diary of Dr. R. J. Bell, Parsons Division Missouri Troops, C.S.A., Mosby Monroe Parsons Papers, Missouri Historical Society, 10; Banasik, *Missouri Brothers in Gray*, 55.

38. Bearss, "Battle of Helena," 260–64; "Sketch of the Life of J. C. Dyer," Alphabetical File, Missouri Historical Society; Fragment of the Diary of Dr. R. J. Bell, Parsons Papers, 11–12; Webb, *Battles and Biographies of Missourians*, 189.

39. Bearss, "Battle of Helena," 261–65; Crisler, *Battle of Helena Centennial*, 22.

40. Kerby, *Kirby Smith's Confederacy*, 132; Bearss, "Battle of Helena," 265–66; Castel, "Fiasco at Helena," 14–15; Urwin, "A Very Disastrous Defeat," 29.

41. Warner, *Generals in Blue*, 386. For a detailed analysis and historiography of Prentiss's career, see Bates, "'History Will Do the Gallant Hero Justice.'" Bates argues that despite a rocky relationship with Grant that began with a row over seniority early in the war, Grant held no enmity toward Prentiss and was grateful for his service at Shiloh, reflected in his appointing Prentiss to the east Arkansas command.

42. Ammi Hawks to Dear Friend Allie, June 4–6, 1863, Ammi Doubleday Hawks Letters, Nelson P. Hawks Collection, Hawks Inn Historical Society; Popchock, *Soldier Boy*, 55; "Personal Reminiscences of August Bondi," August Bondi Papers, 1833–1907, Kansas State Historical Society, chap. 4, pp. 30–31; George Cook Diaries, Wisconsin Historical Society, 6; Reynolds Family Papers, Indiana Historical Society; Capt. Youngs to My Dear Sister Mary, July 15, 1863, Youngs Civil War Collection; "Wisconsin Troops at Helena: X," 8–9.

43. Your loving Husband Ben to Dear Wife, July 3, 1863, Palmer Collection; Gaston, *Civil War Diary*, 21; W. A. Jenkins, "A Leaf from Army Life," in *Military Essays and Recollections*, 438; Jones, "Logs of the USS *Tyler*," 27; Edward to Dear Mary, July 3, 1863, "Edward S. Redington Papers, 1862–1867," *University of Wisconsin Digital Collections*, http://digital.library .wisc.edu/1711.dl/WI.EdRed01 (accessed Aug. 7, 2006).

CHAPTER 4

1. Bearss, "Battle of Helena," 269; Urwin, "A Very Disastrous Defeat," 29.

2. *OR*, 22(1):424, 428, 430.

3. W. C. Braly to My Dear Ma, July 21, 1863, Amanda Malvina Fitzallen McClelland Braly Family Papers, Special Collections Division, University of Arkansas Libraries; Kirkman, "28th Wisconsin Infantry Regiment at Helena," 13; Kirkman, "28th Wisconsin Infantry Regiment at Helena, II," 14; Bearss, "Battle of Helena," 272–73; Jones, "Logs of the USS *Tyler*," 29. Brooks reported that three Yankees were killed and six captured in the initial contact with Helena's defenders. *OR*, 22(1):430.

4. *OR*, 22(1):424, 428, 432–33.

5. Urwin, "A Very Disastrous Defeat," 33; Edwin C. Bearss, "John Sappington Marmaduke," in Davis and Hoffman, *Confederate General*, 4: 155–56; Mayfield, *William Physick Zuber*, 166.

6. *OR*, 22(1):436–37; Bearss, "Battle of Helena," 276–77; Urwin, "A Very Disastrous Defeat," 33; Elder, *Love amid the Turmoil*, 155; Banasik, *Missouri Brothers in Gray*, 111.

7. Bearss, "Battle of Helena," 278–81; W. A. Jenkins, "A Leaf from Army Life," in *Military Essays and Recollections*, 441; Warner, *Generals in Blue*, 401–402, 417–18; Urwin, "A Very Disastrous Defeat," 31; Diary of Adam B. Smith, Missouri Historical Society, 59; Frederick Salomon, "The Battle of Helena," *Twenty-Eighth Wisconsin Volunteer Infantry*, http://www.28th

wisconsin.com/service/battle.html (accessed Feb. 18, 2009); Your affectionate Eben to My Dear Augusta, July 4, 1863, Ebenezer S. Peake Letters, Butler Center for Arkansas Studies, Central Arkansas Library System. Salomon had commanded the Federal troops in and around Helena since June 2, 1863, while Prentiss commanded the District of Eastern Arkansas. Quiner, *Military History of Wisconsin*, 770.

8. Reynolds Family Papers, Indiana Historical Society, 15; *OR*, 22(1): 425, 428. Even for the torrid Arkansas delta, July 4, 1863, was notably hot. One Kansan recorded: "The day had opened out intensely hot—and the sun came down fiery and scorching among the naked ridges, occupied by the rebels; many of whom were without water in their canteens." William F. Creitz Diary, William F. Creitz Papers, Kansas State Historical Society, 49.

9. *OR*, 22(1):395, 397, 437; Edwards, *Shelby and His Men*, 167; Urwin, "A Very Disastrous Defeat," 34. Benjamin Pearson of the Thirty-sixth Iowa recorded that six companies of his regiment were ordered to Battery A, while four companies were ordered to support the Dubuque Battery to the right of Battery A. Pearson, "War Diary," 204. John N. Edwards is notorious for hyperbole and prevarication, but his account of the fighting at Helena, while florid, is relatively accurate and in agreement with other sources.

10. *OR*, 22(1):433–36.

11. Ibid., 402; Floyd Thurman to Marions (?), Brother & Friend, July 7, 1863, O. V. Brown Collection, Manuscripts Section, Indiana State Library; Creitz Diary, Creitz Papers, 47; "Personal Reminiscences of August Bondi," August Bondi Papers, 1833–1907, Kansas State Historical Society, chap. 4, p. 33; Capt. Youngs to My Dear Sister Mary, July 15, 1863, John F. Youngs Civil War Collection, Missouri Historical Society.

12. Bearss, "Battle of Helena," 274; *OR*, 22(1):413; William N. Hoskins Civil War Diary, 1862–65, Western Historical Manuscripts Collection, University of Missouri–Columbia, 22; Banasik, *Missouri Brothers in Gray*, 55; "Sketch of the Life of J. C. Dyer," Alphabetical File, Missouri Historical Society.

13. Banasik, *Missouri Brothers in Gray*, 55; Bearss, "Battle of Helena," 275; James T. Wallace Diary, 1862–65 (3059), Southern Historical Collection, Wilson Library, University of North Carolina, 28. No known record survives of Holmes's meeting with Price. The senior general merely cites Price's report, while Price gingerly noted, "I explained the facts to him." *OR*, 22(1):410, 414.

14. Banasik, *Missouri Brothers in Gray*, 57; Bearss, "Battle of Helena," 421, 410; "Civil War Letters of J. D. Cummings," 20; Barnhill, "Greene County Youth," 82–83. In a column of divisions, "the lead regiment in each brigade deployed in a column two companies wide by five companies deep, the men in each column aligned in a double-ranked line of battle. All the other regiments in the brigade stacked up behind the first in the same formation." Urwin, "A Very Disastrous Defeat," 5.

15. John F. Lacy, "A Battle Scene at Helena, Ark., July 4, 1863," in Hutchins, *War of the 'Sixties*, 195; Minos Miller to Dear Mother, June [July] 6, 1863, Minos Miller Civil War Letters, Special Collections Division, University of Arkansas Libraries; Urwin, "A Very Disastrous Defeat," 35; "McRae's March to Helena Retraced," 15.

16. *OR*, 22(1):388, 400; Ingersoll, *Iowa and the Rebellion*, 617; Urwin, "A Very Disastrous Defeat," 35; Davis, "Death Take No Holiday," 26; Blackburn, *Dear Carrie*, 126.

17. Floyd Thurman to Marions (?), Brother & Friend, July 7, 1863, O. V. Brown Papers; "The Attack on Helena," in Brock, *Southern Historical Society Papers*, 199–200; Scott, "Letters from an Iowa Soldier," 34; Bearss, "Battle of Helena," 282. The armless Southerner was philosophical about his terrible injuries: "Since that day at Helena I tell the boys I would rather buck against a hoodoo than try to down Old Glory on the Fourth of July." "Attack on Helena," 199–200.

18. Pitcock and Gurley, *I Acted from Principal*, 38–39; Fragment of Diary of Dr. R. J. Bell, Parsons Division Missouri Troops, C.S.A., Mosby Monroe Parsons Papers, Missouri Historical Society, 14.

19. *OR*, 22(1):400, 425, 428–29, 432; John G. Hudson Collection, 1850–67, Western Historical Manuscripts Collection, University of Missouri–Columbia (copy).

20. *OR*, 22(1):411, 418, 421–22.

21. Bearss, "Battle of Helena," 282–83; Urwin, "A Very Disastrous Defeat," 35; *OR*, 22(1):403; Henry S. Carroll to Dear Mother, July 5, 1863, "Battle of Helena, Arkansas," *Twenty-Eighth Wisconsin Volunteer Infantry*, http://www.28thwisconsin.com/helena2.html (accessed Feb. 18, 2009).

22. Your affectionate Eben to My Dear Augusta, July 4, 1863, Peake Letters; Henry S. Carroll to Dear Mother, July 5, 1863, "Battle of Helena, Arkansas," *Twenty-Eighth Wisconsin Volunteer Infantry*,.

23. E. S. Redington to Dear Mary, July 7, 1863, "Edward S. Redington Papers, 1862–1867," *University of Wisconsin Digital Collections*, http://digital.library.wisc.edu/1711.dl/WI.EdRed01 (accessed Aug. 7, 2006); Floyd Thurman to Marions(?), Brother & Friend, July 7, 1863, O. V. Brown Papers; *OR*, 22(1):422; C. H. Glines to Dear Brother, July 8, 1863, Letter to Albert Glines, Special Collections Department, University of Iowa Libraries.

24. E. S. Redington to Dear Mary, July 7, 1863, "Edward S. Redington Papers, 1862–1867," *University of Wisconsin Digital Collections*; Floyd Thurman to Marions(?), Brother & Friend, July 7, 1863, O. V. Brown Papers; Henry S. Carroll to Dear Mother, July 5, 1863, "Battle of Helena, Arkansas," *Twenty-Eighth Wisconsin Volunteer Infantry*; *OR*, 22(1):403; Lacy, "Battle Scene at Helena, Ark., July 4, 1863," 196.

25. *OR*, 22(1):403, 411; Walton, *Epitome of My Life*, 67; Banasik, *Missouri Brothers in Gray*, 59; Baker, "In the Fight at Helena," 237; Wallace Diary, 30. A Confederate officer claimed that after the battle Holmes "remarked gloomily . . . that to him death upon the field was preferable to disaster and that he had prayed for it earnestly when the attack proved a failure." Castel, "Fiasco at Helena," 17. The Union troops were impressed by the desperate valor of Price's division, with one Kansan concluding, "if the balance of the rebel force had fought with equal perseverance, your correspondent is privately of the opinion, we might be on the road to Little Rock, eating pone and bacon with our rebel admirers." Creitz Diary, Creitz Papers, 53.

26. *OR*, 22(1):426, 429, 433; Urwin, "A Very Disastrous Defeat," 37; Wm. H. Heath to Sir, July 6, 1863, William H. Heath Papers, 1863–64, Pearce

Civil War Collection, Navarro College. Colonel Bell and Lt. Col. J. C. Johnson of the Thirty-seventh Arkansas were among those captured below Battery D, leaving Maj. T. H. Blacknall in charge of the remnants of the regiment. Bearss, "Battle of Helena," 287.

27. *OR,* 22(1):430; Bruce Allardice, e-mail to author, Feb. 1, 2007; Bearss, "Battle of Helena," 287–88.

28. *OR,* 22(1):437; Popchock, *Soldier Boy,* 64; Edwards, *Shelby and His Men,* 167, 169; "Personal Reminiscences of August Bondi," Bondi Papers, chap. 4, p. 33. Major Smith had reported a presentiment that he would be killed during the fighting at Helena. Scott, "Diminished Landscape," 369.

29. Creitz Diary, Creitz Papers, 9; *OR,* 22(1):433; Bearss, "Battle of Helena," 290. Marmaduke blamed Walker for the failure of his Missourians to take Battery A, but at least one of Walker's men thought Marmaduke was to blame. Lt. W. W. Garner wrote, "Marmaduke failed; consequently, we had to fail." W. W. Garner to My Dear Wife, July 7, 1863, Mary Hope Moose Papers, Special Collections Division, University of Arkansas Libraries.

30. Aurelius T. Bartlett Collection, Missouri Historical Society; Blackburn, *Dear Carrie,* 127; "Civil War Letters of J. D. Cummings," 22; *OR,* 22(1):441. Confederate doctor R. J. Bell reported that all of the wounded, Union and Confederate, who were well enough to travel were sent upriver on July 6, while "those who are mortally wounded, are left in hospital." Fragment of Diary of Dr. R. J. Bell, Parsons Papers, 17.

31. Kirkman, "28th Wisconsin Infantry Regiment at Helena," 15; John to My Darling, July 4, 1863, John A. Savage, Jr., Letters, Hargrett Rare Book and Manuscript Library, University of Georgia Libraries; *(St. Louis) Daily Missouri Democrat,* July 13, 1863. James Loughney of the Twenty-eighth Wisconsin wrote, "[at] about noon on the 4th on one boat we sent 870 up the river, and another boat load afterwards." Kirkman, "28th Wisconsin Infantry Regiment, II," 17.

32. Letter, July 5, 1863, Savage Letters; Creitz Diary, Creitz Papers, 54; Blackburn, *Dear Carrie,* 127; Urwin and Urwin, *History of the 33d Iowa Infantry,* 43; Kirkman, "28th Wisconsin Infantry Regiment at Helena, II," 22; "Civil War Letters of J. D. Cummings," 21.

33. *OR,* 22(1):389, 411–12; Urwin, "A Very Disastrous Defeat," 37; Scott, "Letters from an Iowa Soldier," 36. Scott, fighting with the Second Arkansas, wrote: "We was not in Gun Shot of them But Could See them Fighting all the time & there Balls whistled all around us & Amongst us[.] one Ball wounded 2 Darkies in the Arm not Dangerous." Ibid., 34. The disparity in casualties led Riley Jessup of the Thirty-third Iowa to muse, "it is and always will be a mystery to me how we killed so many of them and they killed so few of us." Meyer, *Iowa Valor,* 204.

34. *OR,* 22(1):411; Wallace Diary, 31–32. Holmes also blamed Dandridge McRae for the failure of the attack on Battery C, accusing him of "misbehavior before the enemy," a charge for which a court of inquiry later found McRae innocent. *OR,* 22(1):438. Early drafts of Holmes's official report of the battle reveal that the general blamed Price for the failure of the attack. Writing of the enfilading fire on Fagan's division from Battery C, Holmes crossed out the words "which Gen. Price had failed to engage at the proper

time," inserting the words "previous to the attack by Gen. Price." It is possible that Price's popularity and political influence led the irascible North Carolinian to ease his criticism, settling his wrath instead on the unfortunate Arkansian McRae. Theophilus Hunter Holmes Papers, Rare Books, Manuscripts, and Special Collections Library, Duke University.

35. John G. Hudson Papers; Jones, "Logs of the USS *Tyler*," 29; "Thomas J. Barb Diary, 1863" (MSN/CW 8002-1), 6, University of Notre Dame Rare Books and Special Collections, *Manuscripts of the American Civil War*, http://www.rarebooks.nd.edu/digital/civil_war/diaries_journals/barb/; W. W. Garner to My Dear Wife, July 7, 1863, Moose Papers. Captain Stevens of the Twenty-eighth Wisconsin praised Salomon for the strength of Helena's defenses, writing that "he has kept large parties of the soldiers here at work almost constantly for several weeks past digging rifle pits, building Batteries & other defenses, and now we appreciate his sagacity." Blackburn, *Dear Carrie*, 129.

36. Pearson, "War Diary," 205; Rea, "Diary of Private John P. Wright," 310; Geo. E. Flanders to Dear Mother, July 9, 1863, George E. Flanders Civil War Letters, Kansas State Historical Society; Creitz Diary, Creitz Papers, 56.

37. Urwin and Urwin, *History of the 33d Iowa Infantry*, 43; Fragment of Diary of R. J. Bell, Parsons Papers, 16; Bearss, "Battle of Helena," 292.

38. Bearss, "Battle of Helena," 293; E. S. Redington to Dear Mary, July 7, 1863, "Edward S. Redington Papers, 1862–1867," *University of Wisconsin Digital Collections*. Frost's troops left their works on July 5 and moved toward Bayou Bartholomew. After months of garrison duty, the Missourians were in poor physical condition. Captain Pinnell of the Eighth Missouri wrote, "we passed a number of men lying by the road side unable to go farther, completely exhausted by the heat." Banasik, *Serving with Honor*, 81.

39. "Personal Reminiscences of August Bondi," Bondi Papers, chap. 4, p. 35; Geo. E. Flanders to Dear Mother, July 9, 1863, Flanders Civil War Letters; Pitcock and Gurley, *I Acted from Principal*, 40–53.

40. Long and Long, *Civil War Day by Day*, 378–81; James Munns Jr. to Capt. F. M. Davis, July 10, 1863, James Munns Papers, Union Miscellany Collection, Special Collections and Archives Division, Robert W. Woodruff Library, Emory University; Geo. Flanders to Dear Mother, July 9, 1863, Flanders Civil War Letters; Urwin and Urwin, *History of the 33d Iowa Infantry*, 40.

41. Pitcock and Gurley, *I Acted from Principle*, 40–42; Meyer, *Iowa Valor*, 204; Waterman and Rothrock, "Earle-Buchanan Letters," 138.

42. W. C. Braly to My Dear Ma, July 21, 1863, Amanda Malvina Fitzallen McClelland Braly Family Papers; Castel, *General Sterling Price*, 153.

43. Skinner, *Autobiography of Henry Merrell*, 340.

CHAPTER 5

This chapter is a revised version of "'As Much as Humanity Can Stand': The Little Rock Campaign of 1863," which appeared in Christ, *The Earth Reeled and Trees Trembled: Civil War Arkansas, 1863–1864*, and Christ, "'Here in the Wilds of Arkansas': Interpreting the Little Rock Campaign," the author's MLS thesis at the University of Oklahoma.

1. "Civil War Letters," *Phillips County Historical Quarterly*, 28; Kirkman, "28th Wisconsin Infantry Regiment at Helena," 18; Pearson, "War Diary," 207.

2. Williams, *Lincoln Finds a General*, 5:322n; *OR*, 22(2):376.

3. Castel, *General Sterling Price*, 153; *OR*, 22(2):924–25, 935; James T. Wallace Diary, 1862–65 (3059), Southern Historical Collection, Wilson Library, University of North Carolina, 33–34.

4. Woodworth, *Jefferson Davis and His Generals*, 121; Castel, "Theophilus Holmes," 11; *OR*, 22(2):936; Huff, "Union Expedition against Little Rock," 226.

5. *OR*, 22(2):376, 377, 384, 921.

6. Ibid., 382–83, 937. Kitchen's estimate was about twice Davidson's actual strength, which on August 11 was 6,000 cavalry and three batteries of artillery. Huff, "Union Expedition against Little Rock," 228.

7. Warner, *Generals in Blue*, 112; Guyer, "Journal and Letters of Corporal William O. Gulick," 594; Petty, *Third Missouri Cavalry*, 28–29; James S. Rogers to My Dearest Emilie, June 29, 1863, James S. Rogers Papers, Western Historical Manuscript Collection, University of Missouri–Rolla.

8. *OR*, 22(2):483–84; Dyer, *Compendium*, 1178; Scott, *32nd Iowa Infantry Volunteers*, 58. A sergeant with the Thirty-second Iowa wrote that "an extra pair of shoes was issued to each man with orders that 'he must carry them in his knapsack' The men also must carry their tents, 40 rounds of cartridges, three days rations, and march to keep up with the cavalry." Ibid., 58–59.

9. Turnbo, *Twenty-Seventh Arkansas Confederate Infantry*, 165; Warner, *Generals in Gray*, 247; Skinner, *Autobiography of Henry Merrell*, 342; *OR*, 22(2):520.

10. *OR*, 22(2):944.

11. Ibid., 947; Petty, *Third Missouri Cavalry*, 43; Robert T. McMahan Diary, July 28, 1863, Robert T. McMahan Papers, Western Historical Manuscripts Collection, University of Missouri–Columbia.

12. McMahan Diary, July 29, 1863; Scott, *32nd Iowa Infantry Volunteers*, 59; Abram Brokaw Civil War Diary, Stuttgart (Ark.) Public Library, 2; Henry Ellison Skaggs Diary, Aug. 1, 1863, Henry Ellison Skaggs Papers, 1862–95, Western Historical Manuscripts Collection, University of Missouri–Rolla; *OR*, 22(2):483–84; Elder, *Love amid the Turmoil*, 188. Franklin Denny of the First Missouri wrote in his diary on July 29 that "the General had a large detail sent out to day to chop timber and throw up fortifications here I can't see any necesity for it." Franklin Spillman Denny Diary, July 29, 1863, Franklin Spillman Denny Papers, 1853–1917, Western Historical Manuscript Collection, University of Missouri–Rolla.

13. Skaggs Diary, Aug. 6, 1863; Denny Diary, Aug. 5–7, 1863.

14. *OR*, 22(2):484; Skaggs Diary, Aug. 3, 1863; Letter to General, Sept. 12, 1863, Frederick Steele Papers, Department of Special Collections and University Archives, Stanford University Libraries. The murdered scout was J. W. Glenn. Banasik, *Reluctant Cannoneer*, 172n.

15. *ORN*, 25:353–54.

16. *OR*, 22(2):483, 511.

17. Ibid., 483, 511; Scott, *32nd Iowa Infantry Volunteers*, 60.

18. Edwards, *Shelby and His Men*, 172; *OR*, 22(2):511–12, 528; *ORN*, 25:357; Scott, *32nd Iowa Infantry Volunteers*, 61.

19. *OR*, 22(2):483, 512. The Little Red River expedition was not the only Union excursion from Clarendon. A gunboat and four hundred men of the First Iowa Cavalry went up the White River to Aberdeen on August 13, then rode inland to Brownsville, where they determined that the Confederates were entrenched on Bayou Meto. This intelligence would be useful in the days ahead as Davidson headed west toward Little Rock. The Iowans encountered little resistance. One trooper wrote: "A squad of Rebs about our number came in sight. We took after them and they dusted. We didn't follow." Lothrop, *First Regiment Iowa Cavalry*, 123–24; Civil War Diary of M. S. Andrews, State Historical Society of Iowa, 17.

20. *OR*, 22(2):512; Behlendorff, *Thirteenth Illinois Cavalry*, 15–16; W. W. Garner to My Dear Wife, Aug. 18, 1863, Mary Hope Moose Papers, Special Collections Division, University of Arkansas Libraries.

21. *OR*, 22(2):385, 387, 389; Thomas A. DeBlack, "1863: 'We Must Stand or Fall Alone,'" in Christ, *Rugged and Sublime*, 89; Warner, *Generals in Blue*, 474; Grant, *Memoirs and Selected Letters*, 1045; Adolph to Dear Mina, Aug. 8, 1863, Engelmann-Kirchner Family Papers, Abraham Lincoln Presidential Library; M. Miller to Dear Mother, Aug. 3, 1863, Minos Miller Civil War Letters, Special Collections Division, University of Arkansas Libraries. Miller's complaint that Steele favored a soft policy toward the Confederacy was echoed by many and would follow the general throughout his time in command of Union troops in Arkansas.

22. Williams, *Lincoln Finds a General*, 5:109; Letter to Dear Davidson, Aug. 9, 1863, Steele Papers. The War Department accepted Prentiss's resignation on October 28 "on the grounds of his . . . health and the situation of his family." The hero of the Hornets' Nest at Shiloh and of the Battle of Helena, Prentiss would see no more action in the Civil War. Warner, *Generals in Blue*, 386.

23. Letter to General, Aug. 11, 1863, Steele Papers; H. O. Brown and M. A. W. Brown, *Soldiers' and Citizens' Album*, 597; Letter to Dear Davidson, Aug. 9, 1863, Steele Papers.

24. M. P. Chambers to Dear Brother, Aug. 11, 1863, Milton P. Chambers Papers, Special Collections Division, University of Arkansas Libraries; Floyd Thurman to Dear Brother, Aug. 11, 1863, O. V. Brown Collection, Indiana Historical Society, Manuscripts Division; George E. Flanders to My Dear Brother, Aug. 12, 1863, George E. Flanders Civil War Letters, Kansas State Historical Society; Elder, *Love amid the Turmoil*, 193; William H. Storrs Diary, Aug. 6–8, 1863, Merrill G. Burlingame Special Collections, Montana State University.

25. Popchock, *Soldier Boy*, 76–77; Letter to My Dear Wife, Aug. 31, 1863, Charles Oscar Torrey Papers, Library of Congress.

26. Blackburn, *Dear Carrie*, 148, 149–50; William Dinsmore Hale to "Dear Folks at Home," Aug. 19, 1863, William D. Hale and Family Papers, Minnesota Historical Society (cited courtesy of Floyd E. Risvold, Edina, Minn.); John Talbut to Dear Sister, Aug. 11, 1863, John Talbut Civil War

Letters, Butler Center for Arkansas Studies, Central Arkansas Library System; James M. Bowler to Dear Libby, Sept. 16, 1863, James M. Bowler Correspondence, Minnesota Historical Society; Steiner, *Disease in the Civil War*, 223; Popchock, *Soldier Boy*, 79; "Personal Reminiscences of August Bondi," August Bondi Papers, 1833–1907, Kansas State Historical Society, chap. 4, p. 30; Storrs Diary, Aug. 13, 1863.

27. George Cook Diaries, Wisconsin Historical Society, 8; *Minnesota in the Civil and Indian Wars*, 1:167; Edward to Dear Mary, Aug. 20, 1863, "Edward S. Redington Papers, 1862–1867," *University of Wisconsin Digital Collections*, http://digital.library.wisc.edu/1711.dl/WI.EdRed01 (accessed Aug. 7, 2006); Reynolds Family Papers, Indiana Historical Society, 18; Guyer, "Journal and Letters of Corporal William O. Gulick," 598.

28. Urwin and Urwin, *History of the 33d Iowa Infantry*, 40–41; Reid, *Ohio in the War*, 840, 885; Dyer, *Compendium*, 1494; Henry Hunt Reminiscences, Missouri Historical Society, 82. The cross-trained Illinoisans did benefit some from their new duties as artillerymen, Hunt noted: "It was an improvement in marching, as we rode on the horses or cayisons [caissons] as our place might be."

29. Guyer, "Journal and Letters of Corporal William O. Gulick," 599; Edward to Dear Mary, Aug. 20, 1863, "Edward S. Redington Papers, 1862–1867," *University of Wisconsin Digital Collections*; Minos Miller to Dear Mother, Aug. 12, 1863, Minos Miller Civil War Letters; Douglas E. Larson, "Alfred Gales and the Third Minnesota in Arkansas," in Christ, *Earth Reeled and Trees Trembled*, 52–53, 62. The widespread flight of slaves to Steele's army led one Confederate to sourly note, "a Negro is as certain as Confederate money." W. W. Garner to My Dear Wife, Aug. 24, 1863, Moose Papers. Alfred Gales died in Minnesota in 1892 and was buried in the Soldier's Rest section of St. Paul's Elmhurst Cemetery.

30. Denny Papers; Petty, *Third Missouri Cavalry*, 34; McLean, *43d Regiment of Indiana Volunteers*, 106. Henry Skaggs also noted in his diary on August 16, "Big Fire in town tonight." Skaggs Diary.

31. *OR*, 22(2):472; Behlendorf, *History of the Thirteenth Illinois Cavalry*, 18; Blackburn, *Dear Carrie*, 155. An Iowa soldier confirmed Stevens's account, writing: "we have to leave a great many men here sick and a force to guard them. thirty of our regiment took sick since we left Helena. the complaint is Swamp fever and the ague." Popchock, *Soldier Boy*, 80.

32. James R. Shirey, ed., *Civil War Journal of James B. Lockney*, Wis. 28th Regmt., Co. G [diary online], Aug. 24, 1863, *Twenty-Eighth Wisconsin Volunteer Infantry*, http://pws.cablespeed.com/~jshirey/CivilWar/ (accessed Feb. 19, 2009); Blackburn, *Dear Carrie*, 158; Lillibridge, *A Civil War Soldier Describes his Army Life*, 78; Edward to Dear Mary, Aug. 20, 1863, "Edward S. Redington Papers, 1862–1867," *University of Wisconsin Digital Collections*.

33. Bobby Roberts, "Rivers of No Return," in Christ, *Earth Reeled and Trees Trembled*, 74–75; *OR*, 22(2):472; Huff, "Memphis and Little Rock Railroad," 267.

34. Annegan, *With Merrill's Cavalry*, 13; Petty, *Third Missouri Cavalry*, 35. The historian of the Thirteenth Illinois Cavalry also remembered the horsemen on the Grand Prairie: "We moved in three columns on a prairie

only two or three miles in width and a large train of five hundred wagons. We could look around and see the whole army with the naked eye." Field, *Three Years in the Saddle*, 42.

35. S. T. Wells to "My Dear Lizzie," Sept. 7, 1863, Samuel T. Wells Papers, Filson Historical Society; Behlendorff, *Thirteenth Illinois Cavalry*, 16; Brokaw Diary, 3.

36. *OR*, 22(2):520–21, 526; Gaughan, *Letters of a Confederate Surgeon*, 169; W. W. Garner to My Dear Wife, Aug. 7, 1863, Moose Papers; W. W. Garner to My Dear Wife, Aug. 4, 1863, ibid.

37. Lothrop, *First Regiment Iowa Cavalry*, 126; DeBlack, "1863," 91; Allardice, *More Generals in Gray*, 102; *OR*, 22(2):530, 532. An Iowa soldier succinctly described Brownsville: "Nice court House and Yard. Brick jail. Town Small." Rea, "Diary of Private John P. Wright," 311.

38. *OR*, 22(2):530,532; Frank M. Emmons to Folks at Home, Sept. 16, 1863, Francis Marion Emmons Letters, Western Historical Manuscripts Collection, University of Missouri–Columbia; Petty, *Third Missouri Cavalry*, 35; Hewett, *Supplement to the Official Records*, 35:341; Petty, *Third Missouri Cavalry*, 35; Banasik, *Serving with Honor*, 378–80; Burford and McBride, *The Division*, 43–44.

39. *OR*, 22(2):530; Reid, *Ohio in the War*, 885–86; Huff, *Civil War Letters of Albert Demuth*, 33, 35; Edwards, *Shelby and His Men*, 174. Even as the Rebels sought to slow the Yankee advance at Brownsville, Confederate surgeon Junius Bragg made an astute observation of the likely result of Steele's advance, writing on August 2: "[T]he enemy will doubtless flank our present position in front of Little Rock. . . . It is not to be supposed that they would attempt to force our works, if there was any way to flank them, and such ways usually exist." Gaughan, *Letters of a Confederate Surgeon*, 179. Later events proved Bragg correct.

40. Crowley, *Tennessee Cavalier*, 109; Edwards, *Shelby and His Men*, 174; "Thomas J. Barb Diary, 1863" (MSN/CW 8002-1), 23, University of Notre Dame Rare Books and Special Collections, *Manuscripts of the American Civil War*, http://www.rarebooks.nd.edu/digital/civil_war/diaries_journals /barb/. John Moore wrote that "Marmaduke performed his part, but General Walker did not stop nor leave a man in the timber, and Marmaduke came near being captured instead of capturing the Federal advance." John C. Moore, *Confederate Military History of Missouri*, vol. 12 in Evans, *Confederate Military History*, 137. Davidson suspected an ambush, according to the historian of the Thirty-second Iowa Infantry, who wrote: "He suspected the decoy. The timber was planted with masked batteries, and men in ambush. Davidson preferred a flank movement to being caught in such a trap." Scott, *32nd Iowa Infantry Volunteers*, 62.

41. *OR*, 22(2):533, 535.

42. Ibid., 484, 501; Petty, *Third Missouri Cavalry*, 36.

43. Edwards, *Shelby and His Men*, 175.

44. *OR*, 22(2):501–502.

45. Ibid., 527, 530.

46. Ibid., 502, 513, 530; Francis M. Emmons to "To All at Home," Sept. 16, 1863, Emmons Letters; "Thomas J. Barb Diary," *Manuscripts of*

the American Civil War, 24; Edwards, *Shelby and His Men,* 176. Davidson's ruse also was recorded by an Iowa historian, who wrote: "The expedient which he adopted to dislodge the enemy was a novel one. He directed a bass drum to be beaten to infer the approach of infantry; and the ruse succeeded admirably, for they left without offering further resistance." Stuart, *Iowa Colonels and Regiments,* 555.

47. *OR,* 22(2):502, 508, 531; Civil War Diary of M. S. Andrews, 18; Ingersoll, *Iowa and the Rebellion,* 367–68; Annegan, *With Merrill's Cavalry,* 17. The historian of the Third Missouri Cavalry made a subtle dig at Davidson's order for the First Iowa to charge: "We are told General Davidson ordered the regiment, when making the charge, to 'draw sabers,' and that too a mile from the enemy and he on the other side of the stream at that, with a burning bridge between them." Petty, *Third Missouri Cavalry,* 36.

48. *OR,* 22(2):502, 531; Edwards, *Shelby and His Men,* 176.

49. *OR,* 22(2):178; Field, *Three Years in the Saddle,* 43.

50. *OR,* 22(2):533; Edwards, *Shelby and His Men,* 177.

51. *OR,* 22(2):502, 527, 532; Petty, *Third Missouri Cavalry,* 37.

52. Wallace Diary, 37; Gaughan, *Letters of a Confederate Surgeon,* 176, 179–80. Artillerist William Hoskins had noticed the movement southward as early as August 6, when he wrote, "Sittizens are emigrating south with their negros—the feds are scaring them badly." William N. Hoskins Civil War Diary, 1862–65, Western Historical Manuscripts Collection, University of Missouri–Columbia, 26.

53. *OR,* 22(2):485, 536, 537.

54. Ibid., 476; Ingersoll, *Iowa and the Rebellion,* 568.

55. *OR,* 22(2):476; Huff, "Union Expedition against Little Rock," 231; DeBlack, "1863," 92; Thomas C. Reynolds to My Dear General, Sept. 4, 1863, Thomas Caute Reynolds Papers, 1821–77, Library of Congress; Frank M. Emmons to "To All at Home," Sept. 16, 1863, Emmons Letters. Despite the rigors of the march, the Federal troops maintained relatively good morale.

56. *OR,* 22(2):476; Blackburn, *Dear Carrie,* 167; Popchock, *Soldier Boy,* 84; Petty, *Third Missouri Cavalry,* 37.

57. Hoskins Diary; Park, *Civil War Letters of the Shibley Brothers,* n.p.

58. Bearss, "Battle of Helena," 290; Huff, "Last Duel," 37–38, 39–40; Moore, *Confederate Military History of Missouri,* vol. 12 of Evans, *Confederate Military History,* 137; Edwards, *Shelby and His Men,* 177–81; John M. Harrell, *Confederate Military History of Arkansas,* vol. 14 of Evans, *Confederate Military History,* 220; *OR,* 22(2):525.

59. Huff, "Last Duel," 44, 45; *(Little Rock) Arkansas Democrat,* Nov. 11, 1928.

60. *OR,* 22(2):525; Turnbo, *Twenty-Seventh Arkansas Confederate Infantry,* 162–63; Personal Reminiscences, 2nd ser., Josephine B. Crump Papers, Special Collections Division, University of Arkansas Libraries, 3; Scott, *32nd Iowa Infantry Volunteers,* 62.

61. *OR,* 22(2):524, 538.

62. Ibid., 476, 524, 528; Frank M. Emmons to "To All at Home," Sept. 16, 1863, Emmons Letters; Stevens, *Dear Carrie,* 168. Edward Redington of the Twenty-eighth Wisconsin Infantry wrote of the Ashley's Mill area, "If it

were not for the ague, six or eight kinds of vermin, snakes, a smart sprinkling of alligators, and several other little annoyances, it would be a nice place to live." Edward to Dear Mary, Sept. 19, 1863, "Edward S. Redington Papers, 1862–1867," *University of Wisconsin Digital Collections.*

63. *OR,* 22(2):476, 523–24; "Stood by His Gun," *National Tribune,* Nov. 12, 1881.

64. *OR,* 22(2):476, 489, 510, 524; Field, *Three Years in the Saddle,* 46–47.

65. *OR,* 22(2):503; Hoskins Diary, 29.

66. *OR,* 22(2):486, 517.

67. Ibid., 489, 524, 525, 529, 539; Adolph to Dear Mina, Sept. 12, 1863, Engelmann-Kircher Family Papers; Reid, *Ohio in the War,* 857.

68. *OR,* 22(2):489, 492, 503, 514; Stuart, *Iowa Colonels and Regiments,* 535; William Hale to "Dear Folks at Home," Sept. 15, 1863, Hale and Family Papers. Engelmann noted, "General Davidson got dissatisfied because my artillery did not fire more rapidly, although every one, the gl. [general] included, admitted that considering the long range they fired with great precision." Adolph to Dear Mina, Sept. 12, 1863, Engelmann-Kircher Family Papers. "Long home" was Civil War slang for a burial trench or grave. Garrison, *Encyclopedia of Civil War Usage,* 149.

69. *OR,* 22(2):522; Thomas L. Snead, "The Conquest of Arkansas," in Johnson and Buel, *Battles and Leaders,* 3:457; Huff, "Union Expedition against Little Rock," 236; Hoskins Diary, 29.

70. *OR,* 22(2):504, 525, 526, 539; "Thomas J. Barb Diary," *Manuscripts of the American Civil War,* 30–31. Theophilus Holmes did not forgive Dobbins for his actions at Bayou Fourche and, following a lenient November court-martial, issued a general order that "the offence of which he was convicted is of a character so grave, and in an army like ours, might result in consequences so ruinous, that the recommendations of the members of the court cannot be regarded. Col. Arch S. Dobbins accordingly ceases to be an officer in the C.S. Army from this date." Dalehite, "Arch S. Dobbins," 20. Dobbins soon returned to command, however, leading cavalry in east Arkansas during the summer of 1864 and accompanying Price's doomed Missouri raid that fall. After the war he tried to establish a business in the Amazon jungle, where he disappeared around 1870, probably being murdered by his native workers. Allardice, *More Generals in Gray,* 79–80; Mark K. Christ, "The Queen City was a Helpless Wreck: J. O. Shelby's Summer of '64," in Christ, *Earth Reeled and Trees Trembled,* 141–43.

71. *OR,* 22(2):492, 504, 534.

72. Ibid., 492, 539.

73. Ibid., 539, 504–505, 507, 534; Edwards, *Shelby and His Men,* 183; Yeary, *Reminiscences of the Boys in Gray,* 534. The Confederates did not keep the captured cannon for long. The historian of the First Iowa Cavalry recorded that the Iowans "at one time during the day . . . recaptured two howitzers which had been captured from the Tenth Illinois Cavalry." Lothrop, *First Regiment Iowa Cavalry,* 129.

74. *OR,* 22(2):505, 492.

75. Ibid., 484, 494, 505, 539.

76. Ibid., 539; Huff, *Civil War Letters of Albert Demuth*, 38.

77. *OR*, 22(2):494–95.

78. Ibid., 529.

79. Ibid., 490, 495, 505.

80. Ibid., 480, 522; Wallace Diary, 41; Hoskins Diary, 29. It is possible that the *Blue Wing*, whose capture precipitated the Union attack on Arkansas Post, was among the vessels burned at Little Rock. Woodruff, *With the Light Guns*, 99–102. The "bull battery" does not appear in any of the official reports of the battle, but a woman who witnessed the fighting and retreat wrote to her soldier-husband that "Pratt's Battery did good work also Woodruff's made up of Volunteers." Ewing, "Retreat from Little Rock," 4.

81. S. T. Wells to My Dear Lizzie, Sept. 16, 1863, Wells Papers; *OR*, 22(2):518–19.

82. Personal Reminiscences, 3rd ser., Crump Papers, 2.

83. *OR*, 22(2):487, 510; James S. Rogers to My Dear Wife, Sept. 16, 1863, Rogers Papers.

84. Turnbo, *Twenty-Seventh Arkansas Confederate Infantry*, 165; Crowley, *Tennessee Cavalier*, 118; "Thomas J. Barb Diary," *Manuscripts of the American Civil War*, 31.

85. Edwards, *Shelby and His Men*, 185; DeBlack, "1863," 94; *OR*, 22(2): 477, 487; Duckett, *Glimpses of Glory*, 60; Reynolds Family Papers, Indiana Historical Society, 20; Thomas, *Arkansas in War and Reconstruction*, 218; Kerby, *Kirby Smith's Confederacy*, 230; Adolph Engelmann to Dear Mina, Sept. 20, 1863, Engelmann-Kirchner Family Papers. One of the recovered cannon, which began its odyssey aboard the *Pontchartrain* before being damaged at Arkansas Post, is now on permanent display in front of the Old State House Museum in Little Rock.

86. Banasik, *Missouri Brothers in Gray*, 62; Annegan, *With Merrill's Cavalry*, 16; Urwin and Urwin, *History of the 33d Iowa Infantry*, 47; Andrews, *Christopher C. Andrews*, 182; Shirey, *Civil War Journal of James B. Lockney*, Sept. 11, 1863 [diary online], *Twenty-Eighth Wisconsin Volunteer Infantry*; Lillibridge, *A Civil War Soldier Describes His Army Life*, 81.

87. John P. Quesenberry Diary, Sept. 10, 1863, Western Historical Manuscripts Collection, University of Missouri–Columbia; Turnbo, *Twenty-seventh Arkansas Confederate Infantry*, 165; Castel, *General Sterling Price*, 158.

88. *OR*, 22(2):479, 496.

89. Ibid., 497, 498, 529, 533.

90. Yours to Dear Annie, Sept. 22, 1863, Lorraine Blore Ragland Collection, Special Collections Division, University of Arkansas Libraries; Turnbo, *Twenty-Seventh Arkansas Confederate Infantry*, 168; Wallace Diary, 43–44.

91. *OR*, 22(2):329, 499; Behlendorff, *Thirteenth Illinois Cavalry*, 18. Davidson wrote to Col. Francis H. Manter, chief of staff, on September 14, 1863: "I regret to state that the expedition returned the day after its march without accomplishing anything and, in my opinion, did not pursue the enemy with the necessary vigor. The reports from officers of the expedition make it advisable this should be inquired into." Hewett, *Supplement to the Official Records*, 4:152. Despite his lukewarm performance at Bayou

Fourche and his desultory pursuit of Price, Merrill ended the war with the rank of brevet brigadier general "for gallant and meritorious services during the war." Hunt and Brown, *Brevet Brigadier Generals,* 411. Merrill would serve in the Seventh U.S. Cavalry after the war, but he was absent from the ranks, serving as military chief of staff to the president during the International Exhibit of 1876 at Philadelphia, when many of his comrades met their ends in the fighting at Little Big Horn. "Lewis Merrill, Brigadier General, United States Army," *Arlington National Cemetery,* http://www .arlingtoncemetery.net/lmerrill.htm (accessed Feb. 16, 2008).

92. *OR,* 22(2):488; Frank M. Emmons to ?, Sept. 17, 1863, Emmons Letters. The troops' opinion of Davidson had softened to the point that "a beautiful and costly saber was presented him, purchased by the privates of the regiment as a token and love for their old commander." Lothrop, *First Regiment Iowa Cavalry,* 139.

93. Petty, *Third Missouri Cavalry,* 40; Bowler to My Dear Libby, Sept. 16, 1863, Bowler Correspondence.

94. Huff, "Union Expedition against Little Rock," 235–36.

95. Castel, *General Sterling Price,* 158; Huff, *Civil War Letters of Albert Demuth,* 40; Quesenberry Diary, Sept. 13, 1863; Lillibridge, *A Civil War Soldier Describes His Army Life,* 81; Turnbo, *Twenty-Seventh Arkansas Confederate Infantry,* 166; Hoskins Diary, 29; Moneyhon, *Impact of the Civil War,* 113; Proclamation, Sept. 16, 1863, Harris Flanagin Papers, Arkansas History Commission. A soldier in the Forty-ninth Indiana also recorded the desertions, writing in his diary on September 11, "A great many deserters and strag(g)lers," and on September 12, "Deserters still coming in." Reynolds Family Papers, Indiana Historical Society.

96. Crowley, *Tennessee Cavalier,* 120. Some of the men and junior officers also agreed. Arkansian Richard Fontaine Earle wrote to his sweetheart that "if it had not been for a number of *cowardly desertions* we would not have been worsted. The retreat was necessary—the enemy being vastly superior." Waterman and Rothrock, "Earle-Buchanan Letters," 143.

97. Ingersoll, *Iowa and the Rebellion,* 543; Sude, "Federal Military Policy and Strategy in Missouri and Arkansas"; Foote, *Civil War,* 2:707; Elder, *Love amid the Turmoil,* 222.

98. DeBlack, "1863," 95.

CHAPTER 6

1. Gaines, *Confederate Cherokees,* 91–94. Despite the dissatisfaction with the Confederacy, five regiments of Cherokee, Choctaw, Chickasaw, Creek, and Seminole Indians would fight for the South, providing some 10,000 men over the course of the Civil War. Fischer and Gill, "Confederate Indian Forces," 249–50.

2. Confer, *Cherokee Nation in the Civil War,* 75; Edwards, *Prairie Was on Fire,* 16; Britton, *Union Indian Brigade,* 62.

3. Edwards, *Prairie Was on Fire,* 16–18; Wright and Fischer, "Civil War Sites in Oklahoma," 174; Tenney, *War Diary,* 17; Cunningham, *General Stand Watie's Confederate Indians,* 67.

4. Britton, *Union Indian Brigade*, 62–63; Tenney, *War Diary*, 17; Edwards, *Prairie Was on Fire*, 18–19; Gaines, *Confederate Cherokees*, 98–99; Gause, *Four Years with Five Armies*, 89–90.

5. Edwards, *Prairie Was on Fire*, 19–21; Rampp and Rampp, *Civil War in the Indian Territory*, 12; Gaines, *Confederate Cherokees*, 103.

6. Britton, *Union Indian Brigade*, 66; Tenney, *War Diary*, 20. In a letter dated a week later, Tenney wrote of the bacchanalia on July 4, 1862: "[O]ne officer even told his men that the one who wasn't drunk that night should be ducked in the Grand River. . . . One reason everybody liked Col. Doubleday so well was, that he never drank." Ibid.

7. Edwards, *Prairie Was on Fire*, 21–22; Confer, *Cherokee Nation in the Civil War*, 78–79; Gaines, *Confederate Cherokees*, 105.

8. Gaines, *Confederate Cherokees*, 109–12; Edwards, *Prairie Was on Fire*, 22; Rampp and Rampp, *Civil War in the Indian Territory*, 13–14; Confer, *Cherokee Nation in the Civil War*, 79.

9. Edwards, *Prairie Was on Fire*, 22–23; Britton, *Union Indian Brigade*, 73.

10. Edwards, *Prairie Was on Fire*, 23–24; Tenney, *War Diary*, 21; Gaines, *Confederate Cherokees*, 112–13.

11. Gaines, *Confederate Cherokees*, 113–14.

12. Ibid., 116–17; Edwards, *Prairie Was on Fire*, 24–27.

13. Wright, "General Douglas Cooper," 146; Anne Bailey, "Douglas Hancock Cooper," in Davis and Hoffman, *Confederate General*, 2:6–7. For a solid account of Pike's stormy relationship with Hindman, see W. L. Brown, *Life of Albert Pike*, 405–12.

14. Edwards, *Prairie Was on Fire*, 29; Warner, *Generals in Blue*, 418; Collins, *General James G. Blunt*, 76–78.

15. Collins, *General James G. Blunt*, 78; *OR*, 12:325–26.

16. *OR*, 12:326–28, 335–36; Crawford, *Kansas in the Sixties*, 59–60; Edwards, *Prairie Was on Fire*, 31–32; Willey, "Second Federal Invasion of Indian Territory," 423.

17. Edwards, *Prairie Was on Fire*, 35–36.

18. Anne Bailey, "William Steele," in Davis and Hoffman, *Confederate General*, 5:200; Kerby, *Kirby Smith's Confederacy*, 42.

19. Eliot, *West Point in the Confederacy*, 311–12; Anne Bailey, "William Lewis Cabell," in Davis and Hoffman, *Confederate General*, 1:155–57; Kerby, *Kirby Smith's Confederacy*, 122–24. Cabell would enjoy a successful postwar career as a lawyer and prominent Democrat. He served as mayor of Dallas for four terms and was a U.S. marshal during Grover Cleveland's first administration. The old warrior volunteered at the age of seventy-one to serve in the Spanish-American War, an offer that was declined. "Gen. William L. Cabell," 68; Bailey, "William Lewis Cabell," 157.

20. Rampp and Rampp, *Civil War in the Indian Territory*, 20; Edwards, *Prairie Was on Fire*, 38; Kerby, *Kirby Smith's Confederacy*, 123–24; Williams, *Lincoln Finds a General*, 5:103.

21. Edwards, *Prairie Was on Fire*, 40–41; Britton, *Union Indian Brigade*, 209–13; Rampp and Rampp, *Civil War in the Indian Territory*, 19. To avoid confusion, the fort will be referred to as Fort Gibson throughout this chapter.

22. Edwards, *Prairie Was on Fire*, 41–42; Rampp and Rampp, *Civil War*

in Indian Territory, 20; Britton, *Union Indian Brigade*, 222–23; Collins, *General James G. Blunt*, 138.

23. Edwards, *Prairie Was on Fire*, 44–46; Britton, *Union Indian Brigade*, 225.

24. Edwards, *Prairie Was on Fire*, 47–50.

25. Ibid., 50–51.

26. Ibid., 57–58.

27. Ibid., 58–61; Britton, *Union Indian Brigade*, 265.

28. Edwards, *Prairie Was on Fire*, 61–62; Blunt, "Civil War Experiences," 243–44; Ashcraft, "Letter of General William Steele," 280.

29. Edwards, *Prairie Was on Fire*, 62, 66–67, 71; Blunt, "Civil War Experiences," 244; Collins, *General James G. Blunt*, 142–44; Frank Arey, "The First Kansas Colored at Honey Springs," in Christ, *All Cut to Pieces*, 80, 88–89.

30. Sude, "Federal Military Policy and Strategy in Missouri and Arkansas," 162; Ashcraft, "Letter of General William Steele," 281.

31. Edwards, *Prairie Was on Fire*, 71; Bearss and Gibson, *Fort Smith*, 266; Britton, *Union Indian Brigade*, 288; Hood, "Twilight of the Confederacy in Indian Territory," 425–26; Bailey, "Douglas Hancock Cooper," 27. It would be nearly a year before Cooper would return to command in the Indian Territory. The general's talents were summed up by one of his foes: "Cooper— well, he had missed his calling. . . . His comrades and the Confederacy should look with compassion on his blunders." Crawford, *Kansas in the Sixties*, 96.

32. Blunt, "Civil War Experiences," 245; Britton, *Union Indian Brigade*, 268–88; Hewett, *Supplement to the Official Records*, 2:126, 35:271; *OR*, 22(1): 597; Bearss and Gibson, *Fort Smith*, 267; Edwards, *Prairie Was on Fire*, 73.

33. *OR*, 22(1):597–600; Edwards, *Prairie Was on Fire*, 73–74; Furry, *Preacher's Tale*, 72. Steele reported that only half of his Choctaw reinforcements were armed.

34. *OR*, 22(1):597–98; Britton, *Union Indian Brigade*, 289–90; Crawford, *Kansas in the Sixties*, 98–99; Edwards, *Prairie Was on Fire*, 75.

35. *OR*, 22(1):604–605; Oneill's Cavalry Company, Berry-Dickinson-Peel Family Papers, Special Collections Division, University of Arkansas Libraries, n.p.; Rieff Manuscript, ibid., n.p.

36. Britton, *Union Indian Brigade*, 290–91; Thomas A. DeBlack, "1863: 'We Must Stand or Fall Alone,'" in Christ, *Rugged and Sublime*, 86; Furry, *Preacher's Tale*, 73–74.

37. *OR*, 22(1):602, 606; John M. Harrell, *Confederate Military History of Arkansas*, vol. 14 of Evans, *Confederate Military History*, 202–203.

38. DeBlack, "1863," 86–87; Blunt, "Civil War Experiences," 247; Hewett, *Supplement to the Official Records*, S. 14, 2(2):117; Furry, *Preacher's Tale*, 74; "A Run from the Feds," no. 11, box 45, Small Manuscripts Collection, Arkansas History Commission.

39. *OR*, 22(1):602–603, 606; Rieff Manuscript. The ambush of Captain Lines's troops outraged the Kansans, with Colonel Cloud decrying it "nothing but *murder* and *bushwhacking*" and Samuel Crawford smugly declaring: "[T]his was a species of warfare to which the Second Kansas never conde-

scended. That regiment fought in the open. . . . [N]ever once did any soldier of the regiment sneak around in the brush and shoot the enemy in the back." Ibid.; Crawford, *Kansas in the Sixties*, 101.

40. Crawford, *Kansas in the Sixties*, 99–100; Wright, *Memoirs*, 112; *OR*, 22(1):603.

41. *OR*, 22(1):603, 606–607; Crawford, *Kansas in the Sixties*, 100; Wright, *Memoirs*, 120. Cabell reported that the fighting lasted three and a half hours; Cloud and Crawford stated only two.

42. Wright, *Memoirs*, 120–21; *OR*, 22(1):602, 606–607; Hood, "Twilight of the Confederacy in Indian Territory," 427; Britton, *Union Indian Brigade*, 294.

43. "A Run from the Feds"; Crawford, *Kansas in the Sixties*, 101–102; Williams, *Lincoln Finds a General*, 5:107–108. Medical historian Jack Walsh notes that a doctor who treated the general at the time attributed his condition to "sunstroke with softening of the brain." When Blunt died in 1881, his immediate cause of death was listed as "paresis, three years duration." Walsh, *Medical Histories of Union Generals*, 32.

44. Britton, *Union Indian Brigade*, 297–98; *OR*, 22(1):603; Carr, *In Fine Spirits*, 65.

45. *OR*, 22(1):603–604.

46. For a detailed account of Confederate operations in Indian Territory and western Arkansas during the fall and winter of 1863, see Bearss, "Confederate Attempt to Regain Fort Smith," 342–80.

47. Carolyn Pollan, "Fort Smith under Union Military Rule," 7; Tom Wing, "'The Sink of Inequity and Corruption': The Civil War in Fort Smith and Indian Territory," in Christ, *Earth Reeled and Trees Trembled*, 129.

48. For an analysis of the results of Devil's Backbone and occupation of Fort Smith, see Franzman, "Battle of Devil's Backbone Mountain," 426–27.

CHAPTER 7

1. William H. Storrs Diary, Sept. 11, 1863, Merrill G. Burlingame Special Collections, Montana State University; Swanson, "Civil War Letters of Olof Liljegren," 108; Adolph Engelmann to Dear Mina, Sept. 22, 1863, Engelmann-Kirchner Family Papers, Abraham Lincoln Presidential Library.

2. Capt. Youngs to Brother Thos., Oct. 1, 1863, John F. Youngs Civil War Collection, Missouri Historical Society; W. W. Garner to My Dear Wife, Sept. 24, 1863, Mary Hope Moose Papers, Special Collections Division, University of Arkansas Libraries; Ross, "Civil War Letters from James Mitchell to his Wife," 314; John P. Quesenberry Diary, Sept. 13, 1863, Western Historical Manuscripts Collection, University of Missouri–Columbia.

3. Swanson, "Civil War Letters of Olof Liljegren," 108; Lillibridge, *A Civil War Soldier Describes His Army Life*, 81; Edward to Dear Mary, Sept. 13, 1863, "Edward S. Redington Papers, 1862–1867," *University of Wisconsin Digital Collections*, http://digital.library.wisc.edu/1711.dl/WI.EdRed01 (accessed Aug. 7, 2006); [Francis M. Emmons] to All at Home, Sept. 17, 1863, Francis Marion Emmons Letters, Western Historical Manuscripts Collection, University of Missouri–Columbia.

4. Richards, *Story of a Rivertown*, 75; Bunch, "Confederate Women of Arkansas," 179.

5. Letter, Feb. 17, 1867, Horace Allis Letters, Rauner Special Collections, Dartmouth College Library; William F. Creitz Diary, William F. Creitz Papers, Kansas State Historical Society, 11; "Personal Reminiscences of August Bondi," August Bondi Papers, 1833–1907, Kansas State Historical Society, chap. 4, p. 39.

6. "Personal Reminiscences of August Bondi," Bondi Papers, chap. 4, p. 39; *Military History of the Kansas Regiments*, 115; Perdue, "Battle of Pine Bluff," 14; Thomas A. DeBlack, "1863: 'We Must Stand or Fall Alone,'" in Christ, *Rugged and Sublime*, 97.

7. Heartsill, *Fourteen Hundred and 91 Days*, 84; Blessington, *Campaigns of Walker's Texas Division*, 68; Lothrop, *First Regiment Iowa Cavalry*, 141; "Battle of Pine Bluff," 5.

8. Kohl, "Raising Thunder with the Secesh," 148; Popchock, *Soldier Boy*, 72; Benjamin J. Riggs, "Autobiographical Sketch," Tennessee State Library and Archives, 4. The Fifth Kansas's Helena patrols often were led by Maj. Samuel Walker, earning them the nickname "Walker's Jayhawkers."

9. DeBlack, "1863," 97; "Personal Reminiscences of August Bondi," Bondi Papers, chap. 4, p. 39; Capt. Young to Brother Thos, Oct. 1, 1863, Youngs Civil War Collection.

10. Burnside, *Honorable Powell Clayton*, 3, 7; Creitz Diary, Creitz Papers, 53; DeBlack, "1863," 97; Edwards, *Shelby and His Men*, 240–41.

11. Rawick, *American Slave*, 8(1):169, 9(1):177; DeBlack, "1863," 97.

12. Bearss, "Marmaduke Attacks Pine Bluff," 291. For an account of Shelby's raid, see Kerby, *Kirby Smith's Confederacy*, 233–36. The raid accomplished little except to give the troopers bragging rights: "You've heard of . . . Jeb Stuart's ride around McClellan? Hell, brother, Jo Shelby rode around MISSOURI!" Shelby's raiders included elements of the Fifth Missouri Cavalry, Shanks's and Jean's Missouri Cavalry, Elliott's Battalion, and Bledsoe's Battery. The remainder of the Iron Brigade stayed in Arkansas under the command of Col. G. W. Thompson. Bearss, "Marmaduke Attacks Pine Bluff," 296n.

13. Bearss, "Marmaduke Attacks Pine Bluff," 293; *Report of the Adjutant General of the State of Kansas*, 2:115; OR, 22(2):1042–43.

14. Bearss, "Marmaduke Attacks Pine Bluff," 293–94; "Personal Reminiscences of August Bondi," Bondi Papers, chap. 4, 39.

15. Walton, *Epitome of My Life*, 72; Riggs, "Autobiographical Sketch," 4–6.

16. Edwin C. Bearss, "John Sappington Marmaduke," in Davis and Hoffman, *Confederate General*, 4:155; Bearss, "Marmaduke Attacks Pine Bluff," 294; DeBlack, "1863," 99; Hewett, *Supplement to the Official Records*, 4(1):160.

17. Bearss, "Marmaduke Attacks Pine Bluff," 295.

18. Ibid., 295–96; Edwards, *Shelby and His Men*, 241; OR, 22(1):733.

19. Bearss, "Marmaduke Attacks Pine Bluff," 296, 301; DeBlack, "1863," 99.

20. OR, 22(1):723, 725; "Battle of Pine Bluff," 6; Bearss, "Marmaduke Attacks Pine Bluff," 297–98.

21. *OR*, 22(1):723–24; "Battle of Pine Bluff," 13; DeBlack, "1863," 97.

22. *OR*, 22(1):723–27; "Personal Reminiscences of August Bondi," Bondi Papers, chap. 4, p. 40.

23. *OR*, 22(1):723, 727; "Personal Reminiscences of August Bondi," Bondi Papers, chap. 4, p. 40.

24. *OR*, 22(1):731–32; Bearss, "Marmaduke Attacks Pine Bluff," 300.

25. *OR*, 22(1):735.

26. Ibid., 733–34; Bearss, "Marmaduke Attacks Pine Bluff," 302–304.

27. "Battle of Pine Bluff," 7; H. B. Allis to Dear Sir, Feb. 17, 1867, Allis Letters.

28. H. B. Allis to Dear Sir, Feb. 17, 1867, Allis Letters; "Battle of Pine Bluff," 8, 13; "Personal Reminiscences of August Bondi," Bondi Papers, chap. 4, p. 40.

29. "Personal Reminiscences of August Bondi," Bondi Papers, chap. 5, p. 1.

30. *OR*, 22(1):723, 726, 731; H. B. Allis to Dear Sir, Feb. 17, 1867, Allis Letters; "Battle of Pine Bluff," 8. Clement L. Vallandigham was an Ohio congressman whose pro-Southern views eventually led to his being exiled beyond the Confederate lines.

31. *OR*, 22(1):735–37.

32. Ibid., 725, 737. A. D. Brown confirmed the capture of a Rebel by a contraband: "[W]e saw one seize the long gun of a captured prisoner, and scanning the barricades, disappear among the skirmishers. Soon after he returned, marching a confederate before him he had succeeded in capturing and disarming." "Battle of Pine Bluff," 8. See also Bearss, "Marmaduke Attacks Pine Bluff," 306–307.

33. "Battle of Pine Bluff," 9; H. B. Allis to Dear Sir, Feb. 17, 1867, Allis Letters; Hewett, *Supplement to the Official Records*, 4(1):162–63. Marmaduke noted Rieff's death, calling him an officer "whom the Army could ill afford to lose," but claimed in a supplementary report that the fires were started as a result of artillery fire. *OR*, 22(1):724. An Ohio artilleryman writing about the battle later claimed that after Rieff fell, he was "plundered by the Kansans of 3 beautiful revolvers, one splendid gold watch plus 3 to 400 dollars in money." Banasik, *Reluctant Cannoneer*, 313.

34. *OR*, 22(1):723; Fry, *Following the Fifth Kansas Cavalry*, 51; "Battle of Pine Bluff," 13. Clayton reported that sixty-two mules were missing after the battle. *OR*, 22(1):724.

35. *OR*, 22(1):730; Bearss, "Marmaduke Attacks Pine Bluff," 308; Hewett, *Supplement to the Official Records*, 4(1):162–63; H. B. Allis to Dear Sir, Feb. 17, 1867, Allis Letters. Artillerist Robert McMahan also reported that the Confederates "plundered every house, with a very few exceptions, that was in their possession." Banasik, *Reluctant Cannoneer*, 313.

36. *OR*, 22(1):730–32.

37. Bearss, "Marmaduke Attacks Pine Bluff," 310–11; *OR*, 22(1):728; Banasik, *Reluctant Cannoneer*, 202.

38. Bearss, "Marmaduke Attacks Pine Bluff, 311; *OR*, 22(1):728–29; Lothrop, *First Regiment Iowa Cavalry*, 141.

39. *OR*, 22(1):729; Bearss, "Marmaduke Attacks Pine Bluff," 311–12.

40. *OR*, 22(1):723–24; Capt. Youngs to Siss Mary, Nov. 15, 1863, Youngs Civil War Collection. A. D. Brown places the Union casualties slightly differently, listing twelve killed and eighteen wounded, each by name. "Battle of Pine Bluff," 11–12.

41. "Battle of Pine Bluff," 13; Banasik, *Reluctant Cannoneer*, 314.

42. Leslie, "Arabella Lanktree Wilson's Civil War Letter," 267; *OR*, 22(1):724; Blackburn, *Dear Carrie*, 199; Banasik, *Reluctant Cannoneer*, 311.

43. "Battle of Pine Bluff," 4, 8; Banasik, *Reluctant Cannoneer*, 314; Fry, *Following the Fifth Kansas Cavalry*, 61. A. D. Brown also noted that "the state militia . . . took a hand in the fight and rendered good service throughout the day." "Battle of Pine Bluff," 13.

44. Hewett, *Supplement to the Official Records*, 4(1):162–63; *OR*, 22(1): 730. Marmaduke's supplemental report on the fighting, written a month after the battle, concluded by saying: "My troops behaved gallantly in this fight and came away with great reluctance. The enemy fought vindictively and with a persevering courage which does them and their commander honor." Hewett, *Supplement to the Official Records*, 4(1):163.

45. Bartels, *Confederate States Army Trans-Mississippi Order Book*, 290; Walton, *Epitome of My Life*, 76; Joel M. Bolton Memoir, Western Historical Manuscripts Collection, University of Missouri–Columbia, 13; Skinner, *Autobiography of Henry Merrell*, 348.

46. *Washington (Ark.) Telegraph*, Nov. 11, 1863. For an analysis of Marmaduke's errors at Pine Bluff, see Bearss, "Marmaduke Attacks Pine Bluff," 313.

EPILOGUE

1. Kerby, *Kirby Smith's Confederacy*, 232–33; "Personal Reminiscences of August Bondi," August Bondi Papers, 1833–1907, Kansas State Historical Society, chap. 5, p. 2; Geo E. Flanders to Dear Mother, Dec. 22, 1863, George E. Flanders Civil War Letters, Kansas State Historical Society.

2. DeBlack, *With Fire and Sword*, 102; Foote, *Civil War*, 2:780; *OR*, 22(2):1060.

3. Kerby, *Kirby Smith's Confederacy*, 232, 238; Fortin, "Confederate Military Operations in Arkansas," 84–85.

4. Bearss, "Confederate Attempt to Regain Fort Smith," 363–65, 372–76.

5. Confer, *Cherokee Nation in the Civil War*, 89–92. Supplying Forts Smith and Gibson would remain a problem throughout the war. The quirky nature of the Arkansas River kept it from being a dependable lifeline, and the constant threat of guerrillas made farming in the verdant valley dangerous. Despite the distance, supply trains from Fort Scott, Kansas, remained essential for both posts. See also Bearss, "Confederate Attempt to Regain Fort Smith," 345–46.

6. Mackey, *Uncivil War*, 38–40.

7. In the same letter Steele observed: "[I]n a short time matters may assume a different aspect. Arkansas troops are being mustered into service, and when the water rises Saline river will be a barrier to the rebels and the 'Tin clads' will protect the lower Arkansas." Unsigned draft to Dear General,

Nov. 9, 1863, Frederick Steele Papers, Department of Special Collections and University Archives, Stanford University Libraries; Smith, "Confederate Attempt to Counteract Reunion Propaganda," 55; Stuart, *Iowa Colonels and Regiments*, 181.

8. Cowen, "Reorganization of Federal Arkansas," 39–41.

9. Ibid., 43–45.

10. Ibid., 50, 57; Dougan, *Confederate Arkansas*, 120.

11. Heartsill, *Fourteen Hundred and 91 Days*, 89; Urwin and Urwin, *History of the 33d Iowa Infantry*, 66–67; Pitcock and Gurley, *I Acted from Principal*, 95; Britton, *Memoirs of the Rebellion on the Border*, 458.

Bibliography

SPECIAL COLLECTIONS AND ARCHIVES

Abraham Lincoln Presidential Library, Springfield, Ill.

Engelmann-Kircher Family Papers
Samuel L. Gordon Papers
John Harper Letters
William J. Kennedy Letters, 1861–65
George W. Russell Papers

Arkansas History Commission, Little Rock

Adams-Miller Family of Clark County, Ark., Letters, 1860–63
Civil War Letters of Capt. William F. Vermilya [Vermillion], Co. C, 36th
    Iowa Inf., U.S.A., 1863–64
Harris Flanagin Papers
Small Manuscripts Collection

Arkansas Post National Memorial

Pvt. D. W. Hitchcock Journal

Bentley Historical Library, University of Michigan, Ann Arbor

Calvin Ainsworth Diary
Ralph Muncy Memoir

Butler Center for Arkansas Studies,
Central Arkansas Library System, Little Rock

Arkansas Civil War Materials
Benjamin Palmer Collection
Ebenezer S. Peake Letters
John Talbut Civil War Letters

Center for Archival Collections,
Bowling Green State University, Bowling Green, Ky.

Kehrwecker Family Papers

Community Archives, Vigo CountyPublic Library, Terre Haute, Ind.

"Diary of John E. Wilkins, a Veteran of the Civil War"

Department of Special Collections and University Archives,
Stanford University Libraries, Stanford, Calif.

Frederick Steele Papers

Filson Historical Society, Louisville, Ky.

Isaac A. Craig Diary
Samuel T. Wells Papers

Hargett Rare Book and Manuscript Library,
University of Georgia Libraries, Athens

John A. Savage, Jr., Letters

Hawks Inn Historical Society, Delafield, Wis.

Ammi Doubleday Hawks Letters

Historical Research Center,
Texas Heritage Museum, Hill College, Hillsboro, Tex.

Estes Letters (collected and transcribed by Floyd Smith)
John Faulk Memoir
Isaiah Harlan's Civil War Letters
William Gates Hubert, Civil War Reminiscences
John Porter Memoir

Indiana Historical Society, Indianapolis

George F. Chittenden Letters
Reynolds Family Papers
Rowland-Shilliday Papers

Iowa State University Library Special Collections Department, Ames

Cyrus Bussey Civil War Reminiscences

Kansas State Historical Society, Topeka

August Bondi Papers, 1833–1907
William F. Creitz Papers
George E. Flanders Civil War Letters

Kentucky Historical Society, Frankfort

John T. Harrington Letter

Library of Congress, Washington, D.C.

Mrs. Douglas W. Clark Papers
Thomas Ewing Family Papers
Lucretia Rudolph Garfield Letters
John Griffith Jones Papers
Thomas Caute Reynolds Papers, 1821–77
Charles Oscar Torrey Papers

Lilly Library, Indiana University, Bloomington

Owen Mss.

Manuscripts Section, Indiana State Library, Indianapolis

O. V. Brown Collection
George B. Marshall Reminiscences
Reminiscences of John M. Roberts, Ripley County Civil War Papers
Asa E. Sample Diary

*Merrill G. Burlingame Special Collections,
Montana State University, Bozeman*

William H. Storrs Diary

Minnesota Historical Society, St. Paul

James M. Bowler Correspondence
William D. Hale and Family Papers (courtesy, Floyd E. Risvold, Edina, Minn.)

*Miscellaneous American Manuscripts Unassigned,
Pierpoint Morgan Library, New York*

John W. Dunnington Papers

Missouri Historical Society, St. Louis

Aurelius T. Bartlett Collection
Diary of an Unidentified Soldier of the 31st Iowa Infantry, Civil War Collection
Henry Hunt Reminiscences
David T. Massey Papers, Civil War Collection
Johann Wilhelm Osterhorn Papers
Mosby Monroe Parsons Papers
David D. Porter Papers, Bixby Collection
"Sketch of the Life of J. C. Dyer," Alphabetical File
Diary of Adam B. Smith
John F. Youngs Civil War Collection

National Archives and Records Administration, Washington, D.C.

Compiled Service Records of Confederate Soldiers Who Served in Organizations from the State or Arkansas

Pearce Civil War Collection, Navarro College, Corsicana, Tex.

Schuyler P. Coe Papers, 1863
William H. Heath Papers

*Rare Books, Manuscripts, and Special Collections Library,
Duke University, Durham, N.C.*

Theophilus Hunter Holmes Papers
S. S. Marrett Papers

Rauner Special Collections, Dartmouth College Library, Hanover, N.H.

Horace Allis Letters

*Schoff Civil War Soldiers Letters, William L. Clements Library,
University of Michigan, Ann Arbor*

Sidney O. Little Papers
Virgil Moats Letters

*Southern Historical Collection, Wilson Library,
University of North Carolina, Chapel Hill*

James T. Wallace Diary, 1862–65 (3059)
Adoniram Judson Withrow Papers (3679)

*Special Collections and Archives Division,
Robert W. Woodruff Library, Emory University, Atlanta*

Frederic E. Davis Papers, 1860–63
James Munns Papers

Special Collections Division,
University of Arkansas Libraries, Fayetteville

Amanda Malvina Fitzallen McClelland Braly Family Papers
Berry-Dickinson-Peel Family Papers
Milton C. Chambers Papers
Josephine B. Crump Papers
Minos Miller Civil War Letters
Mary Hope Moose Papers
Lorraine Blore Ragland Collection
John B. Scott Letter, 1862

Special Collections Department, University of Iowa Libraries, Iowa City

Letter to Albert Glines, Helena, Ark., July 8, 1863
David James Palmer Papers

State Historical Society of Iowa, Des Moines

Civil War Diary of M. S. Andrews

Stuttgart (Ark.) Public Library

Abram Brokaw Civil War Diary

Tennessee State Library and Archives, Nashville

Benjamin J. Riggs, "Autobiographical Sketch"
Miller, Roy Gilman, trans. "A Narrative of the Services of Brevet Major
  Charles Dana Miller in the War of the Great Rebellion, 1861–1865"

University of Arkansas at Little Rock Archives

John T. Buegel Reminiscences
J. N. Heiskell Civil War Collection
Roger Q. Mills Papers

Walter Havighurst Special Collections, Miami University, Oxford, Ohio

Diaries of Thomas B. Marshall

Western Historical Manuscripts Collection,
University of Missouri–Columbia

Joel M. Bolton Memoir
John T. Buegel Civil War Diary
Francis Marion Emmons Letters

William N. Hoskins Civil War Diary, 1862–65
John G. Hudson Collection, 1850–67 (copy)
Robert T. McMahan Papers
John P. Quesenberry Diary

Western Historical Manuscripts Collection, University of Missouri–Rolla

Franklin Spillman Denny Papers, 1853–1917
Phillip A. Reilly Collection
James S. Rogers Papers
Henry Ellison Skaggs Papers, 1862–95

Wisconsin Historical Society, Madison

George Cook Diaries

GOVERNMENT DOCUMENTS

Beers, Henry Putney. *Guide to the Archives of the Confederate States of America.* Washington, D.C.: Government Printing Office, 1968.
Official Records of the Union and Confederate Navies in the War of the Rebellion. 30 vols. Washington, D.C.: Government Printing Office, 1894. In *The Civil War CD-ROM.* Disc 2. CD-ROM; Carmel, Ind.: Guild Press of Indiana, 1999.
U.S. Bureau of the Census. *Agriculture of the United States in 1860.* Prepared by Joseph G. Kennedy, Superintendent of Census, under the Direction of the Secretary of the Interior. Washington, D.C.: Government Printing Office, 1864.
U.S. House of Representatives. *Survey of the Arkansas River.* 41st Cong., 2d sess., 1870. Exec. Doc. 295.
War of the Rebellion: A Compilation of the Official Records of the Union and Confederate Armies. 70 vols. in 128 books and index. Washington, D.C.: Government Printing Office, 1880–91. In *The Civil War CD-ROM.* CD-ROM; Carmel, Ind.: Guild Press of Indiana, 1996.

NEWSPAPERS AND MAGAZINES

Arkansas Democrat
Arkansas Gazette
Arkansas True Democrat
Douglass' Monthly
Frank Leslie's Illustrated Newspaper
Harper's Weekly
Harper's New Monthly Magazine
National Tribune
The (Pine Bluff) War Bulletin
Rolla (Mo.) Express
St. Louis Daily Missouri Democrat
Washington (Ark.) Telegraph

BOOKS

Allardice, Bruce. *More Generals in Gray*. Baton Rouge: Louisiana State University Press, 1995.

Anderson, John Q., ed. *Campaigning with Parsons' Texas Cavalry Brigade, CSA*. Hillsboro, Tex.: Hill Junior College Press, 1967.

Andrews, Alice E., ed. *Christopher Columbus Andrews, Recollections, 1829–1922*. Cleveland: Arthur H. Clark, 1928.

Annegan, Charles, ed. *With Merrill's Cavalry: The Civil War Experiences of Samuel Baird, 2nd Missouri Cavalry , U.S.A*. San Marcos, Calif.: Book Habit, 1981.

Bailey, Anne J. *Between the Enemy and Texas: Parsons's Texas Cavalry in the Civil War*. Fort Worth: Texas Christian University Press, 1989.

Banasik, Michael E., ed. *Missouri Brothers in Gray: Reminiscences and Letters of William J. Bull and John P. Bull*. Iowa City, Iowa: Camp Pope Bookshop, 1998.

———. *Reluctant Cannoneer: The Diary of Robert T. McMahan of the Twenty-Fifth Independent Ohio Light Artillery*. Iowa City, Iowa: Camp Pope Bookshop, 2000.

———. *Serving with Honor: The Diary of Captain Eathan Allen Pinnell of the Eighth Missouri Infantry (Confederate)*. Iowa City, Iowa: Camp Pope Bookshop, 1998.

Bartels, Carolyn M., ed. *Confederate States Army Trans-Mississippi Order Book, 1862–1864, Brigadier-General John S, Marmaduke*. 2 vols. Independence, Mo.: Two Trails, 2000.

Bearss, Edwin C. *The Campaign for Vicksburg*. 3 vols. Wilmington, N.C.: Morningside, 1985.

Bearss, Edwin C., and Arrell M. Gibson. *Fort Smith: Little Gibraltar on the Arkansas*. Norman, Okla.: University of Oklahoma Press, 1969.

Behlendorff, Frederick. *The History of the Thirteenth Illinois Cavalry Regiment Volunteers*. Grand Rapids, Mich.: 1888.

Bentley, William H. *History of the 77th Illinois Volunteer Infantry, Sept. 2, 1862–July 10, 1863*. Peoria, Ill.: E. Hine, Printer, 1883.

Bering, John A., and Thomas Montgomery. *History of the Forty-Eighth Ohio Veteran Volunteer Infantry*. Hillsboro, Ohio: Highland News Office, 1880.

Black, Samuel. *A Soldier's Recollections of the Civil War*. Minco, Okla.: Minco Minstrel, 1911–12.

Blackburn, George M., ed. *Dear Carrie, . . . The Civil War Letters of Thomas N. Stevens*. Mount Pleasant, Mich.: Clarke Historical Library, 1984.

Blessington, Joseph P. *The Campaigns of Walker's Texas Division*. New York: Lange, Little, 1875.

Bolton, S. Charles. *Arkansas, 1800–1860: Remote and Restless*. Fayetteville: University of Arkansas Press, 1998.

Bond, Otto F., ed. *Under the Flag of the Nation: Diaries and Letters of a Yankee Volunteer in the Civil War*. Columbus: Ohio State University Press, 1961.

Britton, Wiley. *Memoirs of the Rebellion on the Border, 1863*. Lincoln: University of Nebraska Press, 1993.

———. *The Union Indian Brigade in the Civil War.* Kansas City, Mo.: Franklin Hudson, 1922.

Brock, R. A., ed. *Southern Historical Society Papers.* Richmond, Va.: Southern Historical Society, 1896. Vol. 24. Reprint, Wilmington, N.C.: Broadfoot, 1991.

Brown, H. O., and M. A. W. Brown. *Soldiers' and Citizens' Album of Biographical Record.* Chicago: Grand Army, 1890.

Brown, Leonard. *American Patriotism, or Memoirs of "Common Men."* Des Moines, Iowa: Redhead and Wellstager, 1869.

Brown, Norman D. *Journey to Pleasant Hill: The Civil War Letters of Captain Elijah P. Petty, Walker's Texas Division, C.S.A.* San Antonio: University of Texas Institute of Texan Cultures, 1982.

———. *One of Cleburne's Command.* Austin: University of Texas Press, 1980.

Brown, Walter Lee. *A Life of Albert Pike.* Fayetteville: University of Arkansas Press, 1997.

Brown, William Wells. *The Negro in the American Rebellion: His Heroism and His Fidelity.* Reprint, New York: Citadel, 1971.

Burford, Timothy Wayne, and Stephanie Gail McBride. *The Division: Defending Little Rock, Aug. 25–Sept. 10, 1863.* Jacksonville, Ark.: WireStorm, 1999.

Burnside, William H. *The Honorable Powell Clayton.* Conway: University of Central Arkansas Press, 1991.

Byrne, Frank L., and Jean Powers Soman, eds. *Your True Marcus: The Civil War Letters of a Jewish Colonel.* Kent, Ohio: Kent State University Press, 1985.

Campaigns 42nd O.V.I. Historical Sketches of the Campaigns of the 42nd Regiment O.V.I. From Vicksburg to the Close of the War. Vol. 2. N.p., 1912.

Carr, Pat, ed. *In Fine Spirits: The Civil War Letters of Ras Stirman with Historical Comments.* Fayetteville, Ark.: Washington County Historical Society, 1986.

Castel, Albert. *General Sterling Price and the Civil War in the West.* Baton Rouge: Louisiana State University Press, 1968.

Christ, Mark K., ed. *All Cut to Pieces and Gone to Hell: The Civil War, Race Relations, and the Battle of Poison Spring.* Little Rock: August House, 2003.

———, ed. *The Earth Reeled and Trees Trembled: Civil War Arkansas, 1863–1864.* Little Rock: Old State House Museum, 2007.

———, ed. *Getting Used to Being Shot At: The Spence Family Civil War Letters.* Fayetteville: University of Arkansas Press, 2002.

———, ed. *Rugged and Sublime: The Civil War in Arkansas.* Fayetteville: University of Arkansas Press, 1994.

Clark, James Samuel. *Life in the Middle West.* Chicago: Advance, 1916.

———. *The Thirty-Fourth Iowa Regiment Brief History.* Des Moines: Watters-Talbott, 1892.

Coleman, Roger E. *The Arkansas Post Story: Arkansas Post National Memorial.* Professional Papers no. 12. Santa Fe, N.M.: Southwest Cultural Resources Center, 1987.

Collins, R. M. *Chapters from the Unwritten History of the War between the States.* Dayton, Ohio: Morningside, 1982.

Collins, Robert. *General James G. Blunt: Tarnished Glory.* Gretna, La.: Pelican, 2005.

Committee of the Regiment. *The Story of the Fifty-fifth Regiment of Illinois Volunteer Infantry in the Civil War, 1861–1865.* Clinton, Mass.: W. J. Coulter, 1887.

Confer, Clarissa W. *The Cherokee Nation in the Civil War.* Norman: University of Oklahoma Press, 2007.

Connelly, Donald B. *John M. Schofield and the Politics of Generalship.* Chapel Hill: University of North Carolina Press, 2006.

Cornish, Dudley Taylor. *The Sable Arm: Black Troops in the Union Army, 1861–1865.* Reprint, Lawrence: University Press of Kansas, 1987.

Cox, Florence Marie Ankeny, comp. and ed. *Kiss Josey for Me.* Santa Ana, Calif.: Friis-Pioneer, 1974.

Crawford, Samuel J. *Kansas in the Sixties.* Ottawa: Kansas Heritage Press, 1994.

Crisler, E. T., Jr. *Battle of Helena Centennial.* Helena, Ark.: Helena Centennial Association, 1963.

Crowley, William J. *Tennessee Cavalier in the Missouri Cavalry: Major Henry Ewing, C.S.A., of the St. Louis Times.* Columbia, Mo.: Kelly Press, 1978.

Cunningham, Frank. *General Stand Watie's Confederate Indians.* Reprint, Norman: University of Oklahoma Press, 1998.

Curtis, Oscar F., trans. *Civil War Diary of James H. Hougland, Company G, 1st Indiana Cavalry for the Year 1862.* Bloomington, Ind.: Monroe County Civil War Centennial Commission and Monroe County Historical Society, 1962.

Davenport, Edward A. *History of the Ninth Regiment Illinois Cavalry Volunteers.* Chicago: Donahue and Henneberry, 1888.

Davis, William C., and Julie Hoffman, eds. *The Confederate General.* 6 vols. Harrisburg, Pa.: National Historical Society, 1991.

DeBlack, Thomas A. *With Fire and Sword: Arkansas, 1861–1874.* Fayetteville: University of Arkansas Press, 2003.

Dougan, Michael B. *Confederate Arkansas: The People and Policies of a Frontier State in Wartime.* Tuscaloosa: University of Alabama Press, 1976.

Duckett, Drew D. *Glimpses of Glory: The Regimental History of the 61st Illinois Volunteers.* Bowie, Md.: Heritage Books, 1999.

Dyer, Frederick H. *A Compendium of the War of the Rebellion.* Des Moines, Iowa: Dyer, 1908.

Edwards, John N. *Shelby and his Men, or the War in the West.* Cincinnati: Miami, 1867. Reprint, Waverly, Mo.: General Joseph Shelby Memorial Fund, 1993.

Edwards, Whit. *The Prairie Was on Fire: Eyewitness Accounts of the Civil War in the Indian Territory.* Oklahoma City: Oklahoma Historical Society, 2001.

Elder, Donald C. *Love amid the Turmoil.* Iowa City, Iowa: University of Iowa Press, 2003.

Eliot, Ellsworth, Jr. *West Point in the Confederacy.* New York: G. A. Baker, 1941.

Evans, Clement A., ed. *Confederate Military History.* 17 vols. Atlanta: Confederate Publishing, 1899. Reprint with new material, Wilmington, N.C.: Broadfoot, 1988.

Field, Charles D. *Three Years in the Saddle from 1861 to 1865.* Goldenfield, Iowa, 1898.

Foote, Shelby. *The Civil War: A Narrative.* 3 vols. New York: Random House, 1958–74.

Frazier, William A., and Mark K. Christ, eds. *Ready, Booted, and Spurred: Arkansas in the U.S.–Mexican War.* Little Rock: Butler Center Books, 2008.

Frey, Jerry. *Grandpa's Gone: The Adventures of Daniel Buchwalter in the Western Army, 1862–1865.* Shippensburg, Pa.: Burd Street, 1998.

Fry, Alice L. *Following the Fifth Kansas Cavalry: The Letters.* Independence, Mo.: Two Trails, 1998.

Furry, William, ed. *The Preacher's Tale: The Civil War Journal of Rev. Francis Springer, Chaplain, U.S. Army of the Frontier.* Fayetteville: University of Arkansas Press, 2001.

Gaines, W. Craig. *The Confederate Cherokees: John Drew's Regiment of Mounted Rifles.* Baton Rouge: Louisiana State University Press, 1989.

Garrison, Webb, with Cheryl Garrison. *The Encyclopedia of Civil War Usage.* Nashville, Tenn.: Cumberland House, 2001.

Gaston, Ephraim. *The Civil War Diary of Ephraim Cullen Gaston with Material Added by Mark Wm. McGinnis, His Great-Great Grandson.* N.p.

Gaughan, Mrs. T. J., ed. *Letters of a Confederate Surgeon, 1861–1865.* Camden, Ark.: Hurley, 1960.

Gause, Isaac. *Four Years with Five Armies: Army of the Frontier, Army of the Potomac, Army of the Missouri, Army of the Ohio, Army of the Shenandoah.* New York: Neale, 1908.

Gerard, C. W. *A Diary. The Eighty-third Ohio Vol. Inf. In the War, 1862–1865.* Cincinnati: n.p., 1889.

Grant, Ulysses S. *Memoirs and Selected Letters: Personal Memoirs of U.S. Grant, Selected Letters, 1839–1865.* New York: Library of America, 1990.

Grecian, Joseph. *History of the Eighty-Third Regiment, Indiana Volunteer Infantry, for Three Years with Sherman.* Cincinnati: John F. Uhlhorn, 1865.

The Handbook of Victoria County. Austin: Texas Historical Association, 1990.

Hatch, Carl E. *Dearest Susie.* New York: Exposition, 1971.

Heartsill, W. W. *Fourteen Hundred and 91 Days in the Confederate Army.* Jackson, Tenn.: McCowat-Mercer, 1954.

Hegarty, Lela Whitton, comp. *Father Wore Gray.* San Antonio, Tex.: Naylor, 1963.

Hess, Earl J. *A German in the Yankee Fatherland.* Kent, Ohio: Kent State University Press, 1983.

Hewett, Janet B., ed. *Supplement to the Official Records of the Union and Confederate Armies.* 99 vols. Wilmington, N.C.: Broadfoot, 1996.

Howe, M. A. DeWolfe. *Home Letters of General Sherman.* New York: Charles Scribner's Sons, 1909.

Huff, Leo E., ed. *The Civil War Letters of Albert Demuth and Roster 8th Missouri Volunteer Cavalry.* Springfield, Mo.: Greene County Historical Society, 1997.

Hunt, Roger D., and Jack R. Brown. *Brevet Brigadier Generals in Blue.* Gaithersburg, Md.: Olde Soldiers Books, 1991.

Hutchins, E. R., comp. *The War of the 'Sixties.* New York: Neale, 1912.

Ingersoll, Lurton D. *Iowa and the Rebellion.* Philadelphia: J. P. Lippincott, 1867.

Iowa Adjutant General's Office. *Roster and Record of Iowa Soldiers in the War of the Rebellion.* 6 vols. Des Moines: Emory H. English, 1910.

Johnson, Robert Underwood, and Clarence Clough Buel, eds. *Battles and Leaders of the Civil War, Being for the Most Part Contributed by Union or Confederate Officers.* 4 vols. New York: Century, 1888.

Jones, Robert H., ed. *My Dear Carrie: The Civil War Letters of George K. Pardee and Family.* Akron, Ohio: Summit County Historical Society Press, 1994.

Josephy, Alvin M., Jr. *The Civil War in the American West.* New York: Alfred A. Knopf, 1991.

Kerby, Robert L. *Kirby Smith's Confederacy: The Trans-Mississippi South, 1863–1865.* Tuscaloosa: University of Alabama Press, 1972.

Kimbell, Charles B. *History of Battery "A" First Illinois Light Artillery Volunteers.* Chicago: Cushing, 1899.

Kiper, Richard L. *Major General John Alexander McClernand, Politician in Uniform.* Kent, Ohio: Kent State University Press, 1999.

Lacy, Lawson Keener, comp. *Letters from Lawson Jefferson Keener Written during His Confederate Service to Alcesta (Allie) Benson Carter.* Longview, Tex., 1963.

Larimer, Charles F., ed. *Love and Valor.* Western Springs, Ill.: Sigourney, 2000.

Lillibridge, Laurence F., ed. *A Civil War Soldier Describes His Army Life as Three Years of "Hard Marches, Hard Crackers and Hard Beds and Pickett Guard in a Desolate Country."* Prescott Valley, Ariz. : Lillibridge, 1993.

Long, E. B., and Barbara Long. *The Civil War Day by Day.* New York: Da Capo, 1971.

Lothrop, Charles H. *A History of the First Regiment Iowa Cavalry Veteran Volunteers.* Lyons, Iowa: Beers and Eaton, 1890.

Lowe, Richard. *Walker's Texas Division, C.S.A. Greyhounds of the Trans-Mississippi.* Baton Rouge: Louisiana State University Press, 2004.

Mackey, Robert R. *The Uncivil War: Irregular Warfare in the Upper South, 1861–1865.* Norman: University of Oklahoma Press, 2004.

Mason, F. H. *The Forty-Second Ohio Infantry: A History of the Organization and Services of that Regiment in the War of the Rebellion.* Cleveland: Cobb, Andrews, 1876.

Mayfield, Janis Boyle, ed. *William Physick Zuber, My Eighty Years in Texas.* Austin: University of Texas Press, 1971.

McEwen, W. A., and A. H. Lewis. *Encyclopedia of Nautical Knowledge.* Cambridge, Md.: Cornell Maritime Press, 1953.

McLean, William E. *The 43d Regiment of Indiana Volunteers.* Terre Haute, Ind.: C. W. Brown, 1903.

Meyer, Steve. *Iowa Valor.* Garrison, Iowa: Meyer Publishing, 1994.

Military Essays and Recollections: Papers Read before the Commandery of the State of Illinois, Military Order of the Loyal Legion of the United States. Vol. 3. Chicago: Dial, 1899.

Military History of the Kansas Regiments during the War for the Suppression of the Great Rebellion. Leavenworth, Kans.: W. S. Burke, 1870.

Military Order of the Loyal Legion of the United States. 66 vols. Wilmington, N. C.: Broadfoot, 1991–97.

Milligan, John D., ed. *From the Freshwater Navy: 1861–1864.* Annapolis, Md.: U.S. Naval Institute, 1970.

Minnesota in the Civil and Indian Wars, 1861–1865. 2 vols. St. Paul, Minn.: Pioneer, 1890.

Mix, Thomas E., and Ellen M. Earley, trans. *Civil War Journal of Thomas E. Mix, Co. B, 118th Regiment Illinois Volunteers.* Kenosha, Wis.: Earley, 1992.

Moneyhon, Carl H. *The Impact of the Civil War and Reconstruction on Arkansas: Persistence in the Midst of Ruin.* Reprint, Fayetteville: University of Arkansas Press, 2002.

Neal, Diane, and Thomas W. Kremm. *The Lion of the South: General Thomas C. Hindman.* Macon, Ga.: Mercer University Press, 1993.

Park, Ruth Ann Smith, comp. and ed. *The Civil War Letters of the Shibley Brothers.* Fayetteville, Ark.: Washington County Historical Society, 1963.

Petty, A. W. M. *A History of the Third Missouri Cavalry.* Little Rock: J. W. Demby, 1865.

Pitcock, Cynthia DeHaven, and Bill J. Gurley, eds. *I Acted from Principle: The Civil War Diary of Dr. William M. McPheeters, Confederate Surgeon in the Trans-Mississippi.* Fayetteville: University of Arkansas Press, 2002.

Popchock, Barry, ed. *Soldier Boy: The Civil War Letters of Charles O. Musser, 29th Iowa.* Iowa City: University of Iowa Press, 1995.

Puck, Susan T., ed. *Sacrifice at Vicksburg: Letters from the Front.* Shippensburg, Pa.: Burd Street, 1997.

Quarles, Benjamin. *The Negro in the Civil War.* Reprint, New York: Da Capo, 1989.

Quiner, E. B. *The Military History of Wisconsin.* Chicago: Clarke, 1866. Facsimile reprint, Dexter, Mich.: Thomson-Shore, 2000.

Rampp, Larry C., and Donald L. Rampp, *The Civil War in the Indian Territory.* Austin: Presidial, 1975.

Rawick, George P. ed. *The American Slave: A Composite Biography.* Westport, Conn.: Greenwood, 1972.

Reid, Richard J. *Fourth Indiana Cavalry Regiment: A History.* Olaton, Ky.: R. J. Reid, 1994.

Reid, Whitelaw. *Ohio in the War: Her Statesmen, Generals, and Soldiers.* Cincinnati: Robert Clarke, 1895.

Report of the Adjutant General of the State of Kansas. 2 vols. Leavenworth, Kans.: W. S. Burke Bulletin Printing House, 1870.

Richards, Ira Don. *Story of a Rivertown.* Benton, Ark., 1969.

Roberts, Bobby, and Carl Moneyhon. *Portraits of Conflict: A Photographic History of Arkansas in the Civil War.* Fayetteville: University of Arkansas Press, 1987.

Scharf, J. Thomas. *History of the Confederate States Navy from its Organization to the Surrender of its Last Vessel.* New York: Rogers & Sherwood, 1877.

Scott, John, comp. *Story of the 32nd Iowa Infantry Volunteers.* Nevada, Iowa: John Scott, 1896.

Scott, Kim Allen, ed. *Loyalty on the Frontier or Sketches of Union Men of the Southwest.* Fayetteville: University of Arkansas Press, 2003.

Scott, Reuben B., comp. *History of the Sixty-Seventh Regiment Indiana Infantry Volunteers.* Bedford, Ind.: Herald Book and Job Print, 1892.

Shea, William L., and Earl J. Hess. *Pea Ridge: Civil War Campaign in the West.* Chapel Hill: University of North Carolina Press, 1992.

Shea, William L., and Terrence J. Winschel. *Vicksburg Is the Key: The Struggle for the Mississippi River.* Lincoln: University of Nebraska Press, 2003.

Sherman, William T. *Memoirs of General W. T. Sherman.* New York: Library of America, 1990.

Simons, Don R. *In Their Words: A Chronology of the Civil War in Chicot County, Arkansas, and Adjacent Waters on the Mississippi River.* Sulphur, La.: Wise, 1999.

Simpson, Harold B., ed. *The Bugle Softly Blows: The Confederate Diary of Benjamin M. Seaton.* Waco, Tex.: Texian Press, 1965.

Skinner, James L., III. *Autobiography of Henry Merrell, Industrial Missionary to the South.* Athens: University of Georgia Press, 1991.

Smith, Walter George. *Life and Letters of Thomas Kilby Smith, Brevet Major-General, United States Volunteers, 1820–1887.* New York: G. P. Putnam and Sons, 1898.

Steiner, Paul E. *Disease in the Civil War.* Springfield, Ill.: Charles C. Thomas, 1968.

Stevenson, B. F. *Letters from the Army.* Cincinnati: W. E. Dibble, 1884.

Still, William N., Jr. *Confederate Shipbuilding.* Athens: University of Georgia Press, 1969.

Stuart, A. A. *Iowa Colonels and Regiments: Being a History of Iowa Regiments in the War of the Rebellion: and Containing a Description of the Battles in Which They Fought.* Des Moines: Mills, 1865.

Temple, Wayne C., ed. *The Civil War Letters of Henry C. Bear.* Harrogate, Tenn.: Lincoln Memorial University Press, 1961.

Tenney, Luman Harris. *War Diary of Luman Harris Tenney, 1861–1865.* Cleveland: Evangelical Publishing House, 1914.

Thomas, David R. *Arkansas in War and Reconstruction.* Little Rock: Central Printing, 1926.

Thorndike, Rachel Sherman, ed. *The Sherman Letters.* New York: Da Capo, 1969.

Trudeau, Noah Andre. *Like Men of War: Black Troops in the Civil War, 1862–1865.* Boston: Little, Brown, 1998.

Turnbo, Silas Claborn. *History of the Twenty-Seventh Arkansas Confederate Infantry.* Conway: Arkansas Research, 1988.

Urwin, Gregory J. W., and Cathy Kunzinger Urwin, eds. *History of the 33d Iowa Infantry Volunteer Regiment, 1863–6.* Fayetteville: University of Arkansas Press, 1999.

Walsh, Jack D. *Medical Histories of Union Generals.* Kent, Ohio: Kent State University Press, 1996.

Walton, Buck. *An Epitome of My Life: Civil War Reminiscences.* Austin, Tex.: Waterloo, 1965.

Warner, Ezra J. *Generals in Blue: Lives of the Union Commanders.* Baton Rouge, Louisiana State University Press, 1964.

————. *Generals in Gray: Lives of the Confederate Commanders.* Baton Rouge, Louisiana State University Press, 1959.

Webb, W. L. *Battles and Biographies of Missourians or the Civil War Period of Our State.* Kansas City, Mo.: Hudson-Kimberly, 1900.

Webster, Daniel. *History of the First Wisconsin Battery Light Artillery.* Washington, D.C.: National Tribune, 1907.

Williams, Kenneth P. *Lincoln Finds a General.* 5 vols. New York: McMillan, 1959.

Willison, Charles A. *Reminiscences of a Boy's Service with the 76th Ohio in the Fifteenth Army Corps, under General Sherman, during the Civil War, by that "Boy" at Three Score.* 1908. Reprint, Huntington, W.Va.: Blue Acorn, 1995.

Woodruff, W. E. *With the Light Guns in '61–'65: Reminiscences of Eleven Arkansas, Missouri, and Texas Batteries in the Civil War.* Little Rock: Central Printing, 1903.

Woods, J. T. *Services of the Ninety-Sixth Ohio Volunteers.* Toledo, Ohio: Blade Print and Paper, 1874.

Woodworth, Steven E. *Jefferson Davis and His Generals: The Failure of Confederate Command in the West.* Lawrence: University Press of Kansas, 1990.

————, ed. *The Musick of the Mocking Birds, the Roar of the Cannon.* Lincoln: University of Nebraska Press, 1998.

Woolworth, Solomon. *Experiences in the Civil War.* Newark, N.J.: 1903.

Wright, John C. *Memoirs of Colonel John C. Wright.* Pine Bluff, Ark.: Rare Book, 1982.

Yeary, Miss Mamie, comp. *Reminiscences of the Boys in Gray.* McGregor, Tex., 1912.

PERIODICALS

Abbot, John S. C. "Heroic Deeds of Heroic Men: The Wilds of Arkansas." *Harper's New Monthly Magazine* (October 1866): 581–601.

Ashcraft, Allan C., ed. "A Civil War Letter of General William Steele, CSA." *Arkansas Historical Quarterly* 22, no. 3 (Fall 1963): 278–81.

Bailey, Anne J. "Henry McCulloch's Texans and the Defense of Arkansas in 1862." *Arkansas Historical Quarterly* 46, no. 1 (summer 1987): 46–59.

Baker, Jeremiah. "In the Fight at Helena, Ark." *Confederate Veteran* 31, no. 6 (June 1923): 237.

Baker, Russell, ed. "This Old Book: The Civil War Diary of Mrs. Mary Sale Edmondson of Phillips County, Arkansas, Part IV." *Phillips County Historical Quarterly* 11 (March 1973): 1–10.

Barnhill, Floyd R., ed. "Greene County Youth Takes the Lead in Battle of Helena." *Phillips County Historical Quarterly* 34 (spring 1996): 82–83.

"Battle of Pine Bluff, the Yankee View." *Jefferson County Historical Quarterly* 17, no. 1 (1989): 4–16.

Bearss, Edwin C. "The Battle of Helena, July 4, 1863." *Arkansas Historical Quarterly* 20, no. 3 (autumn 1961): 256–97.

———. "The Battle of the Post of Arkansas." *Arkansas Historical Quarterly* 18, no. 3 (autumn 1959): 237–79.

———. "The Confederate Attempt to Regain Fort Smith, 1863." *Arkansas Historical Quarterly* 28, no. 4 (winter 1969): 342–80.

———. "The Federals Raid Van Buren and Threaten Fort Smith." *Arkansas Historical Quarterly* 26, no. 2 (summer 1967): 120–42.

———. "Marmaduke Attacks Pine Bluff." *Arkansas Historical Quarterly* 23, no. 4 (winter 1964): 291–313.

Bilby, Joseph G., ed. "Memoirs of Military Service, Carlos W. Colby, Co. G, 97th Illinois Infantry." *Military Images* 3, no. 2 (1981): 24–29.

Bishop, S. W. "The Battle of Arkansas Post." *Confederate Veteran* 5, no. 4 (April 1897): 151–53.

Blunt, James G. "General Blunt's Account of his Civil War Experiences." *Kansas Historical Quarterly* 1 (May 1932.): 211–65.

Bunch, Clea Lutz. "Confederate Women of Arkansas Face 'the Fiends in Human Shape.'" *Military History of the West* 27, no. 2 (fall 1997): 173–88.

Caraway, L. V. "The Battle of Arkansas Post." *Confederate Veteran* 14, no. 3 (March 1906): 127–28.

Castel, Albert. "Fiasco at Helena." *Civil War Times Illustrated* 7, no. 5 (August 1968): 12–17.

———. "Theophilus Holmes: Pallbearer of the Confederacy." *Civil War Times Illustrated* 16, no. 4 (July 1977): 11–17.

"Civil War Letter." *Grand Prairie Historical Society* 20, nos. 1–2 (April 1977): 36–38.

"Civil War Letters." *Phillips County Historical Quarterly* 29 (September 1990/January 1991): 24–31.

"Civil War Letters of J. D. Cummings." *Phillips County Historical Quarterly* 25, nos. 3–4 (June/September 1987): 19–22.

"Confederate Letters of Bryan Marsh." *Chronicles of Smith County, Texas* 14, no. 2 (winter 1975): 9–55.

Cowen, Ruth Caroline. "Reorganization of Federal Arkansas, 1862–1865." *Arkansas Historical Quarterly* 18, no. 2 (spring 1959): 32–57.

Cuthbertson, Gilbert. "Coller of the Sixth Texas: Correspondence of a Confederate Infantry Man, 1861–64." *Military History of Texas and the Southwest* 9, no. 2 (1971): 129–36.

Cutrer, Thomas W., ed. "'An Experience of Soldier's Life' The Civil War Letters of Volney Ellis, Adjutant Twelfth Texas Infantry Walker's Texas Division, C.S.A." *Military History of the Southwest* 22, no. 2 (fall 1992): 109–72.

Dalehite, Bob. "Arch S. Dobbins." *Phillips County Historical Quarterly* 4 (September 1965): 15–31.

Darst, Maury, ed. "Robert Hodges, Jr.: Confederate Soldier." *East Texas Historical Journal* 9 (March 1971): 20–49.

Davis, Steven R. "Death Takes No Holiday." *America's Civil War* (May 1993): 22–28, 71–74.

Delaney, Norman C. "The Diary and Memoirs of Marshall Samuel Pierson, Company C, 17th Regiment, Texas Cavalry, 1862–1865." *Military History of Texas and the Southwest* 13, no. 3 (1976): n.p.

Ewing, Mrs. Laura. "The Retreat from Little Rock in 1863." *The Independence County Chronicle* 5, No. 4 (October 1963): 3–17.

Ferguson, Hubert L., ed. "Letters of John W. Duncan, Captain, C.S.A." *Arkansas Historical Quarterly* 9, no. 4 (winter 1950): 298–312.

Fischer, LeRoy H. and Jerry Gill. "Confederate Indian Forces outside of Indian Territory." *Chronicles of Oklahoma* 46, no. 3 (autumn 1968): 249–84.

Foster, Samuel T. "We Are Prisoners of War: A Texan's Account of the Capture of Fort Hindman." *Civil War Times Illustrated* 16, no. 2 (May 1977): 24–33.

Franzman, Tom. "The Battle of Devil's Backbone Mountain." *Chronicles of Oklahoma* 62 (1984–85): 420–28.

Geise, William R. "General Holmes Fails to Create a Department, Part VII." *Military History of Texas and the Southwest* 14 (fall 1978): 169–78.

———. "Holmes, Arkansas, and the Defense of the Lower River: August, 1862–February, 1863, Part VIII." *Military History of the Southwest* 14 (winter 1978): 229–36.

"Gen. William L. Cabell." *Confederate Veteran* 11, no. 3 (March 1894): 67–68.

Glover, Robert W., ed. "The War Letters of a Texas Conscript in Arkansas." *Arkansas Historical Quarterly* 20, no. 4 (winter 1961): 355–87.

Guyer, Max, ed. "The Journal and Letters of Corporal William O. Gulick." *Iowa Journal of History and Politics* 28 (1930): 543–603.

Hearn, Chester G. "Admiral Porter and His 'Damned Gunboats.'" *Naval History* 10, no. 1 (May/June 1996): 40–42.

Hood, Fred. "Twilight of the Confederacy in Indian Territory." *Chronicles of Oklahoma* 41, no. 4 (winter 1963): 425–41.

Hubbs, Mark. "A Rebel Shot Causes Torture and Despair." *Naval History* 16, no. 2 (April 2002): 46–50.

Huff, Leo E. "The Last Duel in Arkansas: The Marmaduke-Walker Duel." *Arkansas Historical Quarterly* 23, no. 2 (spring 1964): 36–49.

———. "The Memphis and Little Rock Railroad during the Civil War." *Arkansas Historical Quarterly* 23, no. 3 (autumn 1964): 260–70.

———. "The Union Expedition against Little Rock, August–September 1863." *Arkansas Historical Quarterly* 22, no. 3 (autumn 1963): 224–37.

Huffstot, Robert S. "The Battle of Arkansas Post." *Civil War Times Illustrated* 2 (1963): 35–38.

"Indiana Troops at Helena, Part II." *Phillips County Historical Quarterly* 16 (September 1978): 1–8.

"Indiana Troops at Helena, Part III." *Phillips County Historical Quarterly* 17 (March 1979): 11–21.

"Indiana Troops at Helena, Part IV." *Phillips County Historical Quarterly* 17 (June 1979): 34–42.

"Indiana Troops at Helena, Part V." *Phillips County Historical Quarterly* 18 (June/October 1980): 1–8.

"Indiana Troops at Helena, Part VI." *Phillips County Historical Quarterly* 19 (December 1980/March 1981): 1–7.

"Indiana Troops at Helena, Part VII." *Phillips County Historical Quarterly* 19 (June/September 1981): 74–82.

Jones, Steven W. "The Logs of the USS *Tyler.*" *Phillips County Historical Quarterly* 15 (March 1977): 23–38.

Kaufman, A. F. "The Fifty-Fourth U.S. Colored Infantry: The Forgotten Regiment." *Ozark Historical Review* 16 (spring 1987): 1–7.

Kirkman, Dale P., ed. "The 28th Wisconsin Infantry Regiment at Helena." *Phillips County Historical Quarterly* 12 (March 1974): 11–24.

———. "The 28th Wisconsin Infantry Regiment at Helena, II." *Phillips County Historical Quarterly* 12 (June 1974): 12–24.

Kohl, Rhonda M. "Raising Thunder with the Secesh: Powell Clayton's Federal Cavalry at Taylor's Creek and Mount Vernon, May 11, 1863." *Arkansas Historical Quarterly* 64, no. 2 (summer 2005): 146–70.

———. "'This Godforsaken Town': Death and Disease at Helena, Arkansas, 1862–63." *Civil War History* 50, no. 2 (June 2004): 109–44.

Leslie, James W., ed. "Arabella Lanktree Wilson's Civil War Letter." *Arkansas Historical Quarterly* 48, no. 3 (autumn 1988): 257–72.

Matteson, Elisa C., and Edward Eckert, eds. "Dear Sister—They Fight to Whip." *Civil War Times Illustrated* 30 (May/June 1991): 16–17, 58–59.

McConnell, Maj. G. W. "Up the Arkansas." *United States Service Magazine* 5, no. 3 (March 1866): 234–41.

McConnell, Roland C. "Concerning the Procurement of Negro Troops in the South during the Civil War." *The Journal of Negro History* 35 no. 3 (July 1950): 315–19.

"McRae's March to Helena Retraced." *The Independence County Chronicle* 4 (July 1963): 13–16.

Milligan, John D., ed. "Navy Life on the Mississippi River: An Excerpt from Union Sailor Daniel F. Kemp's Civil War Reminiscences." *Civil War Times Illustrated* 33, no. 2 (May/June 1994): 16, 66–73.

Moneyhon, Carl H. "The Civil War's Impact in Arkansas: Phillips County as a Case Study." *Locus* 5, no. 1 (fall 1992): 19–32.

Oliphant, William J. "Arkansas Post." *Southern Bivouac,* n.s., 1 (1886): 736–39.

Pearson, Benjamin. "Benjamin Pearson's War Diary" *Annals of Iowa,* 3rd ser., 15, no.2 (October1926): 83–129.

Perdue, David. "The Battle of Pine Bluff, October 25, 1863." *Jefferson County Historical Quarterly* 1, no. 2 (1962): 14–19.

Perdue, Karen T., ed. "The Wartime Diary of William Henry Willcox." *Jefferson County Historical Quarterly* 4, no. 1 (1972): 18–28.

Pollan, Carolyn. "Fort Smith under Union Military Rule, September 1, 1863–Fall, 1865." *Journal of the Fort Smith Historical Society* 6, no. 1 (April 1982): 2–33.

Rea, Ralph R., ed. "Diary of Private John P. Wright, U.S.A., 1864–1865." *Arkansas Historical Quarterly* 16, no. 3 (autumn 1957): 304–18.

Robertson, Brian K., ed. "A Civil War Letter: Benjamin Fullager's Account of the Union Expedition against Van Buren." *Arkansas Historical Quarterly* 41, no. 1 (spring 2002): 80–87.

Ross, Frances Mitchell, ed. "Civil War Letters from James Mitchell to his Wife, Sarah Elizabeth Latta Mitchell." *Arkansas Historical Quarterly* 37, no. 4 (winter 1978): 306–17.

Rudolph, Joseph. "Early Life and Civil War Reminiscences of Captain Joseph Rudolph." *Pickups from the American Way*, 2nd ser., 1 (1941): 16–19.

Scheiber, Harry N. "The Pay of Troops and Confederate Morale in the Trans-Mississippi West." *Arkansas Historical Quarterly* 18, no. 4 (winter 1959): 350–65.

Scott, Kim Allen. "A Diminished Landscape: The Life and Death of Major Robert Henry Smith." *Missouri Historical Review* 91, no. 4 (July 1997): 353–72.

Scott, Newton. "Letters from an Iowa Soldier in the Civil War." *Phillips County Historical Review* 35 (spring 1997): 25–49.

Shea, William L. "'Whipped and Routed': Blunt Strikes Marmaduke at Cane Hill." *North and South* 7, no. 6 (October 2004): 26–39.

Sherman, William T. "Vicksburg by New Year's." *Civil War Times Illustrated* 16, no. 9 (January 1978): 44–48.

Simms, L. Moody, Jr., ed. "A Union Volunteer with the Mississippi Ram Fleet." *Lincoln Herald* 70 (winter 1968): 189–92.

Smith, Robert F. "The Confederate Attempt to Counteract Union Propaganda in Arkansas, 1863–1865." *Arkansas Historical Quarterly* 16, no. 2 (spring 1957): 54–62.

Surovic, Arthur F. "Union Assault on Arkansas Post." *Military History* 12, no. 7 (March 1996): 34–40.

Swanson, Alan, ed. and trans. "The Civil War Letters of Olog Liljegren." *Swedish Pioneer Historical Quarterly* 21, no. 2 (April 1980.): 86–121.

"They Were There—The Battle of Arkansas Post." *Grand Prairie Historical Society Bulletin* 18, nos. 1–2 (April 1975): 3–7.

Turner, Jim. "Jim Turner, Co. G., 6th Texas Infantry, C.S.A." *Texana* 12, no. 2 (1974): 149–78.

"The 28th Wisconsin Infantry Regiment at Helena: III." *Phillips County Historical Quarterly* 12 (September 1974): 36–40.

"The 28th Wisconsin Infantry at Helena: IV." *Phillips County Historical Quarterly* 13 (March 1975): 23–33.

"The 28th Wisconsin Infantry Regiment at Helena: V." *Phillips County Historical Quarterly* 13 (September 1975): 7–17.

"The 28th Wisconsin Infantry Regiment at Helena: VI." *Phillips County Historical Quarterly* 14 (December 1975): 7–16.

"The 28th Wisconsin Infantry Regiment at Helena: VII." *Phillips County Historical Quarterly* 14 (March 1976): 30–40.

"The 28th Wisconsin Infantry Regiment at Helena: VIII." *Phillips County Historical Quarterly* 14 (June 1976): 30–38.

Urwin, Gregory J. W. "A Very Disastrous Defeat: The Battle of Helena, Arkansas." *North and South* 6, no. 1 (December 2002): 26–39.

Waterman, Robert E., and Thomas Rothrock. "The Earle-Buchanan Letters of 1861–1876." *Arkansas Historical Quarterly* 33, no. 2 (summer 1974): 99–174.

Willey, William J. "The Second Federal Invasion of Indian Territory." *Chronicles of Oklahoma* 44, no. 4 (winter 1966–67): 420–30.

"Wisconsin Troops at Helena: X." *Phillips County Historical Quarterly* 15 (December 1976): 4–11.

"Wisconsin Troops at Helena: XI." *Phillips County Historical Quarterly* 15 (June 1977): 5–19.

Wise, Joe R., ed. "The Letters of Lt. Flavius W. Perry, 17th Texas Cavalry, 1862–1863." *Military History of Texas and the Southwest* 13, no. 2 (1976): 12–37.

Woodworth, Steven E. "The Scapegoat of Arkansas Post." *MHQ* 13, no. 3 (2001): 58–67.

Wright, Muriel H. "General Douglas Cooper, C.S.A." *Chronicles of Oklahoma* 32, no. 2 (summer 1954): 142–84.

Wright, Muriel H., and LeRoy H. Fischer. "Civil War Sites in Oklahoma." *Chronicles of Oklahoma* 44, no. 2 (summer 1966): 158–215.

THESES AND DISSERTATIONS

Bates, Toby Glenn. "'Without Doubt History Will Do the Gallant Hero Justice': Benjamin Prentiss and the Failure of American History." Master's thesis, University of Mississippi, 2002.

Belser, Thomas A., Jr. "Military Operations in Missouri and Arkansas, 1861–1865." Ph.D. diss., Vanderbilt University, 1958.

Christ, Mark K. "'Here in the Wilds of Arkansas': Interpreting the Little Rock Campaign of 1863." MLS thesis, University of Oklahoma, 2000.

Fortin, Maurice G., Jr. "Confederate Military Operations in Arkansas, 1861–1865." Master's thesis, North Texas State University, 1978.

Philbeck, Larry Gene. "A Union Soldier in Arkansas, 1862–1866: Minos Miller of Iowa." Master's Thesis, University of Arkansas, 1990.

Sude, Barry Richard. "Federal Military Policy and Strategy in Missouri and Arkansas, 1861–1863: A Study of Command Level Conflict." Ph.D. diss., Temple University, 1986.

INTERNET SOURCES

Abraham Lincoln and the Civil War. http://www.lincolnandthecivilwar .com/ (site now discontinued).

Arkansas in the Civil War Message Board. http://history-sites.com/cgi-bin /boards/arcwmb/.

"Edward S. Redington Papers, 1862–1867." The State: Papers, 1862–1867 (Wis Mss EQ, Folder 1): Contents. *University of Wisconsin Digital Collections.* http://digital.library.wisc.edu/1711.dl/WI.EdRed01.

"Lewis Merrill, Brigadier General, United States Army." *Arlington National Cemetery.* http://www.arlingtoncemetery.net/lmerrill.htm.

"Matson3." *They Were the 114th O.V.I.* http://www.fortunecity.com/westwood/makeover/347/id192.htm.

"Thomas J. Barb Diary, 1863" (MSN/CW 8002-1). University of Notre Dame Rare Books and Special Collections. *Manuscripts of the American Civil War.* http://www.rarebooks.nd.edu/digital/civil_war/diaries_journals/barb/.

Twenty-Eighth Wisconsin Volunteer Infantry. http://www.28thwisconsin.com/service/battle.html.

Index